Queer Ear

Queer Ear

Remaking Music Theory

Edited by

GAVIN S. K. LEE

OXFORD
UNIVERSITY PRESS

OXFORD
UNIVERSITY PRESS

Oxford University Press is a department of the University of Oxford. It furthers the University's objective of excellence in research, scholarship, and education by publishing worldwide. Oxford is a registered trade mark of Oxford University Press in the UK and certain other countries.

Published in the United States of America by Oxford University Press
198 Madison Avenue, New York, NY 10016, United States of America.

Library of Congress Cataloging-in-Publication Data
Names: Lee, Gavin S. K., editor.
Title: Queer ear : remaking music theory / edited by Gavin S. K. Lee.
Description: [1.] | New York : Oxford University Press, 2023. |
Includes bibliographical references and index.
Identifiers: LCCN 2023004628 (print) | LCCN 2023004629 (ebook) |
ISBN 9780197536773 (paperback) | ISBN 9780197536766 (hardback) |
ISBN 9780197536797 (epub)
Subjects: LCSH: Queer musicology. | Music theory. | Musical analysis.
Classification: LCC ML3797.4 .Q44 2023 (print) | LCC ML3797.4 (ebook) |
DDC 780.72—dc23/eng/20230131
LC record available at https://lccn.loc.gov/2023004628
LC ebook record available at https://lccn.loc.gov/2023004629

DOI: 10.1093/oso/9780197536766.001.0001

Paperback printed by Marquis Book Printing, Canada
Hardback printed by Bridgeport National Bindery, Inc., United States of America

Contents

QUEER NARRATOLOGY

Contributors

David Bretherton is Associate Professor of Music at the University of Southampton. He is a coeditor of *Heinrich Schenker: Selected Correspondence* (Boydell and Brewer) and author of several articles and book chapters.

James R. Currie is Associate Professor of Music at University at Buffalo. He is author of the article "Music After All," the monograph *Music and the Politics of Negation* (Indiana University Press), and several other articles and book chapters.

Philip Ewell is Professor of Music Theory at Hunter College and the CUNY Graduate Center. In addition to his work on Russian music theory, Ewell is author of the article "Music Theory and the White Racial Frame," the monograph *On Music Theory, and Making Music More Welcoming for Everyone* (forthcoming, University of Michigan Press), and the inclusive textbook *The Engaged Musician: Theory and Analysis for the Twenty-First Century* (forthcoming, Norton).

Kristin Franseen is currently a postdoctoral fellow in history and Affiliate Assistant Professor in the Simone de Beauvoir Institute at Concordia University, where her work is supported by the Fonds de recherche du Québec—Société et culture (FRQSC). Her research is published in *19th-Century Music* and *Music and Letters*. She is also the author of *Imagining Musical Pasts: The Queer Literary Musicology of Vernon Lee, Rosa Newmarch, and Edward Prime-Stevenson* (forthcoming, Clemson University Press).

Robert Hatten is Marlene and Morton Meyerson Professor in Music (Theory) at the University of Texas at Austin. Author of three books, most recently *A Theory of Virtual Agency for Western Art Music* (Indiana University Press), he has also served as President of the Society for Music Theory and the Semiotic Society of America.

Gavin S. K. Lee researches and teaches global and decolonial, Sinophone and Afro Asian, ancient and avant-garde and popular, and queer and trans musics and sounds. He is the author of *Estrangement from Ethnicity: Music and Sinophone Alienation* (forthcoming, University of Michigan Press) and editor of *Rethinking Gender, Sexuality, and Popular Music* (Routledge). Based at Soochow University, China, Lee has presented ten guest lectures on three continents at universities in the US, Australia, Taiwan, and China since 2020.

Judy Lochhead is Professor of Music at Stony Brook University. She is author of *Reconceiving Structure in Contemporary Music* (Routledge) and editor of several volumes from University of Chicago Press, Routledge, and Ashgate.

Vivian Luong is a graduate of the University of Michigan and currently Visiting Lecturer of Music Theory at University of Oklahoma. Her research on feminist music theory and ethics appears in *Music Theory Online*.

Federica Marsico is currently a postdoctoral fellow at McGill University, where she works on a project that has been funded by a Marie Skłodowska-Curie Global fellowship in partnership with Ca' Foscari University of Venice. Her research on Hans Werner Henze appears in several Italian journals and edited volumes.

Fred Everett Maus teaches music at the University of Virginia. He has written about sexuality in relation to music theory and other critical discourse about music, and about queerness in popular music (the Pet Shop Boys, R.E.M., the B-52s). He has also written about music and narrative/drama, musical unity, music through the lens of object relations, music and trauma, and other topics. He was Chair or Cochair of the Queer Resource Group of the Society for Music Theory, 2004–2013, and in 2020 was appointed the first Chair of the Committee on LGBTQ+ Issues of SMT. With the late Sheila Whiteley, he is coeditor of *The Oxford Handbook of Music and Queerness*.

Bill Solomon is Cochair of Music at the Dalton School in New York City and performs as a percussionist. He completed a dissertation on queer influences in the percussion works of West Coast composers.

Chris Stover is Senior Lecturer at Queensland Conservatorium and a composer and improvising trombonist. He is coeditor of *Rancière and Music* and has published articles on music theory, philosophy, and improvisation in many journals and edited volumes. A new monograph, *Timeline Spaces: A Theory of Temporal Process in African and Afrodiasporic Musics*, is forthcoming with Oxford University Press, and he is finishing a volume on inclusive music theory for Routledge.

Introduction

Queer Ear

Gavin S. K. Lee

I once served on a masters thesis committee on set theory together with a violist who had performed with one of the famous orchestras in London (who then later became a professor at the same conservatory as me). The student used the standard theoretical terminology, describing pitch class sets as "chords," to which the violist—a veteran performer of new music—remarked that he could not see how a collection of non-simultaneously sounded notes could be described as a "chord." Although this episode could be written off as being about the vagaries of terminology, it might be better understood as a clash of musical embodiment and expectations. The violist clearly did not hear the collection of pitches *as* a pitch class set, which suggests that the important harmonic aspect of set theory might be a peculiarity of music theorists as opposed to the larger number of professional musicians who perform atonal and twelve-tone music (and who may be more interested in details of expression, articulation, and motivic derivation).

It is because of the highly specialized nature of set theory, which seems to have little appeal even for dedicated music researchers (who are non-music theorists), that Susan McClary referred in 1991 to "pitch class amoebas" (109)—the pitch class sets that are the small musical segments that constitute the building blocks of mainstream post-tonal music theory as transmitted in most US doctoral programs.[1] McClary was reacting then against a common-sense music academia that had for decades occupied itself mostly with verifiable, positivist facts of biography and history, or identifiable pitches in a score. With the rise of (what we might broadly call) postmodern theory (Kramer

---

[1] Certainly, set theory is not just about pitch class amoebas, but it is important to trace the history of the contention between the disciplines of musicology and music theory, and to note the early resistance of feminist and queer musicologists to music theory.

Gavin S. K. Lee, *Introduction* In: *Queer Ear*. Edited by: Gavin S. K. Lee, Oxford University Press.
© Oxford University Press 2023. DOI: 10.1093/oso/9780197536766.003.0001

1995) in music research in the 1990s—which, among other things, questioned the notion of scientific objectivity—music scholars began to call for attention to musical histories and experiences that differed according to one's historical context, race, class, gender, and sexuality. Feminist, queer, postcolonial, literary, and critical-race theory made powerful inroads in music research that valued historical contingencies and differentiated subjectivities. Feminist and queer musicology were natural allies, both opposed to hegemonic powers that most often were aligned with heteronormative, patriarchal masculinity, which in turn was understood to be expressed in the rationality of positivist history and formalist music theory.[2] As opposed to the singular scientific truth, a productive ambiguity was introduced. McClary, for instance, noted that although there may be a relationship between Schubert's (then newly construed) same-sex attraction, on the one hand, and her theorization of a subjectivity open to ambiguous harmonic pleasures in the second movement of the composer's *Unfinished* symphony, on the other, there is no essential link between the two. Schubert may or may not have been same-sex attracted; same-sex attracted male composers may or may not articulate a subjectivity that deviates from the normative goal-directed mold; the information we have on the early eighteenth century is spotty—and musical ambiguity may indeed be musical as opposed to an expression of non-normative masculinity or sexuality (McClary 1994, 226–28).[3]

It is notable that this radical degree of interpretive contingency—which stands in contrast to the generalizable impetus of the "theory" of music (or any theory, really)—was articulated by a scholar generally recognized as a musicologist.[4] Because queer musicology often aims to interpret implicit meanings and hidden secrets, there is a degree of ambiguity that comes with the terrain, leaving room for *degrees* of plausibility. Whether or not it is this ambiguity that has discouraged queer research in music theory, the latter field has not seen the same level of queer vitality as musicology. Musicologists have

---

[2] Feminist and queer theory of the 1990s shared a systemic, deconstructive purview of the binaries of gender and sexuality, which meant that even studies of conventional notions of masculinity or even heterosexuality had a progressive edge that usually (but not always) pointed at least implicitly to a non-normativity that lies beyond. See Borgerding 2002; Smart 2000; Purvis 2013; Dellamora and Fischlin 1997; Case, Brett, and Foster 1995; and Blackmer and Smith 1995.

[3] See also McClary's interpretation and analysis of Tchaikovsky's Fourth Symphony in McClary 1999, 69–79.

[4] Although McClary incorporates music theory and analysis in her work, the relevant passages usually constitute a relatively small section of her publications, and she does not aim for an exhaustive, systematic account of musical workings. McClary is therefore widely recognized as a musicologist, even though she has been invited to present the 2009 keynote speech (published in McClary 2010) at the Society for Music Theory conference in Montréal, Canada.

examined topics ranging from "lesbian" musical experience (Cusick 1994) to musicality as a closet (Brett 1994), from musical queering as ethical prac-tice (Peraino 2005) to ambiguity as an analytic in popular music (Lee 2018). Whereas a noted scholar of queer musicology such as Suzanne Cusick has been elected president of the American Musicological Society (2019–2020), and whereas the LGBTQ Study Group of the society is home to a vibrant community of scholars whose research has only expanded since the field's emergence in the late 1980s and early 1990s, queer scholarship is still in its nascence in the Society for Music Theory, though the publication of this book marks a significant milestone.[5] Part of the explanation is that musicology has by and large come to value minority identities and perspectives, whereas music theory as a discipline is defined as the search for "general principles" (Fallows 2011) of music. Even though recent decades have seen much growth in interdisciplinary approaches to music theory, the fact that the definition of the discipline leans toward generality has major implications for those of us who ground our work in the perspectivism that is central to feminist, queer, and critical-race theories of difference—that is, what music theory looks like and sounds like is *contingent* on one's race, gender, and sexuality, and more generally, on one's positionality (as evinced in my opening anecdote). The "generalist" definition of music theory creates an exclusionary pressure of gatekeeping among music theorists who regard studies of gender and sex-uality as belonging properly to the domain of queer *musicology*. Indeed, it is widely acknowledged that conference program committees of the Society for Music Theory frequently reject abstracts on the basis that they are not about "music theory" (and are instead about musicology, philosophy, cul-tural studies, etc.).[6] As to what precisely music theory seeks to establish gen-eral principles for, evasion can be sometimes discerned, particularly in the wake of New Musicology's critique of music theory's formalism—suffice it to say that a recent award-winning Oxford handbook on music theory (Rehding and Rings 2019) includes chapters on pitch, interval, mode, scale, tonic, timbre, texture, and so on, and not "gender" or "sexuality" (whereas

[5] The Society for Music Theory formed a LGBTQ+ standing committee that is guaranteed panels at annual conferences beginning in 2021. Panels are reviewed internally by the standing committee instead of going through the program committee, thus guaranteeing a queer presence at conferences.

[6] There is some debate about this, but my personal observation is that music theorists who are marginalized by their identities or by their research are more likely to have experienced scholarly exclusion and thus report on it. Music theorists who have not been marginalized, on the other hand, tend to refute that such exclusion exists.

the absence of the latter terms from a parallel volume in musicology would probably cause a scandal).[7]

Before going on, I need to articulate the caveat that the picture I painted above of musicology and music theory is intended as a description of general trends that are not, however, universal. There are certainly promising interdisciplinary developments in music-theory research and pedagogy that are too numerous to enlist here,[8] including work by a new generation of scholars breaking down the musicology–music theory divide that was historically particularly entrenched in the United States—but we only have to take a look at the requirements of US music-theory doctoral programs to understand that much work remains to be done. I will simply state that most US faculty have their disciplinary identities enshrined in their official job titles (e.g., lecturer in music theory), and many music theorists do not recognize me as a "real" music theorist. Though it may be the case that disciplinary boundaries in Europe and Canada may not be maintained to the same degree as in US music studies, which is the adopted frame in this introduction, it is unquestionable that US voices are dominant in English-language music scholarship.

Whereas music theory has largely retained its impetus toward generalization (a theory is meant to be applicable across multiple examples), musicology has largely embraced contingency as an ethical anchor—indeed, there is an almost reflexive recourse to ever smaller parcels of sociohistorical context that can blind us to overarching factors such as global capitalism (Currie 2009). And where music theory has broached relatively murky realms such as musical meaning, it has tended to do so in a systematic, taxonomic manner, premised on extensive theorizations of, for example, what a human gesture versus musical gesture are (Hatten 2004; Hatten 2018). Taken as a whole, then, music theory has not embraced postmodern theory to the same *degree* as musicology. (Morgan 2003 offers a critique—as well as, perhaps

---

[7] *The Oxford Handbook of Critical Concepts in Music Theory* is the winner of the 2020 award for an edited volume from the Society for Music Theory.

[8] The Engaged Music Theory Working Group (accessed March 1, 2022) maintains an interdisciplinary bibliography that brings music theory into relation with issues of race, class, gender, sexuality, and ability:

https://engagedmusictheory.com/

Recent pedagogical projects published online (all accessed March 1, 2022) include:

"Engaging Students: Essays in Music Pedagogy" (https://engagingstudentsmusic.org/), "Composers of Color Resource Project" (https://composersofcolor.hcommons.org/), "Music Theory Examples by Women" (https://musictheoryexamplesbywomen.com/), and "Expanding the Music Theory Canon—A Collection of Inclusive Music Theory Examples" (https://www.expandingthemusictheorycanon.com/).

unintentionally, a useful literature review—of postmodern approaches to music theory; more later.) Even though postmodern theory can hardly be said to be universal or even accepted by a majority of musicologists, there are sizeable bodies of work in musicology in which a certain degree of contingency is acceptable and even valorized. These musicological studies are typically premised on contexts, subjectivities, and identities defined in terms of historical or cultural difference, and gender, sexuality, race, and/or postcolonial relations. In addition, the bracketing of objective truth has meant that *any* claims are contingent and subject to interrogation, raising important questions about methodology—should we proceed via close hermeneutic interpretations of musical texts for musical meaning, or lean back, paying heed instead to the multiple historical discourses from which music emerges as a construct? On the question of necessary historical distance from, versus interpretive proximity to, the musical object, Lawrence Kramer (1993) and Gary Tomlinson (1993) have conducted a highly publicized debate—what they both share is a commitment to the principle of music's contingency.

Among the sectors of musicology that could be described as postmodern in some respect, queer musicology in particular has benefitted from postmodern theory's questioning of objective truth, in that one of queer theory's founding tenets in its moment of emergence is an absolute non-normativity. To quote the classic formulation by David Halperin: "Queer is . . . *whatever is at odds with the normal, the legitimate, the dominant. There is nothing in particular to which it necessarily refers*. It is an identity without an essence" (1995, 62). The relentless production of always differentiating meanings, contexts, identities, and perspectives is the very cornerstone of queer theory that validates minority LGBTQ perspectives and values these perspectives for their potential to challenge hegemonic knowledge structure on a systemic level, pushing back against normative powers. To cite just a few classics of queer and transgender theory, the non-normative impetus is seen in Butler's theory of the accretion of daily, potentially subversive gender performance as opposed to gender as completely pre-determined (Butler 1993, 1999), in Edelman's theory of homosexuality as the cathexis that is the crumbling point of heteronormativity (Edelman 2004), in Halberstam's exploration of the spectrum of transgender embodiment (Halberstam 1998), and in voluminous articles in *Transgender Studies Quarterly*. By calling norms into question, a resolute non-normativity makes room for the contingency characteristic of postmodern theory, so much so that queer theory—in giving voice to an oppressed minority—is perhaps the most effective spokesman for postmodern theories (of textual [Derrida 1974], academic-intellectual [Lyotard 1984], mediatized [Baudrillard 1994], or discursive-structural contingency [Foucault 1982]).

Critics of the non-normative tenet of queer theory have pointed to (i) the perceived dilution of "queer" to encompass far more than LGBTQ lives (are cisgender straights who profess to reject categories of gender and sexuality considered to be "queer"?), and (ii) to the privilege of white, cisgender, homonormative, gays and lesbians, who do not necessarily need a queer identity politics in order to thrive. Identity politics must by definition be anchored in the articulation of a stable group identity (e.g., homosexual, "same-sex" marriage) in the process of demanding political recognition. Critically, identity is central to the struggle for recognition by queers of color (Johnson 2005; Ferguson 2003) and transgender people (Halberstam 2005), especially black transgender women, who are the most vulnerable groups under the LGBTQ+ umbrella; this tradition of thought is indebted to black feminism, particularly that of the Combahee River Collective, for whom "the most profound and potentially most radical politics come directly out of our own identity, as opposed to working to end somebody else's oppression" (Combahee River Collective 1977). In contrast, much of early queer theory, beginning with Butler's foundational theory of gender as quotidian performance, aims to *destabilize* (gender) identity. The contradictions of the non/identity-based strands of queer theory can be seen in the following: pushed to its logical extreme, Butler's theory that gender is performative would imply that "same-sex" marriage (and indeed, the very concepts of homosexuality and heterosexuality) cannot be conceptualized, since gender is fundamentally indeterminate. This is both the power and the Achilles' heel of queer theory, which dismantles oppressive structures at the same that it appears to weaken identity-based political organization.

As a queer of color person myself, I recognize the trickiness of sustaining both the identity and non-identity facets of queer theory, but my life experience also convinces me of the salience of queerness as non-normativity. As queers of a certain age know, the vast majority of us were born into straight families and thus learn from a young age to collect scraps at the heteronormative table, recycling and reusing bits and pieces of an often hostile world to fortify our closets. Many of the queer younger generation in Europe and North America are lucky enough to have been born into a world in which equality is at least partially enshrined in legislation, but this is rarely true for global queer youths who live in fear of state-sanctioned physical and psychological violence. Stigmatized and abject, queers as a whole *live* non-normativity, both in the traumatic sense of marginalization, and, crucially, in the sense of *queering* bits of the heteronormative world in order to survive (Muñoz 1999). Rather than arriving fully formed as an identity, queer, in the global view, usually emerges when we derive secret meanings and uses from ostensibly straight culture, people, and sounds. Same-sex marriage is, after all, modelled on its heteronormative equivalent and, for its problems, presents a significant advancement of LGBTQ+ rights.[9]

Perhaps only the moral universalism of a Kantian hangover (the so-called categorical imperative) would mandate that "queer" can only be defined in one way—as an identity. Later work in queer theory has managed to curb some of the logical extremes to which Halperin's conception of pure anti-normativity could be pushed (Wiegman and Wilson 2015). In particular, theorization of queer temporality has shed light on how livable queer futures are created from the reinvention of pasts (Muñoz 2009), and queer temporal diversions are bound up with the efficient timing of capitalist profit-making and cultural/biological reproduction (Freeman 2010). That is to say, non-normativity is *always anchored in a point of resistance against heteronormativity*. Queer theory's non-normativity has roamed far and wide epistemologically, enabling even temporality and phenomenology (Ahmed 2006) to be queered. The power of epistemological queering lies in the systemic paradigm shift demanded by queer theorists, such that *everyone* is called upon to revise their normative understanding of the world around us. At the same time, queer temporality is anchored in, for example, BDSM practices upon which Elizabeth Freeman based her theory of nonproductive (hence anti-capitalist), "slow" temporality (2010, 138). Johnson's theorization (2005) of the intersectional "quare" identity speaks not just to those who identify as black rather than queer because it is racial identity that speaks best to their lived oppression; Johnson also articulated a valuable framework for analyzing the *ambiguous* outcome of the intersection of multiple identities and subjectivities (he argues that white privilege allows for a *discursive* form of subjectivity, wherein words and concepts of non-normativity

---

[9] The mimicry of heterosexual marriage by same-sex marriage is sometimes considered to be a form of *homo*normativity, which is originally associated with a form of gay rights that is anchored in the notion of private accumulation in a personal capacity in a capitalist economy ("contributing to economic growth"), detached from the larger assemblage of left-wing, LGBTQ+, feminist, anti-racist, and socialist goals (Duggan 2002). In recent usage, homonormativity is often used to refer to queers who are white and/or male.

can be appropriated freely, whereas those without privilege are continually constrained by their *material*, impoverished, racial embodiment).

The authors of this volume recognize the importance of identity while retaining the non-normative stance of queer theory. Embracing the ambiguity that arises from the intersection of both a generic non-normativity and the specificity of LGBTQ lives means navigating the dynamics of what I term in this volume as *generalizable contingency*. Here it is useful for us to distinguish between the specific queer *identity* of LGBTQ+ music-makers, listeners, and music theorists, versus the queer *ethos* of non-normativity, which other people can be inspired by—without, however, earning the right to call themselves "queer." Queer identity is contingent upon LGBTQ+ lives; the queer ethos of non-normativity is up for grabs by writers so inclined and is in that sense generalizable—with the caveat that for a piece of writing to count as expressing a queer ethos, there should be a focus on music-makers or -listeners who are marginalized in some way by race, gender, sexuality, or ability (e.g., a BIPOC woman composer who is not LGBTQ+). *Queer ear* refers to a non-normative *practice* of listening that may be adopted by people inspired by the queer ethos (non-normative musical practices can be learned regardless of one's identity); however, this is to be distinguished from research on specifically LGBTQ+ *listeners and music-makers*, which I will refer to as *queer music theory*. It is worth pointing out that a writer does not need to be queer to engage in queer music theory; conversely, queer writers are naturally free to pursue any kind of research, queer or otherwise. In the following, the specific meaning of "queer" (as identity, as ethos) will emerge from the relation between contingency and generalizability.

The power of queerness lies in both in its generalizability to anyone's experience of being in the world, *and* in its gender and sexual contingency. Our aim is to push queer studies in music—especially within music theory—toward ever more diversity and inclusion while incorporating queer theories' epistemological ambitions to undo the worst forms of oppression. We let music theory speak to all kinds of queer agendas, making room for studies that can speak both to particular lives as well as to broader methodological points, much as the entire field of gender and sexuality studies always has done. While some chapters (Solomon, Stover, Bretherton) in this volume are based on queer music-makers, other contributions (Maus, Franseen, Lee) roam further afield, showing the queer*ing* of ostensibly straight sounds by listeners—including music theorists and music critics—who had no choice but to make a habitable world for themselves. Furthermore, queerness, while linked to gender and sexuality, and to queer theory, in a concrete way, also paves the way for the emergence of *general* spheres of non-normativity, such as a non-anthropocentric conception of musical agency (Luong); an insular, non-instrumental conception of music-theorizing for sake of the pleasure of it, as opposed to the marketing of the music humanities as socially relevant in the neoliberal university (Currie); and new ways of theorizing that attend to non-canonic sounds, necessitating departure from music-theoretical methods that prioritize the normative values of unity (Lochhead) or logical certainty. Crucially, these general aspects of non-normativity are anchored in lives and/or theories that are unambiguously recognized as queer and reveal the targets of resistance (anthropocentrism, instrumentality, unity) to be heteronormative, allowing us to discern how gender and sexuality inflect wide swaths of general existence. Even so, non-normativity is ultimately a *compulsory way of life* for queers, and queer theory is forged in the crucible of closets and homophobic violence.

Of critical importance in this volume is the intersection of gender, sexuality, and race in many of the chapters, whether race is part of the chapter's subject matter and/or shapes the author's history of listening as a facet of the author's identity. The tenet of non-normativity that informs queer theory is relevant in these intersectional chapters as well, marking the alterity of racial marginality. Luong's chapter points out that racial exclusion (along with the marginalization of women and queers) is constitutive of the anthropocentrism that informs music-theoretical conceptions of musical agency, with the human agency of theorists and composers placed above that of the work's "non-human" themes and topics; following post-humanist theory, the key point is that those who have historically been counted as "human" are white, male, and cis-heteronormative. Stover's chapter (an intersectional study of Sun Ra) cites Muñoz 2009 in pointing out that racial liberation movements have always included queers. Solomon's chapter examines the crafting of an orientalist, gamelan-based, erotically charged, static temporality in early twentieth-century US West Coast queer composers' percussion ensemble works, which project a utopian alterity of queer and free sexuality elsewhere. Lee's chapter refers to the homophobic environment of his youth in Singapore to argue that his queering of Schumann is a form of cosmopolitanist escape. Lochhead's chapter focuses on the music of Israeli American composer Chaya Czernowin and is consistent with recent calls for greater inclusion of BIPOCs, especially QTBIPOCs, and women in music theory.

The current work presented in this volume should be understood against the spotty and non-linear history of queer music theory (based on the musical practices of queers), with contributions crisscrossing disciplinary boundaries and often subsisting at disciplinary margins. In queer musicology, authors such as McClary and Brett have made use of analysis, but they did so within a much broader conceptual and cultural framework that is necessitated by the characteristic ambiguity of the topic at hand, requiring careful parsing and erudite exposition as authors grapple with the structural uncertainty that surrounds silences, absences, and closets (see Maus's chapter for a fuller account). Publications that can be categorized under music theory comprise a tiny fraction of the bibliography of LGBTQ music scholarship maintained by the LGBTQ Study Group of the American Musicological Society (Sagrans, Wace, and Whitesell 2018). In tracing the emergence of queer music theory, one starting point is the first conference paper in that area by Nadine Hubbs (on the "sexual politics" of Morrisey's melodic contours) at the Society for Music Theory (SMT) in 1994 (subsequently published as Hubbs 1996; see also Hubbs 2007). A notable exception among scholars of queer music studies, who usually have a primary musicological affiliation, is Fred Everett Maus, who has carved a niche for himself in the study of the subjectivity and practices of music theorists, articulating "masculine," "masochistic," or "bottom" subjectivities (Maus 1993, 2004, 2013). Martin Scherzinger (1997) has examined the late nineteenth-century conception of "inversion" in terms of music (Webern's symmetrical tone row inversions) and homo/heterosexuality. Following the tenet of queer non-normativity, Jennifer Rycenga (2006) writes on the queering of form in the music of the progressive rock band Yes, while Ivan Raykoff (2002) examines formal deviation in piano transcriptions that paraphrase the original Lieder (these book chapters lean toward queer ethos and thus do not belong to a strict definition of queer music theory). Apart from the foregoing publications, panels on queer topics were organized at the SMT conferences in 1999 and 2001, which included papers that eventually made it into print (some cited above), as well as other papers by Charles Fisk, Steven Nuss, Martha Mockus, Joseph Kraus, and Ian Biddle. More recently, queer music-theory panels have featured regularly at SMT conferences since 2014, and some of the papers are featured in this volume. Among the younger generation of scholars, a small handful of QTBIPOC music theorists have been contributing innovative scholarship (e.g., Luong 2017; Sofer 2018), expanding the possibilities of music theory in the examination of music-theoretical practices and electronic music. From the above, we can discern that the history of queer music theory takes the form of a loose web of spidery threads; there has never been a monograph dedicated to the subject prior to this volume.

Queer non-normativity in the narrower sense pertaining to gender and sexuality has always been at least *consistent*—as opposed to identical—with non-normative approaches to music theory. These latter approaches arguably share the same ethos as the scholarship mentioned in the previous paragraph, even if they are not "queer" per se. There has always been a minority voice calling for attention to the contingencies of listening, to the act of theorizing, and to the historicity of music-theoretical values such as unity, which may not be borne out in musical works. A few readings here will suffice in exemplifying music theory's non-normative thread. David Lewin's theory of perception (1986) sought to reflect listening experience more closely than Schenkerian theory, twisting the latter by incorporating the fluidity of musical expectation as a work proceeds. As opposed to a hyper-rational, disembodied practice, music theory in general has been cast by Kofi Agawu (2004) as a performative act (involving repeated listening) in which the theorist exercises his musicality by "composing" an analytical graph based on knowledge of musical conventions. In his defense of a music theory premised on the traditional conception of the coherent synthesis of contrasting elements into musical unity (a vision congruent with that of a singular objective truth), Robert Morgan (2003) grouped together a number of writers who discerned and theorized non-normative musical processes. There is a sense in which the best of music theory has always celebrated ambiguity and bold defiance of structural norms (Schachter 1998; Anson-Cartwright 2001), even as the staid majority dominated music theory—from this perspective, music theory has perhaps always been a little queer in its ethos.

The above overview of queer music theory in relation to both non-normative music theory and to queer musicology raises the question of what precisely queer music theory is. Queer music-theorizing in this volume has its own specificity, distinct from historical, contextual studies in musicology, focusing instead on the experience of listening to particular pieces of music, and the articulation of that experience using concepts that correspond to the inner workings of music, defined as pitch, interval, mode, scale, tonic, timbre, texture, melody, harmony, rhythm, meter, and so on—that is, precisely the elements included in *The Oxford Handbook of Critical Concepts in Music Theory*, but repurposed for our queer uses. To give a crude definition, the most widely held notion of music theory, at its core, is the study of music as abstracted from the vagaries of social and listening context, focusing instead on *compositional* features (which Dahlhaus calls the "practical" tradition of music theory; Dahlhaus 1984, 6–9). Rather than feelings and narratives, then, *hard* music theory in this sense focuses on pitch, interval, mode, and so on—musical elements that have a relatively large measure of verifiability and consistency across listenings. That this kind of objectivity is coded white, male, and cis-heteronormative needs hardly be emphasized for the reader familiar with Donna Haraway's seminal work (1988) in the feminist critique of scientific knowledge, which has influenced generations of writers in queer, critical race, disability, and post-humanist theory—writers from whom authors in this volume generously draw.[10]

Many of the authors of this volume appropriate the apparatuses of hard music theory for queer ends, establishing a link between non-normative gender and sexuality, and non-normative compositional features or music-theoretical approaches. We might think of this as the ultimate sleight of hand as far as queer*ing* goes, dismantling and remaking masculine music-theoretical tools for the study of queer listening and queer music-makers. Bretherton's chapter anchors his hermeneutic queering of Schubert's *Der Atlas* in Schenkerian analysis, proposing that the exaggeration of structural norms represents oppressive homophobic and ableist forces (symbolized by Zeus and the Olympians).[11] Solomon's chapter demonstrates how the exotic, homoerotic stasis of ostinati is situated by West Coast composers in the teleological milieu of Western musical temporality. Stover's queer analysis of Sun Ra's music, emphasizing emergence and transformation within a musical multiplicity (as opposed to a closed logical circuit), is connected with Sun Ra's sexuality as well as with queer theory. Lee's chapter critiques Schenkerian analyses of Schumann's Lieder in terms of the heteronormative temporality of unilinearity, opening space for a queer reading of temporal leaps and short circuits. In all of these chapters, the queerness of the composition or music-theoretical approach is inspired by the queer sexuality of the music-makers (West Coast composers, Sun Ra) and/or of the music theorist who authored the chapter. What precisely the normative music-theoretical values are, which these chapters write against, can be gleaned from Morgan's

---

[10] The binary of human rationality and non-human irrationality—a category to which queers are assigned, along with women and people of color—is a hoary Enlightenment conceptual framework that has informed the exercise of oppressive powers over centuries (Braidotti 2019, 7).

[11] Joseph Straus has written widely about the intersection of musical and social structures from the perspective of disability studies. See Straus 2011, 2018.

defense of the precept of unity (2003), and from the tendency of some music theories to iron out ambiguities in favor of maintaining logical, formal consistency.[12] Against this background, queer music theory undercuts the traditional masculine values of rationality (Maus 1993), unity, unilinearity, teleology, and logical certainty. It privileges provisional, idiosyncratic, non-normative theories and analyses, as well as minority, queer vantage points, narrative, and listening experiences—but in articles that seek, in spite of their queer and experiential contingency, to be generalizable. In relation to the above chapters, what makes queer music theory a "theory"—if we follow Fallows's definition of "general principles"—is the following features: (1) the inextricable intertwining of gender and sexuality, and/or queer theory, with hard music-theoretical apparatuses; and (2) the traversing of *non-normativity* across gender and sexuality, as well as the hard music-theoretical dimensions of the chapters. Queer music theory, contingent on queer gender and sexuality, and queer theory, is generalizable both in the sense that it can challenge a normative view of the entire enterprise of music theory, and in the sense that the tools of music theory allows for the possibility for all readers to experiment with particular conceptions of music theory and musical experience from a minority vantage point. Generalizable contingency, radiating outward from queer gender/sexuality and queer theory, is seen in the *repurposing of hard music theory for queer ends*, constituting one of myriad ways by which queers remake various general aspects of an often hostile world, making those selected aspects contingent to us.

The interweaving of various chapters in this volume into my arguments above shows that there are multiple overlapping cognitive maps of the book, and many pathways built around concepts such as the valences of non-normativity (gender/sexuality versus music theory), the queering of hard music theory, and intersectionality. Yet the book does assume a somewhat

---

[12] David Ferris (2000) discusses the problems of using Schenkerian theory to analyze passages of musical ambiguity (39–43). This is not to say that *all* Schenkerian or other theories (e.g., set theory) necessarily are opposed to ambiguity, uncertainty, non-systematicity, and non-unity, subscribing instead to the notion of a unified, objective truth, but that the dominant approach to these theories, as transmitted by tenured professors who have ruled over music-theory programs for decades, does indeed reflect the rather obvious tenets of unity and logical certainty in these theories. Perhaps a corpus study of the entire literature on music theory will prove my point as to the weightage of articles leaning toward either unity and logical certainty, on the one hand, or contingency, on the other—but that is obviously far beyond the scope of this introduction. To the reader allergic to supposed "straw man" characterizations of a conservative music theory, purportedly ignoring the many advances in the field, I should point out that citing, e.g., Scherzinger 1997 as a queering of set theory does not constitute proof that set theory as a whole welcomes queer theory with open arms, or that music theory as a whole is socially oriented. Work by Scherzinger and others are *exceptions that prove the rule*.

linear structure by convention. Before providing an outline of the three sections of the book, however, a note on the coverage is necessary. Due to a variety of factors (including health, a change in viewpoint, a change in career path, and the impact of COVID-19), a number of authors who originally proposed a wide range of topics (music theory and transgender theory, bisexuality, and BDSM practices) had to withdraw from the project. While the resulting volume has a presence of queers of color in the range of authors and topics, the degree of diversity is unfortunately more limited than I had hoped, in spite of two public calls for papers in the mailing list of the Society for Music Theory in 2017 and 2018—this is in addition to personal invitations to authors, several of whom declined because of existing commitments. As the first monograph on queer music theory, this book signals the arrival of the field and the formation of a critical mass of authors, which, however, is still relatively thin in comparison with the thriving community of queer musicologists. The thinness of the field goes some way in explaining the difficulty of editorial curation and the regrettable lacunas of this book. As noted, queer of-color topics and authors are present in this book, but barely so, a situation that I find to be highly unsatisfactory; there is regrettably no transgender representation in this volume. I had faced real difficulty in curating chapters on queer/trans of-color composers,[13] and received no proposals on queer/trans of-color ways of listening as articulated in music theory, but I am hopeful that this book will lay the foundation for future research in these areas. As a queer of-color person myself, I feel especially responsible for the inadequate representation of queer/trans of-color composers and music-makers in this volume. I recognize my inadequacies in not attending to them from an earlier stage in the conception of this project, so that I could perhaps have written about them myself, or have innovated a theory of queer/trans of-color listening. To address the situation, I have created the QTBIPOC Composers Project, publishing online profiles for US-based composers who identify as transgender or non-binary, and have begun making related research presentations.[14] Composers include Mari Esabel Valverde, Holland

---

[13] Research on queer/trans of-color composers is scarce, especially in the discipline of music theory. For example, Barg 2013 contains some analysis of Billy Strayhorn's music, while Hisama 2015 has more extended analyses of Julius Eastman's music, but neither is conventionally classified as belonging to the discipline of music theory.

[14] QTBIPOC Composers Project folder, *Global Musical Modernisms* (created in March–April 2022, accessed April 30, 2022), https://hcommons.org/groups/global-musical-modernisms/docs/.

Gavin Lee, "How Not to Talk About Mari Esabel Valverde's Music: A Trans Indigenous Mexican Composer's Perspective," SMT Queer Resource Group panel, joint AMS/SEM/SMT conference (New Orleans, Louisiana).

Andrews, Nebal Maysaud, Ahmed Al Abaca, James Vitz-Wong, Mária Grand, Janelle Lawrence, Melika M. Fitzhugh, and Spencer Arias.

When a field such as music theory is full of white men, and as graduate students we are taught the primacy of citation, the products of our scholarship are going to cite a lot of white men. There have been calls to break off from mainstream scholarly conventions as well as established citational habits (Ahmed 2017, 8; Ewell, foreword to this volume; Luong 2022), accompanied by the emergence of innovative queer and feminist work from QTBIPOC scholars, for example, analysis of electronic music in Sofer 2018 (by composer Barry Truax), or reflexive articles on the gendered qualities of the very practice of music theory itself (Luong 2017). However, there is an immense "narrative scarcity" (Lee and Ramakrishnan 2021) of *both* QTBIPOC *scholars* and QTBIPOC *composers* because of the "white racial frame" (Ewell 2020). As noted by Eric Hung (2018), QTBIPOC composers such as Julius Eastman faced resistance, particularly when he made overt political statements about race and sexuality, thus leading to marginalization and loss of his music. Furthermore, queer and trans music-makers living in homophobic and transphobic regimes are often in the closet (as in Singapore, where I grew up, where gay sex remained criminalized until the prime minister in 2022 announced plans to remove the relevant statute from the penal code[15]) and even have their existence scrubbed from the internet entirely (as in China, where I now work, and where queer conferences—which have now ceased—used to scrub the word "queer" completely from their paper abstracts).[16] Even for places like the United States, where LGBTQ+ rights have advanced to a certain degree, the discussion of QTBIPOC music-makers (as in the Race-ing Queer Music Scholarship symposium of 2016 at the AMS/SEM/SMT conference in Vancouver) concentrates virtually entirely on popular music, such that Eastman to this day remains one of a very small handful of QTBIPOC concert-music composers on the radar of music theory.

As someone who is marginalized by the intersection of race and sexuality myself, I can speak in the first-person register on the importance of

---

[15] Chen Lin, "Singapore Will Decriminalize Sex between Men, Prime Minister Says," *Reuters*, August 22, 2022 (accessed October 13, 2022), https://www.reuters.com/world/asia-pacific/singapore-will-decriminalise-sex-between-men-pm-2022-08-21/.

[16] All references to lesbian singer Qiao Qiao have been scrubbed from the Chinese internet. Gabriel Gima, "An Inspiring Collection of Chinese LGBTQ+ Musicians," *Fashion School Daily*, May 19, 2020 (accessed October 13, 2022), https://fashionschooldaily.com/an-inspiring-collection-of-chinese-lgbtq-musicians-2/63459/.

considering multiple aspects of oppression, emerging out of the whiteness of early queer music studies (try scrolling through the LGBTQ+ music bibliography; Sagrans, Wace, and Whitesell 2018). Gay Asian men like me are subject to caricaturization as effeminate in the United States, such that whenever I speak, others feel the need to speak over me—this is not the same as the oppression faced by women, but gender binarism is the shared axis of oppression for women and "racially castrated" Asian men (Eng 2001). People speak over me at conference panels I have chaired, and in the process of putting together books and special journal issues I have edited. They feel uncomfortable having me, an Asian male, as a leader and try to "teach" me how to chair panels (I have chaired thirty-one of these), or they try to take my place, appropriating my labor and my arguments. They assume I know next to nothing, that I am drawing from outdated theories, that my statements are based on guesswork rather than research, that my research methodology is faulty—the list goes on. It is within this context that I have a special investment in redefining Asian masculinity as well as gay masculinity; this will be part of a new edited book volume on queer Chinese music that I am putting together. Such a project is parallel to earlier queer theorists who appropriated the originally derogatory "queer." It involves taking years of marginalization as a gay Asian man by US music scholars, sexual racism in the United States (on Grindr: "No Asians"), exoticization and being talked over by white rice queens attracted to specifically only Asian men, and erasure by Chinese and Singaporean regimes—and reappropriating that stereotypically effeminate positionality of the gay bottom, which is the presumed default position of gay Asians as featured in the white gay pornographic imaginary. We might take a page here from BDSM practice, wherein it is the bottom who is in charge of the scenario, who controls the intensity of the sensations that may be visited upon them with permission (note that the "bottom" role applies in lesbian and heterosexual BDSM scenarios too). While we might be tempted to read the sexual practices of (misrecognized) "passive" bottoms as allegories of gender relations in real life, this may be too much of an exercise in positivist mapping after three decades of debate over hermeneutics since the 1990s—straight male BDSM bottoms do not signify a new matriarchy; indeed, "a hatred of what is projected as 'passive' and therefore female" might be an expression of the heteronormative subject's "displaced misogyny" (Watney 1987, 50). It should be noted as well that active/passive are not cultural universals. Tops and bottoms are certainly found among gay Chinese folks, but Chinese culture as a whole contains a plethora of tropes that counter the Western masculine image of aggressive action or confrontation, most notably the Taoist notion of *wuwei* or non-action, the philosophy of moderation known as *zhong yong zhi dao*, and colloquial expressions such as *da shi hua xiao, xiao shi hua wu*, meaning to mediate a major conflict so that it becomes a minor conflict, and to resolve the minor conflict altogether.

With regard to earlier queer studies that may not have considered race, we can build on that research foundation where appropriate, while focusing our criticism on the "white racial frame." We learned from Maus 1993 that music theory is a gendered practice: masculine music theorists impose analytic structures over listening experience in order to ameliorate their anxiety over becoming overwhelmed. It is important that a distinction is made between queer theorists who are trying to counter cis-heteromasculinity, on the one hand, versus racist gays like Andrew Sullivan, who supported the Iraq war (Johnson 2005), and the depoliticized gay Republicans discussed by Lisa Duggan (2002), whose idea of emancipation is individual economic success in the capitalist economy. I find the earlier racist masculine-military homonationalism of Sullivan to be especially appalling (he has since renounced his earlier position, after reports on the torture of prisoners and the lack of evidence of weapons of mass destruction in Iraq).[17]

It is because of the white racial frame that there is such a narrative scarcity of BIPOC and QTBIPOC research in music theory, resulting in heightened scrutiny of every piece of related research. But when the key methodology is reflexive contemplation about one's own listening practice as in Maus 1993, ranging over multiple subject positions might not be possible. Perhaps the most appropriate response was what actually unfolded a year later, that is, when a woman, Suzanne Cusick, theorized feminine embodiment through the lens of the physical act of performance (Cusick 1994). This is not to say that we may only ever write about our identities—for example, there are many articles in which writers approach composers who are of a different race, gender, and sexuality than themselves. I would suggest, however, that reflexive articles that involve navel gazing about one's own musical or listening practice is akin to autoethnography, and it would be impossible for a writer to attempt an autoethnography of another person. The crux of the matter is not whether someone is writing from particular majority perspectives—it is *how* they are doing so that should inform our response. Writings that

---

[17] "Andrew Sullivan: Dishing It Out Daily For A Decade," NPR website, October 17, 2010 (accessed October 12, 2022), https://www.npr.org/templates/story/story.php?storyId=130629716.

aim to subvert *cis-hetero*masculinity should not lumped together with chauvinistic texts; such an approach risks essentializing masculine gender itself as a vector of oppression when it is *cis-hetero*masculinity and *right-wing* homonormativity that oppresses women and gay BIPOC men alike. Queer writings that fail to consider race may not be ideal, but it is the *white racial frame*, which results in the narrative scarcity of BIPOC and QTBIPOC music-makers as well as music theorists, that should be castigated, with harsh critique directed at the appropriate targets. Jackson 2019 may not have mentioned QTBIPOCs explicitly, but it contributed to our invisibilization all the same by refusing to recognize Schenker's racism.

I think a truly inclusive approach that covers myriad identities may be more practical in a book, such as our present volume, than a stand-alone article. Each chapter allows its author to fully explore wide-ranging discussions (as in Luong's chapter) or specific intersections of race, gender, and sexuality (as in Stover's chapter on Sun Ra; beyond this book, see Sofer 2022 on non-binary black singer Janelle Monáe). The spectrum of race, gender, and sexuality among the authors and topics covered in this book venture beyond marginalized QTBIPOCs, and I consider this to be a concrete manifestation of alliance. I observe that alliance formation that was important from the early days of queer intersectional theory (e.g., Cohen 1997) has given way to an increasingly ghettoized modality of thinking based on the identity differences that are critiqued by the very founder of Black Lives Matter, Alicia Garza, who distinguishes between *strategic* "popular fronts" based on alliance and "united fronts" that are internally integrated on all counts (Garza 2020, 233). We should remember that there is such a thing as LGBTQ+ rights because of the democratic alliance. There is the SMT LGBTQ+ standing committee because of alliance. Readers will find that there are chapters in this book that do not deal with intersections of race with gender and sexuality. However, those chapters are complemented by others that consider a diverse set of positionalities, and there remains much to be done to show straight scholars how we can discuss white queer and trans music-makers, listeners, and music theorists in a way that is cognizant of cis-heteronormativity. This book is only the start of a much longer conversation that urgently needs to be had.

While I cannot write in a reflexive way about other marginalized positionalities other than my own, I do want to ensure that a discursive space is opened up here for envoicing them. It is well known that the most oppressed of QTBIPOCs are trans women, and while my work in this area is still under peer review and will be found only beyond this book, I thought it was important to provide some reflections on how one can approach identities beyond one's own. For my project on trans Indigenous Mexican composer Mari Esabel Valverde, I took a page from ethnomusicologists who have long emphasized collaborative knowledge production (Barz and Cooley 1997; Stobart 2008; Pettan and Titon 2019) and drew as well from my previous experience interviewing women and queer composers from Singapore. The first thing I did was to refer to writings on QTBIPOCs on trans musicology and trans theory, specifically articles by Stephan Pennington and C. Riley Snorton, sieving through what is by now quite a large bibliography on trans theory that includes mainly white authors. Having educated myself to the extent possible on my own, I then conducted an interview with Valverde[18] and also showed her excerpts of my analysis of her work *Our Phoenix* (2016), which is a piece that confronts transphobia and the murder of trans people, but also celebrates their survival against all odds.[19] Valverde provided me with notes on how to talk about trans people, including the importance of adjectival sequence, for example, if we mention "white cis male" (i.e., race then gender), the appropriate phrasing for Valverde's identity would be "BIPOC trans woman," not "trans BIPOC woman" (which would be gender then race).[20] From this research experience, what I learned above all was the limits of (literary, queer) theory—trans people need material assistance in addition to representation,[21] and the multiplicity of their life experiences exceed what theory alone can capture (Baitz 2022). There are lessons here that are relevant too for those of us who write about queer music-makers.

In this book, the first section, "Queer Music Analysis," contains narratological-hermeneutic, philosophical, and counter-disciplinary essays that converge on music analysis as methodology. Currie's chapter positions music analysis as the foundation of a queer academy that repurposes the neoliberal university's dictate that the humanities, unlike the profitable sciences, must justify their existence by being *socially* relevant, thereby fulfilling a "minimal" *function* in the education of young adults. Noting the disturbing resonance between the neoliberalized, functional conception of humanities,

[18] Interview with me on August 27, 2022 (accessed September 1, 2022), https://www.youtube.com/watch?v=tr8f5wl0Jzo.

[19] For more information, see composer profile for Mari Esabel Valverde, in Lee, ed., *Global Musical Modernisms* (accessed September 1, 2022), https://hcommons.org/docs/mari-esabel-valverde-2/.

[20] Email communication from Valverde on August 29, 2022.

[21] Valverde emphasized this in an interview. "Engender" podcast, The Choral Commons website (accessed September 1, 2022), https://www.thechoralcommons.com/engender.

on the one hand, and the turn to social relevance in the musicology of recent decades, on the other, Currie proposes a function*less* music analysis (what I have called hard music theory), which intentionally rejects connection to other socially oriented musicological arguments. Music analysis is coded queer—in its lack of status in the neoliberal university, in the turn to the pleasure of music analysis (pleasure being a touchstone of queer and feminist theory), and in its "shameful" lack of social content, when seen from the perspective of the contemporary musicological consensus over sociality (queer shame is the result of heteronormativity). The next three chapters proceed via music analysis to construct and interrogate queer and intersectional narratives. Bretherton's chapter (as mentioned earlier) proposes queer and disabled interpretations of the Schubert's "Der Atlas," departing from the conventional reading of unrequited heterosexual love. Marsico's chapter analyzes Henze's operas through inexplicit queer codings of homosociality, deviant human-animal pairings, and constricting, oppressive social norms. In the final chapter in this section, Lochhead proposes a method of analysis that focuses on the assembling of gestures in the twenty-first-century music of Czernowin, modelling a music-theoretical approach that actually is suited for such music, unlike mainstream post-tonal music theory. In both its selection of music and in the music analysis, Lochhead's chapter is marked by an avowedly queer ethos.

The second section, "Queer Temporality," contains chapters by Stover, Lee, and Solomon, which have all been mentioned above in brief. The promise of queer temporality for music studies was raised early on in Peraino 2013 (827). Chapters in this section expand on the musical implications of theories of queer temporality, exploring models of linear and non-linear temporality (Lee, Solomon), on the one hand, and models of music-theorizing that attends to process, ceding analytical control to the becoming of music (Stover). These chapters appropriate hard music-theoretical apparatuses for queer ends, showing how non-normativity in gender and sexuality infects music theory.

The final section, "Queer Narratology," explores the linkages between narratology and queerness, covering and critiquing case studies across the twentieth century, thereby establishing an outlook on future work in this area. Making relatively little use of hard music-theoretical apparatuses, the chapters in this section primarily engage with "theory" in the form of *conceptualizations* of queer narratology. Fred Maus's chapter articulates the foundational nature of narrative for early queer musicological writings that sought meaning in orchestral music. Maus begins with McClary's work on Tchaikovsky and Schubert. Rather than conventional structuralist plot archetypes (victory, defeat, etc.[22]), McClary's readings weaved queer-world elements into minority narratives, envoicing lives that subsisted at the margins of heteronormativity. Crucially, McClary's narratives are anchored in music analysis and, together with Brett's analysis and interpretation (1997) of Schubert's four-hand piano music from the vantage point of a contemporary queer pianist, marks one of the points of origins of an explicitly queer music theory (although she is considered to be a musicologist). Maus's chapter then proceeds to make its main claim that the intimate relation between queerness and narratology serves as a foundation for projecting queerness back onto the earlier narratological work of scholars who did not construct queer musical narratives but were themselves queer. In a variety of writings by the scholars Edward Cone and Anthony Newcomb, and by the former's life partner, queer sexuality was not explicit, but their narratives nevertheless resonated with a mixed bag of queer life experiences, including the terror of being different, the pleasure of sexuality, the uncertainty that stems from being out of place, and the struggle to overcome myriad difficulties.

Kristin Franseen's chapter continues the narratological thread in her examination of US writer and music critic Edward Irenaeus Prime-Stevenson (1858–1942), who created gay characters (in the author's novel *Imre: A Memorandum*) that recur in his musical writings, which included a queerly coded narratological study of Beethoven's Ninth Symphony. Franseen's work points to an alternative and promising form of queer music theory that turns away from hard music-theoretical apparatuses, relying instead on literary writing to explicate queer listening. The final chapter by Vivian Luong (mentioned earlier) criticizes anthropocentric accounts of musical agency, raising the question of who or what has agency in a narrative. Rather than presuming a clear human protagonist, Luong expands on Maus's argument (1988) that close attention to listening experience reveals that musical agency is indeterminate. As opposed to the analyst or composer, Luong argues for a modality of music theory that cedes control and agency to musical elements (themes, topics), thereby decentering an exclusionary (white, male, cis-heteronormative) conception of rational control, allowing for the emergence of voices that have previously been silenced. The three chapters

---

[22] The archetypes are nascent in a lot of early narratological work but formally theorized in Almén 2003.

in this section explore the boundaries of queer narratology from various perspectives, ranging from the examination of early narratological scholarship (Maus), to the use of narratives in music criticism (Franseen), to posthumanist critique (Luong).

If readers had picked up this volume expecting *general principles* of musical queerness in the form of a catalogue of "queer musical traits," they would be disappointed. This volume is not just about queer composers whose music can be heard differently from that of their straight counterparts, but also about queer appropriation of musical conventions that are made ambivalent in the process. Methodologically, what is most important in this book is not the production of a checklist of distinctive differences, which are shaped by the vagaries of context and chance, but the queer repurposing that results in ambiguities, and the semantic ephemerality of often-secret meanings. Another way to say this is that this volume is balanced between the interrelated dynamics of expressive sound versus listening; one might say that in addition to queering the "pitch," as it were, this volume, like previous work, is also invested in *queering the ear*, which is particularly evident in chapters (Maus, Luong, Franseen, Currie, Lee) focused primarily on the practices and apparatuses of music theory, music theorists, other music scholars, and music critics—rather than on queer composers.

Queering the ear can be seen as being anchored in the reflexive exercise already evident in the earliest work in queer music studies, examining how musical and music-theoretical practices and pleasures are conditioned by the power dynamics of gender and sexuality. Music's power—its ability to overwhelm the listener—has been explicated as the "other" that alienates the listener, prompting the masculine response of rational music theorizing (Maus 1993), or the reconfiguration of the dynamics of power in "lesbian" listening that puts listener and music on an equal footing (Cusick 1994). Representing a vast, multi-faceted expansion of that earlier work, chapters in this volume retain a counterhegemonic positionality against the key form of modern power—normativity (Foucault 1995, 184), while articulating myriad manifestations of queer agency, as seen with both queer listeners (scholars, critics) and queer composers. With sounds unmarked by the queer gender and sexuality of the composer, the filter of a queer ear is needed to discern emergence, transformation, gestures, stasis, non-unilinearity, danger, allure, overcoming, agency, choral voices, human-animal pairings, oppressive social norms, storylines, *Urlinie*, and even the act of music analysis itself, as queer. One of the things that we have accomplished in this book is to show

how a queer ear transposes the non-normativity of gender and sexuality onto music-theoretical apparatuses broadly conceived (ranging from hard music theory to narratology, etc.), such that "normal" compositional features become irradiated with rainbow colors. On the one hand, queer listening is contingent on the queer music-maker or music theorist; on the other hand, queer listening is a generalizable ethos if a sympathetic listener dons a queer ear and hears emergence, gestures, and so on in the way we in this volume have intended. This ambivalence is a *fact of life* and *matter of survival* for musical queers, who, like queers in general, are often "born into the homes of the oppressors" (Attinello 2018, 187) and forced to remake heteronormative culture. It is in recognition of this embodied history that I make the distinction between "queer music theory" as music-theoretical research related to queer listeners and music-makers, on the one hand, and "queer ear" as a modality of non-normative hearing that anyone can adopt, on the other. Through the queer ear, writers can acknowledge their debt to non-normative queer (music) theory, but without claiming the queer identity. If it is strategically important to limit who can claim to be queer, it is just as necessary to acknowledge that queer culture has had an impact beyond the immediate queer community. Retaining the professional designation of "music theory" for queer identity (queer music theory), while allowing for the malleability of listening habits (queer ear), seems to be a good compromise, if not a perfect one.

As Brett noted (1994), musicality itself, long synonymous with homosexuality,[23] entails similar *ambiguities*, conceptualized as the dynamics of "universalization" versus "minoritization."[24] That is, there a fundamental ambiguity about musical queerness that resonates with the specific ambiguity of non-normativity teased out in this volume. Musicality may be synonymous with homosexuality (music itself—*all* music—is "universally" queered), but queers may minoritize themselves and their own kind through closeting. It is unsurprising that queer music theory, too, exhibits this vacillation, with

---

[23] Certainly, singing and sports are assigned the conventional codes of queer and straight in the hit TV show *Glee*.

[24] Brett argues that musical queerness operates in accordance with the logics of universality and minoritization, identified by Eve Sedgwick (1990) as structural features of the closet. On the one hand, universality is observed in putative homosexual panic, which is used as a legal justification for homophobic violence; in this case, homosexuality infects everyone such that straight men experience homosexual desire and thus "panic." On the other hand, minoritization is observed in the enclosure of the closet, keeping queers out of sight (don't ask, don't tell). In music studies, Brett notes minoritizing efforts (sometimes by closeted queers) to block the advancement of out queers and of queer research.

non-normativity carrying different valences and resonances, encompassing both the queer gender and sexuality of music-makers and music theorists, and the queer ethos of non-normative modalities of music theory. Once one hears with a queer ear, it seems as if vast swathes of music become queer (from Beethoven to musical ambiguity to ostinati), but then again, maybe not in the cold daylight of normativity. This speaks to the *fragility* of the queer semiotic reclamation of heteronormative spaces that is easily reversed by a shift in perspective. It is imperative that we keep this fragility in mind, remembering that whatever queer sounds we hear are vibrations anchored in the work of generations of queer music-makers and music scholars who have fought to remake oppressive pasts in service of habitable futures.

In putting this volume together, I have been humbled and inspired by the work of our authors, but it is important to note again that this book merely marks the beginning of queer music theory, and much work remains to be done, particularly in the bridging of the gap between music theory (the discipline to which most of the authors belong) and its sister disciplines, in which a vast literature on listening has developed, and in which many insightful, descriptive, expressive, and hermeneutic passages based on close listening can be found (e.g., Feld 1982; Kramer 1995). There is an urgent need to expand beyond the limits of this book in terms of musical genre, and interdisciplinary bridges to musicology and ethnomusicology will become increasingly important in the future, as the discipline of music theory seeks to overcome its traditional boundaries. That evocative descriptions of musical passages often contain some kind of reference to melody, harmony, and timbre suggests to me that it is a matter of time before innovative interdisciplinary scholarship on queer listening emerges, encompassing and moving beyond the spheres of hard music theory and narratology that we have addressed in this volume. I am hopeful that interdisciplinarity will stretch toward non-music disciplines as well, with scholars in the fields of world, jazz, and popular music theory becoming acquainted with queer theory, which currently is still mainly adopted by scholars of Western art music in the discipline of music theory.

A final note here for some readers who may have a nagging feeling that perhaps the ambit of queer should just be limited to queer gender and sexuality. Since "queer" has become diluted as a code for the cool indie hipster, and there has been pushback against the appropriation of queer by straight media figures,[25] we as academic queer music theorists need to interrogate the

---

[25] For example, in 2015, Lily Rose Depp, the daughter of Johnny Depp, took part in a public campaign for LGBTQ+ awareness by posing for a photograph, but later stated that her non-normativity

meaning of "queer." But this does not mean positioning social media dictates as our ethical compass. It is arguably *our* academic responsibility to conduct a comprehensive ethical review of the multitudes encapsulated in "queer," and to elaborate on the complexities, ambiguities, and, yes, contingencies and generalities that are so often ironed out of universalist social-media pronouncements, as if complex cultural problems could be solved if one just read a blog post and followed the six-point guidelines in *all* situations—no need to consider contextual differences.[26] On the one hand, there are queer people of color committed to changing music theory, and writing about queer music-makers of color; on the other hand, music theorists in general may be inspired by the queer ethos to innovate non-normative methods, breaking from heteronormative masculine values. But I believe it is worth taking the risk of navigating conceptual complexities in the hope that this volume will be the beginning of a larger queering, as music theorists of all genders and sexualities—our *allies*—join us in our project. I leave it to the reader to take actions that have bearing on whether we might convincingly claim that the age of "pitch class amoebas" is over.

Finally, a note of thanks. The preparatory work for this volume took place over a long period of time. I am grateful to the authors in this book who originally took part in conference panels held in 2014 (James Currie) and 2015 (Fred Maus, Judith Lochhead) on the subject of queer approaches to music theory, plus a special panel dedicated to Fred Maus in 2017 (in which Vivian Luong participated). These were panels that I organized as chair of the Queer Resource Group of the Society for Music Theory (SMT). I was later invited to join an ad hoc committee tasked by then–society president Robert Hatten in 2019 with reviewing the diversity committees; it was this ad hoc committee that recommended the formation of a new SMT LGBTQ+ standing committee. Robert serves as a model of what an ally should be. I am also grateful to other authors who responded either to personal invitations or to public

---

extends only to protesting against sexuality *labels*, and not to her actual sexuality. Olivia Blair, "Lily-Rose Depp Clarifies Comments on Her Sexuality," *The Independent*, February 4, 2016 (accessed May 17, 2021), https://www.independent.co.uk/news/people/lily-rose-depp-clarifies-comments-about-her-sexuality-a6853151.html.

[26] A refreshing exception is found in a blog post on how to focus on actual ethical accountability instead of the public *perception* of ethical accountability. The advice is to avoid the tendency to "use the same strategy for every situation," though that point is part of a six-point plan that presumably works for every situation. Maisha Z. Johnson, "6 Signs Your Call-Out Isn't Actually About Accountability," *Everyday Feminism*, May 6, 2016 (accessed August 2, 2021), https://everydayfeminism.com/2016/05/call-out-accountability/.

calls for contributions posted on the SMT mailing list in 2017 and 2018. I have learned much from everyone's contributions, which reflect different perspectives and positionalities. It was because of our collective work that a monograph became feasible, and the amazing support of my editors Suzanne Melamed, and later Norm Hirschy, at Oxford University Press was indispensable in bringing this work to fruition. I would like to thank everyone who has taken part in, or has been inspired by and associated with, the project of queer music theory across the years. For their invaluable advice on the introduction, I am grateful to Kristin Franseen, Judith Lochhead, Vivian Luong, and Federica Marsico—any shortcomings are of course mine.

When I first embarked on the journey of queer music theory, I was still in the final year of graduate school, and I would not have been able to navigate all of this without many people who have given me advice over the years. I am grateful for the unflagging support from mentors, colleagues, and allies who showed me how to tread the convoluted paths of counterhegemonic scholarship and of the profession in general—Philip Rupprecht, Annie Liu, Daniel Wu, Philip Ewell, James Currie, Paul Attinello, Daniel Chua, Kevin Korsyn, Sarah Weiss, and Sean Williams. Finally, my life and work has meaning because of my parents and my chosen family, Stephen Hitchner, Clement Chau, and Steve Wang.

References

Agawu, Kofi. 2004. "How We Got out of Analysis, and How to Get Back in Again." *Music Analysis* 23, nos. 2–3: 267–86.

Ahmed, Sarah. 2006. *Queer Phenomenology: Orientations, Objects, Others*. Durham, NC: Duke University Press.

Ahmed, Sara. 2017. *Living a Feminist Life*. Durham, NC: Duke University Press.

Almén, Byron. 2003. "Narrative Archetypes: A Critique, Theory, and Method of Narrative Analysis." *Journal of Music Theory* 47, no. 1: 1–39.

Anson-Cartwright, Mark. 2001. "Chasing Rainbows: Wolf's *Phänomen* and Ideas of Coherence." *Journal of Music Theory* 45, no. 2: 233–61.

Attinello, Paul. 2018. "Afterword: The World Only Spins Forward." In *Rethinking Gender, Sexuality, and Popular Music: Theory and Politics of Ambiguity*, edited by Gavin Lee, 184–88. New York: Routledge.

Baitz, Dana. 2022. "Towards a Trans* Methodology in Musicology." In *The Oxford Handbook of Music and Queerness*, edited Fred Everett Maus, Sheila Whiteley, Tavia Nyong'o, and Zoe Sherinian, 367–82. Oxford: Oxford University Press

Barg, Lisa. 2013. "Queer Encounters in the Music of Billy Strayhorn." *Journal of the American Musicological Society* 66, no. 3: 771–824.

Barz, Gregory, and Timothy Cooley, eds. 1997. *Shadows in the Field: New Perspectives for Fieldwork in Ethnomusicology*. Oxford: Oxford University Press.

Baudrillard, Jean. 1994. *Simulacra and Simulation*. Ann Arbor: University of Michigan.

Blackmer, Corinne E., and Patricia Juliana Smith, eds. 1995. *En Travesti: Women, Gender Subversion, Opera*. New York: Columbia University Press,.

Borgerding, Todd, ed. 2002. *Gender, Sexuality, and Early Music*. New York: Routledge.

Braidotti, Rosi. 2019. *Posthuman Knowledge*. Cambridge, UK: Polity Press.

Brett, Philip. 1994; 2nd ed., 2006. "Musicality, Essentialism, and the Closet." In *Queering the Pitch: The New Gay and Lesbian Musicology*, edited by Philip Brett, Elizabeth Wood, and Gary C. Thomas, 9–26. New York: Routledge.

Brett, Philip. 1997. "Piano Four-Hands: Schubert and the Performance of Gay Male Desire." *19th-Century Music* 21, no. 2: 149–76

Butler, Judith. 1988. "Performative Acts and Gender Constitution: An Essay in Phenomenology and Feminist Theory." *Theatre Journal* 40: 519–31.

Butler, Judith. 1993. *Bodies That Matter: On the Discursive Limits of "Sex."* New York: Routledge.

Butler, Judith. 1999. *Gender Trouble: Feminism and the Subversion of Identity*. New York: Routledge.

Case, Sue-Ellen, Philip Brett, and Susan Leigh Foster, eds. 1995. *Cruising the Performative: Interventions into the Representation of Ethnicity, Nationality, and Sexuality*. Bloomington: Indiana University Press.

Cohen, Cathy. 1997. "Punks, Bulldaggers, and Welfare Queens: The Radical Potential of Queer Politics." *GLQ* 3: 437–465.

Combahee River Collective. 1977. "The Combahee River Collective Statement." Accessed March 1, 2022. https://www.blackpast.org/african-american-history/combahee-river-collective-statement-1977/.

Currie, James. 2009. "Music After All." *Journal of the American Musicological Society* 62, no. 1: 145–203.

Cusick, Suzanne G. 1994. "On a Lesbian Relationship with Music: A Serious Effort Not to Think Straight." In *Queering the Pitch: The New Gay and Lesbian Musicology*, edited by Philip Brett, Elizabeth Wood, and Gary C. Thomas, 67–83. New York: Routledge.

Dahlhaus, Carl. 1984. *Die Musiktheorie im 18. und 19. Jahrhundert: Grundzüge einer Systematik*. Darmstadt: Wissenschaftliche Buchgesellschaft.

Dellamora, Richard, and Daniel Fischlin, eds. 1997. *The Work of Opera: Genre, Nationhood, and Sexual Difference*. New York: Columbia University Press.

Derrida, Jacques. 1974. *Of Grammatology*. Baltimore, ML: John Hopkins University.

Duggan, Lisa. 2002. "The New Homonormativity: The Sexual Politics of Neoliberalism." In *Materializing Democracy: Toward a Revitalized Cultural Politics*, edited by Russ Castronovo and Dana D. Nelson, 175–94. Durham, NC: Duke University Press.

Edelman, Lee. 2004. *No Future: Queer Theory and the Death Drive*. Durham, NC: Duke University Press.

Eng, David. 2001. *Racial Castration: Managing Masculinity in Asian America*. Durham, NC: Duke University Press.

Ewell, Philip. 2020. "Music Theory and the White Racial Frame." *Music Theory Online* 26, no. 2. Accessed October 5, 2020. https://mtosmt.org/issues/mto.20.26.2/mto.20.26.2.ewell.html.

Fallows, David. 2011. "Theory." In *The Oxford Companion to Music*, edited by Alison Latham. Accessed September 28, 2018. Oxford Music Online. Oxford University Press.

Feld, Steven. 1982. *Sound and Sentiment: Birds, Weeping, Poetics, and Song in Kaluli Expression*. Philadelphia: University of Pennsylvania Press.

Ferguson, Roderick. 2003. *Aberrations in Black: Toward a Queer of Color Critique*. Minneapolis: University of Minnesota Press.

Foucault, Michel. 1982. *The Archaeology of Knowledge and the Discourse on Language*. New York: Pantheon Books.

Foucault, Michel. 1995 [1978]. *Discipline and Punish: The Birth of the Prison*. Translated by Alan Sheridan. New York: Vintage Books.

Freeman, Elizabeth. 2010. *Time Binds: Queer Temporalities, Queer Histories*. Durham, NC: Duke University Press.

Garza, Alicia. 2020. *The Purpose of Power: How We Come Together When We Fall Apart*. New York: One World.

Halberstam, Judith. 1998. *Female Masculinity*. Durham, NC: Duke University Press.

Halberstam, Judith. 2005. *In a Queer Time and Place: Transgender Bodies, Subcultural Lives*. New York: New York University Press.

Halperin, David M. 1995. *Saint Foucault: Towards a Gay Hagiography*. Oxford: Oxford University Press.

Haraway, Donna. 1988. "Situated Knowledges: The Science Question in Feminism and the Privilege of Partial Perspective." *Feminist Studies* 14: 575–99.

Hatten, Robert. 2004. *Interpreting Musical Gestures, Topics, and Tropes: Mozart, Beethoven, Schubert*. Bloomington: Indiana University Press.

Hatten, Robert S. 2018. *A Theory of Virtual Agency for Western Art Music*. Bloomington: Indiana University Press.

Hisama, Ellie. 2015. "'Diving into the Earth': The Musical Worlds of Julius Eastman." *Rethinking Difference in Music Scholarship*, edited by Olivia Bloechl, Melanie Lowe, and Jeffrey Kallberg, 260–86. Cambridge: Cambridge University Press.

Hubbs, Nadine. 1996. "Music of the 'Fourth Gender': Morrissey and the Sexual Politics of Melodic Contour." In *Genders 23: Bodies of Writing, Bodies in Performance*, edited by Thomas Foster, Carol Siegel, and Ellen E. Berry, 266–96. New York: New York University Press.

Hubbs, Nadine. 2007. "'I Will Survive': Musical Mappings of Queer Social Space in a Disco Anthem." *Popular Music* 26: 231–44.

Hung, Eric. 2018. "Lessons from Archives and Public History for the Race-ing of Queer Music Scholarship." *Women and Music: A Journal of Gender and Culture* 22: 129–40.

Jackson, Timothy L. 2019. "A Preliminary Response to Ewell." *Journal of Schenkerian Studies* 12: 157–66.

Johnson, E. Patrick. 2001. "'Quare' Studies, Or '(Almost) Everything About Queer Studies I Learnt From My Grandmother." *Text and Performance Quarterly* 21, no. 1: 1–25.

Kramer, Lawrence. 1993. "Approaches to the Discipline: Music Criticism and the Postmodernist Turn: In Contrary Motion with Gary Tomlinson." *Current Musicology* 53: 25–35.

Kramer, Lawrence. 1995. *Classical Music and Postmodern Knowledge*. Berkeley: University of California Press.

Lee, Gavin, ed. 2018. *Rethinking Difference in Gender, Sexuality and Popular Music: Theory and Politics of Ambiguity*. New York: Routledge.

Lee, Jennifer, and Karthick Ramakrishnan. 2021. "From Narrative Scarcity to Research Plenitude for Asian Americans." *RSF: The Russell Sage Foundation Journal of the Social Sciences* 7, no. 2: 1–20.

Lewin, David. 1986. "Music Theory, Phenomenology, and Modes of Perception." *Music Perception* 3, no. 4: 327–92.

Luong, Vivian. 2017. "Rethinking Music Loving." *Music Theory Online* 23, no. 2. https://mtosmt.org/issues/mto.17.23.2/mto.17.23.2.luong.html.

Luong, Vivian. 2022. "Musical Bodies: New Work in LGBTQ+ Music Theory." Panel at AMS/SEM/SMT 2022, New Orleans, LA.

Lyotard, Jean-François. 1984. *The Postmodern Condition: A Report on Knowledge.* Minneapolis: University of Minnesota.

Maus, Fred Everett. 1988. "Music as Drama." *Music Theory Spectrum* 10, no. 1: 56–73.

Maus, Fred Everett. 1993. "Masculine Discourse in Music Theory." *Perspectives of New Music* 31, no. 2: 264–93.

Maus, Fred Everett. 2004. "The Disciplined Subject of Musical Analysis." In *Beyond Structural Listening?: Postmodern Modes of Hearing,* edited by Andrew Dell'Antonio, 13–43. Berkeley: University of California Press.

Maus, Fred Everett. 2013. "Classical Concert Music and Queer Listening." *Transposition* 3. http://transposition.revues.org/148.

McClary, Susan. 2002 [1991]. *Feminine Endings: Music, Gender, and Sexuality.* Minneapolis: University of Minnesota Press.

McClary, Susan. 1994; 2nd ed., 2006. "Constructions of Subjectivity in Schubert's Music." In *Queering the Pitch: The New Gay and Lesbian Musicology,* edited by Philip Brett, Elizabeth Wood, and Gary C. Thomas, 205–34. New York: Routledge.

Morgan, Robert. 2003. "The Concept of Unity and Musical Analysis." *Music Analysis* 22: 7–50.

Muñoz, José Esteban. 1999. *Disidentifications: Queers of Color and the Performance of Politics.* Minneapolis: University of Minnesota Press.

Muñoz, José Esteban. 2009. *Cruising Utopia: The Then and There of Queer Futurity.* New York: New York University Press.

Johnson, E. Patrick. 2005. "'Quare' Studies, Or (Almost) Everything I Know About Queer Studies I Learned From My Grandmother." *Black Queer Studies: A Critical Anthology,* edited by E. Patrick Johnson and Mae G. Henderson, 124–60. Durham, NC: Duke University Press.

Pennington, Stephan. 2018. "Willmer Broadnax, Midcentury Gospel, and Black Trans/Masculinities." *Women and Music: A Journal of Gender and Culture* 22: 117–25.

Peraino, Judith. 2005. *Listening to the Sirens: Musical Technologies of Queer Identity from Homer to Hedwig.* Berkeley: University of California Press.

Peraino, Judith. 2013. "The Same, But Different: Sexuality and Musicology, Then and Now." Part of "Colloquy: Music and Sexuality," convened by Judith Peraino and Suzanne Cusick. *Journal of the American Musicological Society* 66, no. 3: 825–72.

Pettan, Svanibor, and Jeff Todd Titon, eds. 2019. *Decolonization, Heritage, and Advocacy: An Oxford Handbook of Applied Ethnomusicology,* Vol. 2. Oxford: Oxford University Press.

Purvis, Philip, ed. 2013. *Masculinity in Opera: Gender, History and New Musicology.* New York: Routledge.

Raykoff, Ivan. 2002. "Transcription, Transgression, and the (Pro)creative Urge." In *Queer Episodes in Music and Modern Identity,* edited by Sophie Fuller and Lloyd Whitesell, 150–76. Urbana: University of Illinois Press.

Rehding, Alexander, and Steven Rings, eds. 2019. *The Oxford Handbook of Critical Concepts in Music Theory.* Oxford: Oxford University Press.

Rycenga, Jennifer. 2006. "Endless Caresses: Queer Exuberance in Large-Scale Form in Rock." In *Queering the Popular Pitch*, edited by Sheila Whiteley and Jennifer Rycenga, 235–48. New York: Routledge.

Sagrans, Jacob, Keith Wace, and Lloyd Whitesell. 2018. "A Cumulative Bibliography of LGBTQ Scholarship."

Schachter, Carl. 1998. "Either/Or." In *Unfoldings: Essays in Schenkerian Theory and Analysis*, edited by Joseph Straus, 121–133. Oxford: Oxford University Press.

Scherzinger, Martin, with Neville Hoad. 1997. "Anton Webern and the Concept of Symmetrical Inversion: A Reconsideration on the Terrain of Gender." *Repercussions* 6: 63–147.

Sedgwick, Eve Kosovsky. 1990. *Epistemology of the Closet*. Berkeley: University of California Press.

Smart, Mary Ann, ed. 2000. *Siren Songs: Representations of Gender and Sexuality in Opera*. Princeton: Princeton University Press.

Snorton C. Riley. 2009. "'A New Hope': The Psychic Life of Passing." *Hypatia* 24, no. 3: 77–92.

Sofer, Danielle. 2018. "The Macropolitics of Microsound: Gender and Sexual Identities in Barry Truax's *Song of Songs*." *Organised Sound* 23, no. 1: 80–90.

Sofer, Danielle. 2022. *Sex Sounds: Vectors of Difference in Electronic Music*. Cambridge, MA: MIT Press.

Stobart, Henry. 2008. *The New (Ethno)musicologies*. Lanham, MD: Scarecrow Press.

Straus, Joseph. 2011. *Extraordinary Measures: Disability in Music*. Oxford: Oxford University Press.

Straus, Joseph. 2018. *Broken Beauty: Modernism and the Representation of Disability*. Oxford: Oxford University Press.

Tomlinson, Gary. 1993. "Approaches to the Discipline: Tomlinson Responds." *Current Musicology* 53: 36–40.

Watney, Simon. 1987. *Policing Desire: Pornography, AIDS, and the Media*. Minneapolis: University of Minnesota Press.

Wiegman, Robin, and Elizabeth Wilson, eds. 2015. "Queer Theory without Antinormativity." *Differences* 26, no. 1: 1–187.

1

Queer and Critical Race Theory

Figuring Out Music Theory

Gavin S. K. Lee, Philip Ewell, and Robert Hatten

GL: *Thank you for agreeing to take part in this conversation on queer studies in music theory. Most of our authors identify primarily as music theorists, though our work may in a sense occupy an ambiguous terrain between music theory and musicology. As this is the first book-length publication entirely dedicated to what we might call "queer music theory" (as opposed to queer musicology or ethnomusicology), I wanted to have a forum in which we can think broadly and contextualize the subfield in relation both to mainstream music theory and other minoritarian approaches. Philip, I am interested in your views on anti-racism in music theory, which you have written perhaps the most forcefully about in recent memory, and the connections between anti-racism and queer approaches to music theory. Robert, I am interested in your view point because the SMT LGBTQ+ standing committee originated in the review of diversity committees undertaken during your SMT presidency in 2017–2019. Could you both say a little about what made you agree to take part in this conversation? What are your initial thoughts?*

RH: My willingness to take part in this conversation stems from a growing concern for defending and promoting the rights and opportunities of the LGBTQ+ music theory community of scholars. I read Fred Maus's recent *Music Theory Online* article[1] in which he reprinted his two presentations to SMT that included anonymous survey responses from scholars who have experienced discrimination in our field, and my heart went out to them. On June 15, 2019, the Supreme Court in a landmark decision ruled that LGBTQ+ individuals have the same rights against discrimination in hiring/firing as guaranteed to all Americans

---

[1] Fred Everett Maus, "LGBTQ+ Lives in Professional Music Theory," *Music Theory Online* 26, no. 1 (2020), accessed October 5, 2020, https://mtosmt.org/issues/mto.20.26.1/mto.20.26.1.maus.html.

Gavin S. K. Lee, Philip Ewell, and Robert Hatten, *Queer and Critical Race Theory* In: *Queer Ear*. Edited by: Gavin S. K. Lee, Oxford University Press. © Oxford University Press 2023. DOI: 10.1093/oso/9780197536766.003.0002

under the 1964 Civil Rights Act. But that guarantee, long overdue, does not address the further needs of music theory researchers for a forum and collegial support as they pursue innovative research programs. I would hope that music theory has become less exclusionary in the past decades, and that any scholarly resistance may be a result of implicit bias or lack of awareness, but clearly much remains to be done in order to overcome the systemic oppressions in music theory's institutions.

I am interested in learning what kinds of experiences queer subjectivities bring to the table, especially in terms of modes of analysis and interpretation. As an outsider to LGBTQ+ experiences, I am keen to listen and learn, in order to encourage the voices of queer music theorists. One way to understand queer theory is to find similarities to my own experience (and difficulties) as a music scholar. I certainly respect the definitions by which new fields establish their footing, but we may also find that queer theory shares something with other marginalities and counterhegemonies. I look forward to exciting developments as queer music theory finds its place in the academy, transforming the way the music-theoretical field understands musics and theories.

PE: I'm eager to take part in this conversation because it is one that is not often heard in music theory, a field that still has a quite stark divide between what is believed to be traditional music theory, and music theory as it actually is. To be clear, traditional music theory is defined by those who have the power to do so as white, male, and cis-heteronormative. By engaging in an open conversation about what queer music theory is, we can begin to have conversations about power in music theory so that we can begin to dismantle oppressive structures.

Current counterhegemonic work focused around "diversity" is problematic because it can be used as an institutional cudgel in order to silence voices of those who wish to raise legitimate concerns about why things are the way they are. "Diversity" committees obfuscate the core problem: the white, male, cis-heteronormative structure in which they are located. SMT is broken with respect to diversity, as evidenced in its demographics: over four-fifths of the members are white, with increasingly higher proportions if one looks at (i) all full-time faculty and, especially, (ii) tenured faculty. Furthermore, if we truly "embraced all approaches and perspectives" as stated in the SMT Mission

Statement,[2] then we would make them—the music theories of Asia, Africa, or the Americas—part of required music-theory classes in our curricula, from freshman theory to doctoral comprehensive exams, and our undergraduate textbooks would not be based solely on the music of white persons. In the history of American music theory, nonwhiteness has been completely erased. One paper on, say, Aretha Franklin at a conference cannot make up for, say, three required History of Music Theory grad classes that feature, literally, 100% white men. To try to argue otherwise would be less than candid in my opinion.

We in music theory have not acknowledged how we maintain and promote white, male, and cis-heteronormative structures in the field. The lack of this acknowledgment is itself an act of white supremacy, antiblackness, and cis-heteropatriarchy.

RH: I think while diversity committees are in a sense the symptom of an oppressive structure which necessitates their existence, and may exacerbate the problem if they are misunderstood as effective solutions in and of themselves, members of these committees have worked hard to reflect an ethical, inclusive commitment on the part of the Society that is visible and sends a clear message. The committees are guaranteed increasingly well-attended sessions on the program each year (in addition to space and time for their individual business meetings), which provides an ongoing voice in the program, as well as a space for the marginalized and their allies to network and disseminate ideas. They provide valuable services, such as the well-attended diversity luncheon (for current and past recipients of minority travel grants, and which includes local undergraduates who were offered free registration) as well as mentorship programs.

That said, it is clear that diversity committees are tasked with confronting deep-rooted issues that are evidenced in the recent issue of the *Journal of Schenkerian Studies*,[3] where several of the hastily assembled essays were overheated in response to Phil's SMT 2019 plenary talk (without reference to his subsequent and more detailed *Music Theory Online* article, "Music Theory and the White Racial Frame"), specifically,

---

[2] "Administration," Society for Music Theory website, accessed October 5, 2020, https://societymusictheory.org/administration.

[3] "Symposium on Philip Ewell's SMT 2019 Plenary Paper, 'Music Theory's White Racial Frame,'" special issue of *Journal of Schenkerian Studies* 12 (2009).

his claim that Schenker's racism affected his music-theoretical practice.[4] Several authors attempted to dismiss Phil's arguments, ranging from denigrating his professional expertise to accusing him of antisemitism since Schenker was Jewish. Reading Phil's articles and his blog[5] should be sufficient to counter both of these baseless accusations. Compounding the abuse was the absence of sound editorial practice. Why was Phil not given the opportunity to read these critiques in advance, in order to offer his response to them? And why were the unethical attacks not excised by the editors? A more revealing example of how a white racial frame affects music theory could scarcely have been imagined. While some essays such as Suzannah Clark's advanced the examination of race and Schenkerian theory, the issue as a whole was marred by misguided, defensive discourse that makes it more difficult to assess the relation between Schenker's ideological commitments and his framing of music hierarchies. Descriptions of the inevitable hierarchies among pitches (obvious from the lowest analytical level of passing and neighboring tones) need not, and should not, be falsely analogized in racist terms, as Schenker often did.

GL: I'm very appreciative of both of your involvement in this dialogue, which I see as a work in progress, a conversation about the possibility of bringing different perspectives together, rather than a finished product that offers definitive theories or methodologies. My approach in this foreword was to invite people with very different backgrounds to take part, rather than have scholars of queer music studies only. This is because I'm trying to put what I conceive of as alliance formation into scholarly practice. I think alliances are complicated and incomplete, and we should be able to acknowledge that as the actually-existing basis for eventually building what Cathy Cohen calls "interconnected sites of resistance."[6] I am grateful for your perspectives, whether as a scholar whose own work has not touched specifically on diversity, or as someone whose work began in anti-racism, as opposed to LGBTQ+ studies.

    I have a couple of responses to your points above. Robert, I appreciate your sympathy toward queer theory. I would say that it is natural to

---

[4] Philip Ewell, "Music Theory and the White Racial Frame," *Music Theory Online* 26, no. 2 (2002), accessed October 5, 2020, https://mtosmt.org/issues/mto.20.26.2/mto.20.26.2.ewell.html.

[5] Philip Ewell, "Confronting Racism and Sexism in American Music Theory," accessed October 5, 2020, https://musictheoryswhiteracialframe.wordpress.com/.

[6] Cathy Cohen, "Punks, Bulldaggers, and Welfare Queens: The Radical Potential of Queer Politics," *GLQ* 3 (1997): 462 (437–65).

seek to support others by finding resonances within ourselves. I would also add that one thing readers should look out for is to distinguish empathy for others from identifying with others. Allies who are not actually members of a minority should refrain from identifying their work as "queer" because some aspect of their research seems to align with the key, antiestablishment tenet of antinormativity in queer theory (I am not saying that either of you do this). I think that for a publication to count as queer studies, it has to place queer theory, queer listeners, and queer music-makers in a central position.

Philip, I appreciate your powerful statement on the problem of diversity in music theory. I would say that inclusion of LGBTQ+ people, along people of color on committees would be the way forward. Diversification of music-theory curricula to include the sounds of queer and trans people is also necessary, and somewhat more complicated. This is because queer and trans people have not often been visible/audible in history until at least the twentieth century. Thus for music before 1900, we may need to focus not just on queer and trans composers and performers, but queer and trans ways of *listening*. I think Maus and Franseen's contributions in this volume are particularly valuable for the way that they illuminate the workings of the queer ear for pre-1900 music, ranging from Beethoven to Mahler. I hope that the exploration of the queer ear in this book serves as a foundation for future work in areas that we have not addressed sufficiently, particularly trans sounding and listening, and popular and global musics. (See the Introduction for my distinction between "queer music theory" as research on specifically queer listeners and music-makers, and "queer ear" as an ethos and a listening practice that everyone can be inspired by without being able to claim the queer identity.)

GL: *Continuing with our broad, intersectional purview for just a bit more, what would you say are the obstacles to and strategies for gaining recognition for variously defined "diversity" or minoritarian research in music theory?*

RH: If by diversity research you mean studies such as this, and studies of queer stances with respect to compositional, listening, and other social practices involving music, then obstacles would be lack of exposure among theorists to scholarly approaches to these practices, lack of forums for disseminating such research (which this volume is helping to address), and various forms of bias that create systematic barriers. I hope the new SMT LGBTQ+ standing committee will help provide one such forum, especially with a guaranteed session at each annual conference. LGBTQ+ research can be advanced through scholarship (submissions to conferences and journals), networking, making oneself available for service on SMT committees, writing public-facing essays on LGBTQ+ issues, finding public forums to share ideas, and lobbying within SMT for greater visibility.

PE: The main obstacle is that SMT and the field music theory have not acknowledged their racist, sexist, and cis-heteronormative histories, and until they do, nothing can change substantively. In "Truth and Reconciliation" spirit, SMT should in particular acknowledge explicitly the *racist policies* that have led to racial disparities and the erasure of nonwhite voices. We have to begin by dismantling white structures and institutions in music theory, addressing, for instance, the lack of BIPOC (black, indigenous, people of color) members on various SMT committees, such as conference program committees and publication committees, and not only on "diversity" committees to which BIPOC scholars have historically been relegated. The solution is maximal transparency in determining all such committees and, most important, forced inclusion of those marginalized by our white-male-cis-hetero structures. We should openly state that only by insisting on inclusion will it happen—it will not happen organically, since those who currently have power will lose some (but not all I hasten to add) of this power, and they generally want to keep this power because they feel entitled to it.

GL: I agree with Philip and reinforce his message. I would add that SMT should make a public commitment to ending 100% white and 100% straight committees by making sure that there are LGBTQ+ and people of color on board. Music theory departments should make a public commitment to enact hiring practices that put an end to 100% white and 100% straight faculties, especially tenure and tenure-track faculty.

GL: *The chapters in this book involve both abstract queer theorizing on non- and anti-normativity, temporality, and formalism, on the one hand, and more particularized investigations relating to queer composers and music theorists. In relation to our work in this volume, what insights can we draw from the relation between music theory and music analysis, a relation of generality versus particularity?*

RH: My working approach is to consider theories in terms of generalizable principles and flexible strategies within a style competency, and analysis as investigation of the particularities of individual works within a style competency—how they exemplify conventions while recontextualizing to produce distinctive (creative, innovative, interesting) structures/ forms/meanings. There is definitely a dialectic between the two, as analysis leads to generalizations, and generalizations guide further analysis, with unusual musical events demanding further nuancing of theories. Of course, it's much messier, since theories can bias what we perceive as unusual versus normative.

Theories of music, unlike scientific theories of, say, the natural world, face three deterrents to empirical confirmation: musical works are historical, they are aesthetic, and their semiotic understanding depends upon learned behaviors. Thus, our theories cannot be empirically validated in the same way scientific theories are. Empirical approaches to musical cognition can teach us about the potential of listeners, but they can be limited to that which listeners have already learned, making unbiased testing impossible, which is why we need speculative theories that attempt to reconstruct the historical, aesthetic, and learned competencies that we may consider to be presupposed by musical works. I would include all music theories under the umbrella of the speculative in this sense—although some theories hew closer to the structural dimensions of the artifact and thus appear more formalist, while others attempt to reconstruct those underlying competencies that may have motivated the complexities we find in the artefact. There appears to be a growing acknowledgment that theories are not universal, and that they are constantly under construction, whether being refined by interpretations that modify rules to more general principles, or being challenged by competing theories that find new kinds of evidence to topple the assumptions and presuppositions of previous theories. Here, I see much room for queer theories. And I will continue to ponder the ways in which my theorizing as a white male participates in the white racial frame.

PE: Sara Ahmed, in *Living a Feminist Life*,[7] rightly notes how, in calling something a theory (that can reasonably be argued is not a theory), authors (often but not always white men) insulate themselves from potential criticism and narrow the understanding of a subject to the dictates of a select few. By calling something a theory, white men are able to hide whiteness and maleness, and their power structures. Breaking Ahmed's "citational chain," white male theorists citing other white male theorists—that is,

---

[7] Sara Ahmed, *Living a Feminist Life* (Durham, NC: Duke University Press, 2016).

moving beyond the barriers of what our white-male frame has defined to be music theory—is difficult, and generally discouraged. My engagement with race and feminist scholarship is an example of breaking the citational chain of music theory. Many senior scholars in music theory have been skeptical of my work and, in certain cases, even hostile, calling it an "attack" or a "manifesto." This hostility is rooted in the white-male frame's persistent belief in race and gender "neutrality"; once such neutrality is proven to be fallacious, the white-male frame will lose power and prestige, which it wants to hold onto. "Theory" is deployed by white men in music studies in order to keep the racial and gender structure as it is, with white men on top. In his compelling race-scholarship, Ibram Kendi almost never cites from the "theoretical" literature,[8] using plain, accessible, and impactful language to challenge oppressive structures.

GL: I think both of you bring up really good points about "theory." Robert, I appreciate your succinct statement on the issue of generality versus specificity in music theory. I think your explanation of the difference of competency between listeners and composers actually has a lot of resonance for this volume. I think that what we are trying to do in this book is to articulate difference in terms of subjectivity or positionality: queer listening is not the same as straight listening, and the queer ear is distinct from the straight ear. What I have observed is that authors in this volume do make use of basic music-theoretical concepts, but we have different takes on issues of meaning, temporality, narrative, aesthetic precepts, and cultural politics. Philip, I think your caution against "theory" is well founded and resonates with our efforts to produce a different, inclusive kind of theory in this book.

GL: *Is coalition-building and allyship possible in the face of various minoritarian theories' competing claims?*

PE: Yes. It's not just possible, but also of paramount importance. Notably, this is not about donning a Black Lives Matter T-shirt, or attending one protest. It's about a deep individual introspection, examining and reexamining one's core beliefs, that can lead to real antiracist, antisexist, and anti-cis-heteronormative change, which can certainly lead to positive affirmation of LGTBQ+ identities. On a personal note, I've gone through, and still go through, such introspection, and I've had to swallow some bitter pills. Understanding how my own past work has perpetrated whiteness and maleness has not been easy, but it's been eye opening, which comes with

---

[8] Ibram X. Kendi, *How to Be An Antiracist* (New York: One World, 2019).

its own special set of rewards. A key point to note is that allyship needs to be informed by an intersectional perspective. While I learned long ago to never pit someone's suffering against someone else's (white frameworks love that by the way, since it takes the focus off whiteness, which is always a primary goal for whiteness), I need to be clear that the voices of white women, white people with disabilities, and white LGTBQ+ folks can, to an extent, be heard in our fields, precisely because they are white. We in music theory have not yet found our footing with respect to BIPOC, especially blacks since, I hardly need to point out, BIPOC will never be considered white and can therefore never exercise the white agency that other minoritized whites can indeed exercise.

RH: I hope my unmarked identity as a white cis-male or my unwitting participation in white male framing of music theory does not disqualify me from allyship. I want to continue to learn how to be anti-racist, antisexist, and anti-cis-heteronormative, and to continue to be supportive of the scholarship and careers of those who have been disadvantaged by whatever means.

GL: I appreciate your statements of support. I would amplify Philip's point that allyship is of paramount importance. I think that Philip's publications on anti-racism have absolutely assisted the push for equity for LGBTQ+ people. His work has 100% inspired my own thinking in terms of rhetoric and focusing on institutional as well as conceptual issues. I don't think that focusing on one set of issues means that we are neglecting other issues, because counterhegemonic scholars inspire one another, even if we are working on different areas of research. What we ought to be doing is to support and build on one another's work. In a conversation like ours, it is reasonable for each of us to be anchored in our various areas of expertise. All of us have to start somewhere in our work on anti-racist, pro-LGBTQ+, and other initiatives.

GL: *One way of understanding music theory is that it creates musical norms. Given the normalizing function of any theory that claims to be a general principle, there is an inherent tension here between (i) the theorization of queerness as anti-normativity, versus (ii) LGBTQ+ identities that acquire normative status by virtue of having been defined. What are your thoughts on how the two aspects of queer theory are related?*

PE: Disability studies (e.g., Straus 2000) suggest that we, as music theorists, are uncomfortable with things that are abnormal, whether a note in a sonata by Beethoven, or a black trans woman music theorist at a theory conference. I think queer theory represents a treasure trove of useful information to non-LGTBQ+ allies, especially on how cis-heteronormativity, which is baked into the DNA of music theory, can disadvantage people who identify as LGBTQ+.

RH: I think "anti-normativity" is one way that any disadvantaged group will carve out its identity, with respect to changing or overturning the norms of a society that has disadvantaged them. And the universality of that response reflects the operation of markedness: carving out territory for a narrower realm of meaning via some marked opposition. But I would not expect all queer identities to be the same, or that a single queer theory will emerge, even if "anti-normativity" is a frequent distinguishing feature of such identity. And I would imagine that the individual work of LGBTQ+ music theorists will have a profound consequence on ways of thinking among all the individuals who comprise our field, inspiring us all to continue the work of transforming whatever disadvantages anyone.

GL: Very well put! I think everyone has to deal with the complexity that comes with (i) a discursive and cultural field like queer theory, which ranges over concrete identities and abstract tenets, and (ii) the distinct but allied fields of anti-racist, queer, disability, and other subfields of music theory. The fact of the matter is that cultural tropes and symbols of race, gender, sexuality, and disability are intersecting, travelling across people with discrete identities. I may be a gay man who does not identify as woman, but the gender stereotype of femininity used to dismiss gay men has 100% effected its damage on us. And this is connected with ableism and the masculine, muscular ideal that gay men pursue in a bid to raise our self-esteem, which is impacted by sexual racism as well.

As a person of color, I completely understand Philip's view point and I have learned much from him, just as I hope both of you may be inspired by our work in this volume. This brings us to the complexity of relations among minority groups. In my view, minorities have to recognize our interconnectedness and not just our differences—to put it simply, what a black music theorist and a gay Chinese theorist share in common is a racist, cis-heteropatriarchal context. On the other hand, it is equally important that we emphasize that certain segments of the community of minority music theorists are more disadvantaged than others, due to a combination of one or more of the factors of race, gender, sexuality, disability, and socioeconomic status; in particular, LGBTQ+ women, especially LGBTQ+ women of color, are underrepresented in music theory. This is something I have sought to address through public calls for contributions to this book on the mailing list of the Society for Music Theory, but the submissions I received do not cover as broad a range of authors' identities and topics as I would have liked (more on this in the introduction). I tried to address this imbalance by making it a practice to seek out peer comments on my writing from readers with different identities than myself.

GL: *Any final thoughts?*

RH: Much more work needs to be done to support research in LGBTQ+ composers. I checked a database on 4000+ composers compiled by the Institute for Composer Diversity, housed at SUNY Fredonia and available online.[9] When I did a search specifying for LGBTQ+ composers who are also Black, six names appeared. I was familiar with only the two who were deceased: Billy Strayhorn and Julius Eastman, and all six deserve closer scholarly attention. Databases such as this can be starting points in considering a wider range of composers that can be explored to enlarge our repertoire for teaching, performing, and analyzing, as well as to expand our theories' inclusiveness. I also think that in pursuing this research, one would want to be sure not to: (i) inadvertently "out" a theorist who would prefer to remain unidentified, (ii) assume a theorist is LGBTQ+-identified because they work on LGBTQ+ issues, or (iii) assume a LGBTQ+ music theorist wants to work on LGBTQ+ issues and inadvertently shame them for not having done so. I find that Gavin's theory of generalized contingency (see introduction) is a great way to address the complex negotiation between the specific characterization of an identity and the individual members of the marginalized social group who may identify as such. What Gavin brings to the fore is how the relationship between individuals and group must be sensitively construed, and how those of us outside these experiential identities may, wittingly or unwittingly, misunderstand or misrepresent LGBTQ+ identities, individuals, and groups. In my case, I need to be sure that my attempt to find common theoretical ground in the concept of, e.g., "anti-normativity" does not obscure or dilute the significance of this concept as contextualized by the LGBTQ+ experience.

---

[9] Institute for Composer Diversity website, accessed October 5, 2020, https://www.composerdiversity.com.

There is clearly a marked or contingent LGBTQ+ application of "anti-normativity" that distinguishes it from the unmarked or generalized use I might make of it (as in my discussion of unusual musical structures), and it is important that I, and others attempting to engage with queer theory, become more sensitive to this distinction. I want to thank Gavin for the invitation to participate in this illuminating exchange, and to thank Phil, whose perspective has enlarged my own.

PE: I'm excited to see this final monograph in print, and I'm honored to have taken part in this dialogue at the beginning. I'm grateful to Gavin for the invite, and I'd like to thank Robert for conversing with me and Gavin. I find that the more seniority one gets in a field, any field really, the harder self-reflection becomes, especially if one has been a key player like Robert, and I commend him for his openness and his hard work here. More broadly, I think it's important to stress that, with this work, it's not about assigning guilt or casting blame but, rather, it's about responsibility and accountability—we should all hold ourselves accountable as we seek to make our field more welcoming for everyone. Also, since I've seen quite a few confused looks from white persons on my Zoom galleries over the past year and a half, I should say here how important I believe it is to welcome white persons to the table as we all chart a just and equitable path for music theory's future.[10] No, this does not mean welcoming anyone who believes, for example, that blacks are inferior to other races, that women can't lead orchestras, or that there's no such thing as an anti-LGTBQ+ bias in music theory since the field is "neutral" with respect to such things—such views are wrong and people who hold them are not welcome at my table. But otherwise, I welcome everyone, and I've been honored that so many white persons, many of whom are in fact cisgender straight men, have taken me up on difficult discussions about making music theory more welcoming. Finally, I'd point out just how much white persons themselves will benefit by letting go of the "neutrality" arguments that have plagued music theory since its inception in the mid-twentieth century. The intersectionality of all marginalized and minoritized groups is of the utmost importance, and *Queer Ear* will surely be a landmark volume in helping understand these issues from a new and significant perspective.

GL: Thank you both!

---

[10] Philip Ewell, "New Music Theory," part 4 of *Confronting Racism and Sexism in American Music Theory* (2020), accessed May 3, 2022, https://musictheoryswhiteracialframe.wordpress.com/2020/05/01/new-music-theory/.

QUEER MUSIC ANALYSIS

2

Music Analysis; Queer Academy

James R. Currie

The activity from which I experienced most pleasure in my studies as a music undergraduate was music analysis. Maybe it is the nostalgia of hindsight, or just a truth about the relatively unfettered quality of the engagements one has earlier in one's life—particularly in comparison with the cramped conditions that later professional complicities impose—but I remember it distinctly as an activity into which I could, and happily would, disappear. I would hazard a guess that my blithe memories of music analysis are not unique and that others have had similar experiences of the pleasures of forgetting attendant upon its practice. Looking back on it, there is something about these experiences that now resonates to me with some famous words of Walter Benjamin. In his book about his childhood years in Berlin, he wrote: "Not to find one's way around a city does not mean much. But to lose one's way in a city, as one loses one's way in a forest, requires some schooling." For Benjamin, this was an art that he "acquired rather late in life." And it held the possibility of a certain childlike happiness for him, for "it fulfilled a dream, of which the first traces were labyrinths on the blotting papers in my school notebooks."[1] And so how wonderful it seemed back then to lose track of time as I followed, searched for, or found once more the thread of a motif through a piece! How oddly happy I could feel when I looked up, disorientated, and realized what a taste I had for not being able to remember what had led me to where I now found myself! How liberating it felt to encounter my aptitude for getting lost and for taking pleasure for a moment in my own modest *dérèglement* of the senses! Hadn't I been trying to prove a point about sonata form? Why then was I now standing agog in front of some strange, isolated rhythmic feature?

---

[1] Walter 2006, 53–54.

James R. Currie, *Music Analysis; Queer Academy* In: *Queer Ear*. Edited by: Gavin S. K. Lee, Oxford University Press.
© Oxford University Press 2023. DOI: 10.1093/oso/9780197536766.003.0003

Such moments produce next to no exterior manifestations and are almost completely without dramatic interest for, and maybe even imperceptible to, anyone watching me at my desk bowed over some score. They are unimpressive. But they have made my life while I was in them feel like a strangely clandestine privilege: rich without threat that the magnitude of my abundance would produce the ostentation of display. Nevertheless, indulging in such pleasures is a risky business in the contemporary North American academy, for it has become an entrenched discursive convention for everyone in that scene, angels and devils alike, social-justice scholar-warriors as much as crass neoliberal middle-management administrators, to talk of what ought to be happening in the academy only in terms of quite literal-minded interpretations of use (of relevance, worldly application, engagement, effectivity, austerity measures, transferable skills, community outreach, and so forth). So, it is testament to the genuine queerness of this essay that I find myself distracted by imaginings of an academy founded rather on a principle of luxury. Is it not possible to consider that such uselessness might indeed have some use? This is my abiding question.

By the early 2000s, I would set off to music analysis more like some obedient goose, full of all the good professional intentions that graduate school and conference participation had rammed down my throat. Getting lost had been replaced by the desire to be delicious enough for a university to want to consume me through employment. I was trying to become part of that world of professionalized knowledge production of which Theodor Adorno was so often so scathing: a world where "[d]ivergence from the facts becomes mere wrongness, the moment of play a luxury in a world where the intellectual functions have to account for their every moment with a stop-watch."[2] So I would get on the correct train at the correct time with the intention of making sure I would arrive at the correct destination.

As Fred Maus has so carefully explained, such disciplinary protocols go deep into the details of key texts of music theory and, thus, hinder the realizations of other potentialities.[3] For example, in his virtuosic reading of Allen Forte's seminal 1959 essay, "Schenker's Conception of Musical Structure," Maus shows how Forte's rhetorical and figurative language works "to create and circulate an image of a particular kind of person," with the resulting function of helping both to propose what should constitute the

---

[2] Adorno 1991, 127.
[3] Maus 2004, 13–43.

professionalized identity of a music theorist and also to encourage us to emulate it.[4] Forte's text thus "not only says 'Read and evaluate the following claims,' but also: 'Be like me. Do as I do,'"[5] . . . and for heaven's sake, get on the right train. Nevertheless, on the occasions when the train of my professional life came to rest in some nowhere spot, waiting perhaps for more important freight to pass, I could still, as if I were in a mild trance, watch myself stand up, move to the door, disembark, and then walk off into the landscape and out of sight. For it was only once I was invisible to others and their validating gaze, only when the train, not even noticing my absence, had departed that the music analysis I had tried to forget could really have its way with me once more. There was, and has remained, something secretive to it, something hesitant in its response to injunctions to socialize.

Thankfully, it transpires that old habits die hard. And so what first as an undergraduate had seduced me, and what had then troubled and threatened to derail my early attempts at professional rectitude, I now in this essay seek to recoup, perhaps free of guilty conscience: a music analysis that constitutes a self-validating activity, one practiced for the tautological reason of me having a proclivity for wanting to practice it; something indifferent to aspirations toward efficiency. For as Kofi Agawu has put it, once music analysis has entered into this register, it "guarantees nothing save the pleasure—or edification, if you want to get pious about it—of doing."[6] Indeed, even Joseph Kerman, who argued so polemically against music analysis, and whom Agawu in turn sought to refute, could admit that, "taken on its own terms, [it] is one of the most deeply satisfying of all known critical systems."[7] If pushed, I would take the point further still and argue that at its most focused—and thus for me most pleasurable—the doing of music analysis is tantamount to a form of Being, and thus calibrated toward existential rather than instrumental concerns. At any rate, queerness in this essay is reserved primarily for academic practices that take pleasure in that which is in excess of, and even indifferent to, instrumentality.

I certainly did not articulate my burgeoning relationship with music analysis quite so expansively and in such loaded terms in the early 1990s, when I was first setting forth. But even if the thirty somewhat-sad and difficult years since have imbued the thought of music analysis with a kind of vexed

---

[4] Ibid., 14. Forte's article first appeared in *Journal of Music Theory* 3, no. 1 (1959): 1–30.

[5] Ibid., 14.

[6] Agawu 2004, 275.

[7] Kerman 1980, 321.

poignancy, the feelings were nevertheless still strong enough in 1992 to inspire me to pack up my life in London, where I was not unhappy, and ship it off to New York, where I had been accepted into a PhD program. Here I hoped to write a music-theory dissertation on Berg's *Lulu*. God writes in crooked lines, so I ended up writing a historical-musicology dissertation instead—and moreover, on a completely different topic, fugal counterpoint in the instrumental music of Haydn, Mozart, and Beethoven.[8] Because musicology has often offered hospitality to those wishing to engage in music analysis, I did not envision that jumping ship from music theory would ultimately come at the price of having to leave behind the founding pleasures that had led me toward seeking a life within the academy in the first place. Music analysis intersects with the activities of both disciplines and in some instances creates a reliable gangplank between the two—an important image for my argument. It is partly for this reason that in the following essay I flip-flop between musicology and music theory without feeling particularly obliged to be overly pedantic about their distinctions.

This essay is therefore not completely qualified to appear in this volume. My primary interest is in providing an initial framing for the queer potentiality of musical analysis, not the potential queerness of music theory per se. In part, my reasoning is that since musical analysis is *not* merely a subset of music theory, it should be allowed to open out onto other things as the whim takes it. By framing the queer potentiality of music analysis in this way, I therefore afford myself the opportunity for getting at a variety of other questions about the forces that either aid or hinder our attempts to pursue happiness and habitation within academic life. So this is a very queer essay indeed. For as David M. Halperin has famously stated, queerness is not an inherent condition of something, but a quality arising from something's position with regard to a norm; it is relational, not ontological: "Queer is . . . whatever is at odds with the normal, the legitimate, the dominant. There is nothing in particular to which it necessarily refers."[9] Policed by a small army of editors and production managers, what's not "normal," "legitimate," and "dominant" about the assumption that an essay in a collection should remain strictly within the boundaries of the collection's presiding theme? Or, to put it another way, if queer music theory necessitates that we stick to music theory, how queer is it anyway?

[8] Currie 2001.
[9] Halperin 1995, 62.

Indeed, I would argue that there is potentially something both self-defeating *and* craven about attempts to sustain disciplinary identifications amid talk of a desire to queer. Such endeavors, common as they are, exude the distinct odor of a desire to bat on both teams: a suspicious proclivity for trying to keep everyone happy by, on the one hand, reaping the undeniable rewards that come these days from having one's moral and political profile validated by one's cutting-edge credentials while, on the other, simultaneously performing one's role as a good citizen of the discipline and its continuing health. However, even though this is an essay that propounds the value of luxury, I would argue that in this instance it is difficult to have one's cake and eat it.

My reasoning is informed by consideration of a broad background of transformation in the nature of academic professionalism over the past thirty-or-so years. In the early 1990s, for example, Edward Said could define academic professionalism as that which keeps one attentive to "what is considered to be proper, professional behavior—not rocking the boat, not straying outside the accepted paradigms or limits, making yourself marketable and above all presentable."[10] For Said, back then, such professionalism was precisely what prohibited the possibility of radical inquiry and action. Now, by comparison, professions across the board are bending over backward to proclaim their radical status. The result is a very particular symptom of our times, which, for want of a better term, we might label *the professionalized radical*. For this type, "what is considered to be proper, professional behavior," and what therefore allows the academic to be "marketable and above all presentable," is precisely the "rocking the boat" that had previously constituted academic professionalism's outside. No doubt for some the fact that the circumference of academic professionalism has expanded over the past thirty years to consume what once lay beyond its purview is cause for celebration. (And so what's not to love about a queer music theory?) But I argue that such an image of professionalism's progressive elasticity has been purchased through an extensive colonization of discursive space by forms of unquestioned instrumental thinking. And to ignore that fact is to choose to ignore the invasive degree to which the increased economic pressures of recent times have intruded into (and manipulated, distorted, and even debased) thinking life within a professionalized academic context—a topic that I turn to consider in the next section of this essay.

[10] Said 1996, 74.

Certainly beyond the level of undergraduate classes, and thus certainly *within* the professionalized confines of North American music theory and musicology, music analysis is often instrumentalized into various related functions: as proof, example, elaboration, and so forth. It is frequently put to work for the theory or historical claim by which it has been employed, so that even when it works harder than anything else, and even when it is drenched in a profligacy of exquisite insights and stunning observations, it is mostly not considered the thing itself. As Agawu observed early on, there exists a certain moral injunction against the possibility of music analysis existing in-and-of-itself: "you must attach the [formalist] patterns you have observed to something else: a plot, a program, an emotional scenario, a context, an agenda, a fantasy, or a narrative."[11] In the North American scene, music analysis thus functions once more like a gangplank, for it is the means not the end; it is there to transport us within a professional context from hypothesis to verification. As Agawu continues, "[t]he findings of formalist analysis are like a severed phallus; they should be re-attached."[12] And to follow through on the psychoanalytic implications, if the phallus is allowed to be free-floating, we might then realize that the Father is impotent. Or, similarly, we might suspect that he is merely playing with himself—music analysis as masturbation. Certainly, if music analysis is left to its own devices, Daddy will end up queer.

In order to protect authority from embarrassing itself, we therefore all jump to the tune. Even in my own work, I have felt the pressure to show willingness to employ music analysis as a means of verification rather than in the queer form that I envisage for it here. In my *Music and the Politics of Negation*, for example, music analysis is conscripted to give weight to involved arguments regarding, among other things, music's non-mimetic relationship to culture and society, the destabilizing excess inherent to all stylistic categorizations, the fundamentally exilic nature of music's historical inscriptions, and the feminist potential in music when it is perceived as having presence.[13] Music analysis here does a *lot* of work; it *doesn't* play. Similarly, things are no different when music analysis appears in queer musicology and music theory in the Anglo-American world. Writing of a choice passage in the slow movement of Schubert's piano duet Sonata in C, D. 812

[11] Agawu 1997, 299. The famous Kerman 1980, 311–31
[12] Ibid., 299.
[13] Currie 2012.

(the so-called Grand Duo), Philip Brett is adamant: "This is not a drama of neighbor notes."[14] The critical momentum set in motion by his analytic observations must either expand outward like reverberations of a struck bell, justifying their relevance, or be damned for the parochialism of never having left home. And since worldliness is *de riguer* in the modern academy, expansion is what happens, and journeying forth ensues. We travel first to the assertion that the notes of Schubert's passage create the affect of "a carefully constructed undecidability."[15] But we have still not traveled far enough, and Brett, sensing we might capitalize on the fact of having made it this far to justify turning back, reasserts the message just quoted from his previous sentence: this is an "undecidability" that "affects the very identity of *more than notes.*"[16] Suitably disciplined, we fasten our seatbelts and submit to the inevitable, and Brett's interpretation accelerates rapidly off into increasingly weighty issues. Out of this "carefully constructed undecidability" can be woven "dramas of public and private, illusion and reality, and more precise and important still, the 'not-knowing-which is-which,' the intense confusion of thought and feeling that is connected with the image of the emasculated male in the age of sensibility and that, for different reasons, homosexual children and adolescents grow up with today."[17] It is for these reasons, I assume, that Brett concludes by stating that "[o]n supersensitive days," when playing this passage with his piano duet partner, "our pianissimo rubato here has been breathtaking."[18] Asphyxiation as guarantor of relevance—I wonder if it is not too high a price to pay.

Of course, exceptions to this pervasive tendency exist. For example, there is the exceedingly important question, which I can only touch upon here, of what other potentialities for music analysis might be afforded by different global locations, and how these might inform future queer endeavors for North American music theory. The disciplinary controls imposed upon music analysis in the North American scene are, after all, very far indeed from being universally valid. Even in somewhere as culturally similar to the United States as the United Kingdom, things function quite differently. This, in part, is because the relationship there among the different music disciplines is somewhat less bureaucratically formalized than it is in the United States;

[14] Brett 1997, 159.
[15] Ibid.
[16] Ibid., my emphasis.
[17] Ibid.
[18] Ibid.

and so music theory does not exist there as such a definitive entity. As a result, it is interesting to note that the journal *Music Analysis* originates in the United Kingdom and still resides there. By comparison, the major journals where extensive music analyses occur in the United States are predominantly advertised as venues for music theory (*Music Theory Spectrum, Journal of Music Theory*, etc.), and thus music analysis appears therein as being more *in service* to music theory. A temporary working theory to draw from this would be that increasing disciplinary specialization within an economically and institutionally loaded professionalized setting works to create an environment hostile to intellectual activities that cannot be immediately domesticated in terms of their function. Or, alternatively, that the bureaucratic instantiation of particular academic disciplines and their societies creates an exponential increase in the demand that all activities that take place within the confines of that discipline must be capable of being mapped according to accepted paths of functionality according to the discipline's goals. Such working theories are given credibility by the findings of recent critical-historical investigations into the foundations and development of the modern music disciplines and societies.[19]

If a global perspective on music analysis might offer a fledgling queer music-theory inspiration, so too should the smattering of exceptions provided by the few prominent cases where musical analysis has been marveled at for its own sake, such as Scott Burnhman's haunting work on Mozart, or certain choice essays by David Lewin. But even here, validation has not occurred uncontested. Burnhman's own *Mozart's Grace* was winner of one of the American Musicological Society's most prestigious awards, the Otto Kinkeldey Award. Yet its introduction is troubled by self-consciousness, and the venture not therefore so blithe an act of unfettered, self-validating music analysis as a queer scholar such as myself might like. There are worries that "one might suspect that my project is rather more *self-indulgent* than systematic," and confessions that "nor would it be incorrect to do so."[20] There is an acknowledgment that the expectation is that scholarship should labor to get something done, and that some of his colleagues "*working hard* on the broad and complex *front lines* of musicological inquiry may well regard my enterprise as *a retreat into some hopelessly Romantic engagement*."[21] So often

---

[19] Notably, see Levitz 2018, 9–80.
[20] Burnham 2012, 5 (my emphasis).
[21] Ibid., 5–6 (my emphasis).

we are told that our scholarship must engage with the world and wake it up when it looks like it might be asleep on the job. We must, in short, disenchant! And yet, as Burnham admits, his own work looks as if its goal were "to *escape reality* by *drifting* into an *enchanted realm*."[22] Similarly, Lewin's impressive canonical stature as a music theorist is indisputable. But the strangeness of certain aspects of his work has either been humored because he so powerfully fulfilled elsewhere the criteria for professional validation—through being eminently capable of laying out complete music theories—or has been celebrated precisely for the dissonance it creates in relationship to such criteria. It is therefore ultimately unsurprising that, in an attempt to move toward a queer music theory, Gavin S. K. Lee focuses in on such aspects of Lewin's work.[23] Lee, for example, emphasizes how, moving beyond theoretical closure, Lewin deliberately "disorients himself immediately";[24] or, how he makes the "attempt to catapult himself outside" of the stability of his own models;[25] or, how he exposes us to a world that "no longer contains the promise of stability, but is filled with uncertainty";[26] or, how he allows through his "poetics of analysis" for the emergence of "a non-normative subject who no longer feels the need to exert systematized control."[27] For Lee, drawing on the "queer phenomenology" of Sara Ahmed, with Lewin "the world becomes *queer*, disorientated."[28]

Another source of inspiration for the kind of non-instrumental queer music theory that I seek could also be found in the past. This essay, after all, is very far from being the first to draw to attention to already-existent but nevertheless alternative modes of academic practice and being centered around music analysis. Nearly twenty years ago now, Agawu could similarly assert that with music analysis there is "always a surplus to be contended with because the materiality of the proceeding is its own reward."[29] In part, Agawu's decision in the early 2000s to adopt a different rhetorical register than mine may well have resulted from a sense of confidence that the position from which he was writing (from music theory outward) was less corseted by disciplinary protocols than his addressee (the new musicology) had wanted

[22] Ibid., 6 (my emphasis).
[23] Lee 2020, 143–53.
[24] Ibid., 3.
[25] Ibid., 4.
[26] Ibid., 4.
[27] Ibid., 6.
[28] Ibid. 4. In this article, Lee works in detail with Ahmed 2006.
[29] Agawu 2004, 276.

to believe (in order rhetorically to clinch its own deal) and maybe even less self-censored than the addressee itself (since the new musicology comes out of Agawu's account looking like they have made a straw man out of music theory in order to disavow a more difficult self-realization).

Indeed, in the competition since the 1990s to see who among the music sub-disciplines can appear most cutting-edge, musicology has frequently relied upon a pretty crass representation of the practices of music theory in order to justify its (quite annoying) swagger. This, I would argue, has helped many—especially musicologists, but perhaps music theorists too—to forget the significant moments of radical activity that have constituted music theory's disciplinary history and might put musicology to shame. For as far as I know, there is *nothing* in North American musicology of the 1970s and early 1980s that is *even close* to the radical stance, and queer potentiality, of, for example, the phenomenologically driven, and often experimental, literary activities of writers such as Elaine Barkin, Marjorie Tichenor, Benjamin Boretz, and J. K. Randall. Forty-plus years ago, Boretz could regularly be found pronouncing on how the "reification of competence and skill enables us to substitute the visible tokens of approval, admiration, and status for the non-negotiable needs, interest and expression." Fully worked out was an understanding that, as a result of professionalization, "[s]tatus replaces identity, erudition replaces experience, technique replaces awareness. Discipline replaces engagement. Knowing replaces searching. Self-congratulation replaces self-fulfillment."[30] If, at the beginning of the third decade of this century, I therefore feel the need to recapitulate these themes in a queer key, then that is as much cause for melancholy as it is a sign of my empowering determination. Through a dark paradox, I have been forced to instrumentalize the attention that attributing a queer label can garner in order to attempt to salvage non-instrumental modes of academic being from some perhaps-final state of obsolescence. Queering, in this instance, merely constitutes the last stop before exhaustion, giving up, and abandonment of academia for other locales where life-enhancing practices might (*just might*) still be possible.

If music analysis is but a means to an end, it is, to invoke a recurring image of mine, a gangplank. And if it is but a gangplank, it can easily just be overlooked as merely the conduit for getting us from one side to the other. The authority of usage easily distracts from the experience and appreciation of the occasion or thing that is being used. To nod toward Heidegger,

---

[30] Boretz 1981/1982, 505 and 507.

we could say that we become so habituated that the thing, in its instrumental condition of being a tool, becomes all but invisible and only attracts our attention when it breaks.[31] And so this essay is therefore an attempt to make music analysis break so that, to continue the Heideggerian theme, it might finally give its Being up to us. But in our present context, where instrumentality is so strongly valued, such a form of musical analysis will easily start to seem a little sad, abandoned, or abject. A gangplank, after all, is neither here nor there (nowhere); it is a place where it is potentially embarrassing or even professionally dangerous to be found loitering. And so, once more, it is queer, since there is a long lineage of pronouncements by queer writers regarding the fact that queers have always been involved either in having to take up habitation and functioning in spaces not normally intended for such things, or in spaces not intended for queers per se. George Chauncey has even argued that there is "no queer space, there are only spaces used by queers or put to queer use." He continues: "Nothing illustrates this general principle more clearly than the tactics developed by gay men and lesbians to put the spaces of the dominant culture to queer uses."[32] Indeed, this is especially so when one considers the question of sex in public that has been so important in the history of queer lives.[33]

In a similar vein, Ahmed notes that heterosexuality, like a gangplank, "can function as a path," indeed as a "straight path," one that "you follow if you are living your life in the right way." If you are living in this "right way" then "you have to reach certain points in order for a life to count as a good life." As a result, you need "not to be distracted by what happens or by what you encounter along the way."[34] In this formulation, the path of heterosexuality, like musical analysis in its present disciplinary inscriptions, is to be used to get from one place to another. By comparison, as Ahmed then shows through a riff on a passage from Freud's *Three Essays on the Theory of Sexuality*, a "pervert gets lost on the way." Not unlike music analysis considered as a self-justifying activity, sexual perversion thus constitutes a form of "delay" in which "you take up time that could have been used to get to the point." And so she concludes: "Queer use: we linger; we do not get to the point."[35]

---

[31] For example, see Heidegger 1971, 17–87.
[32] Chauncey 1996, 224.
[33] Califa 1994.
[34] Ahmed 2019, 204.
[35] Ibid., 206.

I will return to this important theoretical provocation in the third section of this essay.

At this historical moment of its subaltern positioning within the hierarchy of agendas in the North American academy, music analysis considered as a self-justifying activity is self-evidently suspiciously queer. I assert this unambiguously. The fact that this may ultimately be a good thing does not cancel out attendant difficulties. Ahmed writes about the queer experience of the heterosexual family in the following fashion:

> When you inhabit such a world, you can feel like you are watching yourself disappear: watching your own life unravel, thread by thread. No one has willed or intended your disappearance. They are kind; they are welcoming. But slowly, just slowly, as talk of family, of heterosexuality as the future, of lives that you do not live, just slowly, just slowly, you disappear.[36]

And I would argue that trying to set up home in the academy in activities that do not immediately justify their functionality in terms of agendas that have been sanctioned as those that are important will likewise lead you as a scholar into analogously ghostly forms of dissipating existence. Even as a graduate student, I found it difficult to pull off fashioning the appropriate disciplinary stance, and I felt as awkward as a musicologist as I had as a music theorist. It was my impression at the time that I was a bit too bloated with history to be able to slip into something minimalist off the rack from Pitch Class Set Theory, and a bit too thin on contextual specifics effectively to butch out a tight white t-shirt from the New Musicology. Looking back on it, I see now that the problem was that I was always trying to find the means of doing as much music analysis as possible; that I was seeking that pleasure, and hoping it could avoid getting snagged on other disciplinary agendas. And so if it often felt lonely back then, it still often does; academia has not felt particularly hospitable.

But if, as Ahmed argues, "[c]reating a shelter and disrupting usage can refer to the same action," and if, as a result, "[a] doorway becomes a meeting place,"[37] then a home can also be made on a gangplank, or in the practice of the art of music analysis—however precarious either of them might at first glance seem. So what would it mean for the North American academy to

---

[36] Ibid., 201.
[37] Ibid., 229.

become hospitable to music analysis not in its presently instrumentalized form (as means to an end), but performed as a self-justifying activity (as an end in itself, a pleasure, and even a form of Being)? And in what ways, however modest, would offering hospitality to the pleasures of such a practice of music analysis contribute to the creation of a queer academy? I would argue that if such practices could be given voice, the effect would be radically transformative. But the forces that conspire against this happening are of immense power and venerability, and increasingly global reach. Indeed, they are of such magnitude, and their effect on the academy so disastrously invasive, that they have created an ingrained and tacit self-loathing among academics that is analogous to internalized forms of homophobia. So before we can start patting ourselves on the back by imagining what a queer academy might look like, we have first to come out about how vigilant we remain (queer scholars too) at making sure the academy never turns queer. It is to the articulation of what some of these forces are that I now turn.

* * *

The question of whether academia is hospitable enough to offer us a home is a topical one. One of the most salient and highly colored threads within the ongoing weave of present academic discourse is constituted by politically and ethically committed endeavors to bring to light the inhospitable conditions of professional academic institutions, disciplines, and their assigned professional societies for certain of their members. A certain assumed consensus of opinion has arisen regarding the aims to which our political and ethical value systems ought to be directed: academic disciplines and their professional societies should offer a kind of radical democratic hospitality to the array of human differences constituting their actually and also potentially existing membership. Since very few within the academy tend to come out publicly against such basic assumptions, the larger part of this critique has therefore been taken up with acts of calling to account when a purported allegiance to assumed democratic responsibilities as hosts has been shown to be profoundly wanting in terms of actual material realizations—or, to put it otherwise, when a theory of what kind of home the academy should offer has been shamed by display of what kinds of practices to date have resulted.

Since I think that those who go about cashing in on the performance of their ethical and political credentials should have to include a scene in their stage shows where they are made to put their money where their mouth is, I have found the spectacle of most of this greatly to my liking. It is also quite interesting in terms of what it suggests for our long-term historical under-standing of the music disciplines. With regard to musicology, for example, I note how present acts of calling out discrepancies between the theory and practice of scholars' disciplinary responsibilities makes sense as itself the his-torical playing out of the final act of a theory-to-practice drama stretching back to the second half of the 1980s. After all, the places where cutting-edge musicology of the late 1980s and 1990s had its most consistently undeniable success and impact were to be found in the strikingly effective rhetoric of its characteristic assertion: that if we believe our role as citizens is to foster the creation of an increasingly pluralistic democracy, then that belief must also be made to intrude far into the intimate details of our academic practice as well; the questions that motivate us in our non-academic life must be allowed to resonate in the issues we bring to bear on our academic research. The result was an exponential deregulation of what was deemed acceptable as research and a refreshing efflorescence of inquiry into politics, gender, sexuality, em-bodiment, race, popular culture, colonialism, and more.

By necessity, attendant upon this was a requisite condemnation of musical autonomy. If such a thing as the music itself actually existed, then that would present a significant push-back to the inviolability of emergent assumptions that academics were ethically and politically beholden unto making connections between that which happens within the boundaries of academic research and that which happens beyond its purview.[38] Neither music nor the academy could be allowed to remain autonomous, and so musical au-tonomy got written off as but a mere chimera of history, the symptom of a set of broader ideological strategies.[39] In certain cases, music even started to be conceptualized as *ontologically* heteronymous and relational. For Lawrence Kramer, for example, "Music is our premier embodiment of the drive for attachment."[40] In this formulation, music's purported ability to link things together (to attach) nicely mirrors the politically and ethically enlightened scholar's desire to make connections between academic and extra-academic concerns. As a result, and metaphorically speaking, connecting extra-academic democratic life to academic practices could itself start to appear

---

[38] Writing against this assumption of postmodern musicology of the 1990s, a small minority of scholars has sought to show how musical autonomy (and its related concepts: formalism, abso-lute music, and so forth) might in fact do all sorts of tangible things in the world. See, for example, Scherzinger 2001, 5–117; Scherzinger 2004, 252–77; Currie 2017.

[39] As for example in McClary 2000, and Chua 1999.

[40] Kramer 2007, 33.

as a means of acting musically; practicing music analysis as a self-justifying activity, in-and-of-itself, therefore became implicitly unmusical.

Such discursive developments by scholars in the later 1980s and throughout the 1990s were instrumental in breaking down the rhetorical distinctions between the concerns of the academy and those of the so-called real world, and that inheritance is tangible in present debates over the discipline's hospitality ratings. So, for example, when Susan McClary is to be found writing the preface to William Cheng's *Just Vibrations: The Purpose of Sounding Good*—a text that, among other things, registered contemporary questions of disciplinary hospitality at a relatively early date within North American music studies—that can be interpreted as an act of inheritance within the lineage of the discipline's theory-to-practice traditions.[41] Crudely put: where McClary fought primarily to make musicological research hospitable to a wider array of inquiries, Cheng and others now seek to make the social realities of disciplinary life more hospitable to a wider array of actually existing human subjects. There would seem to be very little to question about this in such a volume. Queer theory develops in part from the overflowing of a wave, into both academic research and the discursive and material constitution of its disciplines and professional societies, of historical energies accumulated from the experience of generations of scholars who, in their extra-academic existence, have been subject to social and political forms of violence that have directly impacted the possibility of their access to full representation within the *Demos*. It would seem inconceivable that a queer scholar versed in this literature would not therefore wish to constitute part of a united vanguard pressing for the implementation of radically democratic practices of disciplinary hospitality. And indeed, this particular queer scholar has no desire to be extraordinary in this regard.

What does give pause, however, is the accompanying assumption that the academy resulting from the implementation of such democratic principles should be one constituted by a plane of consistency that, free from conceptual turbulence, can pass across and link together the particular ethical and political hopes and dreams of our extra-academic life with academic life itself. What threatens here, at least from a theoretical perspective, is that any positive possibility of academic life constituting a tangible form of authentic *difference* in relationship to extra-academic life is annulled. As a result, in order to implement a rigorous ethics of respect for difference within the academy,

[41] Cheng 2016.

it has therefore been necessary sometimes to eradicate either any potential positive difference that the academy might constitute in and of itself, or anything that might help bring such a difference into being. And regarding the latter, I would argue that a self-justifying practice of musical analysis, queerly conceived as a kind of indifference to instrumentality, could indeed participate in its small way in the creation of such a difference.

The irony of this complicit relationship between diversity politics and patterns of ideological exclusion is something that I have examined before, primarily through the optic musicological discourse regarding the question of context.[42] More recent critical work on racial capitalism, however, takes some of these ironies into the realms of the more materially tangible economic repercussions for institutional life writ large. Nancy Leong, for example, makes the brilliantly blunt observation that in a "society preoccupied with diversity, nonwhiteness is a valued commodity. And where that society is founded on capitalism, it is unsurprising that the commodity of nonwhites is exploited for its market value."[43] As a result, affiliation with nonwhite individuals "becomes merely a useful means for white individuals *and predominantly white institutions* to acquire social and economic benefits while deflecting potential charges of racism and avoiding more difficult questions of racial equality."[44] By definition, actions aimed at increasing diversity in the academy are congruent with the assumption that a plane of consistency can and should be drawn to pass across and link together the particular ethical and political hopes and dreams of our extra-academic life with academic life, in and of itself. But the easy coexistence of a capitalist commodity economy with diversity initiatives within the academy leads ultimately, according to Leong, to a degrading of nonwhiteness. Further, because racial capitalism within the academy is, as Leung argues, a systemic problem, the university diversity initiatives that help to sustain it are, therefore, tantamount to forms of coloniality. And this is particularly the case, as Tamara Levitz has for example argued, when we are dealing with academic life in the North American context.[45]

After all, capitalism is the predominant means by which colonial power came into being. And since, according to Nelson Maldonado-Torres, coloniality means "a logic, metaphysics, ontology, and a matrix of power

---

[42] Currie 2009, 145–203.
[43] Leong 2013, 2154.
[44] Ibid., 2155. My emphasis.
[45] Levitz 2017, 1–13.

that can continue existing *after* formal independence and desegregation,"[46] then to talk seriously about decolonizing the academy must on some level mean to start the process of formally amputating the deep structures of our thinking and institutional Being from the unquestioned logic of the capitalist worldview in which they have long been historically entrenched. We must create relations of critical *discontinuity* between, on the one side, diversity initiatives within the academy and, on the other side, the relationship between capitalism and race as it exists pervasively elsewhere. Such an act of severance could work toward "rehumanizing the world," and to "breaking hierarchies of difference that dehumanize subjects and communities," including those within the academy itself.[47]

But if capitalism is the problem, then it is one whose roots stretch deeply, maybe even constitutively, into the form and function of the academy. Economically speaking, the modern university has never been a tower made of unblemished ivory. The only thing different about our present moment is that universities have now lost whatever squeamishness they once had about appearing in the raw in this regard. And so, as a result of the exponential increase in the intrusion of neoliberal economic thinking into the very heart and structure of the academy's functioning, the construction of the academy's towers are now increasingly indistinguishable (metaphorically) from the tall buildings of any corporate or financial zone. Most academics I know claim to be horrified by such developments. And yet one of the most typical ways in which neoliberal deans and their recently hired hordes of middle-management cronies confront us is in terms of demanding that we justify the real-world relevance and applicability of our research—or, to recast it in the terms of this section of my essay, that we prove a line of continuity between one and the other. If we are made anxious by this demand, part of our unease must then surely come from the experience of its uncanny dialectical reversal. For in a strange act of ventriloquism, out of the mouths of neoliberal administrators now come our own calls for the eradication of the distinction between the concerns of the academy and the concerns of the world beyond its parameters. Of course, not all mouths are the same. And so even though the forces do in fact significantly overlap, those that compel academics into speech are not identical with those that mediate the mouths of university bureaucrats. Nevertheless, I argue that it is precisely the ease

---

[46] Nelson Maldonado-Torres, "Outline of Ten Theses on Coloniality and Decoloniality," 10, https://fondation-frantzfanon.com/outline-of-ten-theses-on-coloniality-and-decoloniality/, my emphasis.
[47] Ibid., 10.

with which, at a cursory glance, the different antagonists seem actually to be employing the same rhetoric that constitutes a significant reason for why neoliberal rhetoric went so rapidly and effectively viral in the academy in the first place. Academics have mostly been left reeling from the narcissistic wound they have received from having had to confront—or tried to *avoid* confronting—the presently existing historical fact of the relative ease with which aspects of their own position have been recruited for negative ends. Therefore, from a politically strategic point of view, it seems acceptable to propose that perhaps the neoliberal business model would not have been able to gain such impressive degrees of traction so rapidly had it encountered a confident rhetoric extolling the credible values of (once more) a productive *discontinuity* between the concerns of the academy and its purported outside. And it is one of the wagers of this essay (once more) that, within the North American context, practice of music analysis as a self-validating activity—one performed for the tautological reason of the pleasure to be gained from performing it—would contribute, in however modest a fashion, toward such a goal.

To summarize, then, the present need for the academy to address its mostly appalling track record with regard to hospitality needs to be supplemented. Transformations in access availability and the diversification of who it is that constitutes the population of the academy need to be accompanied by increased hospitality to a conceptual diversification of what, in an almost existential sense, we think life in the academy could be. We need a vibrant, and experimentally open, attempt to inhabit the potential *differences* that could be constituted by academic life in and of itself. In making this statement, I am en route to asserting that the need to think that the difference of academic life is, among other things, a strongly queer one. I am in part asking: what is the university to be used for? And since I am asking that from a queer vantage, I am assuming that there is something problematic about our present usages that we are failing to notice. As Ahmed writes, "[t]o queer use is to make use audible, to listen to use, to bring to the front what ordinarily recedes into the background." And so ultimately, "to make use strange."[48] Might not academic life itself be something queer? Do we need to become open not only to those who have been cast as the *academy's* Other, but also to the fundamental *otherness* of the academy itself?

---

[48] Ahmed 2019, 198.

I make such statements self-consciously against the background of one of the most canonical texts of queer studies in the Anglo-American academy, "Friendship as a Way of Life," the interview with Michel Foucault that appeared in April of 1981 in the French magazine *Gai Pied*.[49] Here Foucault famously asks: "Is it possible to create a homosexual mode of life?"[50] And so, likewise, I ask: is it possible to create an academic mode of life? As is typical in his late work, such a life for Foucault would not come from defining some essence, called homosexuality, and then finding the best way for one's life to be an expression of it: "we have to work at becoming homosexuals and not be obstinate in recognizing that we are." Rather, homosexuals need to "work on ourselves and invent—I do not say discover—a manner of being that is still improbable."[51] Likewise, I seek less to find the means by which academics could identify themselves and then act accordingly (according, at the present moment, to economically manipulated professional *aprioris*) and more to attempting to formulate what the incipient moves might be toward imagining habitation in the academy as constituting a kind of experimental life practice.

Principles of radical democratic equality are presently being mobilized transformatively to diversify the demographic of the academy. Rightly so. But once the citizens of the academy have been gathered, is it not possible that they could be afforded the opportunity to be inspired by other principles of social relationality without having to assume that in doing so they are capitulating to a regressive politics? Likewise for Foucault it is not so much a case of trying to "re-introduce homosexuality into the general norm of social relations," but rather trying to create and become within a new "empty space."[52] And so in "Friendship as a Way of Life," for example, "[t]he problem is not to discover in oneself the truth of one's sex, but rather, to use one's sexuality henceforth *to arrive at a multiplicity of relationships*."[53] Accompanying this in the essay is also the possibility of making ourselves "infinitely more susceptible to pleasure [*plaisirs*]."[54]

One does not need to indulge in specious analogies in order to make Foucault's remarks regarding the new potential socialities attendant on homosexuality resonate with questions of academic and intellectual life.

[49] Foucault 1997b, 135–40.
[50] Ibid., 137.
[51] Ibid., 136, 137.
[52] Foucault 1997e, 160.
[53] Foucault 1997b, 135 (my emphasis).
[54] Ibid., 137.

Foucault himself draws out the social potentialities of academic and intellectual life frequently and in a manner perfectly congruent with what he says about homosexuality. For example, in an interview with Paul Rabinow, he explains his intellectual tendency toward dialogue precisely because it opens up possibilities of as-of-yet unknown socialities, rather than being driven by unquestioned ethical and political aprioris. In the "serious play of questions and answers, in the work of reciprocal elucidation, the rights of each person are in some sense *immanent* in the discussion."[55] Regarding academic life in general, in an interview with Stephen Riggings, he claims that he has "worked like a dog" not because he is "interested in the academic status of what I am doing." His activities are not performed so as to circulate within the professional economy of validating gazes and the undeniable (and mostly repellent) resulting social formations (driven by jealousy, gossip, and corrosive forms of narcissistic wounding) that so frequently monopolize the lives and behaviors of academics. Rather, it is "because my problem is my own transformation." And for Foucault, this "transformation of one's self by one's own knowledge is . . . something rather close to the aesthetic experience." It is therefore a *pleasure* taken in such transformation, since"[w]hy should a painter work if he is not transformed by his own painting?"[56] Admittedly, such a pleasure would seem at first glance to erase the question of the social, since it is pursued only in terms of a singularly individual goal ("my own transformation"). But since the pursuit is perfectly available at one time to more than just Foucault himself, it implicitly opens up the possibility of envisioning collections of those involved in intellectual activity in a highly provocative and paradoxical form: as a community of isolates. And so precisely by means of confessing to a certain prioritization of pleasure within the conceptualization of his intellectual activity, Foucault affords us the possibility of encountering as-of-yet non-existent forms of sociality. As such, it is a fundamentally queer maneuver, and it was for similar reasons that I began this essay by acknowledging that the instigation for pursuit of an academic life arose in part from the pleasures I had once experienced in participating in the practice of music analysis for its own sake.

---

[55] Foucault 1997a, 111 (my emphasis). In his later work, Foucault repeatedly turns to repositioning traditional notions of rights with respect to a new mode of being. So, for example: "Rather than arguing that rights are fundamental and natural to the individual, we should try to imagine and create a new relational right that permits all possible types of relations to exist and not be prevented, blocked, or annulled by impoverished relational institutions." In Foucault 1997e, 158.

[56] Foucault 1997d, 131.

But it is important to note that such queer maneuvers would *also* afford us the possibility of creating the kinds of productive discontinuities between academic and non-academic life that would help to hinder the effective functioning of, among other things, racial capitalism and all it does to derail the possibility of us properly making good on the project to diversify the academy and making it credible as a kind of home. So while it would be conceptually violent to conflate queer theory with the project to decolonize the academy, it is still worth noting that they can significantly overlap and offer a generosity of resources to each other. They are available to each other in the form of a kind of theoretical comradeship. For Maldonado-Torres, we need "counterdiscourses, counter-knowledges, counter-creative acts, and counter-practices that seek to dismantle coloniality." And such things could ultimately "open up multiple other forms of being in the world."[57] Not only being in the world at large, but also being in the world of the academy. And in a queer academy, too.

* * *

Why has the productive Otherness of academic life yet to manifest itself in any significantly progressive fashion? In the early 1980s Foucault could state directly that it is "the prospect that gays will create as of yet unforeseen kinds of relationship that many people cannot tolerate."[58] And I would suggest that similar animosities breed and fester in relationship to whatever arcane, pretentious, and elitist activities and ways of being academics and intellectuals are purportedly guilty of being engaged. The fact that academic life constitutes a certain kind of privilege—although one that is still, even if one comes from privilege, relatively hard won—does not cancel out the fact of how tenuous is the guarantee of respect that academics can expect from those many more who look in askance at us in from the expanses of extra-academic life. Academics and those in pursuit of the life of the mind have been surrounded by a wealth of negative representations of themselves for a long time. Ridicule of the moribund impotence of intellectual pursuits in comparison to the vibrancy of the real has had a prominent history and is encapsulated in the standard insult that academic work is just so much intellectual masturbation—as opposed (one assumes) to intellectual copulation, which (one assumes) is to be valued for being on the side of life and

---

[57] Ibid., 10.
[58] Foucault 1997f, 153.

working to give birth to realities as opposed to spawning fantasies. From this perspective, academics are pleasing themselves rather than participating in the good work of making sure they are always also pleasing others, and so they are guilty in terms of the strictures of a relational morality.[59] In the literary fiction of the West, for example, this insult is personified with particular loathing in the figure of Edward Casaubon, the dry and intellectually worn-out scholar who marries the young, intelligent, and idealistic Dorothea Brooke in George Eliot's *Middlemarch* (1871–72). His ongoing and never-to-be-finished work, *A Key to All Mythologies*—irrelevant even in scholarly terms, since he cannot read German, in which language the cutting-edge debates take place—is the altar on which he sacrifices his ability to love and engage with life, and on which he almost sacrifices Dorothea's life forces too.

Condemnations of academic activity have also been easily found closer to home. After all, so much of the work that presently circulates today in the academic humanities tends to take place according to intellectual models whose political allegiances are mostly advertised as left-leaning. As a result, even when no allegiance to a Marxist lineage is purported, it is difficult not to hear the eleventh of Marx's mighty *Theses on Feuerbach* (1845) booming somewhere in the background: "Philosophers have hitherto only interpreted the world; the point is to change it."[60] As academics, we are pursued by an always-looming threat, which for many of us in the profession probably began with being ostracized (and worse) at school for being bookish. I have long felt that lurking around every corner is an unproductive encounter with the shame of being called out for my irrelevance, or ridiculed from the position of a kind of realist authoritarianism for the moribund impotence of my intellectual pursuits in comparison with the vitality of life itself (or some such other undigested ideological standard). What I ought to be doing, purportedly, is transforming my thinking into action, becoming relevant, engaged, useful, and social, and showing myself willing at attempting to cure myself of addictions to such unnatural desires and impotent passivities. And so, if there is any credibility to my earlier assertion, that since the later 1980s, Anglo-American academics have sought out their radical credentials through an increased commitment to making their activities more continuous with the

---

[59] I would argue that it is fear of being called out for not being relational enough that accounts for the somewhat uncritical reception and success of certain noted publications, rather than the fact that readers have been impressed by the novelty or penetration of the arguments to which they have been exposed. In this regard, consider Born 2010, 205–43. I return to this topic later in this essay in my reading of Abbate 2004, 505–36.

[60] Marx 1978, 145.

authority with which they have imbued real-world activities, then academics now simply self-legislate the terms by which they themselves can so easily be condemned.

It sounds, of course, a lot like the internalized self-loathing that has traditionally, and efficiently, accompanied homophobia. And if there is any credibility to the analogy—between hatred of queers and hatred of academics—then maybe academics (like queers) also struggle with internalized injunctions against what they love. So what *do* academics love? One way of approaching the question would be to say that academics love that which they study. And that being the case, it would seem that we are proceeding from the assumption that the act of studying and the act of loving are therefore analogous. Certainly, it is a normative assumption that love is a relationship and that relationships require commitment. And certainly, commitment would seem to be proven by the extensive and not-infrequently harrowing professional training that academics must go through in graduate school—with, to boot, next to no possibility of employment at the conclusion of often having studied much longer than most doctors and lawyers; and, even if you do land a job, no choice whatsoever as to its location, unless you are some kind of academic rockstar or just distastefully slick at playing the scene. So if we are academics involved in the study of music, it is therefore not difficult to postulate our love for music too. For in one of its most recognizable forms, to fall in love with someone is to be made, against one's will, prisoner of a regime of attention upon the radical singularity of a particular being. All other contextual claims are potentially expendable. Academics likewise have mostly been prepared to gamble just about everything on the slim chance of maximizing the amount of time they might spend with music more directly in their lives.

So what is there to worry about? Even at a really middling drinks party, it is quite possible, as an academic working professionally within music studies, to encounter a stranger who goes weak at the knees when they find out what you do. Their response is usually some variation on the leitmotif: "How wonderful! I love music too!" This being the case, maybe the only people who really have a problem with loving music are precisely those academics who have organized their lives around music. And so, to return to one of my primary formulations, perhaps if academics could just work more effectively to create a continuity between themselves and life beyond the academy, this would then help to cancel out their shame, and their problems would be resolved. For if the world is ready to love us for what we love, then all we have to do to love ourselves is love the love already in existence for what it is we do (which, one here assumes, is loving music). If, in this instance, we assume that love is what we need, and that such loving means opening ourselves up to the already existent, then the problem with academics is that they are too squeamish and try to uphold boundaries to keep such things at bay. Once more, what is needed is thus continuity—connection, relationship formation, openness, and so forth. If those involved in the academic study of music could only accept this, then their shame would be cancelled out.

How could music analysis relate to all of this? Certainly, back in the 1990s, the idea was floated that music analysis could be part of the love cure rather than a symptom of the psychological complaint of academic self-loathing. In a well-known statement on "music loving," for example, Marion Guck in 1996 wrote:

> Though presumably we all came to our present positions through a strong attraction to music and to specific pieces, most theorists and musicologists, whether old or new, are not comfortable with "music loving." Or perhaps I should say I think that no one is comfortable with "loving." We do not call ourselves music lovers; we call amateurs music lovers.[61]

For Guck, music analysis ought to be the means "to understand the extreme sense of intimacy one can feel for a musical work—an intimacy akin to the what one feels for a lover."[62] Moreover, music analysis for Guck does not only constitute "the articulation of a process of growing awareness, increasing closeness, of 'immersion in pleasure,' to quote [Suzanne] Cusick"[63]; it is, therefore, not merely good PR for "the powers of music, powers of attraction, engagement."[64] Rather, music analysis *is* such intimacy itself, and it is only by means of denying love and intimacy that it has been possible for music analysis to create "a fiction whereby one speaks purely about a piece, out there, lying on a desk perhaps, unperceived by anyone." For Guck, to talk as if "one really could stand at a distance" from music "is an illusion."[65] And so the logic of her argument opens up the following possible conclusion: that a music analysis founded on love would return us, through the cancelling out

---

[61] Guck 1996, paragraph 2.

[62] Ibid., paragraph 34.

[63] Ibid., paragraph 34. Guck is referring here, and throughout the rest of the article, to Cusick 1993, 67–83.

[64] Ibid.

[65] Ibid., sections 13 and 14.

of "illusion," to reality, and so, perhaps, to truth. If this truth is therefore to our benefit, then love of music is therefore tantamount to love of truth, and if music analysis also has fidelity to this love, it therefore acts likewise.

But if Guck in 1996 could be found wondering why we were all so worried about getting our feet wet, by the early 2000s it seemed we were all more than up for getting wasted at pool parties. This would account for the extraordinary self-confidence of assumption regarding what it means to love music that fuels the opening rhetoric of Carolyn Abbate's iconic "Music: Drastic or Gnostic?":

> What does it mean to write about performed music? About an opera live and unfolding in time and not an operatic work? Shouldn't this be what we do, since we love music for its reality, for voices and sounds that linger long after they are no longer there? Love is not based on great works as un-performed abstractions or even as subtended by an imagined or hypothetical performance. But would considering actual performances simply involve concert or record reviews? And would musicology—which generally by-passes performance, seeking meanings or formal designs in the immortal musical work itself—find itself a wallflower at the ball?[66]

What clinches the deal in this paragraph's direct assault is the unquestioned authority that is given to the experience of being directly exposed to live, present-tense happening. Live musical performance has value precisely *because* it necessitates such exposure, rather than it having value in and of itself.[67] It follows that if music scholarship is to have value, then it must act accordingly. However, through a series of brilliantly damning comic observations, Abbate paints a picture of music scholarship in thrall instead to what she calls the "cryptographic sublime." Rather than the dramatic sonic *immediacy* of live performance, music scholars are attracted by *delay*. They get sidetracked by the hermeneutic pleasures attendant on the resistance that music, scripted as social text, exhibits to the giving up of its meaning. For music scholarship, "the carnal and material in their evident and common form, as actual live performances, seem somehow too hot to handle."[68] Music

---

[66] Abbate 2004, 505.

[67] Abbate's essay is strongly influenced by the thinking of Hans Urlicht Gumbrecht, which is likewise concerned with arguing for the value of presence in live-action happening. Gumbrecht's most focused articulation of his value system appears in the same year as Abbate's essay (2004).

[68] Abbate 2004, 529.

scholarship (music analysis included) must therefore be symptomatic of a lack of courage for getting at the thing itself—of not loving well enough. And if the image of that fate is not enough to make musicology change its tune, then threatening it with being called out as sissy clinches the deal: "would musicology—which generally by-passes performance, seeking meanings or formal designs in the immortal musical work itself—find itself a wallflower at the ball?"[69] Man up to the haptic, or else! Not a particularly queer sentiment.

Abbate's essay is driven by the tacit assumption that the *sine qua non* of true love is *detourphobia*: that if we study music, it must be because we love music; and if we love music, then we should love it its most immediate fashion possible. It is a staggeringly literal-minded philosophy—and also, as I argue, not nearly literal-minded enough. But it does provide a good cue for moving toward wrapping things up by reminding us of some observations of Ahmed's discussed in the first part of my essay. Ahmed was there shown positing that sexual perversion is a form of "delay" in which "you take up time that could have been used to get to the point." And if Ahmed is right, and "[q]ueer use" means "we linger; we do not get to the point,"[70] then "Music—Drastic or Gnostic?" is a very straight thing indeed, and the historical fact of its almost immediate success might therefore give us pause within this context where I am considering the possibility of a queer academy. For it seems more than a little disingenuous to say that we become academics involved in the study of music in order to replicate a certain immediacy characteristic of an initial love relationship with music. We certainly need to have an initial *relationship* with music; if we eventually become academics who study music, it is not unlikely that that relationship must have been a pretty serious one, maybe even at first love. But from the perspective of queer theory, why should musicology have to be quite such a monogamous form of fidelity, like the sentimental image of childhood sweethearts who remain together for life?

Queer scholars have long been involved with questioning the assumptions of our notions of love and relationality, and their conceptualizations can be shown to resonate directly with cutting-edge work in music theory. Take, for example, Leo Bersani's famous reading of the scene in Jean Genet's 1948 novel *Funeral Rites* (*Pompes funèbres*), in which one man fucks another from behind on the roof of a building at night during the liberation of Paris at the end of the Second World War. The fact that they do not fuck face-to-face is

---

[69] Ibid., 505.
[70] Ibid., 206.

immensely important to both Genet and Bersani, and it transforms the scene from a kind of relational intimacy—analogous to that valorized as the predominant form of loving music in scholars such as Guck and Abbate—into a form of cosmological opening out. The two men are thus "elevated" to a kind of "objectless or generalized ejaculation, a fucking of the world rather than each other." They "come not with each other but, as it were, *to the world*, and in so doing they have the strange but empowering impression of looking at the night as one looks at the future."[71] And now take Vivan Luong's powerful recent critique of our scholarly models for loving music.[72] Luong takes inspiration from Gilles Deleuze and Félix Guattari's insistence that, rather like Genet's guys fucking on the roof, "we always make love to worlds."[73] As a result, she seeks to explore "what might happen if we viewed love and more specifically, music loving, not just as relations among two (a person and a piece), but among and within dynamic multiplicities or assemblages—networked, vibrant landscapes [*paysages*] comprised of many people, things, and forces."[74] And so likewise, when I started to be aware back in the early 1990s that music analysis was making me happy, it came with a dawning realization that music analysis was more than just an expression of a couple in love: of just me and music. It also had other hues—of polyamory and productive forms of betrayal.

For what I loved and, to return to Foucault's terms, wished to take pleasure in, was something *even more* immediately present and intimate to me within the scene of scholarship than the music that I loved. It was the deep attraction, excitement, and pleasure that I was easily able to gain from the activity of *thinking* about music—*not* the fact that I was thinking *about* music. Indeed, from my own experience, the ease with which I can experience a disconnect between what music I love, and prefer to listen to and perform, and the music I like to teach and think about is testament to the fact that music affords me just as much a ruse that allows me take pleasure in the act of thinking as it does a reason that ameliorates for the inconvenience of having to suffer the ignominy of living a life of the mind. It was because of *this* event in my life, and not, I might add, because I was not up to scratch, that I was inspired to betray the commitment I had made and give up pursuing a career as a classical viola player. The symptom of this betrayal was the new attachment

---

[71] Bersani 1995, 166.
[72] Luong 2017.
[73] Deleuze and Guattari 1983, 294.
[74] Luong 2017, section 1:10.

I made to the pleasures that the act of music analysis, performed for its own sake, could afford.

In this essay, I have scripted these pleasures as queer because of the way they grate against the dark complicities between neoliberal forms of instrumentality and the strategies academics perform to escape the shame of their own internalized sense of impotence and irrelevance. They are queer pleasures because they offer glimpses of habitation in the nowhere places between the disciplinary boundaries and thus offer the potential of loosening the grip that disciplinary professionalism holds over us and that keeps us bound to a capitalist worldview. If at this point of conclusion I have still not yet extensively articulated what the queer academy that music analysis intimates might be, that is in part testament to the huge resistance to it that must first be brought to light. But it is also because that academy *does not yet exist*. And so, to invoke Foucault's words once more, we have still to work on ourselves and invent that manner of being that is still improbable. It is my belief that such work would best begin by coming out about, and becoming infinitely more susceptible to, the pleasures that led us to the academy in the first place. We need to develop fidelity to the possible fact that once we were happy and that that was good enough. Or is that simply *too* queer an acknowledgment to contemplate as foundational?

References

Abbate, Carolyn. 2005. "Music—Drastic or Gnostic?" *Critical Inquiry* 30, no. 3: 505–36.

Adorno, Theodor. 1991. "Keeping One's Distance." In *Minima Moralia: Reflections from Damaged Life*, translated by E. F. N. Jephcott, aphorism 82, 126. London: Verso.

Agawu, Kofi. 1997. "Analyzing Music Under the New Musicological Regime." *The Journal of Musicology* vol 15, no. 3: 297–307.

Agawu, Kofi. 2004. "How We Got out of Analysis, and How to Get Back in Again." *Music Analysis* 23, nos. 2–3 (July–October): 267–86.

Ahmed, Sara. 2006. *Queer Phenomenology: Orientations, Objects, Others*. Durham, NC: Duke University Press.

Ahmed, Sara. *What's the Use? On the Uses of Use*. Durham, NC: Duke University Press, 2019.

Benjamin, Walter. 2006. *Berlin Childhood Around 1900*. Translated by Howard Eiland. Cambridge, MA: Harvard University Press.

Bersani, Leo. 1995. *Homos*. Cambridge, MA: Harvard University Press.

Born, Georgina. 2010. "For a Relational Musicology: Music and Interdisciplinarity, Beyond the Practice Turn: The 2007 Dent Medal Address." *Journal of the Royal Musical Association* 135, no. 2: 205–43.

Boretz, Benjamin. 1981/1982. "If I am a musical thinker . . ." *Perspectives of New Music* 20 (Fall–Winter/Spring–Summer): 464–517.

Brett, Philip. 1997. "Piano Four-Hands: Schubert and the Performance of Gay Male Desire." *19th-Century Music* 21, no. 2: 149–76.

Brodsky, Seth. 2017. *From 1989, or European Music and the Modernist Unconscious.* Berkeley: University of California Press.

Burnham, Scott. 2012. *Mozart's Grace.* Princeton, NJ: Princeton University Press.

Califa, Pat. 1994. *Public Sex: The Cult of Radical Sex.* Pittsburgh: Cleiss Press.

Chauncey, George. 1996. "Privacy Could Only Be Had in Public: Gay Uses of the Streets." In Stud: Architectures of Masculinity, edited by Joel Sanders, 224–61. New York: Princeton Architectural Press.

Cheng, William. 2016. *Just Vibrations: The Purpose of Sounding Good.* Ann Arbor: University of Michigan Press.

Chua, Daniel K. L. 1999 *Absolute Music and the Construction of Meaning.* Cambridge: Cambridge University Press.

Chuang, Tzu. 1996. *The Book of Chuang Tzu,* translated by Martin Palmer, with Elizabeth Breuilly, Chang Wai Ming, and Jay Ramsay. London: Penguin Books,

Currie, James Robert. 2001. "Disagreeable Pleasures: Negotiating Fugal Counterpoint in Classical Instrumental Music." PhD dissertation, Columbia University.

Currie, James Robert. 2009. "Music After All." *Journal of the American Musicological Society* 62, no. I (Spring): 145–203.

Currie, James Robert. 2012. *Music and the Politics of Negation.* Bloomington: University of Indiana Press.

Cusick, Suzanne. 1993. "On a Lesbian Relationship with Music: A Serious Effort Not to Think Straight." In *Queering the Pitch,* edited by Philip Brett, Gary C. Thomas, and Elizabeth Wood, 67–83. New York and London: Routledge.

Deleuze, Gilles, and Félix Guattari. 1983. *Anti-Opedipus: Capitalism and Schizophrenia,* translated by Robert Hurley, Mark Seem, and Helen R Lane. Minneapolis: University of Minnesota Press.

Foucault, Michel. 1997a. *Ethics: Subjectivity and Truth,* edited by Paul Rabinow, translated by Robert Hurley and others. New York: The New Press.

Foucault, Michel. 1997b. "Friendship as a Way of Life." In Michel Foucault, *Ethics: Subjectivity and Truth,* edited by Paul Rabinow, translated by Robert Hurley and others, 135–40. New York: The New Press.

Foucault, Michel. 1997c. "Polemics, Politics, and Problematizations." In Michel Foucault, *Ethics: Subjectivity and Truth,* edited by Paul Rabinow, translated by Robert Hurley and others, 112–19. New York: The New Press.

Foucault, Michel. 1997d. "Michael Foucault: An Interview by Stephen Riggins." In Michel Foucault, *Ethics: Subjectivity and Truth,* edited by Paul Rabinow, translated by Robert Hurley and others, 121–33. New York: The New Press.

Foucault, Michel. 1997e. "The Social Triumph of the Sexual Will." In Michel Foucault, *Ethics: Subjectivity and Truth,* edited by Paul Rabinow, translated by Robert Hurley and others, 157–62. New York: The New Press.

Foucault, Michel. 1997f. "Sexual Choice, Sexual Act." In Michel Foucault, *Ethics: Subjectivity and Truth,* edited by Paul Rabinow, translated by Robert Hurley and others, 141–57. New York: The New Press.

Guck, Marion A. 1996. "Music Loving, Or the Relationship with the Piece." *Music Theory Online* 2: paragraph 2. Accessed March 2, 2022. https://mtosmt.org/issues/mto.96.2.2/mto.96.2.2.guck.html.

Gumbrecht, Hans Urlicht. 2004. *Production of Presence: What Meaning Cannot Convey.* Stanford, CA: Stanford University Press.

Halperin, David M. 1995. *Saint-Foucault: Towards a Gay Hagiography*. Oxford: Oxford University Press.

Heidegger, Martin. 1971. "The Origin of the Work of Art." In *Poetry, Language, Thought*, translated by Albert Hofstadter, 15–86. New York: Harper and Row.

Kerman, Joseph. 1980. "How We Got Into analysis, and How to Get Out." *Critical Inquiry* 7: 311–31.

Kramer, Lawrence. 2007. *Why Classical Music Still Matters*. Berkeley: University of California Press.

Lee, Gavin. 2020. "Queer Music Theory." *Music Theory Spectrum* 42, no. 1: 143–53.

Leong, Nancy. 2013. "Racial Capitalism." *Harvard Law Review* 126, no. 8: 2151–26.

Levitz, Tamara. 2017. "Decolonizing the Society for American Music." *The Bulletin of the Society for American Music* 43, no. 3 (Fall): 1–13.

Levitz, Tamara. 2018. "The Musicological Elite." *Current Musicology* 102 (Spring): 9–80.

Luong, Vivan. 2017. "Rethinking Music Loving." *Music Theory Online* 23, no. 2. Accessed March 2, 2022. https://mtosmt.org/issues/mto.17.23.2/mto.17.23.2.luong. html#:~:text=Vivian%20Luong&text=ABSTRACT%3A%20Building%20on%20 an%20implicit,Deleuzian%20sense%20of%20the%20term.

Maldonado-Torres, Nelson. "Outline of Ten Theses on Coloniality and Decoloniality." https://fondation-frantzfanon.com/outline-of-ten-theses-on-coloniality-and-decolo niality/.

Marx, Karl. 1978. "Theses on Feuerbach." In *The Marx-Engels Reader*, 2nd edition, edited by Robert C. Tucker, 143–45. New York and London: W.W. Norton and Company.

Maus, Fred Everett. 2004. "The Disciplined Subject of Musical Analysis." In *Beyond Structural Listening? Postmodern Modes of Hearing*, edited by Andrew Dell'Antonio, 13–43. Berkeley: University of California Press, 204.

McClary, Susan. 2000. *Conventional Wisdom: The Content of Musical Form*. Berkeley: University of California Press.

Said, Edward. 1996. *Representations of the Intellectual: The 1993 Reith Lectures*. New York: Vintage Books.

Scherzinger, Martin. 2001. "Negotiating the Music-Theory/African-Music Nexus: A Political Critique of Ethnomusicological Anti-Formalism and a Strategic Analysis of the Harmonic Pattering of the Shona Mbira Song 'Nyamaropa.'" *Perspectives of New Music* 39: 5–117.

Scherzinger, Martin. 2004. "The Return of the Aesthetic: Musical Formalism and Its Place in Political Critique." In *Beyond Structural Listening? Postmodern Modes of Hearing*, edited by Andrew Dell'Antonio, 252–77. Berkeley: University of California Press.

3

Queering Schubert's "Der Atlas"

Reflections on Positionality and Close Reading

David Bretherton

On January 6, 2017, I received a cancer diagnosis and was booked in for urgent surgery.[1] I remember thinking that my convalescence would provide the ideal opportunity to catch up on research, perhaps by writing an essay on Franz Schubert's "Der Atlas." This attitude to work is now common among academics in UK universities and beyond, where excessive workloads have become the norm and annual leave is routinely (even expectedly) used for writing and research. The year before, despite plummeting weight, and like a fool, I had delayed—by months—medical investigations that ultimately revealed severe Crohn's disease, because I was "too busy" to be ill; I had a grant application deadline to meet, and academia waits for no one, least of all the sick or disabled.[2] This time, though, I was a "bad" academic: after surgery in mid-January, I spent my sick leave being sick.

At home a few days after surgery, I woke up gloriously late one morning, and descended the steep and narrow staircase of the Victorian terrace where my husband and I then lived. I had only managed a few steps before my legs began to shake and then give way. Luckily, I fell just a short distance before I managed to grab the handrail and regain my footing. I was more exhilarated than alarmed; I had been emotionally numb since my cancer

[1] I would like to acknowledge the support of the United Kingdom's Arts and Humanities Research Council (Grant Reference: AH/P007740/1).

[2] A recent UK Research and Innovation report on diversity among grant applicants to the United Kingdom's nine research councils reveals both that "[t]he proportion of applicants who say they have a disability ranges from 1% to 3% [. . .], which is below the proportion of people with disabilities employed in universities on both teaching and research contracts (4%) and in the labour market (13%)," and that "[w]hite applicants and applicants without disabilities respectively have higher award rates by value than ethnic minority applicants and applicants with disabilities." See UK Research and Innovation, "Diversity Results for UKRI Funding Data 2014–15 to 2019–20" (Swindon: UK Research and Innovation, n.d. [2021]), 2, https://www.ukri.org/wp-content/uploads/2021/03/UKRI-300321-DiversityResultsForUKRIFundingData2014-20.pdf.

David Bretherton, *Queering Schubert's "Der Atlas"* In: *Queer Ear*. Edited by: Gavin S. K. Lee, Oxford University Press.
© Oxford University Press 2023. DOI: 10.1093/oso/9780197536766.003.0004

diagnosis, but now I felt alive again. I might have been at risk of serious injury, but for a few moments I had enjoyed the adrenaline rush. In the midst of this micro-drama—mid-flight, as it were—I had what I was then convinced was an epiphany: this must have been how Schubert's self-pitying Atlas felt, struggling to bear the weight of the heavens while standing on trembling tremolo legs, cursing his wretched luck, no longer in control of his life, but nevertheless knowing he had lived.

By this time, I had known Schubert's song "Der Atlas" for almost two decades; I had written a master's essay on *Schwanengesang* (D. 957) (the so-called song cycle that includes "Der Atlas," which was assembled by Tobias Haslinger after Schubert's death) and had also analyzed the song for my doctoral thesis. Its eponymous protagonist, Atlas, is a figure from Greek mythology who was sentenced to hold up the heavens for eternity by Zeus, after the Olympians had overthrown the Titans, whom Atlas had led in battle. The song, which sets a text from Heinrich Heine's *Die Heimkehr*, presents Atlas as he endures this sentence. Schubert's musical setting is superficially straightforward: a strongly characterized ternary form, in which the outer sections depict Atlas's suffering and feature piano tremolos that memorably evoke his extreme physical exertion, and an inner Section B that sees Atlas briefly reflect on the infinitely happier fate he might have had, had he not listened to the desires of his "proud heart." But analyze the music a little deeper, and odd structural quirks emerge, particularly in relation to Schubert's unusual treatment of the reprise. Within the narrative context of the six Heine settings found in Schubert's *Schwanengesang*, the Atlas myth is generally understood as a metaphor for unrequited love. But the symphonic grandiosity of "Der Atlas," and its curious reprise, have always left me feeling unsatisfied with this reading; Schubert, it seems to me, hints at something far more tragic. The strength of this feeling has waxed and waned as I have aged and as my positionality has changed, and I often find myself returning to "Der Atlas" to try to solve this conundrum.

For whatever reason (self-pity?), "Der Atlas" was lurking in my mind again in January 2017, at a point when I was taking powerful medication. And so the interpretative "epiphany" I had about "Der Atlas" when I tripped on the stairs looks less significant now that my head is clear. Yet this event is still personally significant for me for the effect it had on my academic outlook: after previously being somewhat skeptical of the notion that people's lived experiences might give them particular insights that are not easily accessible to or appreciable by others, my trip caused me to reassess that position. My skepticism was then completely overcome as a result of events (which I will come to) that caused me to realize just how endemic ableism is in academia.[3]

In this chapter, I finally write my essay on "Der Atlas." I first highlight some technical details of the music, before outlining four musico-poetic readings of "Der Atlas," each of which I have ascribed to over the years that I have known the song. These readings chart not only my developing understanding of the song, but also the changing relationship between my positionality and my scholarship. In contrast to the overconfidence and veneers of objectivity that still pervade the discipline of music theory and analysis, the subjective, self-reflective, and provisional approach that I take toward interpreting the song here is intended to be methodologically queer. Toward the end of the chapter, I reflect on my queer positionality, and also consider the possibility of a queer (fifth) reading of Schubert's "Der Atlas" itself.

A Music Analysis of "Der Atlas"

While the song's ternary form is strongly characterized, I disagree with Edward T. Cone's description of it as "typical" and "simple."[4] Rather, the apparent simplicity is deceptive. The way Schubert reworks reprised material, so that the tonal areas opened up by Section A are completely closed down in Section A', is highly sophisticated. "Der Atlas" is Schubert at the height of his powers, and is an example of what I would describe as "deep" word painting. Let me start with an overview of the setting, before examining some details.[5]

In Stanza 1 of Heine's poem, Atlas speaks of his unbearable punishment, before blaming his downfall on his proud heart in Stanza 2. As Table 3.1 shows,[6] Schubert sets these two stanzas as two contrasting musical sections, A and B. Section A' (a varied thematic reprise of Section A) follows, setting a repetition of the opening two lines of text from Stanza 1. Note that this textual repetition, which I will call "Stanza 3," is Schubert's, not Heine's.

---

[3] Nicole Brown and Jennifer Leigh have highlighted the significant underrepresentation of disabled and neurodivergent academics in UK universities; see Brown and Leigh 2018, 985–89, https://doi.org/10.1080/09687599.2018.1455627.

[4] Cone 2000, 73–74.

[5] The following technical analysis of the song is heavily based on that found in my doctoral thesis: "The Poetics of Schubert's Song-Forms" (Bretherton 2008, 73–91).

[6] Table 1 does not show immediate repetitions of lines or parts of lines.

Table 3.1 Text and formal outline of "Der Atlas"

Mm.	Text	Translation	Key	Section
1			g	A
5	Ich unglücksel'ger Atlas! Eine Welt, Die ganze Welt der Schmerzen muß ich tragen, Ich trage Unerträgliches, und brechen Will mir das Herz im Leibe.	I, unhappy Atlas! A world, The whole world of sorrows must I bear, I bear the unbearable, and The heart within me wants to break.	 b	
22			B	B
	Du stolzes Herz, du hast es ja gewollt! Du wolltest glücklich sein, unendlich glücklich, Oder unendlich elend, stolzes Herz, Und jetzo bist du elend.	You proud heart, you wanted it so! You wanted to be happy, infinitely happy, Or infinitely miserable, proud heart, And now you are miserable.	 g	
40	Ich unglücksel'ger Atlas! Die ganze Welt der Schmerzen muß ich tragen!	I, unhappy Atlas! The whole world of sorrows must I bear!		A'

The idea of Atlas holding up the heavens seems to have captured Schubert's imagination during Sections A and A' (see Example 3.1, which shows the opening of the song).[7] Here, the vocal line is generally shadowed at the compound-octave by the bass line, perhaps to depict the distance between the heavens and earth that Atlas holds apart. In between, the tremolos in the pianist's right hand could be thought to represent Atlas's mental turmoil, or the toll of his extreme physical exertion, or perhaps both. Toward the end of Section A, the chromatic alteration of G to G♯ in m. 17 instigates a modulation from the home key of G minor toward the distantly related key of B minor (see Example 3.2). The arrival of B minor is then announced by a rhetorically strong perfect authentic cadence in mm. 19–20, but, at the start of Section B (m. 22), the key switches to the parallel mode, B major.

Schubert's choice of B minor/major as the goal of this modulation is significant: it is as if he takes the normative goal of the secondary key area, B♭ major

[7] The music examples of Schubert's "Der Atlas" appearing in this chapter were created with reference to the digitized holograph manuscript and editions available from the International Music Score Library Project / Petrucci Music Library at https://imslp.org/. Written-out thirty-second notes in mm. 2^1, 3^1, 10^3, 15^1, 18^3, 19^3, 38^3, 44^3, 53^1, and 54^1 have been replaced with tremolo symbols to save space.

Example 3.1 "Der Atlas," mm. 1–11², showing the start of the song and the start of Section A

(the relative major of G minor), and wrenches it up by a semitone to B♭ minor, aurally reflecting Atlas's words "the heart within me wants to break." Such a modulation, from a tonic minor to the raised mediant minor (by which I mean to the minor key on the note a major third above a minor tonic, G minor to B minor in this case), is in fact relatively rare in Schubert's songs.

Example 3.2 "Der Atlas," mm. 14–24[1], showing the end of Section A and the start of Section B

The other examples I know of—"Auf dem Flusse" and "Der Doppelgänger"—are, like "Der Atlas," very emotionally wrought settings, particularly at the points where this modulation occurs. "Der Atlas" additionally features a change in mode from B minor to B major (mm. 20–22), which reflects a

change in the focus of the text at that point: Atlas addresses his heart and briefly dwells on the happier outcome he had hoped for. Without digressing too far into neo-Riemannian theory, it is worth noting that B major is the "hexatonic pole" of G minor,[8] that is, the furthest point from G minor in the hexatonic cycle (a method of organizing tonal space that Schubert sometimes appears to have used). The complete key change in mm. 16–22, from G minor to B major, is thus unusual, remote, and marked, taking us to a very different tonal world from the one in which the song started. Of course, this tonal change is accompanied by a stark thematic change, as Section B is cast as a compound waltz.

Atlas now proceeds to blame and mock his heart (which he addresses in the second person, "You proud heart") for its (his) earlier foolish desires. He derides his heart's desire to be either infinitely happy, set to the B major just reached, or infinitely miserable, appropriately harmonized with a turn to E minor (m. 32). Section B concludes with the words "And now you are miserable," at which point another rhetorically strong perfect authentic cadence (mm. 38–39)—using identical rhetoric to the one in mm. 19–20—returns the tonality to G minor and reintroduces the thematicism of Section A (see Example 3.3). This "double return" marks the start of Section A'.

As noted above, Schubert reuses the opening two lines of Stanza 1 ("I, unhappy Atlas! A world, / The whole world of sorrows must I bear") to provide the text for the song's reprise. While it is not unheard of for Schubert to alter the poetic texts he set, his creation of a new "Stanza 3" in this way is rather unusual. By returning to the misery of the song's opening text at its conclusion, Schubert seems to have wanted to emphasize that Atlas cannot escape his fate. It is crucial to appreciate, however, that in "Der Atlas," Section A' is not simply a written-out da capo repetition of Section A. Rather, Schubert makes a number of often very subtle changes that have a profound effect on the song's structure.

The most easily recognizable change between Section A and A' is that, when the singer enters in m. 40 at the start of "Stanza 3," they do so with a different melodic line to the one used at m. 5 onward at the start of Stanza 1 (compare Examples 3.1 and 3.3). This does not detract from the sense of reprise, however, due to the return of G minor and of other prominent thematic elements (the tremolos and bass line). The obvious difference and obvious sameness of these two passages obscure a significant change in

---

[8] Cohn 1996, 19.

Example 3.3 "Der Atlas," mm. 35–44, showing the end of Section B and the start of Section A'

the music's harmonic structure: in Section A, the singer's first downbeat of Stanza 1 falls on tonic harmony (m. 5), while in Section A', their first downbeat of "Stanza 3" falls on dominant harmony (m. 40); moreover, in Section A the two-measure vocal units in mm. 5–6 and 7–8 each present a i – V harmonic motion, while in Section A' the two-measure vocal units in mm. 40–41 and 42–43 instead each present V – i (compare Examples 3.1 and 3.3). The i – V motions of Section A open up tonal space, whereas the V – i motions of Section A' shut it down, reinforcing the closure obtained with the strong G minor perfect authentic cadence concluding in m. 39. Of course, the singer's aforementioned new melodic line in mm. 40–43 (a repeated stepwise descent, $d'' - g'$,[9] or $\hat{5} - \hat{1}$) also contributes to this strong sense of tonal closure.

There is then a small but potentially significant change: the $d' - bb'$ leap that sets the words "A world" ("Eine Welt") in mm. $8^3 – 9^2$ of Section A is omitted from the equivalent point in Section A' (compare Examples 3.1 and 3.3). The leap's omission in Section A' has implications for how we might interpret the song's Schenkerian structure, as I will discuss shortly. But for now, in non-Schenkerian terms, we could think of this leap as a gesture that again opens up tonal space, and that it is therefore appropriate to omit from the tonally closed Section A'. In terms of meter, whereas Sections A and A' have been "out of sync" with respect to the ordering of their tonic/dominant juxtapositions in mm. 5–8 (i – V, i – V) and 40–43 (V – i, V – i), respectively, with the omission of the "A world" leap in Section A', the two now come into alignment, and mm. 10–14 and 44–48 are essentially identical.

This alignment is short-lived, however, as the two sections again diverge at the point where Section A began to modulate, so that Section A' (and the song as a whole) can end in the tonic. The modulatory phrase is reworked, rather than being cut or replaced (compare Examples 3.2 and 3.4): the brief piano interlude in Section A at mm. $14^3 – 15^2$ is omitted in Section A'; the singer's repeated g' (m. 16) becomes an arpeggiation to g'' (m. 49); and then the $g\sharp'$ (m. 17)—crucial to the earlier modulation—is respelled as ab'' (m. 50), which pulls back to g''. Modulation is thus averted. The vocal line of Section A' concludes with a downward octave register transfer $g'' - g'$ (mm. 51–52), which uses rhetoric comparable to the earlier perfect authentic cadences (mm. 19–20 and 38–39, shown in Examples 3.2 and 3.3, respectively). Thus, in Section A', return to or closure in G minor is stressed both by a genuine perfect authentic cadence at the start (mm. 38–39), and by a cadence-imitating register transfer at the end (mm. 51–52).

The features I have discussed in the previous few paragraphs contribute to an incessant emphasis throughout Section A' on tonal closure in the home key of G minor, and they have implications for the song's Schenkerian

---

[9] Throughout this chapter, I give the register of vocal notes as they are written in the score, regardless of the register in which they might be sung in performance.

Example 3.4 "Der Atlas," mm. 48–56, showing the end of the song and the end of Section A'

structure.[10] $\hat{3}$ would be my choice of primary tone for this song, as it allows the tonicization of B♮ at m. 20 to be represented as mixture of the primary tone. The song's fundamental structure thus looks set to conform to the model of three-part (i.e., ternary) form arising from mixture of primary tone $\hat{3}$, which Schenker laid out in *Free Composition*.[11] An important characteristic of all types of three-part form that Schenker considers in *Free Composition* is that there is a clear structural parallelism between the arrival of the primary tone in the opening part of the structure, and the "retaking" of the primary tone in the final part, which is thus implicitly linked to the thematic parallelism that exists between Sections A and A' of a ternary form in standard formal

---

[10] I am still reflecting on the significance of Philip Ewell's recent critique of Schenkerian theory for my analytical practice; in the meantime, I acknowledge the influence that Schenkerian thinking has had on my understanding of "Der Atlas." As I noted in the introduction to this chapter, my analytical work on this song dates from my days as a graduate student, at which point I was deeply immersed in Schenker's work. See Ewell 2020, https://mtosmt.org/issues/mto.20.26.2/mto.20.26.2.ewell.html.

[11] Schenker 1979, §310.

Example 3.5 (a) Schenker's model of three-part form arising from mixture of primary-tone $\hat{3}$; (b) the Schenkerian structure of "Der Atlas"

analysis.[12] With respect to three-part form arising from mixture of primary-tone $\hat{3}$ in particular, it is the mixture itself that stakes out the sections of the form. As Example 3.5(a) (cast in G minor) illustrates, the chromatic alteration $\flat\hat{3}$ to $\natural\hat{3}$ gives rise to part 2 (i.e., Section B), while the reversal of this chromatic alteration and the retaking of the primary tone, $\natural\hat{3}$ returning to $\flat\hat{3}$, gives rise to part 3 (Section A').

Yet "Der Atlas" deviates significantly from this model, as Example 3.5(b) illustrates. The tonicization of B minor is completed slightly "early," and the start of Section B is thus marked not by mixture (the alteration of B♭ to B♮), but by mixture within mixture (i.e., the alteration of D♮ to D♯, as B minor switches to B major). Similarly, the retaking of the primary tone $\flat\hat{3}$ occurs

---

[12] In his codification of Schenker's formal theory, Charles J. Smith retains this link, writing that "a reprise is best analysed by a return to the same background configuration that represents its original (first-section) appearance." See Smith 1996, 243.

"early," toward the end of Section B (albeit tucked away in the piano accompaniment), rather than at the start of Section A'. More significantly, $\hat{2}$ and $\hat{1}$ arrive in mm. 37 and 39 respectively, during the perfect authentic cadence that elides the end of Section B with the start of Section A'; in other words, the descent of the fundamental line concludes at the very point at which—according to Schenker—we might have expected to find the retaking of the primary tone, $\hat{3}$. Having arrived so very prematurely, $\hat{1}$ is then retained throughout Section A' until the end of the song.

If you accept the middle-ground analysis I have presented in Example 3.5(b), in "Der Atlas" there is no structural parallelism between Sections A and A', despite their strong thematic link. Instead, the structural events that Schenker suggested should generate the song's three-part form are all bunched up into the first two sections of its ternary design. And, following the conclusion of the fundamental line in m. 39, there is no further structural motion, only the continued prolongation of $\hat{1}$, making Section A' a coda in the Schenkerian sense. This reading of the structure is entirely consistent with my earlier observations about the changes that Schubert makes to reprised material: the i – V motions of Section A becoming V – i in Section A', the d' – $b\flat'$ leap that emphasizes $\hat{3}$ in Section A that is omitted from the $\hat{1}$-prolonging Section A', the respelling of Section A's G♯ as A♭ in Section A' to avoid modulation; all of these changes rework a structurally open Section A into a resolutely structurally closed Section A'.

I therefore suggest that the song's form, at both a foreground and middle-ground levels, evokes Atlas's inescapable and unbearable fate. Central to this is the reprise, with its (over)emphasized closure in the miserable home key of G minor. This is something that I believe a reading of "Der Atlas" ought to take into account.

Four Readings

Having focused on technical aspects of the music in the previous section, I now turn to consider interpretative matters. I will present four readings of "Der Atlas": Surface, Straight, Gay, and Disabled. These readings are not contrived for this chapter, but rather they are ones that I have held as credible at various points over the years I have known the song; as I outline each reading, I will briefly comment on the circumstances by which I came to it.

In revising these readings for this chapter, I have borne in mind the following questions, which arise from the song's text:

1. Who is Atlas and who are the Titans? (Note that although the Titans are not explicitly mentioned in the text, their existence is implied by the use of the Atlas myth.)
2. Who is Zeus and who are the Olympians? (Again, although Zeus and the Olympians are not explicitly mentioned in the text, their existence is implied by the use of the Atlas myth.)
3. Atlas('s heart) wanted to be "infinitely happy or infinitely miserable"; what did Atlas want so much that he was prepared to risk infinite misery for?
4. What is the implicit middle path (between the two extremes causing infinite happiness and infinite misery) that Atlas('s heart) did not want to take?

Surface Reading

A Surface Reading of "Der Atlas" understands the song simply as a presentation of the Atlas myth itself. That is, Atlas, of Greek mythology, enduring his punishment from Zeus, after the Olympians won their war with the Titans. With regard to the four questions I just raised: (1) Atlas and the Titans appear as themselves, (2) as do Zeus and the Olympians; (3) Atlas was hungry for power and was willing to risk his life to get it, (4) whereas he was unwilling—due to his "proud heart"?—to be neutral in the conflict between the Titans and Olympians.

From this perspective, Schubert's setting of Heine's text is unproblematic. The music is suitably dramatic, with a quasi-orchestral piano accompaniment, a wide dynamic range, strident vocal lines, and clearly directed harmonic progressions. The wrenching modulation to B minor/major at the end of Section A is appropriate for evoking the magnitude of what Atlas risked and lost. Similarly, Schubert's reworking of the reprise to emphasize tonal closure in the depressing home key suitably reflects Atlas's unbearable eternal fate. In this Surface Reading, Schubert's setting—monumental in everything but duration—fits its legendary subject matter like a glove.

This also happens to be a very common reading of the song. It is generally the first reading that people construct on hearing, learning or writing about the song; this was certainly the case for me. Furthermore, it is also the reading presented or implied (by the omission of any deeper interpretation) in countless program notes, CD/download liner notes, and fan websites. In this way, the Surface Reading of the song is also the default reading. But there is a snag: Schubert's circle was literary, and there is evidence that Heine's *Die Heimkehr* (which includes the Atlas poem) was discussed at one of their reading parties in January 1828.[13] We might presume, therefore, that Schubert was aware of the potential broader context of the poem within *Die Heimkehr*, and that he also knew that myths generally function as metaphors. Therefore, we might expect his artistic vision to reflect this, which makes the Surface Reading of the song rather unambitious.

Straight Reading

Schwanengesang, the song cycle that includes "Der Atlas," was posthumously assembled by Haslinger, and several scholars have argued that Schubert's Heine settings can be extracted from it to form a coherent cycle in their own right. There is some debate as to the correct sequence of songs in this "Heine cycle." On one side, Maurice J. E. Brown, Harry Goldschmidt, and Richard Kramer advocate reordering the songs to match the order in which their texts occur in *Die Heimkehr* ("Das Fischermädchen," "Am Meer," "Die Stadt," "Der Doppelgänger," "Ihr Bild," and "Der Atlas").[14] On the other side, Louise Litterick, Michael Hall, and others advocate preserving the order found in Schubert's sole surviving manuscript and in *Schwanengesang* ("Der Atlas," "Ihr Bild," "Das Fischermädchen," "Die Stadt," "Am Meer," and "Der Doppelgänger").[15] While the position of "Der Atlas" in these two orderings of the Heine cycle could not be more different (last vs. first), there is neverthe-less apparent agreement among prominent scholars on both sides (Kramer and Litterick) that "Der Atlas" acts as a metaphor for unrequited love within the narrative that emerges from either ordering.

---

[13] Reed 1997, 259.

[14] Brown 1967; Goldschmidt 1974, 52–62; Kramer 1985, 213–25; Kramer 1994, ch. 6; Kramer 1996, 185–89.

[15] Litterick 1996, 77–95; Hall 2003. In addition to Litterick and Hall, Kurt von Fischer and Douglass Seaton also appear to support the manuscript and published ordering; however, due to difficulties with accessing library materials during the COVID-19 pandemic, I have been unable to consult their work directly and base this assessment on Martin Chusid's discussion of their work. See: von Fischer 1989, 122–32; Seaton 1992, 85–99; Chusid 2000, 159–73.

I have called this "unrequited love" interpretation of "Der Atlas" the Straight Reading, on the basis that the protagonist's beloved is understood to be the young woman he serenades in "Das Fischermädchen," making this a heterosexual relationship. But this reading is also "straight" in the colloquial sense of being conventional and studious: it is a very literary reading whose roots are in academia, and it is frequently discussed in student essays and seminars (indeed, I first came across it when writing a master's essay on Schubert's Heine settings). While it certainly offers a coherent, even pleasing, reading of "Der Atlas," I have gradually come to find it wanting, perhaps in part because of overfamiliarity, but also because the Atlas-myth-as-unrequited-love metaphor has imperfections. These can be drawn out by considering the four questions that I raised earlier.

Let us start with the first two questions: (1) who is Atlas and who are the Titans; and (2) who is Zeus and who are the Olympians? In the Straight Reading, Atlas is a jilted lover, and Zeus is his usurper (the same usurper who takes the protagonist's place in "Der Doppelgänger"). But who are the Titans and who are the Olympians in this metaphor? One might suppose that the Titans could represent some sort of "brotherhood of the jilted" and, by the same token, that the Olympians could represent some sort of "brotherhood of usurping womanizers," but the former (and, by the same token, the latter?) hardy seems credible, because the protagonist appears to be completely alienated during the cycle. Thus these aspects of the metaphor are arguably left empty in this reading.

To continue: (3) what did Atlas want so much that he was prepared to risk infinite misery for; and (4) what is the implicit middle path that Atlas did not want to take? In this Straight Reading, Atlas felt that the chance of living happily ever after with his beloved was worth risking the misery that might come from rejection. We can also assume that the middle path between the two, which Atlas chose not to take, would have been to never have pursued the maiden in the first place. These aspects of the metaphor work in principle, but it seems to me that Schubert's tragic setting (particularly with regard to his emotive treatment of the reprise), and the metaphor's epic mythological vehicle, are excessive for such a commonplace tenor. In other words, while the protagonist of the Straight Reading is understandably upset at being cast aside for someone else, there is something very self-indulgent, even adolescent, about his likening of his relationship woes to a war between gods, and melodramatically claiming his life to be ruined because he was dumped. So, for me, this interpretation is unsatisfactory.

There are potential solutions to this apparent mismatch between the tragedy of the setting and the supposed tenor of the Straight Reading's unrequited-love metaphor. For example, Jack Stein and Susan Youens have suggested that Heine's protagonist is self-mocking,[16] which Schubert could have reflected in his setting. Yet in my view, although the song's protagonist mocks his heart for its ambition in Section B, there does not seem to be any mockery or self-mockery of his suffering, and no hint that Schubert considers the metaphor to be ridiculous. An alternative solution would be to presume that the protagonist has mental health difficulties. This explanation is perhaps most convincing when the song is performed as part of a Heine cycle in the Brown-Goldschmidt-Kramer sequence. That is, with "Der Atlas" last, and proceeded by the three other minor-key songs, "Die Stadt," "Der Doppelgänger," and "Ihr Bild," so that the protagonist becomes increasingly depressed as the cycle reaches its conclusion. But this solution essentially concedes the point: "Der Atlas" is not understood as a song about unrequited love per se, but rather as one about an inability to deal with unrequited love. (This possibility looks forward to aspects of the Disabled Reading that I will discuss shortly.)

To summarize, this Straight Reading of "Der Atlas" is plausible, but there are drawbacks that prevent it from being compelling: not all aspects of the Atlas metaphor are utilized (there are no Titans or Olympians), and there is a mismatch between the epically tragic mood of the song, and the relative triviality of the metaphor's supposed tenor of unrequited love.

Gay Reading

The acrimonious debate about Schubert's sexuality had largely exhausted itself by the time I started university in the late 1990s. As an undergraduate, I read Susan McClary's "Constructions of Subjectivity in Schubert's Music,"[17] but it was not until I was a doctoral student in the mid-2000s that I had fully caught up with the literature. I vividly remember reading Maynard Solomon's famous article proposing that Schubert and members of his circle may have been primarily homosexual,[18] and then the very next day reading

[16] Stein 1971, 81–82; Youens 2007, 11.
[17] Published in its definitive form as McClary 1994, 205–34.
[18] Solomon 1989, 193–206.

Rita Steblin's strident rebuttal.[19] The experience was jarring. Regardless of the extant evidence, because Schubert died at the young age of thirty-one, supposedly with if not from syphilis, it was only natural for classical music lovers in the LGBTQ+ community and their allies, particularly those who lived through the peaks of the HIV/AIDS pandemic, to associate and empathize with his plight.

"Der Atlas" seems to me to call out for a Gay Reading. Moreover, following McClary's example, one might interpret the song's non-normative structural features, discussed above, as signifying a homosexual compositional subjectivity on Schubert's part. Thus, while the premise of the Gay Reading I present here is that the song's protagonist is homosexual, this itself is underpinned by the possibility that the song could be a coded statement of Schubert's own homosexuality. Whereas the "unrequited love" tenor of the Straight Reading did not seem to match the tragedy of the Atlas myth, in this Gay Reading we now have one that is sufficiently tragic, if speculative: an autobiographical outpouring about the pain of unrequited love borne of oppressed homosexuality, from a young man suffering with an incurable and potentially terminal sexually transmitted disease.

This Gay Reading equates the song's general tragic mood to the oppressive atmosphere of a homophobic society. Meanwhile, the dichotomy between Atlas and his heart in Stanza 2—a dichotomy Schubert evokes by a remote modulation to B minor/major—can be interpreted as an internal struggle between the protagonist's public presentation and closeted desires, between his knowledge that homosexuality is socially unacceptable and the reality of his sexual attraction to men, two worlds that could not be further apart. And in this split between his head and heart, Atlas blames his heart for its homosexual desires. But perhaps there is a suggestion of emotional fidelity—of being true to oneself—here too: Atlas's heart wanted to be "infinitely happy or infinitely miserable"; we might surmise, therefore, that if he cannot have a homosexual relationship, he is not prepared to live a lie and attempt to maintain a heterosexual relationship for the sake of his public image. And so Atlas's fate is one of emotional alienation.

Let me conclude this Gay Reading by parsing the four questions I raised at the start of this section. (1) In a Gay Reading, Atlas is a homosexual man, who is perhaps also a representation of Schubert; the Titans, meanwhile, are other queers, perhaps even Schubert's circle of gay friends (if we accept

[19] Steblin 1993, 5–33.

Solomon's proposal that they were primarily homosexual).[20] (2) The identity of Zeus is less certain. It does not further the metaphor to interpret him as a romantic competitor. So, perhaps Zeus is a man whom Atlas desires, but who has either rejected Atlas's advances, or whom Atlas has never sought to seduce, because it is clear that Zeus would not welcome an advance from a man. Alternatively, Zeus could represent an authority figure of some sort, perhaps a member of the government or the church. Indeed, perhaps Zeus even represents the Christian God. Regardless, this reading understands the Zeus figure to be homophobic and understands the Olympians to represent homophobic society. (3) The "infinite happiness" that Atlas desired is simply to be able to live as a homosexual man and love men openly, in contrast to the "infinite misery" of remaining single and closeted. (4) The middle path between these extremes, which Atlas does not want to take, would be to have a false heterosexual "relationship of convenience."

If Schubert were homosexual, I fear that he must have had a truly wretched time trying to come to terms with his sexuality.

Disabled Reading

While suggestions that Schubert may have been homosexual led to ill-tempered responses and heated debate, suggestions that he may have had mental-health difficulties, such as Elizabeth McKay's proposal that he had cyclothymia,[21] have been more generously received. At this historical distance, there is little prospect of a sound diagnosis of Schubert's mental health, but his low mood and melancholia are well documented, as is the decline in his physical health. Christopher H. Gibbs notes that, from 1822 onward, Schubert's letters make frequent reference to his "miserable" mood[22] and, from February 1823 onward, to his poor physical health.[23] Schubert's early death is, of course, the stuff of legend, even if there is disagreement as to the cause (typhus, typhoid fever, syphilis, mercury poisoning, etc.).[24] There is thus ample biographical justification for attempting a Disabled Reading of

[20] Solomon 1989, 202.
[21] McKay 1996, 138.
[22] Gibbs 2000, 115.
[23] Gibbs 2000, 92.
[24] See, for example, Sams 1980, 15–22. Or, for a more recent account, Cybulska 2019, 44–47, https://doi.org/10.47513/mmd.v11i1.647.

"Der Atlas," and the malleability of the Atlas metaphor means that there is plenty of space for us to do so.

While I acknowledge that physical and mental disability are separate and enormously broad categories of disability, I will nevertheless offer just a single combined Disability Reading, as constructing individual readings for each potential condition results in ones that are repetitive and fragmentary. In this reading, more so perhaps than even the Gay Reading, the song's protagonist is understood to represent Schubert himself. That the powerful and muscular Atlas, strongest of the Titans, might be associated with disability perhaps confounds expectations, but I think it would have been perfectly possible for a disabled Schubert, whose health began to deteriorate at a relatively young age, to have identified with Atlas, a mythological figure known for his suffering and misery.

The events that I described at the start of this chapter were the inspiration for this Disabled Reading, so let me go back to the song's tremolos, which you will recall caught my imagination as I tripped on the stairs. The term "tremolo" originates from the Italian *tremolare* (to tremble, to shake) and the Latin *tremulus* (trembling, quivering, shaking). I suggested earlier that, in the outer sections of the song, these tremolos represent the extreme physical exertion of Atlas having to hold the heavens on his shoulders, but this Disabled Reading now understands them as embodying the many illnesses and impairments that might cause one to shake and tremble. Schubert's episodes of depression could be indicative of several anxiety and personality disorders, for which trembling and shaking are often potential symptoms. Indeed, depression, anxiety, and bipolar-spectrum disorders, as well as many other conditions, might lead to a lack of energy and disturbed sleep, causing physical fatigue, and ultimately trembling muscles. In terms of physical health, Schubert is widely thought to have had syphilis. In its tertiary (and final) stage, this disease spreads to the nervous system (neurosyphilis), which can lead to difficulties with coordination and control of muscles, problems with walking, tremors, and seizures.[25] The use of mercury as a treatment for syphilis could itself have led to erethism mercurialis (acute mercury poisoning), a neurological condition characterized by anxiety, depression, irritability, mania, and, if mercury exposure continues, muscle

---

[25] "Neurosyphilis: MedlinePlus Medical Encyclopedia," accessed September 6, 2021, https://medl ineplus.gov/ency/article/000703.htm.

tremors.[26] Similarly, the symptoms of typhoid fever, another potential cause of Schubert's death, include shivers and muscle aches. So, there is ample scope for us to interpret the song's characteristic tremolos as representing the physical tremors caused by illness or disability of some kind.

The depressive mood of the outer sections of "Der Atlas," and particularly the sense of resignation in the reprise (created by the technical features noted earlier) might thus be considered a testament of Schubert's declining mental and/or physical health. In terms of the song's text, in Section A (Stanza 1) it is notable that the protagonist refers to himself in both the first and third person ("I, unhappy Atlas!") before, in Section B (Stanza 2), distancing himself from his heart, addressed in the second person ("You proud heart"), which he blames for his situation. This might be indicative of some sort of dissociative-identity disorder or psychosis. With regard specifically to psychosis, which is a symptom of a variety of serious mental-health disorders,[27] it is worth noting that several of the other Heine settings detail events that might suggest that the protagonist is having a psychotic episode: the portrait that comes to life in "Ihr Bild" (hallucination), the protagonist's belief that his beloved has poisoned him with her tears in "Am Meer" (persecutory delusion), and the protagonist's sighting of his double in "Der Doppelgänger" (hallucination, dissociation). Indeed, in "Der Atlas" itself, one wonders if the protagonist's self-identification as a mythical god could even be a grandiose delusion.

Let me conclude this Disabled Reading by addressing the four questions I have used previously. (1) Atlas is a disabled protagonist (i.e., someone with an impairment who is prevented from fully accessing society), while the Titans are disabled people generally.[28] (2) As with the Gay Reading, the role of Zeus is less clear, but he could represent an ableist authority figure, the Olympians represent ableist society. (3) The "infinite happiness" that Atlas longs for is now understood to represent being non-disabled, either because of the absence of an impairment, or because an impairment is accommodated. On the other hand, "infinite misery" could represent the

---

[26] Stone, Angermann, and Sugarman 2021, 190–98.

[27] "Psychosis: MedlinePlus Medical Encyclopedia," accessed September 6, 2021, https://medlinep lus.gov/ency/article/001553.htm.

[28] Note that here I use the terms "impaired" and "disabled" according to their use in the "social model of disability." Thus, "impairment" refers to a mental or physical disadvantage or difference, while "disability" arises from a society creating or failing to remove barriers that prevent people with an impairment from fully participating. For further information about this model, see Shakespeare 2017, 195–203.

disabled Atlas having to withdraw from ableist society. (4) Finally, the middle path, which Atlas did not want to take, could be understood as participating in ableist society as a disabled person without accommodations, and having one's dignity denied as a result.

If this Disabled Reading of "Der Atlas" is credible, and if the song is indeed autobiographical, Schubert must have found his situation truly unbearable.

Queering

My Positionality

I am undoubtedly privileged. I am a white cisgender male. I am relatively securely employed. I am gay, but I was not targeted by bullies at school, even after I came out at seventeen. My family is supportive. My workplace is inclusive of LGBTQ+ people. During my lifetime the legal, political, and social climate in the United Kingdom has become increasingly supportive of queer rights (although, alarmingly, the steady progress of the last two decades has now reversed under the Johnson Government). My domestic life is not especially radical: I have been in a monogamous, long-term, same-sex relationship for twenty-one years, and my partner and I married in 2018. With the exception of a few small incidents while I was a school and university student, and despite my angst about coming out, I have never really felt directly discriminated against because of my sexual orientation. In short, I have never felt especially "queer" or "othered" because of my homosexuality. So if, to paraphrase Sara Ahmed,[29] being queer provides a unique perspective, orientating queer people to see things that are hidden from the view of straight people, then, for much of my adult life to date, I have not lived queerly enough to make an honest claim to such insight.

But this all changed for me a few years ago, following the serious illnesses that I referred to in the introduction to this chapter. Since those diagnoses in 2016 and 2017, I have lived with two chronic illnesses, and although I am incredibly grateful to have regained a good quality of life, managing these conditions takes time and care. One impact of this has been that my ability to overwork is now very restricted—and yet, as a dyslexic academic, I had come to rely on overworking to mask and compensate for my difficulties

[29] Ahmed 2006, 20 and 107.

with reading and writing. To compound matters, the tiredness that some-times results from my chronic illnesses can further exacerbate my dyslexia.

While I would like to say that I was always supported professionally to overcome these difficulties, unfortunately this has not always been the case. (Although I stress that my immediate colleagues have only ever been in-credibly supportive.) After my capacity for overwork diminished, I began discussions with my employer about putting in place appropriate "reason-able adjustments" (United States: "accommodations"), as provided for by the United Kingdom's Equality Act 2010. After a year or so of little progress, I went off work with stress for several months, and my union (the wonderful University and College Union) got involved. Ultimately, the matter was re-solved in my favor, and in a manner that enabled the employment relation-ship to be repaired. My employer has since taken meaningful steps to try to prevent a recurrence of the difficulties I encountered.

I know that many people suffer far worse discrimination than I did, par-ticularly where that discrimination is directed, intentional, or motivated by hate (the discrimination that I faced was, by contrast, structural, and even-tually corrected). Moreover, I recognize that it was only because of my priv-ilege that I was able to challenge my treatment. Even so, at the time and for some months afterward, I was very distressed, hurt, and angry. This has had a lasting and profound impact on my positionality: for the first time I felt I had been meaningfully discriminated against, excluded, othered, and even queered. Consequently, I now believe that I have gained a queer—or at least a queerer—perspective. To borrow Ahmed's words, I now feel I have a "slant-wise" view of the world, and things that were previously hidden from me have now "come into view."[30]

And so, I would like to conclude this chapter by reflecting on the various readings of "Der Atlas" I have given above, making a few further observations from this queerer perspective.

Queer Reading?

I came out as "gay" some twenty-five years ago, but I have only really considered myself "queer" in the last few years, having arrived at this position primarily due to my experiences as a disabled academic. I suspect that most

[30] Ahmed 2006, 107.

readers of this volume will know that "gay" (or for that matter "lesbian," "homosexual," "bisexual," "trans," etc.) is not a direct synonym of "queer." And perhaps also that, within the academic sphere, there is a distinction between the older discipline of LGBT studies and the newer one of queer studies. This distinction is less to do with chronology than it is to do with their respective approaches: LGBT studies implies simply an LGBT/LGBT-related object of study, whereas queer studies, and particularly queer theory, seeks to problematize sexual categories, and to critique encultured heteronormativity and systems of dominance, often using methodology that is purposely "queer" or "queered."[31] It therefore follows that writing about an LGBT object does not necessarily make a study queer, and also that one could write a queer study of a straight object. In short: a "Gay Reading" is not necessarily a "Queer Reading."

Earlier, I proposed a Gay Reading of "Der Atlas," which was constructed from the premise that the song's protagonist is homosexual. While this reading imagined the oppression the protagonist faced, it did not really interrogate heteronormativity; it was not queer. What, then, might a Queer Reading of "Der Atlas" look like? Well, before I address this question, let us first step back and queer the readings that I presented above.

The Straight Reading is, in fact, not only straight but also heteronormative, because its protagonist holds deeply patriarchal and misogynistic attitudes about women. In the protagonist's world, men are given all the agency, while women are denied any; the young woman whom the protagonist desires cannot choose whom she dates, but rather, the Atlas metaphor implies that she is a prize to be claimed by the victor in the battle between Atlas and Zeus. Men are gods; women are chattel. And the protagonist seems perfectly happy with this state of affairs, even though on this occasion it means he loses his woman to his competitor.

Moreover, in this Straight Reading, and actually in all the readings I outlined earlier, the underlying message is decidedly conservative, even anti-revolutionary: submit to the powerful and know your station. Atlas blames his heart (i.e., his own desires) for his predicament, not Zeus and not the Olympians, and he implicitly accepts that his eternal punishment is appropriate. Yes, he grumbles to himself, but only that his punishment is unbearable, not that it is unjust. As the Atlas myth is the vehicle of the song's

---

[31] An informative discussion of the differences between LGBT studies and queer studies can be found in Hall and Jagose 2013, xiv–xx.

metaphor, this outlook is inherited by all other readings: the Straight, Gay and Disabled Readings all feature men who neither challenge authority nor question their fate. This is not queer. If the Straight Reading's protagonist does not value women, then the Gay and Disabled Readings' protagonists do not value themselves, apparently accepting that they are of lesser value than the rest of society, accepting that they should be discriminated against, and making no argument for change, let alone equality. Granted, the oppressed and disadvantaged should not necessarily be expected to have to liberate themselves, but there is no suggestion in these readings that they even want to be liberated. And so, while the Gay and Disabled readings may feature minorities, their message is far from politically radical or progressive. And in this sense, while one can queer readings of "Der Atlas," I am not sure that a compelling Queer Reading of "Der Atlas" is particularly plausible.

Queerness and Disability

On the topic of queerness and political activism, it is worth noting the commonalities between the experiences and oppressions of queer and disabled people, and consequently the close relationship between queer theory and disability studies. Mark Sherry writes:

> Both Disability Studies and Queer Theory problematize the public and the private, the social and the biological, difference, stigma and deviance, and the construction of identities. Both challenge universalizing norms that marginalize those who don't conform to hegemonic normalcy. And both engage with the lives of people who can experience high levels of discrimination, violence and intolerance.[32]

Perhaps unsurprisingly, my earlier Gay and Disabled Readings of "Der Atlas" have many similarities, including first and foremost that they are both narratives of oppression (something they inherit from the Surface Reading, and then particularize). Indeed, regardless of Schubert's sexuality and disability status, and whether or not there is an autobiographical element to the song, the appeal to me of these two readings is that they offer a portrait of

---

[32] Sherry 2004, 769.

the relationship between the oppressed individual and an oppressive society, with which all oppressed people might empathize.

The specific similarities shared by the Gay and Disabled Readings include the following (and I set these out using the same four questions I have used elsewhere):

1. Regardless of whether Atlas is understood to be gay or disabled (not that these categories are mutually exclusive, of course), the Titans are understood as representing the wider oppressed group.
2. Zeus could be seen as representing a homophobic or ableist authority figure, while the Olympians represent homophobic or ableist society itself.
3. Infinite happiness is understood as being allowed or enabled to live one's life unhindered, while infinite misery is understood as remaining isolated in some way.
4. Finally, the middle path that the protagonist did not want to take amounts to participating in society on society's terms, at the cost of one's principles and personal dignity.

From this fourth answer, we might conclude that the message of "Der Atlas" is not wholly irredeemable, for while the protagonists of these readings may not be revolutionaries, their acquiescence to authority does have a limit: if they cannot participate as who they really are, then they will not participate at all. In this, there is perhaps a glimmer of a Queer Reading.

Queer Music Analysis

Within the context of music theory and analysis, the conflation of sexual variance and structural variance—whereby a composer's actual or potential non-heterosexuality is associated with a perceived deviation from music's structural norms—needs to be approached with particular care. It can be a powerful interpretative tool, as McClary has demonstrated,[33] but it is also a controversial one.[34] In the case of "Der Atlas" specifically, there are certainly non-normative structural features, such as the use of the raised mediant as

[33] McClary 1994.
[34] See McClary's own discussion of the reception of her work: McClary 1994, 205–9. Also see the contributions to Kramer 1993.

a modulatory goal, and the (over)emphasis on closure in the reprise. One might interpret these as some sort of homosexual compositional subjectivity on Schubert's part, but in light of the song's potential conservative message I discussed above (the protagonist's near-complete submission to an oppressive authority, and his acceptance of his supposed inferiority), perhaps a more interesting question to address is: do the song's non-normative structural features suggest a queer (rather than homosexual) compositional subjectivity?

I think the answer to this is probably "no." In "Der Atlas," the expected Schenkerian structural events are neither absent nor upturned, but rather premature; out of place, but (crucially) early. Even if we disregard Schenkerian theory, the seeds of my Schenkerian analysis are there in the music (for example, in the obsessive focus on closure in the reprise). Even the exaggerated tonal contrast of the song's central section—that modulation to the raised mediant, the hexatonic poll—might be said ultimately to highlight the dominance of the home key, which is quickly and resolutely restored by the start of the reprise. In "Der Atlas," then, we might say that there is an enthusiasm or exaggeration of structural norms and conventions, rather than an abandonment of them.[35] If one were to make a link between the song's structure and Schubert's compositional subjectivity, it seems to me the enthusiasm for and exaggeration of ternary form in "Der Atlas" might actually be said to suggest the opposite of queerness: a heterosexist heterosexual, or a deeply closeted homosexual, perhaps?

I suppose that this confirms what we realize the moment we hear the song's opening measures: "Der Atlas" is a deeply unhappy work. If Schubert was gay and/or disabled, and if this is song is in anyway autobiographical, then he must have been in a very dark place when he composed it.

Conclusion

The "close reading" of individual works—or what music scholars usually call "music analysis"—is a practice that Eve Kosofsky Sedgwick once bemoaned had become "devalued,"[36] and this often seems to be the case in music studies

---

[35] "Auf der Donau," D. 553, would be a better candidate for the latter, so far as ternary form is concerned.

[36] Sedgwick 1997, 23.

today. But close reading (music analysis) is also a practice that, thanks to McClary's work, was central to the emergence of queer musicology, and one that I believe should remain central to it.

In this chapter, I have offered several readings of Schubert's "Der Atlas" and have sought to critique those readings from a queer perspective. I have foregrounded my own subjectivity in a way that is characteristic of much queer scholarship. And, while I have used some traditional music analysis, this was more to highlight the ways in which the song does not fit music theory's models, than to point to ways in which it does.

Crucially, though, I have endeavored to avoid prescriptive interpretation, and indeed this chapter documents my repeated engagement with and reinterpretation of "Der Atlas" over many years. I have offered multiple perspectives on the song, in a way that perhaps chimes with Ahmed's notion of orientations,[37] and maybe even with Adorno's likening of Schubert's music to changing views of the same landscape.[38] For me, the appeal of "Der Atlas"—and of Schubert's work more generally—lies in its ability to support multiple complementary or even contradictory readings simultaneously. Such ambiguity, of course, was a vital tool to avoid state censorship and persecution in the "Age of Metternich." Yet the queer embrace of ambiguity and subjectivity is at odds with the traditional heteronormative-masculine virtues of certainty and objectivity, which, I would argue, still dominate music theory.[39] There is surely nothing more straight than the notion of a singular, fixed, definitive, and objective interpretation of a "masterwork," and nothing more queer than multiple subjective and speculative readings of an incomplete and posthumously published composition. Close queer readings may be "weak theory," but they are all the stronger for it.[40]

Finally, I have alluded to the possibility that "Der Atlas" could be autobiographical, perhaps representing Schubert's oppressed homosexuality, or even his possible illnesses or disabilities. I am open to the possibility that Schubert may have been heterosexual, but in the queering of a composer's music, the composer's sexuality seems to me to be of lesser importance than the need for their music to engage with or critique power and oppression in some way. It is not necessary for Schubert to have been homosexual for us to offer queer readings of his music; indeed, by decoupling these two things,

---

[37] Ahmed 2006.
[38] Adorno 2005, 3–14.
[39] On which, see Maus 1993, 264–93.
[40] On which, see Cheng 2016, 40.

rather than making the latter contingent on the former, queer music theory becomes more broadly applicable, and more interesting. In any case, there can be little doubt that "Der Atlas" is about oppression, even if the specific type of oppression remains an open question.

References

Adorno, Theodor W. 2005. "Schubert (1928)." Translated by Jonathan Dunsby and Beate Perrey. *19th-Century Music* 29, no. 1: 3–14.

Ahmed, Sara. 2006. *Queer Phenomenology: Orientations, Objects, Others*. London: Duke University Press.

Bretherton, David. 2008. "The Poetics of Schubert's Song-Forms." DPhil, University of Oxford.

Brett, Philip, and Elizabeth Wood, eds. 1994. *Queering the Pitch: The New Gay and Lesbian Musicology*. New York: Routledge.

Brown, Maurice J. E. 1967. *Schubert's Songs*. London: British Broadcasting Corporation.

Brown, Nicole, and Jennifer Leigh. 2018. "Ableism in Academia: Where Are the Disabled and Ill Academics?" *Disability & Society* 33, no. 6: 985–89. https://doi.org/10.1080/09687599.2018.1455627.

Cheng, William. 2016. *Just Vibrations: The Purpose of Sounding Good*. Ann Arbor: University of Michigan Press.

Chusid, Martin. 2000. "The Sequence of the Heine Songs and Cyclicism in *Schwanengesang*." In *A Companion to Schubert's* Schwanengesang: *History, Poets, Analysis, Performance*, edited by Martin Chusid, 159–73. New Haven, CT: Yale University Press.

Cohn, Richard. 1996. "Maximally Smooth Cycles, Hexatonic Systems, and the Analysis of Late-Romantic Triadic Progressions." *Music Analysis* 15, no. 1: 9–40.

Cone, Edward T. 2000. "Repetition and Correspondence in *Schwanengesang*." In *A Companion to Schubert's* Schwanengesang: *History, Poets, Analysis, Performance*, edited by Martin Chusid, 53–89. New Haven, CT: Yale University Press.

Cybulska, Eva Maria. 2019. "The Myth of Schubert's Syphilis: A Critical Approach." *Music and Medicine* 11, no. 1: 44–47. https://doi.org/10.47513/mmd.v11i1.647.

Ewell, Philip A. 2020. "Music Theory and the White Racial Frame." *Music Theory Online* 26, no. 2. https://mtosmt.org/issues/mto.20.26.2/mto.20.26.2.ewell.html.

Fischer, Kurt von. 1989. "Some Thoughts on Key Order in Schubert's Song Cycles." In *Essays in Musicology*, edited by Tamara S. Evans, 122–32. New York: City University of New York.

Gibbs, Christopher H. 2000. *The Life of Schubert*. Cambridge: Cambridge University Press.

Goldschmidt, Harry. 1974. "Welches war die ursprüngliche Reihenfolge in Schuberts Heine-Liedern." *Deutsches Jahrbuch der Musikwissenschaft für 1972*, Jahrg. 17: 52–62.

Hall, Donald E., and Annamarie Jagose. 2013. "Introduction." In *The Routledge Queer Studies Reader*, edited by Donald E. Hall, Annamarie Jagose, Susan Potter, and Andrea Bebell, xiv–xx. New York, Abingdon: Routledge.

Hall, Michael. 2003. *Schubert's Song Sets*. Aldershot: Ashgate.

Kramer, Lawrence, ed. 1993. "Schubert: Music, Sexuality, Culture." Special issue, *19th-Century Music* 17, no. 1: 3–101.

Kramer, Richard. 1994. *Distant Cycles: Schubert and the Conceiving of Song*. Chicago: University of Chicago Press.

Kramer, Richard. 1996. "Against Recycling." *19th-Century Music* 20, no. 2: 185–89.

Lee, Gavin. 2020. "Queer Music Theory." *Music Theory Spectrum* 42, no. 1: 143–53.

Litterick, Louise. 1996. "Recycling Schubert: On Reading Richard Kramer's *Distant Cycles: Schubert and the Conceiving of Song*." *19th-Century Music* 20, no. 1: 77–95.

Maus, Fred Everett. 1993. "Masculine Discourse in Music Theory." *Perspectives of New Music* 31, no. 2: 264–93.

McClary, Susan. 1994. "Constructions of Subjectivity in Schubert's Music." In *Queering the Pitch: The New Gay and Lesbian Musicology*, edited by Philip Brett and Elizabeth Wood, 205–34. New York: Routledge.

McKay, Elizabeth Norman. 1996. *Franz Schubert: A Biography*. Oxford: Oxford University Press.

"Neurosyphilis: MedlinePlus Medical Encyclopedia." 1997–2023. Accessed September 6, 2021. https://medlineplus.gov/ency/article/000703.htm.

"Psychosis: MedlinePlus Medical Encyclopedia." 1997–2023. Accessed September 6, 2021. https://medlineplus.gov/ency/article/001553.htm.

Reed, John. 1997. *The Schubert Song Companion*. New edition. Manchester: Mandolin.

Sams, Eric. 1980. "Schubert's Illness Re-Examined." *The Musical Times* 121, no. 1643: 15–22.

Schenker, Heinrich. 1979. *Free Composition*. Translated by Ernst Oster. New York: Pendragon Press.

Seaton, Douglass. 1992. "Interpreting Schubert's Heine Songs." *The Music Review* 53, no. 2: 85–99.

Sedgwick, Eve Kosofsky. 1997. "Paranoid Reading and Reparative Reading; or, You're So Paranoid, You Probably Think This Introduction Is about You." In *Novel Gazing*, edited by Eve Kosofsky Sedgwick, 1–37. Duke University Press.

Shakespeare, Tom. 2017. "The Social Model of Disability." In *The Disability Studies Reader*, edited by Lennard J. Davis, 5th ed., 195–203. New York: Routledge.

Sherry, Mark. 2004. "Overlaps and Contradictions between Queer Theory and Disability Studies." *Disability & Society* 19, no. 7: 769–83.

Smith, Charles J. 1996. "Musical Form and Fundamental Structure: An Investigation of Schenker's *Formenlehre*." *Music Analysis* 15, no. 2–3: 191–297.

Sofer, Danielle. 2020. "Specters of Sex: Tracing the Tools and Techniques of Contemporary Music Analysis." *Zeitschrift der Gesellschaft für Musiktheorie* 17, no. 1: 31–63.

Solomon, Maynard. 1989. "Franz Schubert and the Peacocks of Benvenuto Cellini." *19th-Century Music* 12, no. 3: 193–206.

Steblin, Rita. 1993. "The Peacock's Tale: Schubert's Sexuality Reconsidered." *19th-Century Music* 17, no. 1: 5–33.

Stein, Jack. 1971. *Poem and Music in the German Lied from Gluck to Hugo Wolf*. Cambridge, MA: Harvard University Press.

Stone, Corey, Jeffrey Angermann, and Jeffrey Sugarman. 2021. "Erethism Mercurialis and Reactions to Elemental Mercury." *Cutis* 107, no. 4: 190–98. https://doi.org/10.12788/cutis.0224.

UK Research and Innovation. 2021. "Diversity Results for UKRI Funding Data 2014–15 to 2019–20." Swindon: UK Research and Innovation. https://www.ukri.org/wp-content/uploads/2021/03/UKRI-300321-DiversityResultsForUKRIFundingData2014-20.pdf.

Whitesell, Lloyd. 2002. *Queer Episodes in Music and Modern Identity*. Edited by Sophie Fuller and Lloyd Whitesell. University of Illinois Press.

Youens, Susan. 2007. *Heinrich Heine and the Lied*. Cambridge: Cambridge University Press.

4

The Expression of Queerness in Hans Werner Henze's Music

Federica Marsico

Unlike an instrumental piece, an opera consists in the masterly blending of a libretto, music, and staging.[1] This peculiarity provides composers with a range of virtually indefinite opportunities to relate to their audiences. The semantic content of a sung text in conjunction with the expressive power of music and staging allows for the establishment of a thoroughly seminal dialogue with one's audience. Opera as a genre has thus made possible many a composer's success in portraying facets of human nature that are either marginalized or outright labeled as taboos in the light of mainstream cultural mindsets. Thanks to the filter of dramatic fiction, a theatrical stage makes for the ideal venue for them to be narrated in an unfettered manner.

The musical theater by Hans Werner Henze (1926–2012), one of the most prominent composers of the second half of the twentieth century,[2] provides an utterly fertile substrate for rendering the condition of individuals deemed as diverse with respect to socially mandated patterns of conduct. Henze's very life experience was likely one of the major determinants of the occurrence and attributes of such subjects within his operas.[3] While enjoying considerable success throughout his career, the composer nonetheless epitomized two tell-tale indicators of marginalization, to wit, his being a homosexual, on the one hand,[4] and his embracing a musical language far removed from

[1] I wish to thank Lloyd Whitesell for his useful suggestions during the writing of this chapter. This text is one of the deliverables of my research project *Sexual and Gender Non-Normativity in Opera after the Second World War*, which has received funding from the European Union's Horizon 2020 research and innovation program under the Marie Skłodowska-Curie grant agreement No. 887530.
[2] For a general look at the composer's figure and production see Jungheinrich 2002; Kerstan and Wolken 2006; Abels and Schmierer 2012.
[3] For the biographical experience of the artist see Henze 2001; Bachmann and Henze 2004.
[4] On his condition as a homosexual composer see Henze 1984d, 322–23; Daolmi 1991.

the experiments of the postwar avant-garde, on the other.[5] Starting from the early 1950s, Henze sought to react to such conditions of marginalization by asserting his personality as a musician. He did mostly so through the genre of opera, which in turn put him on the path to success and, what is more, enabled him to captivate and endear a wide and composite audience to his perspective on marginalized identities, a subject unsurprisingly relevant to him for self-evident biographical reasons.

Some studies on Henze's operas have highlighted his anti-normative stance with respect to one of the dichotomies most inherent in social-conduct regulation, to wit, the one concerning sexual and gender identity.[6] Among the operatic scores by Henze most revealing of anti-normativity, three of them provide some seminal inspiration as to the hermeneutic analysis and interpretation of a score harboring queer meanings. In *Boulevard Solitude* (Hannover, Landestheater, 1952) the vocal roles and musical writing are consistently employed with the aim of lending a homosocial connotation to the relationships relevant to the male protagonist. In addition, *Der Prinz von Homburg* (Hamburg, Staatsoper, 1960) and *Il re cervo* (Kassel, Staatstheater, 1963) both encompass episodes whereby the music all but strengthens the representation of the protagonist or one of the main characters as individuals embodying otherness in terms of either gender identity or sexual-erotic connotation. In the three pieces, some facets of the score thus seem to echo one's rejection of the social norms that ensnare the expression of individuality and, by the same token, one's willingness to indulge in interpersonal relationships deemed as non-normative. A thorough analysis of the way the music highlights such an attitude within each of said pieces will bring to light a peculiar tier of score-specific dramaturgical meaning.

The Choral Writing "in the Masculine" in *Boulevard Solitude*

Boulevard Solitude, the *Lyrisches Drama in sieben Bildern* initiating Henze's opera career, illustrates the extent to which the score can lend suitable expression to one of the queer meanings possibly hidden within the dramaturgy

---

[5] On Henze's stance with respect to the *Ferienkurse* of Darmstadt see Kovács 1997; Marsico 2018. For the composer's perspective, see Henze 1984a, 1984c.

[6] Marsico 2014a, 2014b, 2015, 2017, 2020a. Moreover, this angle was explored in: Puhlmann 1988; Noeske 2019; Tumat 2019.

of an operatic work, to wit the theme of homosociality read from an anti-normative perspective. Male homosocial ties, whose limits dictated by the patriarchal model aim to guarantee the preservation of heteronormativity, become here, on the contrary, the space to depict the empathy between individuals of the same sex, attributing a much greater authenticity to this feeling than to the sexualized relationship between the protagonist and the woman he loves. The emphasis on homosociality is therefore used in the opera to disrupt the masculine norms of behavior imposed by the heteronormative canon.

Based on a libretto by Grete Weil and scenery by Walter Jockisch, *Boulevard Solitude* is an adaptation of Antoine François Prévost's *Histoire du chevalier Des Grieux et de Manon Lescaut*, a novel thrust into the operatic limelight on multiple occasions.[7] The story is set in 1950s Paris and stars Manon (soprano), a *femme fatale* accomplice of the misdeeds of her pimp brother Lescaut, and Armand des Grieux (tenor), a student madly in love with her regardless of her infidelity. The latter, who in the novel is submissive to Manon while nonetheless showing an overall resolute character, in Henze's work takes on the contours of a man who has nothing virile about him, and whose perennial weakness of mind places him at odds with the stereotype of the dominant male. Some intertextual elements of the libretto have recently been highlighted that refer to the homosexual culture (including references to the gay icons of Orpheus and Saint Sebastian and to the novel *Notre-Dame-des-Fleurs* by Jean Genet).[8] In light of the above, moreover, the coming-into-play of the treble voices at the finale of the story—incidentally, the sole presence of a *Kinderchor* within the work—has been construed as a disguised invitation for Armand to search some solace from the sorrows engendered by Manon turning to homosexual love, pursuant to Orpheus, who refused women's love after the definitive loss of Eurydice.[9] Here, on the contrary, I undertake to construe the interventions of the adult voice choir, which sings in the fourth and fifth *tableaux* alone, as aimed at devising an atmosphere of "homosocial empathy." A thorough analysis of some bouts of utmost dismay on the part of the protagonist, uncertain as to the fate of his relationship with Manon, shall further elucidate my hermeneutic perspective.

[7] On the *œuvre* see Goertz 1986; Wagner 1988; Winter 2003; Brzoska 2012; Marsico 2014a, 2020b.
[8] Marsico 2014a.
[9] Marsico 2020b.

Table 4.1 Structure of No. 12 (*Ensemble*) of *Boulevard Solitude*ª

Tableau section	Agogics	Reference to the score	Voices involved
12.a	Ruhige, fast lastende	bb. 1–48	Male choir, A, F
12.b	Tanzvariation – Etwas lebhafter	bb. 49–57	Male choir
12.c		bb. 58–94	Male choir, A, F
12.d	Tanzvariation – Ruhiger	bb. 95–102, G.P., 104–07	Male choir
12.e		bb. 108–40	Male choir, A, M
12.f	Tempo I	bb. 141–211	Male choir, A,

ª The subdivision into sections as reported in the first column of the table does not occur in the score (Henze 2000a) and is outlined herein for explanatory purposes alone.

The fourth *tableau* is set at Sorbonne University library, where Armand resumed his studies after being betrayed by Manon. In spite of his friend (baritone) Francis's attempts at discouraging him from reconciling with her, he cannot seem to stop thinking about his beloved. Unexpectedly, Manon arrives and manages to beguile Armand once again. Some male and female students are present in the library throughout the whole *tableau*. The former (tenors and basses) sing two famous *carmina* composed by Catullus for his beloved Lesbia, which establish a paradigm of comparison between the two couples, as both Catullus and Armand surrender to the *charme* of bewitching and unfaithful women, yet are always willing to reconcile with them, and as Manon's behavior is a source of continuous sorrow for Armand, just as is Lesbia's with regard to Catullus.

By reconnecting to the tradition of the operatic *concertato*, Henze conceives the *tableau* as a single number going by the title of *Ensemble* (No. 12) and consisting of several sections constantly featuring the male choir, with the soloists interspersing their dialogue—to wit, Armand (A) with Francis (F), and thereafter with Manon (M)—with sheer silence. Table 4.1 summarizes the structure of the piece.

At the opening of *tableau* section 12.a, Armand and Francis are immersed in reading, seated at a table in the proscenium, while in the background students move between the shelves of the library.[10] The two friends each sing to themselves and in contrast to each other: while Francis praises the

---

[10] "Armand und Francis sitzen lesend an einem Tisch im Vordergrund. Im Hintergrund Studenten und Studentinnen an den Bücherschränken" (Henze 2000a, 100). The quotations of the verbal text of

pleasures of reading and culture, Armand is obsessively thinking about Manon. The ground bass in the left hand of the piano and the low strings, which accompany the entire section (Example 4.1), effectively construe the protagonist's fixation.

At the same time, the male choir joins Armand's lamentations by intoning the first distich of Catullus's Carmen 92 (Example 4.1).[11] This couplet of verses is repeated four times in a mostly syllabic fashion almost identical in each instance and including several vocal styles (singing, *Sprechgesang*, and melodic line without any reference pitch). The text, in which the Latin poet yearns for Lesbia's love though she would not hesitate to maltreat him, interprets Armand's need to reunite with his beloved despite being the subject of betrayal.

The two friends pause briefly during the attack of the first *Tanzvariation* (12.b). Meanwhile, the choir intones the second distich of the poem,[12] once again interpreting the young man's state of mind. Like Catullus, and irrespective of his beloved's having forsaken him, Armand dispels his torment by persuading himself that his feelings are reciprocated.

After a few bars, the two friends commence a dialogue (12.c) during which Armand flares up in anger when Francis tells him he had seen Manon with a new partner. Once kicked out of home together with his swindler brother by wealthy old Lilaque-*père*, she does not hesitate to supplant her lover. Even in the face of evidence, and despite Francis's warning him of the fickleness of the woman, a character complicit in Lescaut's misdeeds, Armand takes Manon's defense for reasons best known to himself. Faced with Armand's obstinacy, Francis interrupts the conversation and joins the students at the back, leaving his friend alone in the proscenium. The Latin verses that accompany the entire dialogue are, again, the last two of Carmen 92 (repeated four times here).

At the start of the second *Tanzvariation* (12.d), the choir intones the first distich of Carmen 109, written by Catullus to rejoice over the return of Lesbia.[13] Between the first and second verses, a long pause (G.P.) ensues

the *œuvre* are drawn from the score, as the latter sometimes diverges from the libretto (Henze 1951), albeit with minimal differences bearing no influence on the content.

[11] "Lesbia mi dicit semper male nec tacet umquam | de me: Lesbia me dispeream nisi amat" (Henze 2000a, 100–6).

[12] "Quo signo? Quia sunt totidem mea: deprecor illam | assidue, verum dispeream nisi amo" (Henze 2000a, 106–7).

[13] "Iucundum, mea vita, mihi proponis amorem | hunc nostrum inter nos perpetuumque fore" (Henze 2000a, 115).

Example 4.1 Henze, *Boulevard Solitude*, No. 12, mm. 1–9, excerpt (piano, voices, and strings) © by kind permission of SCHOTT MUSIC, Mainz—Germany

during which all attention converges on Manon, who arrives and sits down next to Armand unnoticed. Again, the words of the choir give voice to the feelings of Armand, who, stunned by the woman's unhoped-for comeback, is still pursuing the fallacious hope of a happy romance.

The *Tanzvariation* continues with the lovers singing the German translation of Carmen 92 (12.e). In Manon's part, however, the text has been slightly amended to enable her to play the role of Lesbia and address to Catullus-Armand the words that the poet originally had intended for his woman (see the italics in the following text):

> ARMAND
> Immer spricht Lesbia schlecht
> über mich und kann gar nicht schweigen.
> Und doch möchte ich meine Seele verwetten,
> dass Lesbia mich liebt.
> MANON
> Immer spricht *Catullus* schlecht
> über mich und kann gar nicht schweigen.
> Und doch möchte ich meine Seele verwetten,
> dass *Catullus* mich liebt.
> ARMAND and MANON
> Der Beweis bin ich selbst,
> auch ich verwünsche sie dauernd
> und verwett' doch die Seele, dass ich sie
> ganz und gar liebe.[14]

Manon's singing, which strictly mimics in a higher register the melody sung by Armand, expresses the woman's conspicuous intent to subjugate the student. During the brief duet, the choir again voices Armand's state of mind by obsessively whispering in Latin the final words of the Carmen (Example 4.2). As soon as Armand becomes aware of Manon's presence, the two lovers commence intoning the German translation of Carmen 109, which occurs in the concluding section of the *Ensemble* (12.f). Through the verses of Catullus, Armand pursues the chimera of renewed loyalty on the part of his beloved and prays the gods that she can keep her promises of love. Manon, too,

---

[14] Henze 2000a, 115–20.

Example 4.2 *Boulevard Solitude*, No. 12, mm. 113–18, excerpt (voices). © by kind permission of SCHOTT MUSIC, Mainz—Germany

addresses the gods, whom, incapable as she is of harboring any doubts toward that of Armand, she asks to vouch for "her own" loyalty, and does so based on a slightly amended text.[15] While Armand is dueting with Manon, the choir sings the entire Carmen in Latin.[16]

Henze's choice to use exclusively male voices comes to the foreground in light of the overall spectrum of choral interventions during the *Ensemble*, on the one hand, and the presence in the library of some female students who, however, do not sing, on the other. The sharp separation of the choral sections

---

[15] "Götter, gebt *mir* die Kraft, dieses | Versprechen zu halten. | Macht doch, daß all *meine* Rede echt | aus dem Herzen *mir* kommt! | Damit es gelingt, unser ganzes künftiges Leben | nur dem heiligen Bund unserer Freundschaft zu weihn" (Henze 2000a, 121–25; amendments in italics).

[16] "Iucundum, mea vita, mihi proponis amorem | hunc nostrum inter nos perpetuumque fore. | Di magni, facite ut vere promettere possit, | atque id sincere dicat et ex animo, | ut liceat nobis tota perducere vita | æternum hoc sanctæ fœdus amicitiæ" (Henze 2000a, 120–26).

into female and male voices is reaffirmed in the following *tableau*, to wit the second and last one entailing the presence of the adult voice choir. Armand is in a dive bar, where he finds in the cocaine he has obtained from Lescaut an ephemeral haven from the sufferings triggered by Manon's deserting him for the umpteenth time. When the woman appears to join a new partner provided by Lescaut, Armand despairs in spite of Manon's attempts to comfort him by reasserting she still feels attached to him. Upon leaving the scene in the company of her new lover, she addresses to Armand a letter inviting him to join her in her new home the next day, when the landlord will be temporarily absent. The text of the letter is sung off-stage by Manon and is preceded by a chorus of equally off-stage humming female voices intoning a sweet lullaby melody. As the letter is about to end, the male voices enter to obsessively reiterate its salutation, to wit "Geliebter Armand," by whispering into a microphone (Example 4.3).

Differently than the male section, the recurrence of which is remarkably more consistent, the female choir only occurs in the aforementioned episode. Moreover, it is the choir of male students that empathizes with Armand in the fourth *tableau* by intoning the Catullan verses in which the boy acknowledges his love story. Homosocial empathy, as a sharing of genuine feelings between people of the same sex, is therefore musically "represented" within the scene by way of male-voice singing. The coming into play of the latter at the end of the fifth *tableau* again appears to reconnect to this interpretative category. While the women are just humming with their mouths shut, it is the men who take the floor to utter "Geliebter Armand," hence providing expression to a feeling of homosocial empathy once again. Through an evident imbalance of the choral writing in favor of the male voices of the students, who apparently fully understand what Armand feels, Henze seems to intend to contrast the spontaneity of same-sex feelings with the artificiality

Example 4.3 *Boulevard Solitude*, No. 16, coda, mm. 50–59, excerpt (voices). © by kind permission of SCHOTT MUSIC, Mainz—Germany

of a heterosexual relationship that will surely be a source of further suffering. The social instance hidden in this scene thus seems to be that of freeing same-sex relations from the limits imposed by the patriarchal model and by the consequent heteronormative canon.

Intertextuality as a Means to Recount Otherness in *Il re cervo*

Upon careful reading of the two *tableaux* of *Boulevard Solitude*, the implicit reference made within the work to Armand's queer subjectivity emerges as being mediated not only by the subject of the libretto itself, but also by the musical writing, which alludes to it in an encrypted fashion through the targeted use of the voice registers of the choir. The presence of intertextual references within the score and subsequent pursuit of the pathways connecting a composition with other musical texts referring to the theme of otherness may, for its part, serve as a second royal road toward the identification of a hidden layer of significance.

This is just what happens in the three-act opera *Il re cervo oder die Irrfahrten der Wahrheit* (1963), the abridged version of *König Hirsch* (1956) after a libretto by Heinz von Cramer and based on the tragicomic theatrical fairy tale *Il re cervo* by Carlo Gozzi. The story tells of Leandro, a mild-mannered sovereign in search of a spouse and opposed by lieutenant Tartaglia, who, in his drive for power, considers killing him to obtain the crown. Unable to marry his beloved Costanza, who has been falsely accused of attempted regicide, Leandro leaves the court and takes refuge in an enchanted forest, where he magically transforms into a stag. The clash between the forces antagonistic to the king, on the one hand, to wit the lieutenant and his clumsy hitman Coltellino, and, on the other, those who instead protect him and are embodied by the forest (which, far from being a mere backdrop, acts as a character)—the magician Cigolotti disguised as a parrot, the melancholic musician Checco, and some alchemists—resolves in the victory of the latter party. In the happy ending, the sovereign learns about his lieutenant's true nature and the innocence of the woman he loves, and he marries her after restoring justice at court.

In the second scene of the intermediate act, a piece of music entitled *Canzone* winds up the meeting between Checco and Cigolotti, the latter of whom, in the guise of a parrot, confides to the musician a magic spell aimed at

Example 4.4 *il re cervo*, act II scene 2, m. 185. © by kind permission of SCHOTT MUSIC, Mainz—Germany

Example 4.4 is drawn from Henze 2000b, 294. The piece is devoid of time signature and consists in a single, extensive bar (no. 185).

Example 4.5 *Tammurriata nera*, mm. 10 (arsis)–18

Example 4.5 is drawn from the original score of the song as reproduced in Careri 2014, 280–81.

protecting the king from peril and vanishes immediately thereafter.[17] Checco takes his guitar and intones a song, praying for the winds to blow in the right direction so that the parrot will soon return to him.[18] The *incipit* of the vocal part (Example 4.4) includes a quote from famous Neapolitan song *Tammurriata nera* by E. A. Mario after a text by Eduardo Nicolardi (Example 4.5).[19] Its occurrence, together with the title of the piece (*Canzone*), can at first glance be explained by the fascination the Neapolitan musical atmosphere exerted on Henze during the initial years of his final relocation to Italy, which he spent in

---

[17] Henze 2000b, 294–95.

[18] "*(Cigolotti macht eine Geste des Abschieds)* | CHECCO | Du gehst schon fort? Werd' ich dich wiedersehn? | *(Cigolotti ist schon weit fort)* | STIMMEN DES WALDES | Du mußt warten. Das ist alles. | CHECCO | Alle meine Träume lang hab ich gewartet, doch du kamst nie, und der Himmel und das Wasser waren schwarz. | *(Er nimmt seine kleine Gitarre aus dem Rucksack und setzt sich)* | Als ich mit Vogelzungen noch zum Fisch sprach, | auf Regenbogen kamst du geritten, | hast in die Träume erste Sehnsucht geschnitten, | bis aus dem Meer die Muschel für ewig geglitten. | Wind, der mit meinen Haaren spielt, | trug mir davon, was ich liebe. | Mußt dich nun drehn, Südwind, | Nordwind, mußt dich nun drehn. | Ostwind, wann wirst du dich wenden? | Wann wirst du dich wenden, Westwind?" (Cramer 1964, 26–27).

[19] The quote is not noticed in Oehl 2003, 207–15. I am indebted to Michele Girardi for bringing it to my attention.

Forio d'Ischia and Naples. In the year of *König Hirsch*, in fact, the composer also ran a radio broadcast devoted to the genre of Neapolitan song[20]—upon completion of the opera, he also composed the *Fünf neapolitanische Lieder* for medium voice and chamber orchestra based on seventeenth-century texts written in the Neapolitan dialect.[21] As to the question why Henze quoted this piece of music instead of another, the key to its authentic interpretation will only disclose itself to those discerning Checco's strong bond with Cigolotti (the parrot) as transcending mere friendship.

Tammurriata nera was composed in 1944 in the aftermath of the sensation resulting from the birth at Naples' general hospital of the black daughter of a local girl and a US-American soldier.[22] In this piece of music, the issue of the newborn's race emerges powerfully ("È nato nu criaturo niro niro"; trans.: "A baby is born, he is a very black baby")[23] and cannot be overlooked in spite of his mother's christening him with a quintessentially Neapolitan name ("e 'a mamma 'o chiamma Giro | sissignore, 'o chiamma Giro!"; trans.: "and his mother calls him Cyrus, | yes indeed, she calls him Cyrus"), which also applies to the disturbance arising within the local community ("'O contano 'e ccummare chist'affare"; trans.: "Housewives gossip about this affair"). The intertextual reference to *Tammurriata nera* in the *incipit* of Checco's *Canzone* suggests that the *Re cervo* piece, too, is related to the theme of illegitimate erotic relationships. Indeed, if we observe the evolution within the piece of the bond linking the melancholic musician and Cigolotti (the parrot), the ardent passion Checco feels toward the animal the magician has transformed into displays the hallmarks of true erotic desire. The first time Checco talks about him is during a chance encounter with Coltellino, who, for his part, is in search of the weapons he has lost (act I scene 7). Checco, too, is searching through the forest, namely for a colorful parrot he has been dreaming about in his sleep.[24] After his long-sought encounter with the bird, and at the time

[20] Co-produced by the Süddeutscher and the Nordwestdeutscher Rundfunk, *Die Canzonen von Neapel* was aired on April 3, 1956. For some excerpts, see Henze 1984b.

[21] Henze 1957.

[22] On the song see Catalano Gaeta 2006, 102; Careri 2014; Frasca 2018.

[23] For the transcription of the lyrics of the song see Careri 2014, 277.

[24] "CHECCO *(seine Gitarre vom Rücken nehmend)* | Willst du nicht ein kleines Konzert mit mir machen? | COLTELLINO | Kann nicht. Ohne Messer und Pistol! | CHECCO | Dann lauf ich weiter, meinen bunten Papagei suchen. | COLTELLINO | Deinen bunten Papagei? | CHECCO | Oft, wenn ich schlafe, seh ich Dinge, | die ich nicht versteh. Seltsam: | Windgeister spielen, ein Papagei, der mir winkt, | der Zauberworte weiß, bunt, wie ein Regenbogen. | COLTELLINO | Gibt's das denn wirklich? | CHECCO | Weiß nicht . . . | COLTELLINO | Ach, du träumst! Hab' keine Zeit! | Große Eile . . . Mein Messer, mein Pistol! | *(er wendet sich zum Gehen)* | CHECCO | *(im Abgehen)* | Adieu. Ach fänd ich ihn, den Regenbogenvogel irgendwo im Wald, im großen Wald. Adieu! | Coltellino | Adieu!" (Cramer 1964, 17–18).

of the farewell taking place just before the *Canzone* ensues, Checco recalls his nocturnal visions of it. Such a bird "riding on a rainbow" has awakened in him a primal desire ("erste Sehnsucht") leading him to pursue it relentlessly. After his departure, Checco beseeches the winds to grant him to meet "what he loves" ("was ich liebe") once again. His attachment to the parrot is also manifest during the finale (act III scene 6), where a crestfallen Checco picks up and hugs Cigolotti's winged attire after the latter has taken leave from the public by divesting himself of it.[25]

If we interpret musical intertextuality with a keen eye for queer sensibility, the common denominator we will acknowledge as linking the famous *Tammurriata nera*, on the one hand, to Checco's *Canzone*, on the other, is the celebration of true love within two relationships that are deemed anomalous in the surrounding social context, to wit, in those established between a white woman and black lover and between a man and a parrot, respectively. The *ensemble* for tenor and guitar, which evokes that of a love serenade, further emphasizes the erotic nature of the *Canzone.*

In the light of the intertextual reference, it becomes plausible to interpret the deeply sentimental relationship between Checco and the parrot as the metaphor of an erotic relationship considered deviant from the dominant normative context, such as a homosexual one. Referring to homosexuality understood as deviance is fitting in the queer interpretation of this scene also because the Italian term "checca," from which the character's name derives, indicates homosexuals in an offensive way, emphasizing their effeminacy and therefore their deviance from the norms of masculinity. In addition, the fact that the object of Checco's desire is a bird, a term that is used to also indicate the penis in Italian ("uccello"), seems to further address the interpretation of the relationship between him and the parrot as the expression of Henze's intent of substituting another form of deviance for homosexuality. The effect is partly provocative, partly quasi-comic for those who catch the queer nuances of the scene.

---

[25] "Cigolotti | (*sich die Maske abnehmend, tritt an die Rampe. Sehr leise zum Publikum, als wollte er nicht stören*) | Sie sind glücklich. Mich brauchen sie nicht mehr. | (*Er legt seinen Papageienmantel und die Maske sanft auf den Boden*) | [...] | (*Checco läuft herein und kniet vor dem König nieder, der ihm die Ketten abnimmt. Wie er sich zurückzieht, erblickt er die Papageienkleider des Zauberers, hebt sie auf, drückt sie an sich und bleibt so bis zum Schluß—traurig, vereinsamt—stehen*)" (Cramer 1964, 47–48).

Inner Conflicts within *Der Prinz von Homburg*

The episode of *Il re cervo*, a queer-inflected reading of which has been suggested herein, has shown the extent to which the intertextual analysis of the score can bring to light dramaturgical connotations the composer wanted to hide within the folds of the musical text. The queer-minded interpretation of an operatic text in which one cannot rely on the intertextuality of either the libretto or the score is far more treacherous. Not being able to find support in elements related to queer culture and external to the work, it has much more to do with reading the dramatic evolution of events and the development of the characters' inner conflicts in a queer perspective. The three-act opera *Der Prinz von Homburg*, after a libretto by Ingeborg Bachmann and based on the drama *Prinz Friedrich von Homburg* by Heinrich von Kleist, serves as an archetypal example of this third approach.

The operatic work is set in 1675 against the historical background of the battle of Fehrbellin promoted by the prince-elector Friedrich Wilhelm of Brandenburg against the Swedes and ending in the victory of the Germans. The protagonist is the Elector's nephew, Prince Friedrich von Homburg, in charge of leading the cavalry during the fight. On the eve of the battle, the plan of attack established by the sovereign is outlined in detail to all officers—yet, the Prince does not listen carefully to the orders issued because his attention is mesmerized by Natalie, another one of the Elector's "niblings." Due to negligence, the next day he orders his soldiers to attack the enemy prematurely. As a consequence, the Elector has no alternative but to enforce martial law and sentence him to death for the act of insubordination, albeit still retaining a fond affection for him. Natalie, however, who is in love with the Prince, manages to persuade her uncle to pardon the prisoner on the grounds of the support she enjoys from the other officers. Prince Friedrich will learn about the pardon on the occasion of the work's happy ending.

A pivotal theme of the drama lies in the conflict between the Prince's yearning for freedom and the oppressiveness of a society governed by the axioms of military ethics (this topic is also recurrent in some works by Britten, such as *Billy Budd* and *Owen Wingrave*, confirming the affinity between Henze's musical theater and his English colleague's one). To this end, we ought to mention the first dialogue between the protagonist, who dreamily wanders through the garden of the castle, and his friend the Earl of Hohenzollern, who uselessly strives to remind him of his duties in view of the forthcoming battle, as seen in this brief excerpt:

HOHENZOLLERN
Friedrich!
Die Reiterei ist eine Stunde schon voraus,
und du, du liegst im Garten hier und schläfst!
HOMBURG
[. . .] Ich weiß nicht, lieber Heinrich, wo ich bin.
HOHENZOLLERN
In Fehrbellin, du sinnverwirrter Träumer![26]

Compared to what is typical of Kleistian drama, Bachmann's re-elaboration gives pride of place to the alterity differentiating the protagonist from the surrounding environment, within which he is deemed an odd, if not down-right crazy individual, and with which he comes to clash. The poet did not confine herself to abbreviating the source text for the purpose of rendering it suitable for an operatic version, but instead considerably smoothed the heroic-military quality of the Prince's traits and stance by expunging many a dialogue revolving around the theme of warfare while at the same time highlighting the episodes focusing on the conflict between the dreamy nature of the protagonist and the austerity of a society resting upon the foundations of military discipline. At one juncture, the man is having an altercation with his best friend, the Earl of Hohenzollern, in whom he is vainly trying to con-fide his utmost feelings (scene 1); at another, with the other officers who, during the battle, resist their commander's enthusiastic impetus and opt to stick to martial discipline instead (scene 3); at yet another, with the Princess-Elector who, insensible to the Prince's moving prayer, declines to intercede with her husband to obtain his pardon (scene 6); now, again, with Natalie who, insensitive to Homburg's feelings for his uncle, tries in vain to prompt him to blame the King for being unfair (scene 8). But most prominently of all, it is the Elector himself who incarnates the inhibitions mortifying Homburg's passionate spirit—true to his role as the supreme guardian of martial law, the Sovereign in fact displays a scathing demeanor throughout the entire work, and only at the end of it, driven as he is to pity by his niece's and officers' entreaties, does he forgo his authoritarian attitude.

Almost forty years after the debut, Henze declared himself as identifying with the Prince as well as all the other characters portraying outsider fig-ures within his works.[27] One of the reasons why Henze identified with the

---

[26] Henze 1960, 5–6.
[27] Henze 1999, 124.

Kleistian prince may have been the chance to represent, through the story being narrated, the condition of a queer individual at odds with the repressive context surrounding him. Henze's emphasizing the theme of social oppression to tell the queerness in an encrypted way cannot fail to recall Britten's *Peter Grimes*, about which Brett laid some foundations for the early queer interpretations of twentieth-century opera.[28] The story of the fisherman, in friction with his own community that points to him as a criminal and ultimately causes his suicide, takes on the characteristics of a tragedy resulting from the non-acceptance of a homosexual by the heteronormative society, according to Brett's reading. Through the examination of the Prince's *solos*, which mark the stages of the conflict between his craving for freedom and duty to obey, light can be shed on the role the issue of conflict may have played in prompting Henze's queer-oriented interpretation of Kleist's drama.

The protagonist's four *solos*, arranged throughout the work so as to occur approximately equidistant from each other, speak to the distinct stages of the conflict between Homburg and his environment—if at the beginning he appears willing to play the role of commander entrusted to him by the sovereign and commit himself to sacrifice for his homeland, after his arrest he gradually comes into conflict with military ideals to an extent where he wishes nothing but to escape martial law and save his own life.

The first monologue occurs at the end of the second scene.[29] Homburg remains alone in the castle hall after the military plans have been imparted in detail and the officers hurry to take their fighting positions. In the *Vivace assai* section the leader addresses Fate and declares himself firmly convinced of securing victory in the upcoming battle. A reiterated, tight-rhythm minor third interval performed at the opening by the timpani and piano playing in very low register further enhances the commander's heroic allure (Example 4.6).[30]

The climate turns much more dramatic in the next two *solos*, ruled as it is by the Prince's dreadful fear of death following his failure to abide by martial law. In these two episodes, Homburg relinquishes his role as a hero and voices his desire to regain his status as a free man. In the second monologue, which occurs in the fifth scene, he hurries to the castle and begs the Princess-Elector

---

[28] Brett 1977.

[29] In the libretto and score, the numbering of the scenes is continuous throughout the three acts. The sequence of events within the story will thus be addressed by reference to the number of each scene, providing that: scenes 1–3 = first act; scenes 4–8 = second act; scenes 9–10 = third act.

[30] The musical examples are taken from Henze 1992.

Example 4.6 *Der Prinz von Homburg*, scene 2, mm. 177–79. © by kind permission of SCHOTT MUSIC, Mainz—Germany

Example 4.7 *Der Prinz von Homburg*, scene 5, mm. 7–11. © by kind permission of SCHOTT MUSIC, Mainz—Germany

to intercede with her husband by asking him to repeal the verdict. During the journey he suddenly encounters some undertakers who are busy digging the grave intended for his burial the next day, and he becomes sorely aware of his destiny. In the piece, a gloomy introductory chord is reiterated with anguish in a syncopated form, which encases the anxiety dwelling in Homburg's soul, while the tolling of the tubular bells marks the relentless elapsing of time (Example 4.7).[31] Shortly thereafter, an ominous aura echoes from the sinister

---

[31] Reference is being made to the overlap of two triads of F sharp minor and G minor divided by the interval of ninth B_2–C_4 (de la Motte 1960, 51).

motif of the trombones, marked by the horns and consisting of two large, dissonant intervals (Example 4.8). This motif, which will anew recur in the work to mark the Prince's vivid memory of his ghoulish vision and the looming of his end as decreed in abidance with the inexorable social construct haunting him and which he cannot elude.

In the third *solo*, which occurs in the eighth scene, an aggrieved Homburg lies in prison and feels crushed by his unforgiving, mortal fate. Once his plea with the Electress has fallen unheeded, his only last-ditch recourse remains the help of Natalie, who, in the previous scene, has expressed her determination to obtain from her uncle the pardon that would save his life. The *solo* opens with the gloomy metaphor of life as correlated to a journey leading "from two spans above earth to two below it," while the descending, unaccompanied vocal line seems to follow just that path (Example 4.9). A prominent, mournful violin tritone (Example 4.10) then triggers in Homburg the impetuous desire to regain freedom—yet, his tone is already at peace with the macabre prospect that his eyes will soon putrefy.

Example 4.8 *Der Prinz von Homburg*, scene 5, mm. 13–14. © by kind permission of SCHOTT MUSIC, Mainz—Germany

Example 4.9 Scene 8, mm. 3–6. © by kind permission of SCHOTT MUSIC, Mainz—Germany

In the fourth *solo*, which occurs at the inception of the last scene, the overall mood conversely improves. Homburg is now ready to face death and fancies that his soul will finally depart from all earthly duties only to embrace the effulgence of the afterlife. The diaphanous sounds of the orchestra adumbrate a nebulous, rarefied atmosphere and seem to accompany his body's soaring toward the felicity of Elysium.

Careful scrutiny of the four *solos* shows that the protagonist's inner conflict between his very nature and the heroic role appointed to him by the martial environment he was born to is pivotal to the drama and also emerges from the score. While in the first monologue Homburg strives to assume the role of a brave warrior, in the second and third his true nature emerges as being that of an individual much more inclined to heeding one's inward feelings than yielding to oppressive, empty hierarchies—in the last *solo*, this innermost tension resolves in death, in which he glimpses the etherealness of an afterlife devoid of boundaries to self-expression. If we assume that the Kleistian exploration of the antithesis between freedom and obedience provided Henze with the opportunity of cryptically embedding into his work the theme of conflict between queerness on the one hand and heteronormativity on the other, then we ought to construe the protagonist's four monologues along with their musical atmospheres as being consistent with that perspective. The latter, however, is not restricted to the work's musical domain, but is instead reinforced by extramusical elements to be identified by reference to the literary subject and author's biography.

Kleistian scholars have highlighted the poet as having drawn inspiration, also, from his own life experience to give shape to the characters of his dramas

Example 4.10 Scene 8, mm. 13–17, extract (voice and strings). © by kind permission of SCHOTT MUSIC, Mainz—Germany

who, as in the case of the prince of Homburg, are critical of prearranged social models. The writer, who sprang from a family belonging to the higher echelons of the military establishment, actually began to serve in the army to honor family traditions, only to soon develop a deep aversion to martial ideals and instead cultivate his interest in literature. To that end, Joachim Pfeiffer writes:

> All preexistent models of socialization, all models of societal subject foundation, were problematic for Kleist: officer, scholar, civil servant, husband, and father—what remained for him was literature, which allowed him an imaginary liquefaction of such identities. This avoidance of the expected male role is all the more remarkable because Kleist grew up in a family tradition shaped by a military, heroic ideal of masculinity.[32]

Pfeiffer correlates rejection of martial principles, a feature pervasive throughout Kleist's life, with the repudiation of the concept of masculinity typically consistent with them. The scholar also points out that the poet used literary writing to voice his "unorthodox" sexuality, which in turn has led some to suggest that he was a latent homosexual—as a matter of fact, Kleist never got married and was deeply attached to his friend Ernst von Pfuel.[33] In light of these considerations, we can deem the figure of the Prince of Homburg, too, as mirroring Kleist's status as an outsider. Just like the poet, the leader wishes to evade the rigor of martial life only to cultivate his peculiar sensitivity, which differentiates him from the rest of the army because of its inconsistency with the model of a male aloof and exclusively intent on warfare. The above considerations strongly support the assumption of Henze's identification in both the German poet's refusal to construe his individual self in terms of gender binarism and the manifestations of this biographical feature in the characters of his dramas. In the decade preceding the debut of *Prinz von Homburg*, the composer resolved to leave his country and move to Italy, where, unlike in Germany and despite the Italian culture being just as permeated with homophobia, no explicit discriminatory legislation was in force. Once again, Henze's aesthetics is similar to that of Britten in construing analogies between sexual and military oppression, like the English composer did in *Billy Budd*[34] and *Owen Wingrave*.[35]

---

[32] Pfeiffer 1996, 222.
[33] Hoverland 1980, 67; Weinholz 1993, 206.
[34] Hindley 1999.
[35] McClatchie 1996.

Final Observations

The scrutiny of the three titles by Henze makes possible a more general reflection on the methods suitable for approaching an opera score possibly concealing queer connotations. The study of the two *tableaux* of *Boulevard Solitude* focuses on the vocal registers, which emerge as the instrument by which Henze has characters of the same sex interact with each other, thus implying the existence of shared homosocial empathy. The *Canzone* from *Il re cervo*, on the other hand, shows to what extent musical intertextuality can emerge as the means to allude to a queer relationship between two characters who in themselves embody a dimension of otherness with respect to the surrounding context. Finally, the monologues of *Der Prinz von Homburg* tell us how the dramatization of a violent inner conflict, the progression of which within the character's soul and *vis-à-vis* the context is depicted by the music as well, can serve as a metaphor for the clash between a queer individuality and the surrounding regulatory environment subjugating it.

The analysis of the three works also leads to a further consideration on the queer interpretation of Henze's operatic output as a whole. In the frame of the musical theater of the second half of the twentieth century, his production is pervasively imbued with the encrypted theme of queerness. Although the investigation proposed in this chapter was limited to his early works, Henze shows to have the theme at heart throughout his career up to the titles of his old age (see for example *Phaedra* of 2007, in which the myth of the Cretan queen in love with her stepson is the pretext to focus on the figure of the chaste and misogynist Hippolytus, a symbol of a queer individual who seeks and finds their place in society). The centrality of such a theme makes Henze's output comparable to that of Britten. Unlike the latter, however, the German composer pursues the utopia of a world in which queer people can find their own space and have not to succumb to social oppression. Many of his titles, in fact, have a positive ending, in which the conflict with the community is solved in favor of the outsider individual (for instance, Friedrich is pardoned and reconciles with the elector in *Der Prinz von Homburg*, while Hippolytus is reborn to new life and is crowned king of the woods after being killed by the wrath of Poseidon).

Unlike Britten's output, few of Henze's operas have been studied though a queer approach, although the latter looks absolutely promising for his theater to the point that not taking it into consideration seems to coincide with the loss of something substantial of his artistic expression. In other words, the queer approach to Henze's theater does not represent one of the interpretative possibilities to be applied at the discretion of the musicologist, but as an essential one that is clamoring to be integrated into any hermeneutic approach to his art in order to fully understand its aesthetic instances.

References

Abels, Norbert, and Elisabeth Schmierer, eds. 2012. *Hans Werner Henze und seine Zeit*. Laaber: Laaber.

Bachmann, Ingeborg, and Hans Werner Henze. 2004. *Briefe einer Freundschaft*, edited by Hans Höller. Munich: Piper.

Brett, Philip. 1977. "Britten and Grimes." *The Musical Times* 118, no. 1618: 955–1000. Later published in 1983. *Benjamin Britten: Peter Grimes*, edited by Philip Brett, 180–96. Cambridge: Cambridge University Press; and in 2006. *Music and Sexuality in Britten: Selected Essays*, edited by George E. Haggerty, 11–33. Berkeley; Los Angeles; London: University of California Press.

Brzoska, Matthias. 2012. "Von *Manon Lescaut* zu *Boulevard Solitude*: Dramaturgie eines Sittenromans auf der Opernbühne." In *Hans Werner Henze und seine Zeit*, edited by Norbert Abels and Elisabeth Schmierer, 64–74. Laaber: Laaber.

Careri, Enrico. 2014. "Sull'interpretazione della canzone napoletana classica: il caso di *Tammurriata nera* di E.A. Mario." *Rivista italiana di Musicologia* 49: 267–84.

Catalano Gaeta, Bruna. 2006. *E.A. Mario: leggenda e storia*, second edition. Napoli: Liguori.

Cramer, Heinz von. 1964. *Il re cervo oder Die Irrfahrten der Wahrheit: Oper in drei Akten, Musik von Hans Werner Henze*. Mainz: Schott.

Daolmi, Davide. 1991. "Henze ovvero della coerenza." *Babilonia* 89: 42–44. Republished in Riccardo Panfili and Clemens Wolken, eds. 2019. *In nessun tempo: Hans Werner Henze: diari, saggi e interviste*, 163–68. Lucca: Libreria Musicale Italiana.

De la Motte, Diether. 1960. *Der Prinz von Homburg: Ein Versuch über die Komposition und den Komponisten*. Mainz: Schott.

Frasca, Simona. 2018. "La canzone 'porosa': riflessioni a margine di *Sull'interpretazione della canzone napoletana classica. Il caso di Tammurriata nera di E.A. Mario.*" *Rivista Italiana di Musicologia* 53: 185–95.

Goertz, Harald. 1986. "Die Metamorphosen der Manon." In *Der Komponist Hans Werner Henze*, edited by Dieter Rexroth, 90–99. Mainz: Schott.

Henze, Hans Werner. 1951. *Boulevard Solitude: Lyrisches Drama in sieben Bildern. Text von Grete Weil, Szenarium von Walter Jockisch*. Mainz: Schott.

Henze, Hans Werner. 1957. *Fünf neapolitanische Lieder (Canzoni 'e copp' 'o tammurro) auf anonyme Texte des 17. Jahrhunderts für mittlere Stimme und Kammerorchester*. Mainz: Schott.

Henze, Hans Werner. 1958. "Wo stehen wir heute?" *Darmstädter Beiträge zur neuen Musik* 1: 82–3.

Henze, Hans Werner. 1960. *Der Prinz von Homburg: Oper in drei Akten nach dem Schauspiel von Heinrich von Kleist: Für Musik eingerichtet von Ingeborg Bachmann*. Mainz: Schott.

Henze, Hans Werner. 1984a. "Die Gründerjahre." In *Musik und Politik: Schriften und Gespräche 1955–1984*, edited by Jens Brockmeier, 32–33. Munich: Deutscher Taschenbuch.

Henze, Hans Werner. 1984b. "Neapel." In Henze, Hans Werner. *Musik und Politik: Schriften und Gespräche 1955-1984*, edited by Jens Brockmeier, 41-48. Munich: Deutscher Taschenbuch.

Henze, Hans Werner. 1984c. "Neue Musik." In *Musik und Politik: Schriften und Gespräche 1955-1984*, edited by Jens Brockmeier, 29-30. Munich: Deutscher Taschenbuch.

Henze, Hans Werner. 1984d. "Die Schwierigkeit, ein bundesdeutscher Komponist zu sein: Neue Musik zwischen Isolierung und Engagement." In *Musik und Politik: Schriften und Gespräche 1955-1984*, edited by Jens Brockmeier, 300-31. Munich: Deutscher Taschenbuch.

Henze, Hans Werner. 1992. *Der Prinz von Homburg*. Mainz: Schott.

Henze, Hans Werner. 1999. "Musiksprache und künstlerische Erfindung." In *Musik und Mythos: Neue Aspekte der musikalischen Ästhetik*, edited by Hans Werner Henze, 116-36. Frankfurt am Main: Fisher.

Henze, Hans Werner. 2000a. *Boulevard Solitude: Lyrisches Drama in sieben Bildern: Libretto von Grete Weil, Szenarium von Walter Jockisch*. Mainz: Schott.

Henze, Hans Werner. 2000b. *Il re cervo oder Die Irrfahrten der Wahrheit: Oper in drei Akten, Libretto nach Gozzi von Heinz von Cramer*. Mainz: Schott.

Henze, Hans Werner. 2001. *Reiselieder mit böhmischen Quinten: Autobiographische Mitteilungen 1926-1995*. Frankfurt am Main: Fischer Taschenbuch.

Hindley, Clifford. 1999. "Eros in Life and Death: *Billy Budd* and *Death in Venice*." In *The Cambridge Companion to Benjamin Britten*, edited by Mervyn Cooke, 147-64. Cambridge: Cambridge University Press.

Hoverland, Lilian. 1980. "Heinrich von Kleist and Luce Irigaray: Visions of the Feminine." In *Gestaltet und gestaltend: Frauen in der deutschen Literatur*, edited by Marianne Burkhard, 57-82. Amsterdam: Rodopi.

Jungheinrich, Hans-Klaus, ed. 2002. *Im Laufe der Zeit: Kontinuität und Veränderung bei Hans Werner Henze*. Mainz: Schott.

Kerstan, Michael, and Clemens Wolken, eds. 2006. *Hans Werner Henze: Komponist der Gegenwart*. Berlin: Henschel.

Kovács, Inge. 1997. "Neue Musik abseits der Avantgarde? Zwei Fallbeispiele." In *Im Zenit der Moderne: Die Internationalen Ferienkurse für Neue Musik Darmstadt 1946-1966: Geschichte und Dokumentation*, edited by Gianmario Borio and Hermann Danuser, vol. 2, 13-61. Freiburg im Breisgau: Rombach.

Marsico, Federica. 2014a. "*Boulevard Solitude* di Hans Werner Henze: una lettura intertestuale del libretto." *Rassegna musicale Curci* 67, no. 3: 37-43.

Marsico, Federica. 2014b. "Il poeta e la sua elegia del desiderio inappagato." *La Fenice prima dell'opera* 4: 11-30.

Marsico, Federica. 2015. "Il conflitto fra sogno e realtà in *Der Prinz von Homburg* di Hans Werner Henze." In *Conflitti: arte, musica, pensiero, società*, edited by Nadia Amendola and Giacomo Sciommeri, 137-47. Roma: UniversItalia.

Marsico, Federica. 2017. "A Queer Approach to the Classical Myth of Phaedra in Music." *Kwartalnik Młodych Muzykologów UJ* 34: 7-28.

Marsico, Federica. 2018. "Introduzione a H.W. Henze: dagli esordi all'impegno politico." *Rassegna musicale Curci* 71, no. 3: 25-33.

Marsico, Federica. 2020a. *La seduzione queer di Fedra: il mito secondo Britten, Bussotti e Henze*. Roma: Aracne.

Marsico, Federica. 2020b. "Opera e queer musicology: appunti per un approccio metodologico." *Musica/Realtà* 123: 165-95.

McClatchie, Stephen. 1996. "Benjamin Britten, *Owen Wingrave*, and the Politics of the Closet: or, 'He Shall Be Straightened out at Paramore.'" *Cambridge Opera Journal* 8, no. 1: 59–75.

Noeske, Nina. 2019. "Klang(farbe) als Genderperformance: Anmerkungen zum Musiktheater nach 1945." In *Gattung. Gender. Gesang: Neue Forschungsperspektiven auf Hans Werner Henzes Werk*, edited by Antje Tumat and Michael Zywietz, 133–43. Laaber: Laaber.

Oehl, Klaus. 2003. *Die Oper* König Hirsch *(1953–55) von Hans Werner Henze.* Saarbrücken: PFAU.

Rosteck, Jens. 2009. *Hans Werner Henze: Rosen und Revolutionen.* Berlin: Propyläen.

Pfeiffer, Joachim. 1996. "Friendship and Gender: The Aesthetic Construction of Subjectivity in Kleist." In *Outing Goethe and His Age*, edited by Alice Kuzniar, 215–27. Stanford: Stanford University Press.

Puhlmann, Albrecht. 1988. "Zerrissen und Zerreissungsmächtig: Zur Aktualität der *Bassariden* von Hans Werner Henze." In *Musiktheater im 20. Jahrhundert*, edited by Constantin Floros, Hans Joachim Marx, and Peter Petersen, 205–13. Laaber: Laaber.

Tumat, Antje. 2019. "'Die Zerstörung des Begriffs vom klassischen Helden': Männerbilder in Henzes frühen Opern bis 1966." In *Gattung. Gender. Gesang: Neue Forschungsperspektiven auf Hans Werner Henzes Werk*, edited by Antje Tumat and Michael Zywietz, 117–32. Laaber: Laaber.

Wagner, Hans-Joachim. 1988. *Studie zu* Boulevard Solitude: *Lyrisches Drama in 7 Bildern von Hans Werner Henze.* Cologne: Gustav Bosse.

Weinholz, Gerhard. 1993. *Heinrich von Kleist: Deutsches Dichtergenie, kämpfender Humanist, preußisches Staatsopfer.* Essen: Die Blaue Eule.

Whitesell, Lloyd. 2003. "Britten's Dubious Trysts." *Journal of the American Musicological Society* 56, no. 3: 637–94.

Winter, Hans-Gerd. 2003. "Liebesdiskurse in den Libretti von Grete Weil und Ingeborg Bachmann." In *Hans Werner Henze: Die Vorträge des internationalen Henze-Symposions am Musikwissenschaftlichen Institut der Universität Hamburg (28. bis 30. Juni 2001)*, edited by Peter Petersen, 41–55. Frankfurt am Main: Lang.

5

Multiplicities, Truth, Ethics

A Queering Analysis of Chaya Czernowin's *Anea Crystal*

Judy Lochhead

I have been analytically engaging Chaya Czernowin's *Anea Crystal* over several years, but the writing of this essay did not get started seriously until January 2020. It is now August 2021, and from my perspective in the United States, events over the last sixteen months have rattled the status quo: March 2020 a global pandemic; May 2020 a cry for racial justice that emanated from the murder of George Floyd; November 2020 viral lying about the US election; and January 2021 an assault on bedrock principles of democracy in the United States. But in an unexpected way over this past year, the motivating issues for the essay were amplified as these events blazed into my life.

First motivation; what might it mean to maintain a commitment to an ontology of multiplicity—or what is sometimes referred to as absolute difference—in the context of knowledge production in music studies: specifically for me, the study of music as sonic event? Second motivation: how might I develop modes of analytical understanding that can address Czernowin's *Anea Crystal* while maintaining a commitment to ontological multiplicity? Third motivation: how are perspectives from queer theory intertwined with issues of truth and ethics demanded by ontological multiplicity? These three motivations led me to writings by four authors in the late 1980s who were themselves grappling with an ontology of multiplicity and the attendant questions of truth and ethics that follow from it. These are Donna Haraway and Sandra Harding, both in feminist science studies, and Judith Butler and Alain Badiou in philosophy.[1]

---

[1] The convergence of thought in different disciplines around what I am here calling "situational multiplicities" in the late 1980s proved illuminating for me. What seems very clear and precise in the thought of these authors at that time is how to maintain a commitment both to ontological indeterminacy and to truth and ethics.

My plans for this essay are (1) delineate the outlines of the ontological stance and epistemological strategy that guide my analysis of Czernowin's *Anea Crystal*, including discussion of how it may be understood as a "queering analysis," (2) present the analysis, and (3) conclude with some reflections on truthful and ethical practices in relation to a queering analysis.[2]

Ontological Multiplicities

The seeds for my queering analysis were planted in the late 1980s and early 1990s by authors from assorted disciplines who developed positive theories of situated knowledge and absolute difference as part of their quest for a truthful and ethical accounting of the world. The tendrils of these disciplinary inquiries spread out in several dimensions, including to queer theory, feminist theory, and antiracist theory, to name a few. The "situated-ness" of knowledge was named famously by Donna Haraway in her 1988 "Situated Knowledges: The Science Question in Feminism and the Privilege of Partial Perspective." In addressing naïve claims to absolute objectivity in mid-twentieth-century scientific discourse, Haraway articulated the dilemma for a "feminist objectivity": how to account for the "real" world, which presents itself as a certainty, while at the same time arguing that knowledge itself is "radically" and "historical[ly] contingent" (Haraway 1988, 581, 579). For Haraway, objectivity is achieved as part of a practice of "contestation, deconstruction, passionate construction," or in other words, as part of a process in which one recognizes the "partial perspective" and the "situatedness" of any knowledge claim (Haraway 1988, 583, 585).

Judith Butler, in an article that preceded her well-known *Gender Trouble*, challenges naturalistic and objectivist claims to "binary genders" and shows that these claims serve to enforce a "system of compulsory heterosexuality" (Butler 1988, 524). In this 1988 article, "Performative Acts and Gender Constitution: An Essay in Phenomenology and Feminist Theory," Butler poses gender not as an "expression" of some pre-linguistic biological imperative of sexual difference but rather as a "corporeal field of play" that is both

---

[2] I was lucky to have the opportunity to present the most recent version of this essay to the music studies community at McGill University via video. I thank them for their generous and probing questions. I was also lucky to have Chaya Czernowin among those attending that lecture and to have subsequent discussions with her about *Anea Crystal* and her music in general. Later in this essay I weave in some of her own thoughts about *Anea Crystal*.

"innovative" and "constrained" by social structures. Writing in the context of 1980s feminist thought, Butler turns toward a destabilization of gender concepts, drawing attention to non-normative existential realities in which the lived experience of sex and gender is not "rendered discrete" (Butler 1988, 528). This turn toward non-normative concepts of sex, gender, and sexuality became central to the move to queer theory as both politically charged and more generally disruptive.

An implicit and yet important part of the projects of authors like Haraway and Butler is an ethical commitment to equity, inclusion, and truth. Naïve claims to objectivity—no matter whether in scientific discourse or in the appeals to nature in discussions of sex and gender—are often accompanied by injustice, exclusion, and distortions of reality. Haraway's emphasis on perspectival knowledge and Butler's focus on the "corporeal play" of sex and gender are in fundamental ways ethical stances that aim at the existential truths of a differential world.

Alain Badiou, another author writing in the late 1980s, also looks to difference as a necessary component of an ethical commitment to truth. In *Being and Event* (1988), Badiou articulates an ontology in which being is defined as a "pure multiplicity," or what others have called absolute difference (Hallward 2004, 3). Reality for Badiou is fundamentally multiple, but from this multiplicity specific "situations" exist, and their coherence or structure arises through a process called "count-for-one" (Feltham and Clemens 2004, 11). Truth arises from the structures of particular situations, from their coherence as a count-for-one. A truth then can be understood as universal within a situation, but it is also contingent since the logic of a situation may transform in a new situation. Radical change occurs when an "event" results in a new situation with new logics and new truths. For Badiou, the universality and contingency of truth and of its link to particular situations requires an "ethic of truth" that "is fully subordinate to the particularity of *a* truth" (Hallward 2001, xiv). Ethics is an active project guided by the truth of a situation to assure that it, the truth, operates for all.

Sandra Harding, in her 1986 *The Science Question in Feminism*, similarly maintains that the reality of the world is multiple: the world consists of "many interrelated and smoothly connected realities" (Harding 1986, 194). She argues, like Haraway and Badiou, that knowledge of the world is always partial, and she goes further to maintain that certain modes of knowledge have gained an epistemic privilege through the mechanisms of institutional power. Harding demonstrates that any claim to "objective" knowledge must entail a critical examination of the epistemic frameworks in which that knowledge is produced. The knowledge of the world produced through such a critical examination has a "strong objectivity" since it requires that "the subject of knowledge and the process through which knowledge is produced are . . . scrutinized according to the same standards as the objects of knowledge" (Harding 1992, 458). Or in other words, Harding argues for an ethics of truth about the world that is fully invested in its ontological multiplicity.

These four authors—Haraway, Butler, Badiou, and Harding—were part of broad, interdisciplinary movements that, by establishing new ontologies and epistemologies, brought into focus matters of inclusion, equity, justice, truth, and the possibilities for change.[3] These new ontologies and epistemologies played foundational roles in establishing a theoretical base for a variety of social justice movements around matters of race, ethnicity, gender, and sexuality. I bring the ideas of these four authors from this specific moment of the late 1980s to bear on a what I call here a "queering" approach to music analysis for several reasons. Their insistence on an ontology of multiplicity intersects with queer theory's approach to sexual and gendered subjects as "fluid, blurred and contingent."[4] (Browne and Nash 2010, 11) And their insistence on an ethics of truth intersects with queer method and methodology. Always entangled with questions of identity or identifications, queerness is also conceptualized as "a methodology . . . that gives us a way to articulate a queer ethics and queer politics"—a methodology premised on a "fundamental openness to difference, located in the world and in ourselves" (Salamon 2009, 230). My project here takes up this latter strand of queer theory—that of a methodological commitment to multiplicity specifically in the domain of music analysis. And in taking up this strand, I would be remiss not to recognize the work already done by a wide range of authors who have opened up new and inspiring pathways into queer music studies over the last thirty years.[5] My project here takes up the specific question of methodology but is dependent on this prior scholarship that embraces all dimensions of

---

[3] I have chosen to focus on Haraway, Butler, Badiou, and Harding partly because of the temporal convergence of their work, but also because they articulate the ideas of truth and ethics from multiple perspectives. Another relevant author, suggested to me by Lloyd Whitesell, is Barbara Hernnstein Smith, who in her *Contingencies of Value: Alternative Perspective for Critical Theory*, offers a similar perspective from the humanities. See Hernnstein Smith 1988.

[4] As is well known, Butler's work on the performativity of gender has been a central component of queer theory.

[5] See in particular: Brett/Wood/Thomas 1994, Maus 1993, Cusick 1994, Hubbs 2004, and Fuller/Whitesell 2002, to name just a few. And see *The Oxford Handbook of Music and Queerness*, ed. Maus, Whiteley, Nyong'o, and Sherinian (2022).

queer theory. Here I hope to sketch out and model an approach to music analysis that weaves into its fabric an ontology of multiplicity and an ethics of truth, an analysis fundamentally open to musical differing.

Next, I return to the central ideas from the four authors—Haraway, Butler, Badiou, Harding—to suggest how they might prove useful for developing queering perspectives for music analysis. It is not my intention here to develop some grand methodology or overarching theory, but rather to provide some tools for interested people to engage and interpret musical works in terms of their multiplicities—or in other words to encourage others to develop queering perspectives on music that are true and ethical.

All four of the authors sampled above take as a starting point what Badiou calls the "ontological multiplicity" of being—that the realities of the world are intrinsically differential. This starting point has profound effects on concepts of unity or any forms of oneness that have dominated modern thought. For instance, as Butler points out, the fundamental realities of human embodied experience are not given as simple binaries of woman/man. Rather, there are myriad material and social strands of a lived-world—or what Badiou would call a situation—with which individuals weave together unique modes of existing as gendered or not.[6] That individuals of the early twenty-first century live in societies in which gendering may occur as a binary, as a spectrum, or as non-existent is itself indicative of a lived-world with multiple lived realities. For some, gender occurs as a binary state in the natural world; for others, gender is multiple and malleable; and for others embodiment is not categorically aligned. The situated-ness of knowledge in Haraway's sense comes at the issues of multiplicity from a somewhat different angle, turning toward epistemology. Deriving from the partial perspective taken up by any particular individual or group of individuals, knowledge of the world is "contingent," subject to change and contestation. Recognition of the partiality of perspective is thus a necessary component of knowledge with a viable claim to truth.

In some ways, the idea of approaching music as a multiplicity is banal. Musical works with scores are always multiple in their sounding, every performance different. Improvised music—spontaneous composition—has

---

[6] I have chosen here to use the term "a lived-world" rather than Badiou's term "situation." I do this for two reasons. First, while it is likely not coincidental that Badiou and Haraway use the same term, situation means something slightly different in each case. And second, the term "a lived-world" gives the idea a bit more grounding in a specific historical and social context. It is worth noting that in Badiou's original French text, the term is "situation"—both the English and the French words deriving from the Middle French *situation*.

as a motivating premise differing. And listenings, even to fixed, recorded performances, differ from one instance to the next. While recognizing music's intrinsic multiplicity, I maintain here that explicitly weaving music's multiplicities into our modes of access is crucial to the ethics and truth of analytical accounts of music. Sounds occurring as music have not only an ontological multiplicity but also multiplicities within the lived-world. Affording multiple dimensions of access and innovation, music's sounding comprises a plethora of receptive and creative facets that intertwine in modes of making, listening, and reflecting. Specific named practitioners— composers, improvisers, performers, listeners, scholars, critics—all engage music generatively through these multiple dimensions of access and invention. Composers, improvisers, creators, and performers generate new musical phenomena in proliferating cascades of innovation. Listeners, those engaged bodily with sounding events, generate feelings, affects, actions, stories, and the like to take account of bodily experiences. And scholars, those reflecting on music as worldly phenomena, generate analyses, theories, histories, critiques, interpretations, and the like. For all practitioners, the reflective and creative facets intertwine in a generative process that constitutes music's multiplicities.

Music's multiplicity is well known and much discussed, especially in music-philosophical circles.[7] This multiplicity has challenged modernity's overriding quest for one-ness, resulting in claims for music's sublimity as it "overcomes" reason and for its ineffability.[8] However, music's multiplicity, considered from the vantage of differential thought over the last half century, offers new pathways toward the queering perspectives of music analysis, which are my focus here and which I exemplify with an analysis of Czernowin's *Anea Crystal*. But before embarking on that analysis, consideration of how truth and ethics are refigured in differential thought provides a basis for the claim that analysis premised in music's multiplicities contributes further to its multiplicity through its queering perspectives.

All four of the authors I have sampled turn their attention to the epistemological issues of knowledge and truth raised by ontological multiplicity. While recognizing that in a differential world all knowledge is necessarily

---

[7] Philosophies of music have addressed issues of multiplicity in terms of the relation between score and performance and how this relation affects the status of a "musical work." Andrew Kania gives a good overview of the issues in the *Stanford Encyclopedia of Philosophy* entry "The Philosophy of Music" (Kania 2017).

[8] See some recent discussions music's ineffability: Jankelevitch 2003; Abbate 2004; Lochhead 2008.

contingent and partial, they maintain that the truthfulness of knowledge claims may only be attained through active investigation of the epistemic frameworks in which knowledge is produced. Only then can a "strong objectivity" (Harding) or a passionately argued objectivity (Haraway) be attained. Such a methodological focus on the epistemic frameworks of knowledge entails an ethical commitment to an "ethic of truth" (Badiou) that is equitable and inclusive.

My sampled authors do not, however, address epistemological issues surrounding aesthetic phenomena, and admittedly knowledge claims about music and other artistic forms have discursive functions that differ in some ways from non-artistic disciplines. But if we take the production of knowledge in non-aesthetic realms as a means of grasping the ontological multiplicity of the lived-world, this discursive function applies equally well to discourses about music. And so, discursive accounts of music—including analysis and theory—are not immune to questions of truth and ethics. Indeed, given their historical claims to "objectivity," music analysis and theory have been ripe for scrutiny of the epistemic privilege afforded certain practices and the inequities and exclusions that follow—a scrutiny that flourishes in the present.[9]

Situating the Analysis

In this section of the paper, I situate myself, my analytical goals for my project, and Czernowin's *Anea Crystal*. For most music analytical studies, the situated-ness of the analyst and the music studied is largely implicit. It would be naïve to think that I or any other music scholar could comprehensively uncover those contextualizing circumstances that shape one's perspectives, but some attempt to make explicit one's positionality and scholarly goals will *hopefully* provide some inkling of transparency that allows you the reader to orient yourself to my situation.

My scholarly work has been guided by my academic music training in European-American art music, first as a musician, then as a

---

[9] Critique of music analysis and theory with respect to issues of diversity, equity, and inclusion was intensified recently at the Plenary session of the 2019 annual meeting of the Society for Music Theory. Speakers at that meeting included Philip Ewell, Ellie Hisama, Yayoi Uno Everett, and Joseph Straus. Information about the Plenary Session can be found here. Philip Ewell has published widely on the issue of "Music Theory's White Racial Frame." See in particular: Ewell 2020. Also, see Ewell's website for further information.

musician-turned-scholar. My interests in music of the present grew out of my quest for repertoire as a clarinetist, and my focus on the music of contemporary composers who are female grows out of my commitments at first to feminist politics and now to equity and inclusion movements more generally. And I acknowledge my positionality and privilege as a white, cisgender female who was empowered by the heady activities—musical and political—of the 1960s and 1970s.

As a music analyst my goals are to promote new modes of addressing music of the present because many of the long-established tools of music theory have proven inadequate to many types of music-making nowadays. These new modes or tools are intended to produce queering perspectives and to allow for a multiplicity of interpretive engagements, in keeping with the premise of music's ontological multiplicity. Music analysis, and any attendant music theories, should not limit interpretive possibilities but should allow them to flourish.[10]

With my analysis I offer *an* interpretation of Czernowin's *Anea Crystal* that aims at an ethical and truthful account of the music's material sounding in the present. The analysis not only acknowledges its partial perspective but also, through the analytical process, seeks to take up queering perspectives that help to shape an inclusive interpretation that serves as an invitation to "contestation, deconstruction, passionate construction" (Haraway).

Over the past several years, Czernowin's music has intrigued, me and it has also proved analytically elusive. Czernowin is a major composer, widely recognized in North America and Europe, and I have found the particular ways that she expands the boundaries of musical expression personally exhilarating. *Anea Crystal* lends itself well to scholarly, written analysis: it is a string quartet of moderate length with a detailed score and a professionally recorded performance. And further, the concept for *Anea Crystal* is itself a fascinating exemplar of musical multiplicity from various perspectives.

Anea Crystal was composed in 2008 and premiered by Quatuor Diotima and the Minguet Quartett that same year. Part of a larger series "Shifting Gravity," *Anea Crystal* is itself a cycle consisting of three pieces. The score includes two self-standing pieces, *Seed I* and *Seed II*, and also the instruction

---

[10] There is a sense in which the development of new music theories and the subsequent production of music analyses have always been motivated by a search for new ways of hearing and engaging music. A long historical view of music analytical/theoretical practices certainly supports this sense. Analyses prompted by queering perspectives begin with the premise of this ontological multiplicity and are guided by an ethics of truth as a multiplicity.

to play the two quartets simultaneously to realize *Anea Crystal*. Example 5.1 shows the first two pages of the score. The performance instructions indicate that *Seed I* or *Seed II* can be performed separately and that the two may be combined as *Anea Crystal*, either with two live quartets or with *Seed II* recorded and projected with loudspeakers, while *Seed I* is played live. The score indicates that *Seed I* is 6:00, *Seed II* is 7:30, and together as *Anea Crystal* they

Example 5.1 Chaya Czernowin, *Anea Crystal*, First two pages of the score, mm. 1–16 *Seed I*, mm. 1–4 *Seed II*

are 8:30, the extra length a result of some additional passages in *Seed I* played only during *Anea Crystal*. The recorded performance has different durations, however: *Seed I*—6:50; *Seed II*—8:10, and *Anea Crystal*—9:10.

In a score note, Czernowin writes about the meaning of the titles and her generative idea for the cycle.[11] The music is motivated by the forces of attraction in the physical world and especially those forces producing crystalline structures. Czernowin invented the term "anea" to refer to a "music crystal," that is, the musical work resulting from the combination of *Seed I* and *Seed II*. Czernowin relates the emergence of this music crystal to that of an ionic crystal that forms from the attractive forces between differently charged ions.[12] The two *Seeds* serve as the catalyst for the formation of the musical crystal, much the way seed crystals function in the physical world by generating larger crystals. Czernowin's music in the *Anea Crystal* cycle, and in the larger series "Shifting Gravity," is motivated by forces of the physical world. Specifically, Czernowin relates that each piece focuses in a "concise and concentrated" way on a "singular physical gesture" that "reveals the strange physical laws of the world . . . " (Czernowin 2008). Through such a concise and concentrated exploration of a single gesture, the music engenders a sonic multiplicity of the gesture in a spiraling flow of novelty.

The sonic exploration of a gesture during each of the two *Seeds* is itself an instance of multiplicity as each of the two gestures transforms temporally. Another sort of multiplicity arises from the combination of the two *Seeds* since the two quartets are not meant to be highly coordinated temporally. As Czernowin notes in the score, there are "points of orientation" as formal articulations and occasionally coordination at the beat-level, but there are also other passages during which the music of the quartets is independent and the interactions not notationally specified (Czernowin 2008). The combination of the two Seeds generates new "musical crystals" from performance to performance, creating a multiplicity on a longer time scale.[13]

Analyzing *Seed I* and *Seed II*

My analysis focuses on the two *Seeds* primarily because this allows a closer investigation of what Czernowin has called the "singular gesture" of each piece

---

[11] After the analysis of *Seed I* and *Seed II*, I return to a discussion of *Anea Crystal* and weave in Czernowin's reflections on experiential memory in relation to the combination of the *Seeds*.

[12] A familiar instance of an ionic crystal is rock salt.

[13] It is worth pointing out that each distinct performance of a "work" also generates a multiplicity. The combination of the two *Seeds* in this instance injects another, distinct sort of multiplicity which I address after the analysis of the two *Seeds*.

and the nature of its exploration over the course of the music. My analysis does not identify "a gesture" and then show how it is explored, but rather proceeds from a gestural profile that undergoes a constant change in a process of emergence during *Seed I* and a process of juxtaposition and difference in *Seed II*.

The analysis relies on both the published recording by the Quatuor Diotima and the published score.[14] Since the music involves an expansive timbral palette requiring the players to employ advanced string techniques, I used the score and sound recording together, checking one against the other to take account of the music. *Seed I* and *Seed II* are alike in that both are organized around gestural profiles that are characterized by their timbral and rhythmic profiles. They differ in that each has a unique strategic design. In what follows I consider each *Seed* separately and then conclude with some ideas about their combination in *Anea Crystal*. My analysis is not a sketch of or a reflection on the multiplicities of performance, a restriction partly born of the fact that only one professionally recorded performance was available to me during my analytical work. Traces of the multiplicities of listening, however, are woven into the analysis since I listened to and reflected on the music over more than a year.[15] The following analyses are detailed material accounts of what happens and my interpretation of these occurrences. It is my argument here, that only by attending to the details of music's sounding can we—myself included—get at its truth in an ethical way.

Seed I

Figure 5.1 is an analytical mapping of *Seed I*.[16] This mapping is my visual, analytical interpretation of the music's sounding events and strategies. Such mapping is like transcribing, but instead of using traditional notation, events are represented with graphical icons whose shapes and colors depict sounding events. This mapping relies on access to a score and a recording, but it is important to note that the depiction of events is not temporally specific as is the case with traditional notation. It is useful to think of such an analytical mapping not as an architectural blueprint but more as a design concept.

[14] Quatour Diotima, Wergo. 6726-2. Recorded January 2009, Studio Gaertnerstrasse, Berlin. Sound engineer, Thomas Mannerjahm, and Sound technician, Susanne Beyer. I have not had opportunity to hear the work live. Score Schott ED 20538; the recorded Quatour Diotima performance is also available at YouTube: *Seed I* and *Seed II*.

[15] It is worth emphasizing here that the analysis is not meant to capture a single listening or analytical engagement. It might be helpful to think of the analysis as depicting the extended process of developing an "analytical-listening."

[16] I have used such analytical mappings in other contexts, such as in 2016a and 2016b. I discuss mapping as a method of analysis in more detail in these two publications.

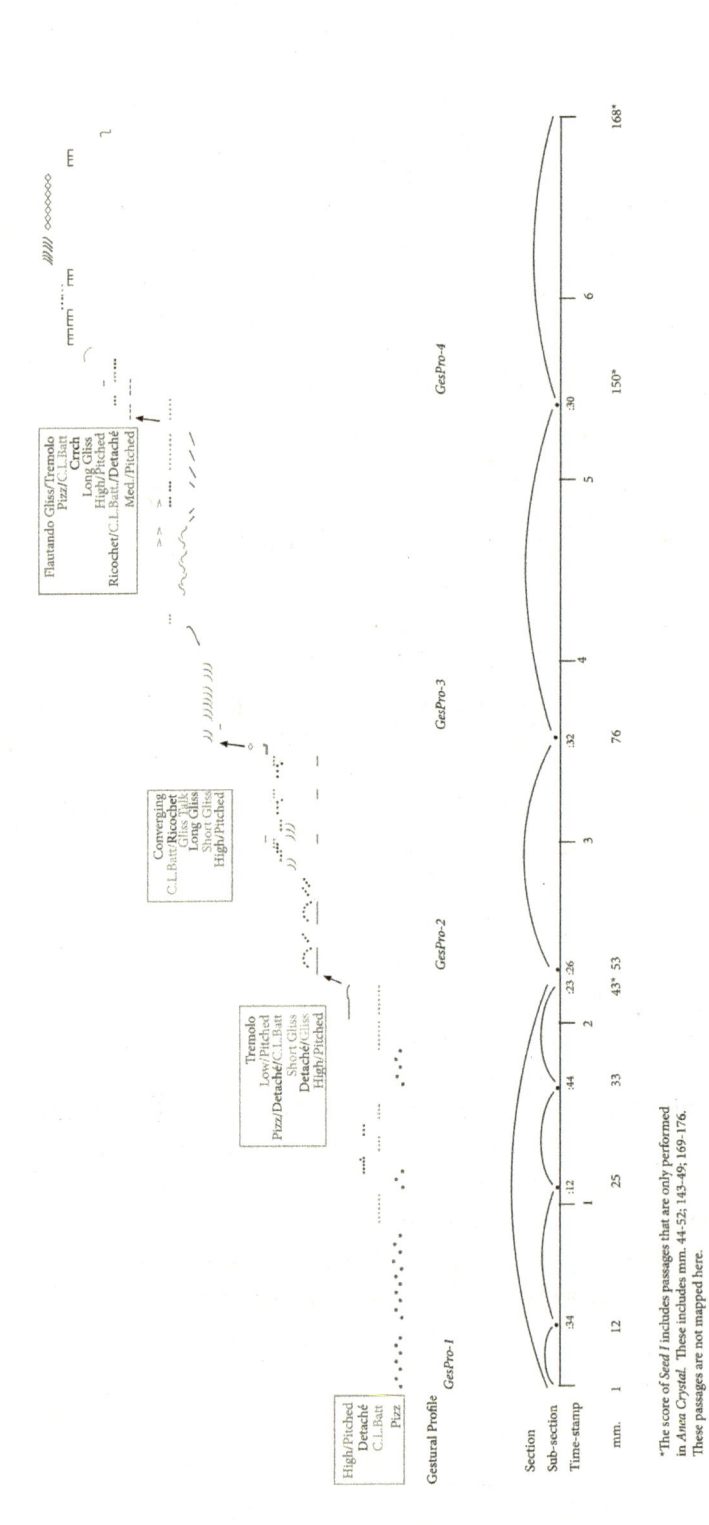

Figure 5.1 Analytical Mapping of Chaya Czernowin, *Seed I*
Based on a performance by Quatuor Diotima

Figure 5.1 depicts the temporal succession of events for *Seed I* along the x axis. The bottom layer of the mapping shows the formal outline with arcs indicating sections and sub-sections, time stamps derived from the Quatour Diotima recording, and measure numbers from the score. Each of the sections presents a Gestural Profile (*GesPro*), which I have labelled according to the chronology. Each *GesPro* consists of several timbral events. For instance, *GesPro-1* consists of four: a *Pizzicato* event, a repeated-note succession that meanders microtonally; a *col legno Battuto* event, played in the violin's 5 register; a *Detaché* repeated-note event; and a *High/Pitched* event, which is the first for which pitch is a prominent feature (the / indicating it is High and Pitched). The successive *GesPros* re-present one or more of a previously occurring timbral event, often by varying it in some way or by combining and recontextualizing it with some other timbral event. A *GesPro* may also present a new timbral event, but these are contextualized by another reoccurring timbral type. Shortly, I consider the nature of this sequence of transformed and new events while considering the overall strategy of *Seed I*.

The timbral events depicted in Figure 5.1 are referenced with a descriptive term, a color, and an icon. For the most part, the descriptive terms indicate the mode of sound production on a string instrument, that mode having become associated with a timbral quality. Some timbral events are *High*, *Medium*, or *Low/Pitched* and are notable for the strong presence of pitch as a qualitative feature.[17] A couple of the descriptive terms are not self-explanatory. These are: *Gliss Talk* (in *GesPro-3*), which entails short glisses that resemble human speech; *Converging*, which entails a rhythmic unison during which the instruments either move up or down together, or they move in contrary motion; and *Crrch*, which is an onomatopoeia—indicating a "crunchy" sound produced by applying more bow pressure on the string. The colors used in Figure 5.1 to depict timbral events are not meant to be mimetic of timbral quality but rather are used to visually draw attention to recurrence. The icons are, however, meant to be visually mimetic in some way. So, for instance, dots indicate short, sharp-attack sounds and lines more sustained sounds. In the end, however, the icons are mostly conventional and specific to this analysis.

Seed I has an overall strategy of emergence, whose sense arises from the gradual transformation, recontextualizaton, and introduction of new

---

[17] All of the timbral events have some element of pitch, but the ones including "pitched" in the name involve pitch as a central qualitative feature.

timbral events.[18] This process of emergence is punctuated at three primary moments, each setting into motion a new phase of an ongoing emergence. Each of these phases—more conventionally labelled as sections—spins out a refreshed sequence of transformations and recontextualizations. As pointed out earlier, Section 1 consists of *GesPro-1* and entails four types of timbral event: *Pizzicato, col legno Battuto, Detaché,* and *High/Pitched,* which is paired with *col legno Battuto.*

Section 2 begins, after an articulating silence, with a *High/Pitched* event, bridging to the preceding *High/Pitched* event at the end of Section 1. It continues with a version of *Detaché*—named here *Detaché/Gliss* since it slithers down and up. As Figure 5.1 shows, a sequence of transformed and recontextualized events occur during Section 2, while the *High/Pitched* event recurs over the course of this entire section, and two new timbral events are introduced in Section 2, *Short Gliss* and *Tremolo.* Section 2, like the preceding one, concludes with the introduction of a new timbral event, *Tremolo,* which creates a kind of bridge to the next section—as indicated by the arrow on Figure 5.1.

With this introduction to the analytical mapping of Figure 5.1, the reader is invited to observe on the figure the transformations and recontextualizatons of timbral events during Sections 3 and 4, following the sequence of events visually and aurally if possible. Of particular note are the several recontextualizations of timbral types into such combinations as *col legno Battuto/Ricochet* in *GesPro-3* and *Ricochet/col legno Battuto/Detaché* in *GesPro-4,* and the introduction of new timbral events such as *Converging* in *GesPro-3* and *Crrch,* and *Flautando/Tremolo* in *GesPro-4.* I turn now to consider some additional aspects of the strategic design of emergence during *Seed I.*

As Figure 5.1 shows the first section of *Seed 1* has four sub-sections. The particular way that timbral events occur during Section 1, including the sub-sectional articulations, is instrumental to projecting the sense emergence that characterizes the entirely of *Seed I.* Figure 5.2 provides a more detailed graphic depicting the design of Section 1. This "zoomed-in" figure is

---

[18] I use the term emergence here for processes during which constellations of timbral events form and change over time. This is a process of continual becoming and differs from processes of motivic development in which a motive is defined by particular features that get extended and changed. While not directly relevant to my analysis of *Seeds I* and *II,* it is worth pointing out that crystal formation is an instance of emergence, most specifically of a first-order phase transition. Scholarship on the concept of emergence in both scientific and philosophical circles has become robust over the last seventy years, largely because of developments in science and their ripples in philosophical thought. I use the term here to capture the sense is diachronic novelty through the combination/recombination of timbral events. Two good overviews of recent thinking about emergence (or emergent properties) see O'Connor 2020 and Humphreys 2016.

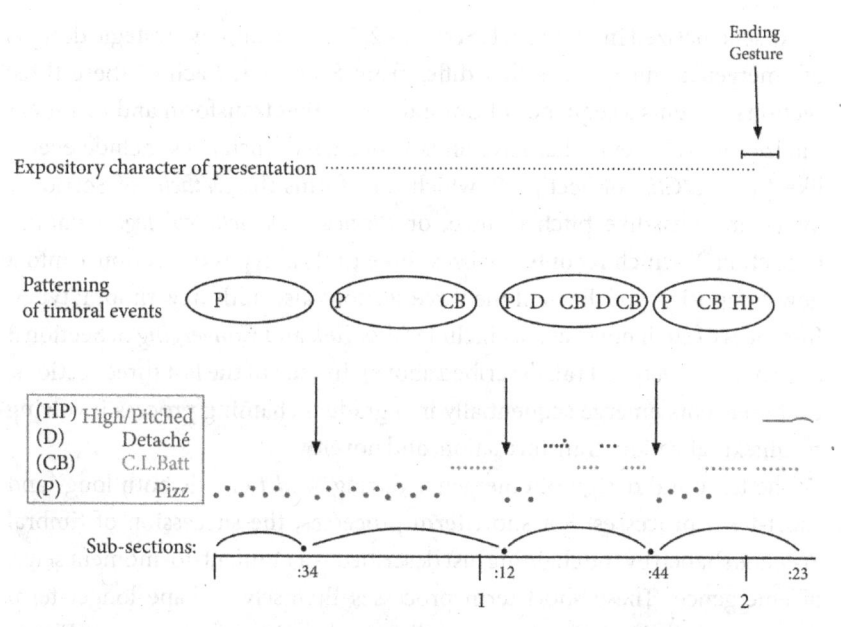

Figure 5.2 Analytical Mapping of Chaya Czernowin, *Seed I*, Section 1
Based on a performance by Quatuor Diotima

organized much like Figure 5.1, showing time on the x axis and the timbral types of *GesPro-1*. The music begins with a relatively slow and deliberate introduction of events, with a predominance of the micro-tonally meandering *Pizzicato*. On Figure 5.2, the downward arrows (at 0:34, 1:12, 1:44) indicate that the recurrence of the *Pizzicato* event is tied to the articulation of the sub-sections. And, as schematized in the Patterning row of Figure 5.2, the sequence and recurrences of timbral events help to shape and articulate the sub-sections. Timbral types are schematized with letters, and the grouping circles illustrate the sequential strategy. For instance, sub-section 1 has a single timbral type; sub-section 2 introduces a new type at its end (*col legno Battuto*); and sub-section 3, after the initial *Pizzicato* event, introduces another new timbral type, *Detaché*, which alternates with *col legno Battuto*. The final sub-section entails the recurrence of the *Pizzicato* and *col legno Battuto* types followed by a new timbral event—*High/Pitched*—which serves as an ending gesture and provides a bridge to the next section. The top row of Figure 5.2 also indicates that the strategic presentation of timbral events and their articulation into sub-sections give Section 1 an expository character. Further, this is an exposition of emergence: a relatively slow introduction of timbral events that invites aural exploration.

As schematized in Figure 5.1, Sections 2, 3, and 4 employ strategic designs of emergence but in ways that differ from Section 1. Each of these three sections presents a sequence of timbral events that transform and recontextualize timbral events that have already occurred. Instances include events like *Detaché/Gliss* of Section 2, which transforms the *Detaché* of Section 1 by adding gliss-like pitch change, or *Pizzicato/Detaché/col legno Batutto* of Section 2, which recontextualizes three timbral types of Section 1 into a new composite type. Each of the three sections also adds new timbral types. Instances of such novel events include *Gliss Talk* and *Converging* of Section 3 and *Crrch* of Section 4 (all described above). In each of the last three sections, timbral events emerge sequentially in a gradual chaining process involving recontextualization, transformation, and novelty.

The temporal design of emergence during *Seed I* entails both long- and short-term processes. For short-term processes, the succession of timbral events is shaped by the chaining just described—a moment-to-moment sense of emergence. These short-term processes themselves shape longer-term processes that characterize an overall formal design of emergence. Figure 5.3 shows a spectral and amplitude display of *Seed 1*. The display has been annotated at the bottom and top with the timeline and also at the bottom with the formal outlines from Figure 5.1, and below the timeline is another row showing the duration of the four sections. From the display of Figure 5.3, some additional features of musical design may be observed. Section 1 is the longest, as befitting its expository function, and the second longest is Section 3. Both Section 1 and 3 are relatively quiet, as a quick glance at the amplitude display confirms. The loudest and most spectrally dense events come during Section 4. As sketched in the mapping of Figure 5.1, those loud moments are the *Crrch* events that occur toward the end of *Seed I*, and on Figure 5.3 the three occurrences have been labelled in the upper right-hand corner. The occurrence of the three *Crrch* timbral events play a role in shaping the conclusion of *Seed I*. Not only are they the loudest and most spectrally dense events of the piece, but they also break the continuity of emergence that has been characteristic of short-term succession: that is, they serve as disruptions of the emergence process. The music following the first and second *Crrch* events renews the sense of emergence, reprising timbral types associated with it. The final *Crrch* event ends abruptly, however, followed by whimpering *High/Pitched* event. This ending gesture generates a pathos that arises not simply from the disruptions of emergence that the *Crrch* events enact but also from the *High/Pitched* events' withdrawal from sounding.

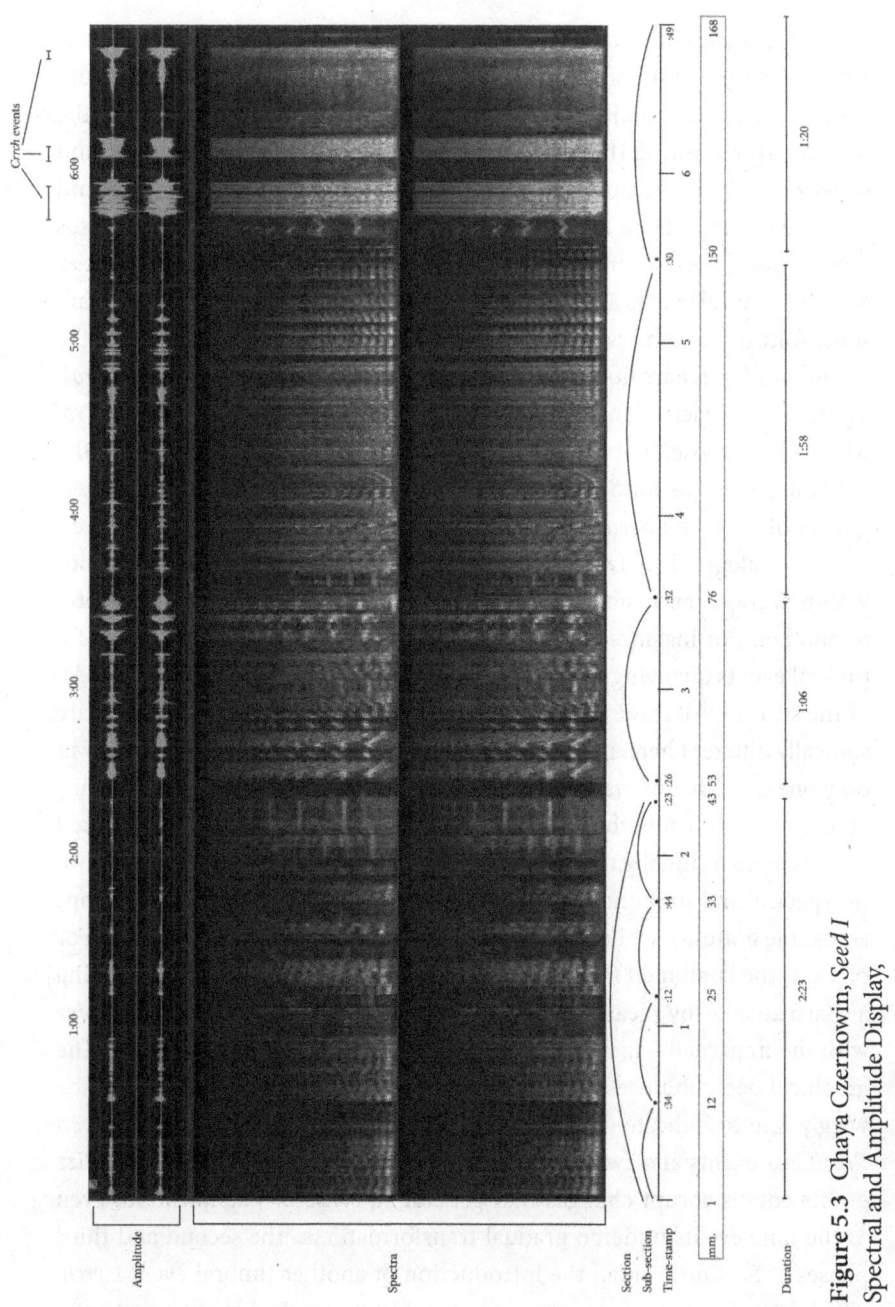

Figure 5.3 Chaya Czernowin, *Seed I* Spectral and Amplitude Display, Showing Formal Outlines

Seed II

Figure 5.4 is an analytical mapping of *Seed II*, and like Figure 5.1, it is an analytical interpretation of the music's sounding events and strategies. Figure 5.4 depicts the temporal succession of events for *Seed II* along the x axis, the bottom layer showing the formal outline with arcs indicating sections and sub-sections, time stamps derived from the Quatour Diotima recording, and measure numbers from the score. As Figure 5.4 indicates, *Seed II* comprises four sections, the last three having sub-sections. As Figure 5.4 also indicates, *Seed II*'s timbral events are not identical to those of *Seed I*, but they do share some features, which I will address shortly. Unlike the sections of *Seed I*, the sections of *Seed II* are not characterized by a single *Gestural Profile (GesPro)*. Section 1 and each of the following sub-sections presents a unique *GesPro*, which I have chosen not to label on the figure for simplicity's sake. Unlike the sequence of events for *Seed I*, which is characterized by emergence, the sequence of events for *Seed II* is characterized by juxtaposition and difference.

This strategy of juxtaposition and difference for *Seed II* operates both within sections and sub-sections and in the succession from one section to another. For instance, the succession in Section 1 involves a series of a timbral events involving *Pizz and Gliss*, with *Crrch* added toward the middle of the section. All three of these timbral types occur in *Seed I*, but they are sonically different here. I have chosen to suggest this difference graphically in only one case, that of *Pizz*. The timbral type of *Seed II* entails a single, sharp plucked sound, while the *Pizzicato* type of *Seed I* entails repeated plucked sounds in microtonally meandering gesture. Figure 5.5 shows a "close-up" of the spectral and amplitude display of Section 1 (mm. 2–33, with time-stamps across the bottom), while also showing that the section has three phases. For phase 1, the combined *Pizz* and *Gliss* (*Pizz/Gliss*) creates an event involving a sharp attack—by means of either a Bartok *pizz*, two-finger *pizz*, or a *pizz* with the fingernail—that is preceded or followed by a glissing gesture. The graphical depiction uses an arrowhead to indicate the sharp attack and the wiggly line to indicate glissing gestures, and it shows that there are seven *Pizz/Gliss* events and two *Pizz* events. The sequence of *Pizz/Gliss* and *Pizz* events entails abrupt changes that generate a sense of juxtaposition, even as the nine events undergo gradual transformations. The second and third phases of Section 1 entail the introduction of another timbral event *Crrch*, which like *Pizz* involves a noisy and temporally marked profile, and as in *Seed I*, *Crrch* is created by increased bow pressure on the strings. For phase

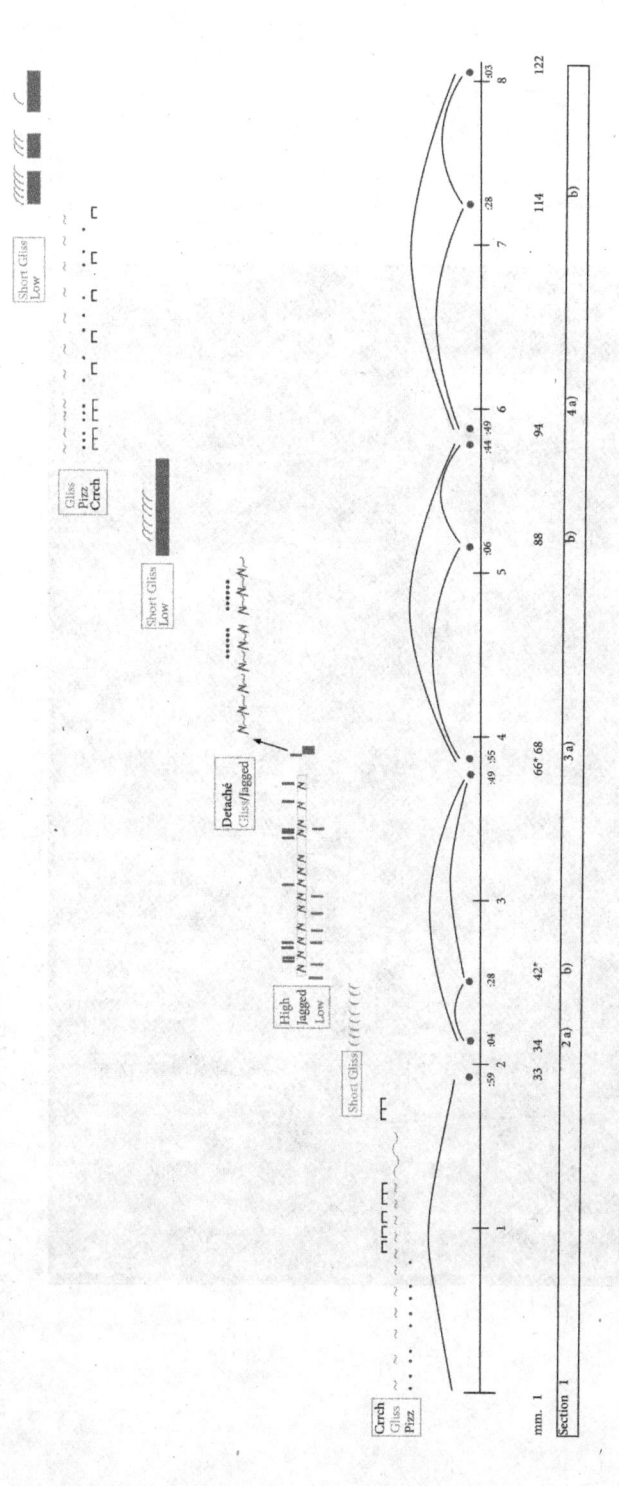

*The score of *Seed II* includes a passage that is only performed in *Area Crystal*. This is mm. 40–41. Measure 67 is a measure of rest.

Figure 5.4 Analytical Mapping of Chaya Czernowin, *Seed II* Based on a performance by Quatuor Diotima

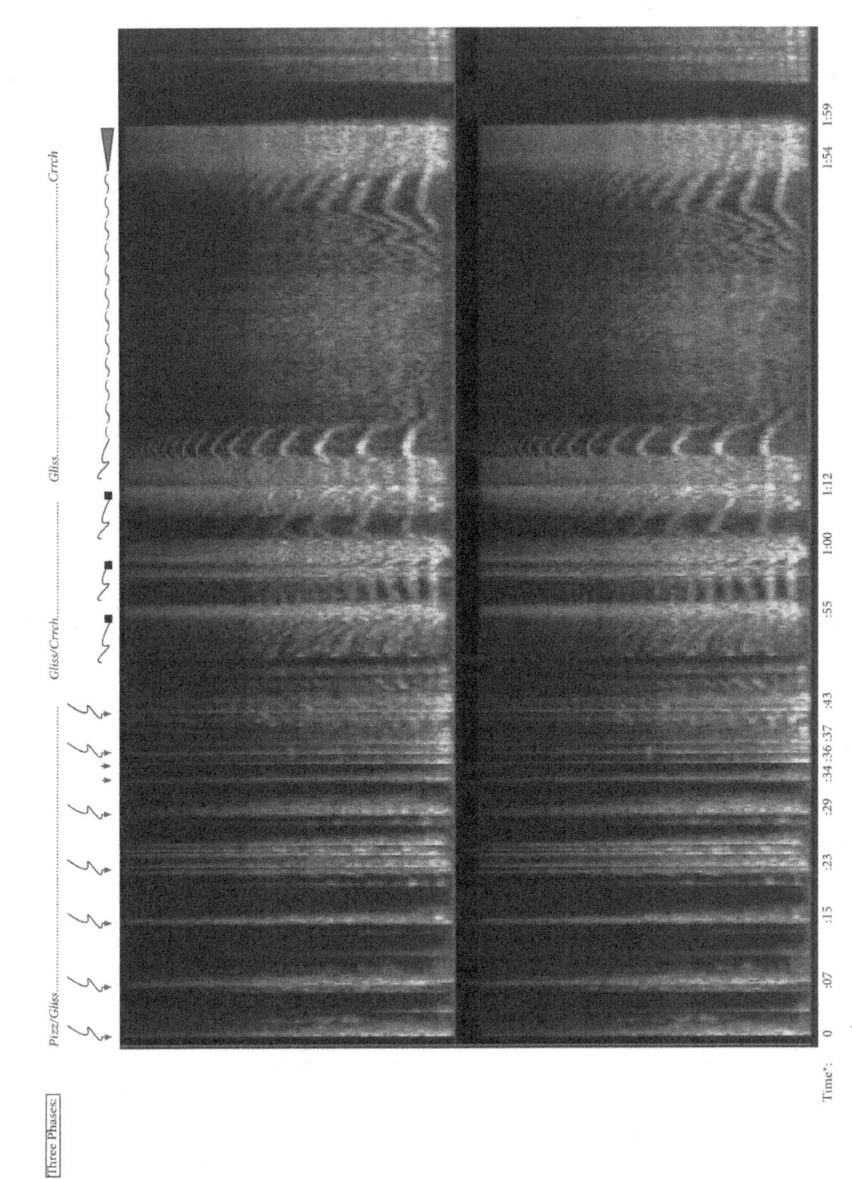

Figure 5.5 Chaya Czernowin, *Seed II*, minutes 0:00–1:59
Timbral Events of Section 1
Spectral display, Performance by Quatuor Diotima

*Times are not exact

2, a square graphically depicts the *Crrch* events and a horizontal wiggly line the *Gliss* events. While the swooping of the *Gliss* events provides a connective tissue between the three *Crrch* events, the sense of abrupt juxtaposition recurs. The third and final phase of Section 1 presents a temporally extended version of the *Gliss/Crrch* gesture, ending the section abruptly with a loud and noisy event.

The strategy of juxtaposition and difference set up by the sequence of timbral events in Section 1 operates for the succession from one sub-section to the next. Since this kind of juxtaposition operates between each of the sub-sections, one might well ask why my analysis does not interpret these sub-sections as simply sections. There are a couple of reasons for my interpretive decision, but the primary one is that between the sections there is a silence that serves as a temporal punctuation: a grand pause at m. 34, a rest at m. 67, and a slow, soft wind-down in m. 93—I will return to these silences in terms of the overall strategy of *Seed II* shortly. Figure 5.4 shows the *GesPro* of each sub-section, and reading from left to right, one may note that the succession from one to the next involves timbral types that have a good degree of difference. For instance, the *Short Gliss* of Sub-section 2a shares no related timbral type with the following *Low-Jagged-High* of Sub-section 2b. Sub-section 3a transforms the *Jagged* type by combining it with a transformed *Gliss* type and it adds a new *Detaché* timbral type. Sub-section 3b recalls *Short Gliss* and combines it with a new *Low* timbral type. While sub-section 4a re-introduces a transformed version of the *GesPro* of Section 1, it differs from the *Short Gliss-Low* of the preceding music only to have that *GesPro* return for Sub-section 4b. So, while there are some threads of continuity across sections and sub-sections for *Seed II*, the overall sense of succession is one of juxtaposition and difference.

Both the short- and long-term strategy for the succession of timbral events and of sections and sub-sections during *Seed II* is characterized by juxtaposition and difference. A more synoptic consideration of overall strategic design reveals some other facets of *Seed II*'s strategic design. Figure 5.6 combines a spectral and amplitude display of *Seed II* with the formal outlines underneath. At the bottom of the figure, I have added the durations of the sections, sub-sections, and silences between sections. These durational annotations show that each of the sections is roughly of the same duration, the exception being Section 4 with a substantially longer duration of 2:14, and that the silences are also roughly of the same duration. Another aspect of sequential design may be observed by highlighting the occurrences of passages that

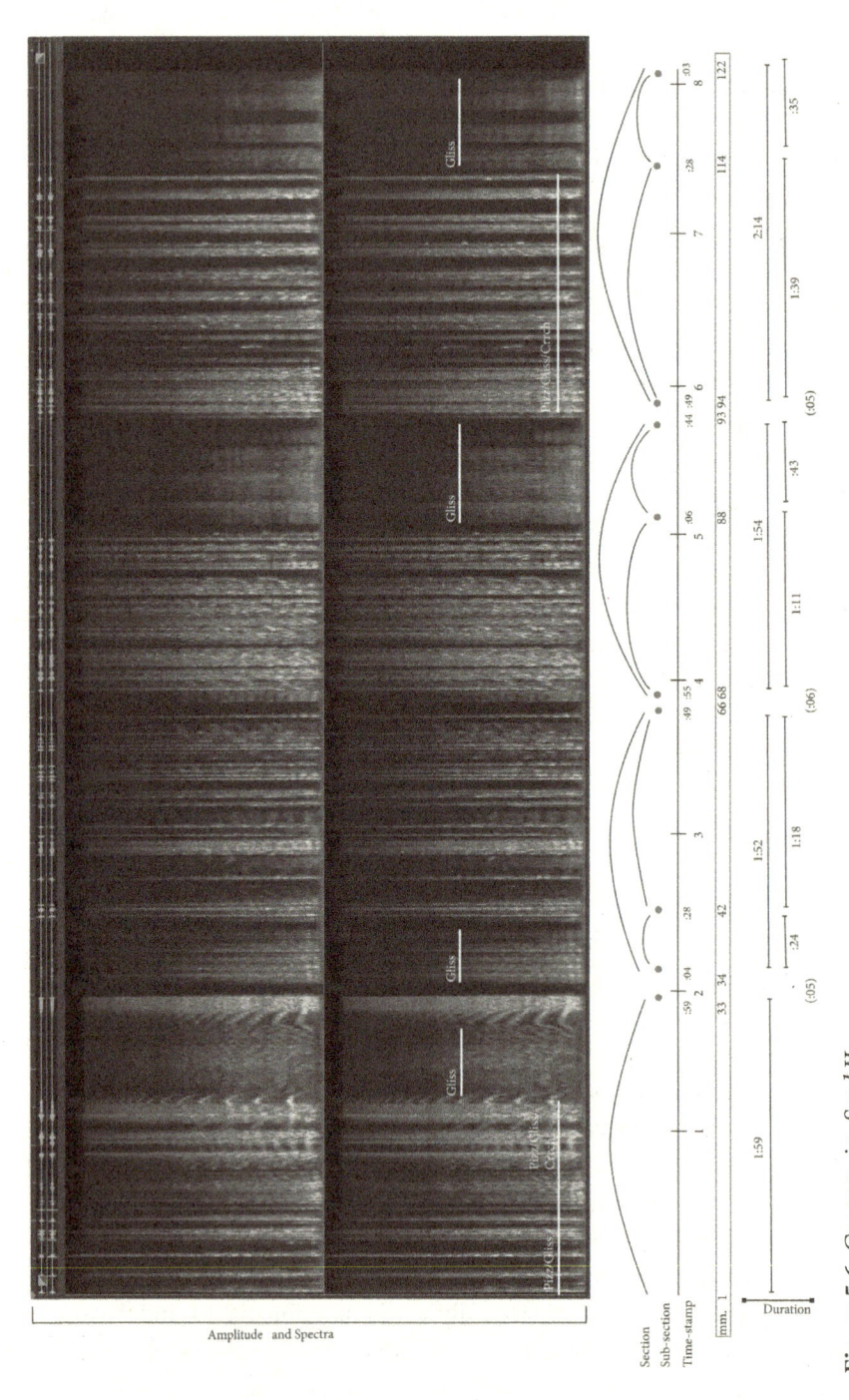

Figure 5.6 Czernowin, *Seed II*
Spectral and Amplitude Display with Formal Outlines

predominantly comprise *Gliss* events. These are annotated on the spectral display of Figure 5.6 and are noticeable there as softer and less spectrally rich. The occurrences of these predominantly *Gliss* passages generate another facet to the formal strategy of juxtaposition and difference. The recurrence of timbral types, such as *Gliss* and also of *Pizz/Gliss/Crrch* in Section 4 a), also annotated on Figure 5.6, provide a cross-current of transformed similarity to the predominant flow of juxtaposition and difference. These patterns of juxtaposition, difference, and recurrence characterize the strategic design of *Seed II* and establish it as different from *Seed I*.

The differences of strategic design between *Seed I* and *II* are several. *Seed I* involves a sense of emergence arising from the transformation and recontextualization of timbral events. Yet that almost seamless sense of emergence ceases abruptly with the ending gestures of the *Crrch* followed by the whimpering *High/Pitched* event. *Seed II*, on the other hand, involves the juxtaposition and difference of timbral events within sub-sections and sections and between sub-sections and sections, while at the same time it includes recurrences of timbral types creating some undercurrents of similarity. Similarities between the two *Seeds* derive from the unique material aspects of the string instruments which produce timbral events such as *Pizzicato*, *Pizz*, *Gliss*, *Crrch*, *Detaché*, and so forth. Yet, there are timbral types that are unique to one of the *Seeds*, such as *col legno Battuto*, *Ricochet*, and *Flautando* for *Seed I*; and *Low*, *Detaché*, and *Jagged* for *Seed II*.

Anea Crystal

Anea Crystal occurs when the two *Seeds* are performed together, either with two live string quartets or with *Seed I* live and *Seed II* recorded. The two *Seeds* individually are of differing lengths, and when combined, there are passages when only one of the quartets is heard while the other is silent. For instance, *Anea Crystal* begins with the viola of *Seed I* playing the *Pizzicato* event for 0:26 seconds before the entrance of *Seed II*'s *Pizz/Gliss*. There are passages in the score which indicate explicit coordination between the two *Seeds*, such as the passage between *Seed I*'s mm. 45–51 and *Seed II*'s 35–40 when each quartet has the same meter. But there are even more passages when the two quartets are playing in different meters and their parts are not coordinated, the score showing an approximate synchronization with systems for each of the quartets on the page (See Example 5.1). And while Czernowin instructs each quartet to "play independently," she has also indicated places for temporal "orientation" to occur (Czernowin 2008).

Anea Crystal and both of its *Seeds* have multiplicities that are typical of music that is notated and then performed and also of music that incorporates indeterminancies as do these pieces.[19] And as is the case with other such works, the conceptual indeterminancies do not have a simple aural analogue for a listener who may not know the compositional concept before hearing a performance. Czernowin takes her inspiration for *Anea Crystal* and its *Seeds* from the natural processes of crystal formation, specifically ionic crystals that emerge from the bonding of ions with negative and positive electrostatic charges. As Czernowin notes, "one could conceive of *Anea Crystal* as an ionic crystal of gestures" (Czernowin 2008). My analysis extends the metaphor of crystal formation to each of *Seeds* as well, the timbral events forming the crystal-like *Gestural Profiles* (*GesPro*). The combination of the two *Seeds* with their differing strategic designs—their differing electrostatic charges—materialize as *Anea Crystal* in a new sonic manifestation with each performance. Through its motivating concept—composer intention, if you will—the work sonically embodies the idea of an ontological multiplicity.

In addition to conceiving *Anea Crystal* in terms of crystal formation, Czernowin articulates another motivating concept: the transience and mutability of human memory. She describes the experience that motivates *Anea Crystal* with a narrative metaphor. Two people go to a party (perhaps drinking a bit too much), and each has a unique memory of the event that is itself shrouded by the effects of alcohol—these two memories are *Seed I* and *Seed II*. These two people come together to share casually their experiences— this is *Anea Crystal*. Each person's memory is preserved in some sense with the simultaneous playing of the two *Seeds*, but the combination of two memories produces another kind of metaphysical memory in which the originating memories get warped and changed. As a combination of disparate memories, *Anea Crystal* enacts a new sounding of remembrances not simply set against each other but transforming into a new experience.[20] *Anea Crystal* does more than simply combine the two *Seeds*, it is an emergent property of their simultaneous sounding.

These two metaphors—ionic crystal formation and mutability of memory—serve as both motivating and descriptive concepts for the music. As motivating concept, they served as spurs to compositional design. And

---

[19] The recording of *Anea Crystal* and the two *Seeds* does, however, fix a single performance, removing the multiplicity of performance.

[20] This account is my paraphrase of Czernowin's description to me in a video chat about *Anea Crystal* and my analysis of the work. See Czernowin 2021.

as descriptive concept, they may serve as imaginative framework for experiential engagement with the music—for listening. But, in keeping with my commitment to ontological multiplicity, the two metaphors should not be understood as authoritative guides to listening, and listeners are free to imaginatively engage the music in diverse ways.[21] It is worth noting, however, that both of these composer-generated musical metaphors are themselves instances of ontological multiplicity. Crystals are generated through a first-order phase transition from one state of being to another, states of being that are constantly in flux. Memories also are in states of flux, constantly transformed through retrieval and interaction with other events and memories. The trick for music analysis is to keep open music's flux, its ontological multiplicity. My analytical mapping and interpretations are intended as invitations to listen imaginatively, intended as frameworks for generative listenings.

Truth, Ethics, and Queering Analysis

I finished writing this essay in August 2021, but much was written when lies created a "reality" for a substantial number of people in the United States that led to violence and the near-overthrow of a democratic government. These events are a reminder that a "reality" can be constructed by those for whom truth can be bent to a corrupt quest for power. Writing nearly forty years ago in their quest for a truthful and ethical world, my sampled authors— Haraway, Butler, Badiou, Harding—were in fact addressing the kinds of situations in which institutional power could create false realities. These authors insisted on a truth arising from a process of "contestation, deconstruction, [and] passionate construction" (Haraway) leading to a "strong objectivity" (Harding), on an "ethic of truth" (Badiou) grounded in an ontology of difference (Butler). They insisted on a truth tethered to ethics.

The truth of an aesthetic reality differs in significant ways from the truth of a political reality, as Luciano Berio noted in the midst of world event in 1968: "We all know that music can't lower the cost of bread, is incapable of stopping (or starting, for that matter) wars, cannot eradicate the slums and injustice" (Berio 1996, 168). But Berio continues: a "responsible composer" must "challenge the meaning of and reasons for their work in relation to the

---

[21] I write about the imaginative aspects of listening in Lochhead 2019.

world of events" (Berio 1996, 168). What or who is this responsible composer? A person who engages musical sounds as an ethical and truthful way of being in the world. The same may be said of those who engage music as scholars, critics, listeners, and—of my concern here—analysts. An ethical quest for truthful accounts of the world permeates all practices and actions, all forms of musical engagement including analytical representations.

What then does my analytical account of the two pieces that form Czernowin's *Anea Crystal* accomplish? A full answer to that question will come from my readers. But here is what I hope it will do. Invite people to listen to and engage Czernowin's *Anea Crystal*, its two *Seeds*, and perhaps her music generally; invite some to develop their own hearings of the pieces; encourage others to develop their own analytical interpretations; and encourage others to develop different modes of taking account of music's sonic realities. I also recognize that what my analysis accomplishes is beyond my control now—it will have its own multiplicities beyond me.

And this is what I intended to do. I hope to acknowledge that a finished musical work is always in a state of differential being, in terms of its performance and its being as the subject of listening. Rather than assuming the structural unity of a musical work, I approach them as multiplicities that allow listeners (broadly construed to include analysts, composers, performers, critics, audiences, etc.) to engage music as a set of interrelated and smoothly connected realities. That my analysis offers "an" interpretation does not preclude other interpretations, either by myself or by others. I arrived at this interpretation through a long process of "contestation, deconstruction, [and] passionate construction" (Haraway) with myself as I was in dialogue with the music over a period of several months, engaging the music in what felt like a process that revealed a truth of *Seed I* and *Seed II*— at least for now. I fully hope that the next stage of intersubjective dialogue about Czernowin's music will come as others engage her music and my analytical interpretation. And finally, I engaged the music of the two *Seeds* from what I hoped was an ethical stance, not forcing the music into preconceived notions of music's structuring and allowing queering perspectives to uncover musical relations I might have initially missed. I fully understand that my intentions may not have been achieved. Whether they have is beyond me now.

Music's prodigious multiplicities are a source of its magical powers. And it is these powers of Czernowin's *Anea Crystal* and its two *Seeds* that I hope my analytical interpretation can illuminate. But as my four sampled authors have shown, an ontology of multiplicity must be tethered to an ethics of truth. An analysis that recognizes music's multiplicity must be guided by an epistemology that seeks not "the" truth of a piece of music but an ethics of truth that illuminates music's being in the world. Such an epistemology engages queering perspectives that uncover new ways of hearing and is committed to truthful and equitable modes of musical engagement.

Works Cited

Abbate, Carolyn. 2004. "Music—Drastic or Gnostic?" *Critical inquiry* 30, no. 3: 505–36. https://doi.org/10.1086/421160.

Badiou, Alain. 1988. *Being and Event*. Translated by Oliver Feltham. New York: Continuum.

Badiou, Alain. 2001. *Ethics: An Essay on the Understanding of Evil*. Translated and introduced by Peter Hallward. New York: Verso.

Badiou, Alain. 2004. *Infinite Thought: Truth and the Return to Philosophy*. Translated and edited by Oliver Feltham and Justin Clemens. New York: Continuum.

Berio, Luciano. 1996 [1968]. "Meditation on a Twelve-Tone Horse." In *Classic Essays On Twentieth-Century Music: A Continuing Symposium*, edited by Kostelanetz, Richard., Joseph Darby, and Matthew Santa, 167–171. New York: Schirmer Books.

Brett, Philip, Elizabeth Wood, and Gary C. Thomas, eds. 1994; 2nd ed., 2006. *Queering the Pitch: The New Gay and Lesbian Musicology*. New York: Routledge.

Browne, Kath, and Catherine Nash. 2010. *Queer Methods and Methodologies: Intersecting Queer Theories and Social Science Research*. New York: Routledge.

Butler, Judith. 1988. "Performative Acts and Gender Constitution: An Essay in Phenomenology and Feminist Theory." *Theatre Journal* 40, no. 4: 519–31.

Cusick, Suzanne. 1994. "Feminist Theory, Music Theory, and the Mind/Body Problem." *Perspectives of New Music* 32, no. 1: 8–27.

Czernowin, Chaya. 2008. *Anea Crystal*. Mainz: Schott.

Czernowin, Chaya. 2011. *Anea Crystal*, on the CD *Shifting Gravity*, Quatuor Diotima. Mainz: Wergo.

Czernowin, Chaya. 2021. Conversation with the author, Monday, May 31.

Ewell, Philip. 2020. "Music Theory and the White Racial Frame." *Music Theory Online* 26, no. 2 (September). https://doi.org/10.30535/mto.26.2.4.

Feltham, Oliver, and Justin Clemens. 2004. "An Introduction to Alain Badiou's Philosophy." *Infinite Thought: Truth and the Return to Philosophy*, 1–30. Translated by Feltham and Clemens. New York: Continuum.

Fuller, Sophie, and Lloyd Whitesell, eds. 2002. *Queer Episodes in Music and Modern Identity*. Urbana: University of Illinois Press.

Hallward, Peter. 2001. "Translator's Introduction." *Alain Badiou, Ethics: An Essay on the Understanding of Evil*, vii–xxxv. Translated by Peter Hallward. New York: Verso.

Hallward, Peter, ed. 2004. *Think Again: Alain Badiou and the Future of Philosophy*. New York: Continuum.

Haraway, Donna. 1988. "Situated Knowledges: The Science Question in Feminism and the Privilege of Partial Perspective." *Feminist Studies* 14, no. 3: 575–99.

Harding, Sandra. 1986. *The Science Question in Feminism*. Ithaca, NY: Cornell University Press.

Harding, Sandra. 1992. "Rethinking Standpoint Epistemology: What Is 'Strong Objectivity'?" *The Centennial Review* 36, no. 3: 437–70.

Hernnstein Smith, Barbara. 1988. *Contingencies of Value: Alternative Perspectives for Critical Theory*. Cambridge, MA: Harvard University Press.

Hubbs, Nadine. 2004. *The Queer Composition of America's Sound: Gay Modernists, American Music, And National Identity*. Berkeley: University of California Press.

Humpreys, Paul. 2016. *Emergence: A Philosophical Account*. Oxford Scholarship Online (November). https://doi.org/10.1093/acprof:oso/9780190620325.001.0001.

Jankélévitch, Vladimir. 2003. *Music and the Ineffable*. Translated by Carolyn Abbate. Princeton, NJ: Princeton University Press.

Kania, Andrew. 2017. "The Philosophy of Music." In *The Stanford Encyclopedia of Philosophy* (Fall ed.), edited by Edward N. Zalta. https://plato.stanford.edu/archives/fall2017/entries/music/.

Lochhead, Judith. 2008. "The Sublime, the Ineffable and other Dangerous Aesthetics." *Women and Music* 12: 63–74.

Lochhead, Judith. 2016a. "Chaotic Mappings: On the Ground with Music." In *Music's Immanent Future: the Deleuzian Turn in Music Studies*, edited by S. Macarthur, J. Lochhead, and J. Shaw, 72–89. New York: Routledge.

Lochhead, Judith. 2016b. *Reconceiving Structure in Contemporary Music: New Tools in Music Theory and Analysis*. New York: Routledge.

Lochhead, Judith. 2019. "Music Places: Imaginative Transports of Listening." In The Oxford Handbook of Sound and Imagination, Vol. 1, edited by Mark Grimshaw-Aagaard, Mads Walther-Hansen, and Martin Knakkergaard. Oxford: Oxford University Press.

Maus, Fred. 1993. "Masculine Discourse in Music Theory." *Perspectives of New Music* 31: 264–93.

Maus, Fred, Sheila Whiteley, Tavia Nyong'o, and Zoe Sherinian, eds. 2022. *The Oxford Handbook of Music and Queerness*. New York: Oxford University Press.

O'Connor, Timothy. 2020. "Emergent Properties." *The Stanford Encyclopedia of Philosophy* (Fall ed.), edited by Edward N. Zalta. https://plato.stanford.edu/archives/fall2020/entries/properties-emergent/.

OED Online. March 2021. "situation, n." Oxford University Press. https://www-oed-com.proxy.library.stonybrook.edu/view/Entry   /180520?redirectedFrom=situation (accessed May 31, 2021).

Salamon, Gayle. 2009. "Justification and Queer Method, or Leaving Philosophy." *Hypatia* 24, no. 1: 225–30.

QUEER TEMPORALITY

6

Sun Ra's Fletcher Henderson

Chris Stover

Sun Ra spins slowly, arms outstretched, head held high, faux-regal.[1] Shimmering silver robes drape from his fully extended body, flowing behind him as his arms move in slow, emphatic gestures, part dance, part ritual, part conducting. His face peers out from beneath a small silver headdress emblazoned with Egyptian symbology, somehow at once intense and expressionless, the aloof transcendence of a drag show impresario and the hyperfocus of a tightrope walker in equal measure. Incommensurabilities forming an "immeasurable equation" (Sun Ra 2005), one might say. He moves in big intentional strides to stage right (probably where his piano/keyboard station is located). The scene cuts to a second figure, writhing on the floor in long flowing white robe before lifting his torso with his arms and practically scurrying, insect-like, off the stage. A third scene, a whirling dervish in tights and cape, and then another, spinning ecstatically. Ailey's Afrodiasporic modernism, Senghor's surrealism, Okorafor's alien otherworldliness. The effect of the cinematic cuts is of a perverse fashion-show catwalk. A big band—Sun Ra's Arkestra—is playing, but we cannot hear them; instead a solo synthesizer improvisation is overlaid across the rapidly shifting visual scenes, Sun Ra alternating waves of dissonant clusters with little snippets of high-register melodic filigree and percussive interjections from the lower range of the instrument. It is a strange range of temporal fissures: the jump-cuts between bodies, the erasure of the music they are interacting with, the desubjectivized presence of musicians who are seen but not heard.

The montage cuts abruptly to the second of several excerpts of Sun Ra being interviewed by an unseen Finnish reporter. He is wearing what might be a different flowing regal gown, now adorned—in a supremely ironic

---

[1] This scene is from a TV interview produced by YLE, the Finnish Broadcasting Company, which aired October 24, 1971. It was later included as part of the two-CD and one-DVD set *Sun Ra—Helsinki 1971—The Complete Concert and Interview* (Transparency 0314, 2009). This excerpt is from 2:57 to 3:45.

Chris Stover, *Sun Ra's Fletcher Henderson* In: *Queer Ear*. Edited by: Gavin S. K. Lee, Oxford University Press.
© Oxford University Press 2023. DOI: 10.1093/oso/9780197536766.003.0007

juxtaposition—with a jester's neckwear. A textured silver tam atop his head resembles an oversized metallic brain. His eyes are hidden behind dark over-sized sunglasses, and he barely suppresses a mischievous smile that signals how much fun he is having speaking in all seriousness to his unseen inter-locutor of aliens and angels and all manner of Others, and of ethical matters that transcend the pragmatic here and now and exemplify what José Esteban Muñoz calls a "field of utopian possibility":

> . . . well the human race has always looked for freedom—they set up rules and all kind of standards for humans, and they never passed any kinds of rules or constitution for other type of beings. For instance, like another type of being comes on the planet, then he hasn't got any rights. . . . (3:53–4:14)

It is no stretch to interpret the "other type of being" Sun Ra invokes as anyone existing at the margins of white-straight-cis-male-able-capitalist orienta-tion, as humanity's undercommons, improvising a life in the interstices of the fabric woven by the partnered forces of neoliberalism and neoconservatism (Brown 2006). Sun Ra's fabulatory re-weaving exemplifies what Sarah Ahmed (2006, 162) describes as a becoming-oblique of the world, an uncanny "diso-rientation in how things are arranged" that queers what she calls the "straight line" (70) of normative modes of being.[2] Another way of saying this (with slightly different implications for the theorization of a queer temporality) is that Sun Ra is in every act, gesture, or utterance contesting what Muñoz calls the "autonaturalizing temporality" of "straight time" (Muñoz 2019, 26). The "presentness" of straight time, for Muñoz, "needs to be phenomenologically questioned, and this is the fundamental value of a queer utopian hermeneu-tics" (27). In contrast to a normative metaphysics of presence, Muñoz orients us toward what could otherwise be: "[t]he future is queerness's domain" (1).

In this chapter I will develop some ideas about how to think and do that phenomenologically questioning queer utopian hermeneutics, through music theory. Music theory, the way I understand and practice it, is always a positioned, partial, enacted engagement with its object (Haraway 1988). It involves the creative invention of a kind of temporality that in two ways refuses the call to *make sense* of a musicking relationship: resisting what we might call the apodicity-drive that begins by assuming that stable

---

[2] Elizabeth Freeman (2010) theorizes this normative mode of being through what she calls a "chronobiopolitical" framework, which I find particularly useful.

knowledge about an object of experience can be acquired, and acting in such a way that one can remain—productively, wondrously—disoriented in the intimate spacetime of feeling-with a musical expression.[3] This is a "willfully eccentric mode of being" (Halberstam 2005, 1). Music theory thought from this perspective strives to communicate with the becoming-other of musical process, in which music's future holds the utopian promise of what might be. In Sun Ra's (2009) conception, it is "reaching outward" toward an "alter-destiny." I suggest that music theory can potentially always be a queer practice, which proceeds by resisting fixing its object (or making an object of it in the first place) and by affirming the theorist's status as merely one constituted, positioned musicking body entering into a relationship with another. Music is a body too: this is a tenet of what we might call first-wave queer musicology.[4]

If music is always a becoming-other, then music theory ought to aim to engage music in terms of that otherness. If music is a kind of body with which we can be in a relationship, then music theory should seek to thematize the nature of that relationship and how it unfolds, at the level of intimate, relational, consensual detail (otherwise is music theory a form of creepy voyeurism?). That relationship is affective, a double constitution of bodies, affecting and affected by one another. It can involve prosthetic or cyborg bodies, non- and post-human bodies, but bodies through and through. By cyborg bodies I mean performer–instrument assemblages and other technological mediations, ranging from the earliest inventions of instrumental

---

[3] I am making a different claim here than what is found in various critiques (and mis-critiques) of a putative over-focus on formalism, unity, organicism, "the music itself," and so on in music theory and analysis. By "apodictity-drive" I mean a shared concern to make an analysis resonate with empirically discoverable features of the experienced music, and to report on them accurately. This is, perhaps, why so much music theory focuses on relatively concrete musical parameters: pitch, rhythm, formal designs, style-specific syntax. To queer this aim amounts to keeping open a kind of creatively productive "what else?" question: not just "how else can music go?" but "how else can I experience it?" See Boretz ([1992] 2003), Dubiel (1992), Guck (1997), Kielian-Gilbert (2005–6), Korsyn (2003), Lochhead (2015), and Scherzinger (2002) for some important theoretical antecedents that ground this idea. See also note 7 below on James K. Randall. I would also draw the reader's attention to Gavin Lee's (2020) recent queer reading of David Lewin's work, since the latter is often associated with, and deployed toward, formalist aims (see also comments in Dubiel 1997, 312).

[4] While there are a number of foundational sources that comprise this loose historical category (the early stirrings of queer musicology that starting gaining critical mass in the early 1990s), I have been especially moved by the work of Philip Brett ([1994] 2006), Suzanne Cusick ([1994] 2006), John Gill (1995), Fred Everett Maus (1988 and 1993), Susan McClary ([1994] 2006), Elizabeth Wood ([1994] 2006), and, not unrelated, Pauline Oliveros (1984). The concept of music as a body can take many forms, for example musical sounds as affecting and affected bodies (Stover 2016), musical compositions as virtual spaces for participating in scenes of intense intimacy (Cusick 1993; Le Guin 2005), or musical instruments as bodies with which one enters into an intimate relationship (Östersjö 2008). All of these perspectives are relevant for Sun Ra's plural, performative embodiment.

means to modify and amplify musical sounds to Laurie Anderson's morphological self-distortions and Pamela Z's technologically afforded spatial/gestural composition, and far beyond. As Kara Keeling (2019, 57) notes, music "imbricates sentient bodies with technologies." By non-human bodies I mean the sonic materiality of musical tones in combinations and the spaces and places in which musical relations unfold. Often these include invisible or virtual spaces: unseen recording studios, unseeable record grooves or mp3 bytes, temporal and geographic dispersals. By post-human, I would like to develop three themes that Sun Ra's music and thought bring into relief: first, the future-directedness of musical processes (the becoming-other I hinted at just above, which can be described in terms of a *queer futurity*). Second, how actions in a living present enact openings onto that future by critically reexamining pasts in the plural. And third, the imaginative and politically pragmatic ways that pasts and futures can be *fabulated*, a practice that music can help animate.

Queer Pasts, Queer Futures

"The present demands our ethical consideration and the task at hand is not to refuse the present altogether, but rather to maneuver from the present's vantage point at the crossroads of life that is lived *after* catastrophe . . . and simultaneously *before* it." Any consideration of a (utopian) queer futurity ought to begin with this cautionary entreaty by Joshua Chambers-Letson, Tavia Nyong'o, and Ann Pellegrini (Muñoz 2019, xiv), from their foreword to the tenth-anniversary edition of Muñoz's *Cruising Utopia*. Muñoz famously insists that

> The present is not enough. It is impoverished and toxic for queers and other people who do not feel the privilege of majoritarian belonging, normative tastes, and "rational" expectations. . . . The present must be known in relation to the alternative temporal and spatial maps provided by a perception of past and future affective worlds. (2019, 27)

But as is already clear from this powerful indictment, this ought not amount to an eschewal of the present, but what we might call a performative becoming-disoriented-with it, a willful and creative appropriation and redeployment of the present enacted by considering the past as "a field of possibility in which subjects can act in the present in the service of a new futurity" (16). In several important senses the present functions as a sign or symptom of its pasts (here Marx, Nietzsche, and Freud might all agree). But Muñoz (and, we will see, Sun Ra) is asking "which pasts?" How, in the present, can we imagine alternative pasts—missed connections, lost horizons, "myth-sciences"—and enact them through new performative gestures in an activist present?[5] How, Muñoz asks (channeling Gloria Anzaldúa), can we "[look] back to a fecund no-longer-conscious in the service of a futurity that resists the various violent asymmetries that dominate the present" (84)? How, Fred Moten (2003, 153) might add (to fold in a slightly different theoretical perspective), can we reinhabit an expansive, effusive present defined by a "temporal-affective disorder, displacement, and disjunction"? I will turn to Moten shortly.

Music theory has the potential to be oriented in this way. In its empirical or phenomenological modes, the music-analytic act is attuned to a present that is *felt with* the musical expression. I described this above in sensuous terms, as an intimate relationship between co-constitutive bodies. To queer this act is to resist taking as simply given either the raw empirical data or the commonly accepted disciplinary frameworks through which those data typically come to be understood. Instead, it involves letting oneself remain open to potential, even contradictory, layers of musical "meaning," to embrace and work to stay within a space of willful disorientation. Indeed, it is to perform that disorientation as a kind of "minor" hermeneutics. This amounts, for example, to finding the little swerve that breaks the formal parsimony of a transformational map, or a "wrong" note revealed by twelve-counting, or conflicting information across two levels in a Schenkerian analysis, and finding a thrill in that transgressive musical moment rather than lamenting a structural aberration.[6] In other words, it is first of all to actively perform what Edmund Husserl calls the bracketing of "the social and familiar character of objects" (Ahmed 2006, 33). This is a creative and, importantly, politically valent act. And second, it is to allow meanings to proliferate wildly by continually asking "what else?" and setting those potential, even contradictory,

---

[5] One way we might frame this question is "How did we get here? And how, if things had gone differently, might we have gotten somewhere else?" This question has relevance for music theory, including but not limited to its more speculative versions relating to compositional practice.

[6] That there are trajectories in Schenkerian analysis that focus on conflicts between different features of musical form and expression without trying to resolve them or subsume one aspect under the authority of the other speaks to the possibility that, in an important sense, music theory has always been a little queer. See Cohn 1992 for an overview and a development of what he calls a "Constructive Conflict" paradigm.

meanings into play with one another, enacting what Jack Halberstam (2005, 5) calls (in somewhat less affirmative terms) a "ludic temporality."[7] The play-space of music-theoretical inquiry, then, becomes not only where analytic identities (or better, what Marion Guck [1994] calls "analytic fictions") begin alternately to coalesce and splinter, but where the "straight line" of conventions and taxonomies can begin to be subverted. Fred Moten (2003, 81) seems to be getting at a similar engagement with the play-space of musical inquiry's temporality: "Music lies before and up ahead of its performance as subsistence, persistence, lingering, and sounded remainder in the breach, in the movement, from and between."

What has this to do with the before and after of catastrophe invoked by Letson, Nyong'o, and Pellegrini? Music theory rarely engages the kinds of real-world catastrophes the contexts and implications of which queer and postcolonial theories strive to account for (the AIDS epidemic, the slave trade, settler colonial genocide). But what if it did? What if we believe Jacques Attali (1985) when he suggests that musical formulations anticipate social ones, and in doing so work to construct a music-theoretical apparatus that aims to illuminate (or fabulate) practicable connections between those domains? I do not know what this would look or feel like, but it is something we ought to be taking seriously. Easier, probably, at least for now, is imagining how music theory can make materially present Muñoz's "past and future affective worlds" (which seems to be Sun Ra's explicit project) through these parallel acts of performative disorientation and ludic disavowal of the discipline's straight lines. This might be a way to lead to the first, more challenging question, by posing music theory not as an explanatory practice but as a liberatory one through which temporally diverse proliferations of relational conjunctions can be imagined and implemented. Among other things, this gives lie to the notion that theory necessarily follows practice.

As Kara Keeling describes, Black liberation has often been assumed to require (or at be facilitated by) a break with the past. She characterizes this as turning toward the "formal and temporal disruption of what Karl Marx calls a 'poetry of the future'" (Keeling 2019, 83). As we will see below, to break with the past is not to eschew it entirely but to refigure it, fabulate it, queer

---

[7] An especially rich early exemplar of this kind of ludic temporality can be found in James K. Randall's ([1972] 1995) *Compose Yourself: A Manual for the Young*; for just one example his absurdist and excessive, yet analytically incisive account of listening to Richard Wagner's *Götterdämmerung* in "Stimulating Speculation no. 1" (see pp. 10–11). See also Gleason 2013 (53) and Maus 2004.

it. To ask what else could have been, or could be. The connection between Black and queer liberation is crucial. Muñoz suggests on one hand that "[i]f the condition of possibility for blackness is a certain radicalness in relation to capitalism's naturalizing temporal logic, the black radical tradition is engaged in a maneuver that helps elucidate queer futurity" (87). But he also draws upon Anzaldúa to make the connection materially manifest and not merely theoretically adjacent: "*jotería* [queers] could be found at the base of every liberationist social movement" (Muñoz 2019, 84), thereby fixing the Black radical tradition as already complexly connected with queer liberation actions. Sun Ra's quAre (Johnson 2005; see below) temporal machinations demonstrate this subtle but crucial connection. The past, for Sun Ra, lingers spectrally in the present, and as Elizabeth Freeman puts it, "[t]his stubborn lingering of pastness (whether it appears as anachronistic style, as the reappearance of bygone events in the symptom, or as arrested development) is a hallmark of queer affect: a 'revolution' in the old sense of the world, as a turning back" (Freeman 2010, 8). Sun Ra continually turns back to multiple concentric circles of pasts: his own life and work, jazz history, African American history during and after slavery, layer upon layer of pre-colonial African historiography. In every performative gesture he folds different, alternative pasts into new presents to newly constitute openings onto imagined futures. And as is well known, his futures are imaginative indeed! They involve not only time but space: interstellar travel, faraway planets, and solar systems. These are metaphors, probably—Afrofuturist retellings of promised-land narratives from the Black American church—but only to a degree. Nothing for Sun Ra—not space or time, not meaning or utility—is fixed.

Fabulated Life

About Sun Ra, then: official records have him born Herman Blount in 1914 in Birmingham, Alabama, but at various points in his life he denied all three of these biographical facts, offering evasive testimony about his geographic origins, his name, and even the fact of having been born. As a young adult he changed his name legally to Le Sony'r Ra, later shortened to Sun Ra, with obvious ancient Egyptian mythological resonances. At times he suggested that he came to Earth from a distant intergalactic civilization. At other times he claimed earthly provenance but suggested he had contact with aliens and had visited Saturn. The contradictions between these fantastical claims matter. He moved to Chicago in 1945, part of the Great Migration that he and many Black American thinkers couched unequivocally in biblical exodus terms. In Chicago, Sun Ra nurtured a profound interest in an astonishing range of arcane subjects from gnosticism and theosophy to numerology, Rosecrucianism, and ancient Egyptian mysticism, to politically valent reclaimings and retellings of African history.[8] All the while he was developing into a progressive pianist (and, soon, synthesizer pioneer), composer, and bandleader, as well as poet, broadside author, teacher, philosopher, activist, inventor of semantic etymologies, self-proclaimed "tone scientist," and progenitor of Afrofuturist thought. Much has been written on these later themes—surprisingly less on Sun Ra's music specifically.[9] Likewise, a great deal has been written about Sun Ra's Blackness, while his sexuality has only been speculated about.[10] I will turn to this last point shortly.

But first I want to weave together three themes to establish some further context. First is Gilles Deleuze's conception of *fabulation*, which refers to the role that fiction, storytelling, and re-worlding can play in developing forms of philosophical thought that might not be possible under conventional regimes. The term "fabulation" first appears as a philosophical concept in Henri Bergson's (1977) *The Two Sources of Morality and Religion*. Deleuze and Félix Guattari appropriate Bergson's concept by insisting that what art does is fabulate alternative temporalities, and what the artist is is a "seer, a becomer" (Deleuze and Guattari 1994, 171). Sun Ra is the archetypal fabulation-artist. Deleuze writes of author T. E. Lawrence's "mythomania" as a continuous effort "to project—into things, into reality, into the future and even into the sky—an image of himself and of others so intense . . . that it has a life of its own. . . . It is a machine for manufacturing giants, what Bergson called a fabulatory function'" (Deleuze 1997, 118). These words could be uttered without change about Sun Ra.

---

[8] A well-known example is the reading list Sun Ra prepared for a course he taught at Berkeley in 1971: https://www.openculture.com/2014/07/full-lecture-and-reading-list-from-sun-ras-1971-uc-berkeley-course.html.

[9] See, e.g., Corbett 1994, Edwards 2017, Heble 2010, Stanley 2014, Stüttgen 2014, Swiboda 2007, Szwed 1998, and Youngquist 2016. Even book-length accounts of Sun Ra's life and work relegate music to somewhat secondary status, with much more space spent on biographical matters and examining his verbal and visual texts: his poetry and philosophical "equations," his dress and visage, his choreography and stage demeanor, his film presence.

[10] Two important exceptions are Stanley 2014 and Stüttgen 2014; see below.

Elsewhere, Deleuze (1983) borrows from Friedrich Nietzsche to suggest that the role of the artist is as diagnostician or symptomatologist. This is not contradictory: as with Sun Ra, Deleuze understands that the past, as with the future, is undetermined, always in a process of becoming. The past is never fixed, but is ever reconfigured as new presents continuously fold back into it. Fabulation in this sense is a tool for actively stimulating the reconfiguration of the past.[11] It is the technique the artist uses not only to read the symptoms of the past and their effects on the ongoing present, but also to invent new pasts that open up possibilities for what can be, for imagining what Deleuze and Guattari call "a people to come." As Deleuze (1995, 142–43) describes, discussing two artists to whom he returns frequently in his work,

> [Proust's] *Recherche* is a general semiology, a symptomatology of different worlds. Kafka's work is a diagnosis of all the diabolical powers around us. As Nietzsche said, artists and philosophers are civilization's doctors. . . . [The signs they diagnose] imply ways of living, possibilities of existence, they're the symptoms of life gushing forth or draining away. . . .

Proust is creatively reassembling a world, in doing so revealing the constructedness of all worlds. Kafka's multivalent alterity is always already Othered and othering, transgressing borders and folding other-worldly encounters into one's own subject-formation. For Nietzsche these are much more than stories: they describe possible ways of being in the world that disidentify with known or accepted narratives.

My second theme is *invagination,* which Jacques Derrida invokes to describe the process in literary texts of folding outside and inside into one another.[12] My usage derives from the chapter "The Sentimental Avant-Garde"

---

[11] Michel Foucault (1977) offers a similar formulation, developing a theory of "counter-memory" that can "transform the temporality of history itself." See also Nyong'o 2019 for a perspective on temporality referred to variably as "contrapuntal" (10) or "poly-" (51) and as a product of a "fugitive present" that makes possible the idea that "representational capture" (of a fixed, accountable past) can be rendered inoperative (93).

[12] See Derrida 1979, 100–1. Among other things, in this account invagination is described as "the apparent outer edge of an enclosure, far from being . . . simply external and circular . . . makes no sign beyond itself, toward what is utterly other, without becoming double or dual, without making itself be 'represented', refolded, superposed, *re-marked* within the enclosure, at least in what the structure produces as an effect of interiority. But it is precisely this structure-effect that is being deconstructed here." Elsewhere, Derrida (1983, 19) describes invagination as "an empty space for chance," which quite radically reconfigures the proliferating movement operating at the putative borderline in the earlier text, and which has compelling implications for Sun Ra's musical formulations.

from Moten's (2003) *In The Break*. There is a sense in which we might think of the scene staged below as a fifth vignette following the creative entanglements with Duke Ellington, Billy Strayhorn and Beauford Delaney, Cecil Taylor, and Eric Dolphy that comprise Moten's chapter. In Moten's account, Blackness "is" only to the extent "that it exceeds itself; it bears the groundedness of an uncontainable outside" (26) that is enacted by improvisation. There is also, fundamentally and irreducibly, an erotics that animates the minor gestures Moten describes: a "shattered erotics of the situation" (81) which we ought to read alongside the cut of Muñoz's affective present. We hear this erotics, for example, in the "outness" of Eric Dolphy's improvisational syntax that still contains "an insistence of the chord" (81) even as it continually exceeds and evades it.

This ties directly into my third theme, what I will call Sun Ra's specific mode of queer temporality, to which I will turn in the last section of this chapter. Sun Ra's primary rhetorical gambit was to invent fantastical, multidirectional spacetimes that channel fabulated pasts and alternative topologies in order to open onto new future possibilities. One of his techniques was to deploy what Deleuze and Guattari (1986) call "minor histories"—narratives and stories that escape or elide State-sanctioned accounts, in doing so constructing alternative genealogies that differently impinge upon ongoing events. This amounts to the creative multiplicitous enactment of *folds* (Deleuze 1993) of past, present, and future into one another. Moten's *invagination* similarly opens onto

> the out of the outside . . . that extends or deepens the totality . . . by way of vio-lation, an extended and deepening violation that is never an erasure or disap-pearance or is only a disappearance in the partial way that erasure performs. . . . (Moten 2003, 158–59)

I am interested, again, in how Sun Ra's specifically *musical* utterances express these creative genealogies and refoldings, these what-ifs, these violations that extend or deepen the totality, that reconfigure history and open onto new futures. Importantly, this fabulated, fabulous, fugitive history is very much *real* in the sense that Sun Ra's own practice of myth-making is in every ut-terance functional, it does *work* that reconfigures his sources by chanelling not what they are or were, but what they could be, or could have been. This is important to keep in mind when, for example, we listen to Sun Ra's late live performances where 1930s swing, stride piano, delta blues, bebop, modal jazz, African drums, funk, disco, and avant-garde flow freely through one another. In keeping with the idea of a queer temporality, I will soon refer to Sun Ra's performances as a kind of drag show.[13]

For Deleuze and Guattari, fabulation is the tool of the minoritarian artist. As Ronald Bogue (2010, 7) describes in his volume on Deleuze and Guattari's fabulatory practice, "the minor [artist's] works are immediately social and political," and the artist, as "an articulator of a collective assemblage of enunciation and practitioner of a deterritorialization of language," is an inventor of a kind of productive excess in the sense of mobilizing existing materials to open them to ever-new meanings, including subversive ones. Moten (2003, 26) puts an Afro-diasporic spin on this: "See, black performance has always been the ongoing improvisation of a kind of lyricism of the surplus—invagination, rupture, collision, augmentation."[14]

Here's Bogue again: "In Deleuze and Guattari's reading, Kafka is neither a religious mystic nor a self-consumed explorer of his personal neuroses, but a thoroughly political writer whose fiction directly confronts and transforms the signs and forces of his world in an experimentation with the real" (Bogue 2010, 6). It is in Deleuze and Guattari's (1986) volume on Kafka that they most fully develop their theory of minoritarianism, which is an important if slightly tacet part of Moten and Stefano Harney's theory of the undercommons. Here is Moten again:

> Like Deleuze. I believe in the world and want to be in it. I want to be in it all the way to the end of it because I believe in another world in the world and I want to be in *that*. And I plan to stay a believer, like Curtis Mayfield. But that's beyond me . . . and out into the world, the other thing, the other world, the joyful noise of the scattered, scatted eschaton, the undercommon refusal of the academy of misery. (Moten and Harney 2013, 10)

Of course the Sun Ra resonances in this passage are promiscuous: not just the direct reference to "joyful noise" (an allusion to Robert Mugge's 1980 documentary film) but the concept of worlds within worlds, of music's (jazz's!) role—as "scatting"—in inaugurating the end of this world and the projection into a new one (such as we hear in Sun Ra's opening monologue in his own film *Space Is the Place*, Sun Ra 2003, where he suggests that we "teleport

---

[13] I am not the first to suggest as much: Tim Stüttgen (2014, 102) describes Sun Ra's stage persona as a "despotic alien drag." See below for more.

[14] All of these ideas are put to vivid work as a specifically (and politically valent) "afro-fabulation" in Tavia Nyong'o's recent work (Nyong'o 2019).

the whole planet here, through music"), of the always-already-political act of refusing to function within the straight line of majoritarian structures. For Sun Ra, being in the world is already stepping beyond it.

Queer Notions

Sun Ra is one of the great inventors of worlds within worlds, of worlds beyond worlds. His grand fabulations are the stuff of jazz legend: his alternative histories, the transcendental empiricisms (and the frank, matter-of-fact delivery) of his linguistic and numerological equations, the ways they adumbrate reality, his double movements from and to outer space and across temporal epochs, his doubled or tripled or quadrupled selves, the continuous process of becoming-other of his polysemous utterances. I would like to take a close look at one small aspect of this proliferating movement, by zooming in on Sun Ra's performative reenactment of the Fletcher Henderson Orchestra's 1933 hit "Queer Notions." There are many names here, though: not just because of Sun Ra's fugitive practice of self-renaming, but because by "Sun Ra" I also, essentially, mean "Sun Ra's Arkestra" that itself went through multiple namings[15] (and also, specifically, the 1980 configuration of the Arkestra to which we will turn shortly), and by Fletcher Henderson I also mean saxophonist Coleman Hawkins, the composer of "Queer Notions," and all the other members of the 1933 incarnation of Henderson's band. All these names enact complex arrays of folds into one another. For example, Hawkins is the named author of "Queer Notions," but as Deleuze and Guattari (1986, 17) insist, in a minoritarian language "there are no possibilities for an individual enunciation that would belong to this or that 'master' and that could be separated from a collective enunciation." It is impossible to separate Hawkins's composition from Henderson's arrangement from the orchestra's playing of it.

Before moving on, I recommend the reader listens to Fletcher Henderson's recording.[16]

Henderson's version already dis-identifies with the jazz practice of its time. "Queer Notions's" harmony is composed largely of symmetrical structures: augmented triads, whole-tone scales, and derived shapes like

---

[15] Over forty different variants (!), according to Stüttgen (2014, 98–99).
[16] A recording can be found at https://open.spotify.com/track/5qDNV2yRJOCyTdymWvj YMZ?si=479f2bd9aa4d43f6.

dominant seven, flat five chords. As composers have known since at least the mid-nineteenth century, these symmetries destabilize tonal expectations by denying perfect-fifth relations such as we find both in major and minor triads and in tonality-defining dominant–tonic bass motions. Perfect fifths earn their hierarchical status in large part because of ideological structures that appeal to the "natural" status of the harmonic series to construct a normalizing ground; it is no stretch to read this history alongside Michel Foucault's (1978) account of the hegemonic normalization of heterosexuality in post-Enlightenment Western culture, and conceptualize it as a "straight line" ripe for twisting open in search of new possibilities.

The symmetrical chords in "Queer Notions" unfold an up-back-down-back oscillation that creates a kind of stasis, a relentless sameness that is at the time same restless, ungrounded. This present opens strangely onto the future: the augmented triad and whole-tone scale, in 1933, indexed newness and other-worldliness, the freedom to imagine alternative futures. Unusually and importantly, the AABA form of Hawkins's song provides little relief from this relentless de-hierarchization: there are small tonal confirmations at the end of each eight-bar A section, but the B section repeats and recontextualizes the symmetrical oscillations of the A sections, rather than providing the textural contrast one might expect in an "exotic" song from this era.[17]

Henderson also reconfigures rhythmic, metric, and formal expectations. For example, Hawkins's saxophone solo starting in m. 4 of the arrangement sounds like a theme, but turns out in retrospect to extend the introduction, the sum of which unfolds as a seven-bar structure, 3 + 4, upsetting sedimented ideas about phrase and hypermetric regularity (especially in dance music). When the actual theme commences, it engenders proliferating layers of syncopated cross-rhythms that pull our attention away from beat 1 as a significant arrival point, transforming the ways we understand meter to behave by redistributing our attention across different temporal spans, opening new possibilities for meaning-enactments.

How does Sun Ra queer "Queer Notions"? Before continuing, I encourage the reader to listen to the recording.[18]

---

[17] A famous "exotic" song from just a few years later is Dizzy Gillespie's "A Night in Tunisia"; in this AABA song, A sections alternate between two chords a semitone apart (E♭7 and D minor), with brief tonal confirmations at each cadence, but the B section provides stark syntactic contrast as it sequences through two four-bar II–V–I progressions. Further contrast is provided by the rhythmic feel of the A and B sections, from a kind of "Afro-Latin" beguine feel to swing and back. Both of these, in conjunction, are highly typical of the period.

[18] A recording can be found at https://open.spotify.com/track/29Qn4ZCPsLcdfFLRKE6JF0?si=80b2d34ea05b443f.

Sun Ra's performance is markedly faster, in both a literal and affective sense. First, Henderson's version orbits around 160 beats per minute; Sun Ra's around 185, with salient temporal ebbs and flows. Second, Henderson's sits back on the back side of the beat, laid-back, cool, mysterioso, while Sun Ra's orients very much toward the front end of the beat, pushing ahead, a bit wild, like it is about to lose control. Part of that wildness is produced by the variable ways different musicians are expressing the musical time-feel: some early, some late, some zig-zagging in and out of temporal dimensions.[19] At every moment producing difference. Fletcher Henderson is cool and mysterious, Sun Ra's Arkestra is bacchanalian.

We hear all of this in the opening moments of the performance: after Sun Ra's solo "pre-intro," the band reproduces Henderson's 3 + 4 false-theme introduction. Everything is a bit wild: loose onsets across the ensemble; the sting–crescendos of Henderson's version raggedly reproduced, each player attacking and shaping their note with a high degree of individual expression. We hear what we might generously call a *creative* approach to intonation, and an ensemble texture orchestrated such that very high and very low notes—lead trumpet and baritone saxophone—are prominent. Every one of these points is analytically interesting, providing openings for developing music-theoretical understandings of musical process and structure and how they express their genealogies. They are interesting *because* of those expressions: in this analytic reading the bent pitches and individualized dynamic arcs and discrepant event onsets attain meaning in relation to the prototypes they performatively mime; wild forward-directed energy takes on important resonances when we have heard the laid-back grooviness of its swing-era antecedent. "This is the dense erotics of arrangement, the whole of the text working like the whole of the body working like the whole of the orchestra—a miraculously autoexpansive, invaginative, erotogenic zone" (Moten 2003, 30). Moten's provocative folding is crucial here as I pivot from (the body of) Sun Ra himself to (that of) his Arkestra, and from the Arkestra to their collective musical enunciation (as a kind of sonic body)—to repeat Deleuze and Guattari's (1986) crucial concept, in a minoritarian seizure of a major language, "there are no possibilities for an individual enunciation

---

[19] As is well known within jazz communities, swing does not involve fixed durational ratios or deviations from normative metric or submetric grids. This is something of a problem in analyses of jazz's micro-temporalities, which often conceive of event placements in terms of "beat-upbeat ratios" (Benadon 2006; Butterfield 2011) that assume at least provisional fixity for the beats against which upbeat locations are measured; I suggest that this normalizes beats in a way that does not correspond with performed reality.

that would belong to this or that 'master' and that could be separated from a collective enunciation."[20] The "throng of dialects and patois" (Deleuze and Guattari 1987, 7) that come together to form the Arkestra's collective assemblage amounts to a multi-directional interpenetration of a multiplicity of individual enunciations. In other words, I would argue, the Arkestra's collective enunciation *needs* those individuated dynamic arcs, those bent notes and intonational proclivities. A clean, homogeneous ensemble expression would quite literally say something different—by erasing difference.

Deleuze-Guattarian machines produce by breaks and flows (Deleuze and Guattari 1983, 286–87). What that means in this case is that as the collective enunciation of Sun Ra's Arkestra connects with its historical contexts, it breaks them apart, intentionally, joyfully, in order to newly figure them. This is a connecting thread we can draw through Moten's sentimental avant-garde too: the Duke Ellington orchestra's approach to group playing, where a "multiply-tongued" glossolalia takes precedence over ensemble homogeneity, is the Arkestra's template. Similarly, Eric Dolphy's melodic torsions deterritorialize the chord changes he is playing, breaking them down to refigure them with new differences, new traces to be differently taken up in new repetitions. Here is Moten again:

> Rigorously un/captured, captured, but you can't capture it again, heard after the fact of its disappearance, the music—organization in the improvisation of principles, nonexclusion of sound in the improvisation (through the relation and opposition of the generation and subversion) of meaning—lies before us. (2003, 81)

Back to "Queer Notions." Still following Henderson's arrangement, the theme begins, with that characteristic up-back-down-back symmetrical oscillation. The texture thickens though, embodying Moten's "expansive, effusive present": brash ornaments in the syncopated trumpet cross-rhythms, an amorphous low-midrange wash of sound produced by Sun Ra's left hand (doubling bass, with the sustain pedal on), and low-tuned tom-toms played by one of Sun Ra's two drummers (one of whom has a name that would be the envy of Afrofuturist drag queens everywhere: Michael "Celestial Star"

---

[20] We ought to compare this formulation productively with Muñoz suggestion that "The queerness of queer futurity, like the blackness of a black radical tradition, is a relational and collective modality of endurance and support" (2019, 91).

Walker). When the melody repeats, Sun Ra's piano (joined by a carnivalesque caricature of Gene Krupa's famous drum banter[21]) begins to really impinge on the ensemble texture; with an increased densification of the low-midrange sonic space and Sun Ra's stabbing upper-range chords adding an additional layer of syncopation, which very quickly transcends any kind of entrainable orientation with the metric matrix. This continues into the bridge, where additional layers of added dissonance stimulate an ever-increasingly expansive spacetime, expressing Moten's "temporal-affective disorder" cited above. Very importantly, everything from Henderson's arrangement is carefully attended to, from harmonic details to the original 1933 solos—for example, saxophonist Marshall Allen reproducing Russell Procope's original twice-repeated lyrical countermelody, now ironically juxtaposed with Sun Ra's harshly dissonant voicings, twice fanning out in opposite directions from the center of the piano, rhythmically echoing Henderson's ensemble voicings but quadruply displaced: in intensity, orchestration, melodic contour, and pitch content. Like Ellington, Sun Ra's "comping marking that rhythmic disruption that animates swing, out of which swing emerges" (Moten 2003, 27). All this is followed by Michael Ray's trumpet solo, who likewise attends carefully to Red Allen's original but distends it rhythmically and timbrally to a kind of nth degree. And on it goes: the frenetic energy of the performance continues to build; there's a moment near the end when it really does seem like things are going to fall apart, but then Sun Ra and band pull everything back into alignment to finish together.

Sun Ra's "Temporal Drag"

There is a long tradition in jazz of riffing on earlier recordings, of signifying on, of re-presenting, one's creative precursors. From the perspective of a queer temporality, these kinds of conscious genealogical expressions are lively events that remind us that every musical utterance is an expression of a vast constellation of real or fabulated pasts that constitute its ever-shifting genealogy. So, for example, when a saxophone player quotes a phrase from an iconic Charlie Parker recording, or a folk song or nursery rhyme, this

---

[21] This is a nice intertextual detail that expands and enriches Sun Ra's queer historiography: Henderson and Krupa worked together in Benny Goodman's orchestra. Sun Ra himself played with Henderson toward the end of the latter's career, which lends a touching gloss to the younger pianist's fabulated musical retellings.

might be an ironic gesture, but more often signals membership in a community marked in large part by such participatory significations. Likewise with jazz arrangers: new versions of canonic songs riff on specific details of their antecedents in ways that go beyond melody and harmony—for example, in certain kinds of ensemble distributions or chord voicings or idiosyncratic formal designs. As Tavia Nyong'o (2019, 4) suggests, "the 'changing same' of black aesthetics and expressivity may have always already been queer." Sun Ra's invaginative fabulations of Fletcher Henderson's music are different, though. Sun Ra and his Arkestra re-create the original arrangement in pretty much exactly its original form, but they performatively change it: by speeding up, by cartoonishly exaggerating aspects of its texture, groove, and improvisational impetus, by adding new musical strata that in turn reinterpret the original material, revealing or inventing new layers of signification. Sun Ra's performance of Fletcher Henderson is a drag show: an exhilarating camp exhibition.[22]

And here I would like to turn back to the question of Sun Ra's sexuality and why it might matter for an analysis of his music. Most accounts (see Stanley 2014) describe Sun Ra as asexual, and indeed, Sun Ra expressed an overt disinterest in sex.[23] Many of these same accounts, perhaps refusing to consider asexuality as a legitimate category, have simply assumed that Sun Ra was gay, but closeted (Murph 2016). Tim Stüttgen's (2014) more nuanced account reads an open range of expressive potentialities through which Sun Ra's queerness, or "quAre-ness" (following E. Patrick Johnson's [2005] analysis of the intersection of black, queer, and US southern identity), might be performed. I do not think it is necessary to pin down the precise nature of

---

[22] There are compelling reasons the framework of drag works for theorizing Sun Ra's positionality and performativity, as well as some ways the latter are inadequate to the concept. If we turn to the first robust theorization of drag (Newton [1972]1979), we find in Su Ra's presentation the flowing robes, jewelry, and other props, as well as the onstage comportment (which I described above as at once intense and aloof), the artist's wry wit and humor, and everywhere what David Halperin (2012, 139) describes as "transgression of the pragmatic conventions of discursive behavior"—in addition to what Esther Newton was troubled to see as a "tendency to laugh at situations that to [her] were horrifying or tragic" (Newton, 109; see Halperin, 138–40). A prime example of this can be seen in a famous scene from Sun Ra's *Space Is the Place* ([1974] 2003), in which a wryly smiling protagonist explains to a group of Black youth how neither he nor they are "real" in white America. While Newton's seminal work on drag remains foundational, it does reflect the epistemological limitations of its time, in that *all* drag queens are assumed straightforwardly to be homosexual men. To frame Sun Ra's (and his music's) performativity in Newton's terms therefore requires a small measure of metaphorical distancing.

[23] This is most clearly evidenced in an oft-cited letter Sun Ra wrote to the US National Service Board For Religious Objectors from 1942; see Szwed (1998, 41) and Stanley (2014, 37). See also Sun Ra's rumination on sex as a "gimmick," as "a lot of child stuff," and even as "a threat to the entire universe" (Sun Ra 2011, 4).

Sun Ra's sexuality, and at any rate, to perform this kind of hermeneutic micromanagement is to fix Sun Ra's sexuality as stable and specific, rather than contingent and malleable. Of course Sun Ra's identity is not exhausted by his sexuality, no more than it is by his Blackness. Furthermore, asexual is certainly a mode of being that qualifies as queer and brings into relief Eve Kosofsky Sedgwick's (1990) important point that object choice is far from the only or even the primary marker of sexual identity. I am drawn to a series of resonances around the word queer that open it beyond sexual identity, although I also take seriously the kinds of epistemological calls for sobriety that insist that queer does not simply get to mean anything we want it to mean. But here are four (non-)definitions that are particularly relevant to the task at hand. First David Halperin (1995, 62): "whatever is at odds with the normal, the legitimate, the dominant . . . [queer] describes a horizon of possibility." Then Lisa Duggan (1992, 11), for whom queer carries first of all "the promise of new meanings, new ways of thinking and acting politically." Third, Sarah Hankins (2014, 87), extending Sherrie Tucker's (2008) Foucauldian resistance to the naturalizing move of sexual categorization: "As Sherrie Tucker writes, 'queer means taking nothing to be natural or normal'; to this I would add that queer assumes answers are always contingent and significations always malleable." And fourth, Muñoz again, whose queer *disidentification* (Muñoz 1999) amounts to an ongoing series of performative acts that resist ideology, reconfigure the self, and subvert binary categories. For Muñoz, disidentification is not an eschewal of dominant power structures or discourses, but a series of actions that work within and dissemble or queer those discourses. For Sun Ra, every such action is a performance that reinscribes his own identity and that of the world with which he interacts: he rewrites histories in order to open new horizons of possibility, he invents new etymologies to map out new meanings and new ways of thinking and doing, and he deconstructs dominant narratives about jazz, Black American identity, world history and religion, even physics and mathematics. There is hardly a discursive thread that Sun Ra does not strategically disidentify with by getting in the middle of it and working out his "equations" that problematize old meanings and construct new ones.

The most important of Sun Ra's acts are in the *aesthetic* realm—in music, poetry, stage, and costume. As Muñoz ([2009] 2019, 1) writes,

> Often we can glimpse the worlds proposed and promised by queerness in the realm of the aesthetic. The . . . queer aesthetic, frequently contains

blueprints and schemata of a forward-dawning futurity. . . . Queerness is . . . performative because it is not simply a being but a doing for and toward the future. Queerness is essentially about the rejection of a here and now and an insistence on potentiality or concrete possibility for another world.

John Murph (2016, 266) enlists these opening thoughts from *Cruising Utopia* in order specifically to theorize elements of Sun Ra's attire, stage presence, and poetry as quintessentially queer. Hankins (2014, 87) similarly turns to the aesthetic as she theorizes a new hermeneutics of musical meaning:

> lived queer experience is itself a hermeneutic, literally an art of interpretation, an ongoing negotiation of selfhood vis-à-vis an omnipresent social text. However, because this text offers mostly inadequate or hostile representations of queerness, queer experiential hermeneutics is necessarily improvisational. A queer relationship with music, then, is fundamentally disoriented with regard to stable or specific musical meanings. [It] disrupts and reworks received macroaccounts of meaning and arrives at no clear declaration or terminus.

Sun Ra's reading of history—as proto-Afrofuturist *and* as what Elizabeth Freeman (2010, 63) would call the iterative performativity of a "temporal drag"—is a dissensual, disruptive act. Sun Ra's creative retelling of history is very much like Deleuze's practice of fabulation, which we see in the latter's creative and strategic readings of the words of his philosophical forebears and the ways he stages the history of philosophy as a dramatic reenactment that eschews the representational personae of State (or straight) narratives.

Nikki Sullivan offers a marvelous example of fabulation that relates to Sun Ra's own storytelling, centered around the character LaMiranda from Nigel Finch's *Stonewall* film. LaMiranda, after describing a version of the old New York story about how everyone has a story, concludes wryly with "Well this is *my* legend, honey, OK?," to which Sullivan (2003, 26) responds:

> This sort of logic . . . pervades the film and recasts history as perspectival, heterogeneous, always-already fictionalized, and in short, "fabulous." History itself becomes a fabulous fable (or a myriad of often camp and contradictory fabulous fables) that no longer conforms to the (hetero)

normative demand for a clear definition of, and distinction between, the real and the unreal, fact and fiction.[24]

This is Sun Ra's uncanny relation with history too: history is always in flux, past and future are always out of joint. Like LaMiranda, Sun Ra puts a trickster gloss on everything he says, blurring truth and fiction in ways that problematize the very notion of truth. But as fabulated and fabulous as Sun Ra's words and actions seem, he performs his interaction with an actual world. As Deleuze and Guattari (1987, 311) write, "to improvise is to join with the world. . . . " Sun Ra's music exemplifies an ontology of world-joining: he performatively seizes the materials and contexts of the world and transforms and transcends them. His is already a queer way of world-joining; those materials and contexts are already being redeployed and reimagined; enacting their own queer positionalities with respect to their own pasts, futures, and creatively disoriented presents.

This is one reason that Sun Ra and his music are particularly fertile spaces for beginning to imagine a queer music theory. A music theory that fabulates alongside its subject, in doing so helping to reveal some of the fabulatory nature of the latter, but also co-creating with it, playfully and provocatively. (Again, I have a sense that music theory does this more often than we sometimes think, which Marion Guck makes overt in her characterization of analysis as fiction[ing]). Sun Ra is something of a philosophical antecedent to, and should certainly be read alongside, the many individual Black musical avant-gardes that emerged in the middle of the 1960s, including Cecil Taylor, Anthony Braxton, Muhal Richard Abrams, and many others. While Taylor, Braxton, and Abrams strove to develop rigorously individualized music-compositional and -improvisational languages, each effecting its own radical break with the discourses of post-bebop jazz (even forcefully disidentifying with the word jazz itself), Sun Ra worked largely within the formal, harmonic, and timbral structures of jazz. So while Braxton might ironically dismantle and reassemble Charlie Parker's music, his primary project has been to constitute a wholly new and personal music-compositional and -improvisational ontology that situates complexly within an array of historical and cultural arcs, but that enacts a series of clear and unimpeachable breaks within those arcs. Sun Ra, on the other hand, continually negotiates

---

[24] See also Freeman (2010, xxi): "Queers have, it is fair to say, fabricated, confabulated, told fables, and done so fabulously."

with his historical and socio-cultural contexts, in ways at once playful and utterly serious. (Compare this to the incommensurable images that began this chapter.) I suggested that Sun Ra's engagement with his musical pasts proceeds as an ongoing series of drag acts, each at once a loving homage and a campily exaggerated re-presentation that transforms his source material into an utterly original and personal expression. All of this is performative and represents a series of specifically musical instantiations of Sun Ra's larger mytho-scientific project. To paraphrase Sarah Hankins (2014, 91), "the raw materials of [Sun Ra's] queer ethos, and [its] performative play, are those of the power structure itself."

"There is no place for you to go / But the in or the out. / Try the out" (Sun Ra 1993[25]). Sun Ra's invitation from a 1973 live performance should be read multiply: out as exteriority, projecting beyond the self, and "out" in the sense jazz musicians use, as "taking it out"; escaping the frame of the formal or harmonic boundaries of the song. Both mark what Paul Youngquist (2016) calls "playing with the beyond," which describes how Sun Ra performs his sources, finding the differentiating movements within them and scrambling them to see what else they are capable of expressing. In an analysis of Sun Ra's verbal "equations," Youngquist describes four techniques—association and permutation, assonance and rearrangement—that Sun Ra uses in his equations, all means of manipulating words to create new etymological connections, new ranges of potential meanings, and new strategies. From this perspective, Sun Ra's texts perfectly encapsulate what Elizabeth Freeman (2010, xix) describes as a "minor literature [that] dislodges referentiality by overloading the dominant language to the point of explosion via neologism, hypotaxis, or semantic overpacking."

I assert that Sun Ra's music functions as an overloaded neologistic, semantically replete text in precisely the same way, and that indeed it *must* if we are to understand Sun Ra's engagement with sound as the opening onto what Amiri Baraka (1968, 135) describes as "the final sum of what we call being." It is therefore crucial to investigate Sun Ra's music, using the tools of a queer music theory, and find in it the kinds of recodings and queerings that are everywhere evident in the equations of his speech, prose, and poetry. And that just like with the latter, we can find in Sun Ra's "tone science" analytical pathways that reveal hermeneutically significant associations and permutations, assonances and rearrangements. For just one example, as we

[25] Also in Youngquist 2016, 76.

have started to see in our engagement with "Queer Notions," Sun Ra's fabulation of Fletcher Henderson functions as what Paul Youngquist (2016) calls a "sound foundation," referring at once to the importance of a profound understanding of one's sources and to the fugitive quality of sound as an elusive but fecund ontological ground. According to Youngquist, sound is a strange, fugitive artistic medium that lacks materiality: sound "disperses as it occurs. As sound happens, it passes away. . . . Sound introduces a hint of dissolution into the heart of creative activity, an undertone of annihilation that tugs toward silence" (80–81). He examines a brief line from Sun Ra's poem "The Sound I Hear" (Sun Ra 2005, 169): "The sounds I hear are nothing / They seem to be but are not." This turns out to be one of Sun Ra's clearest and most effective examples of his "equations" that conjoin philosophical rumination with an activist recipe for the material transformation of the world. Younquist continues, "so the nothing of sound is no simple absence but an active force that transforms the present" (81). Sound "annihilates the present world" by "untuning" it, "open[ing] the present to new possibilities." Sun Ra's poem concludes with a queer conflation of temporal affects, dragging relational times through one another and toward his "alter-future":

> . . . These sometimes bewilderments,
> These haunting memories
> Yesterdays
> And yesterday's now
> How unlike the days I would to be
> How unlike the days I would to horizon-be the future.
> But this is the alter-future I speak of.
> The alternative is the key. (Sun Ra 2005, 169)

* * *

As Hankins (2014, 88) insists, "there is, quite simply, no drag performance absent a deep critical hermeneutic; sociohistorical 'questions' are not 'distracting' or marked by 'metaphysical distance' but rather gripping, immediate, and granular." Sun Ra's drag show is more than an exhilarating, slightly absurd ride. It is also a series of associations and permutations of its source materials, a performative equation that decodes Henderson's swing-era syntaxes and meanings in a provocative reimagining of history, of what could be. It is also a robust engagement with material historical sources

(Henderson's music), with all of its resonances: from jazz's place in the histories of US race relations to whatever it might mean to be reimagining swing-era big band music (as "quotidian gestures . . . laden with potentiality"; Muñoz 2019, 87) in a period when that music was definitely not "cool." This is what *matters* about Sun Ra's performative re-presentation, and it amounts to a way in, an adumbration of Sun Ra's complex, creative relationship with historical trajectories and material sources. To read Sun Ra's Fletcher Henderson as a drag show is to deliberately and strategically read Sun Ra's fabulated biographies into his music, to consider the ways that a musical utterance can express its pasts while also critically interpreting them. This seems to be what Sun Ra means by tone science, or when he suggests that we can "teleport the whole planet through music" (Sun Ra 2003).

References

Ahmed, Sara. 2006. *Queer Phenomenology: Orientations, Objects, Others*. Durham: Duke University Press.

Anzaldúa. Gloria. 2012 [1987]. *Borderlands/La Frontera: The New Mestiza*. San Francisco: Aunt Lute Books.

Attali, Jacques. 1985. *Noise: The Political Economy of Music*, trans. Brian Massumi. Minneapolis: University of Minnesota Press.

Baraka, Amiri. 1968. *Black Music*. Brooklyn: Akashic Books.

Benadon, Fernando. 2006. "Slicing the Beat: Jazz Eighth-Notes as Expressive Microrhythms." *Ethnomusicology* 50, no. 1: 73–98.

Bergson, Henri. 1977. *The Two Sources of Morality and Religion*. Translated by R. Ashley Audra and Cloudesley Brereton. Notre Dame: University of Notre Dame Press.

Bogue, Ronald. 2010. *Deleuzian Fabulation and the Scars of History*. Edinburgh: Edinburgh University Press.

Boretz, Benjamin. 2003 [1992]. "Experiences With No Names." In *Being About Music: Textworks 1960–2003*, Vol. 2, edited by J. K. Randall, 338–352. Red Hook: Open Space.

Brett, Philip. 2006 [1994]. "Musicality, Essentialism, and the Closet." In *Queering the Pitch: The New Gay and Lesbian Musicology*, 2nd edition, edited by Philip Brett, Elizabeth Wood, and Gary C. Thomas, 9–26. New York: Routledge.

Brown, Wendy. 2006. "American Nightmare: Neoliberalism, Neoconservatism, and De-Democratization." *Political Theory* 34, no. 6: 690–714.

Butterfield, Matthew. 2011. "Why Do Jazz Musicians Swing Their Eighth Notes?" *Music Theory Spectrum* 33, no. 1: 3–26.

Cohn, Richard. 1992. "Schenker's Theory, Schenkerian Theory: Pure Unity or Constructive Conflict?" *Indiana Theory Review* 13, no. 1: 1–19.

Corbett, John. 1994. *Extended Play: Sounding Off from John Cage to Dr. Funkenstein*. Durham: Duke University Press.

Cusick, Suzanne. 1994. "Feminist Theory, Music Theory, and the Mind/Body Problem." *Perspectives of New Music* 32, no. 1: 8–27.

Cusick, Suzanne. 2006 [1994]. "On a Lesbian Relationship with Music: A Serious Effort Not to Think Straight." In ·Queering the Pitch: The New Gay and Lesbian Musicology, 2nd edition, edited by Philip Brett, Elizabeth Wood, and Gary C. Thomas, 67–83. New York: Routledge.

Deleuze, Gilles. 1983. Nietzsche and Philosophy. Translated by Hugh Tomlinson. London: Althone.

Deleuze, Gilles. 1993. The Fold: Leibniz and the Baroque, trans. Tom Conley. Minneapolis: University of Minnesota Press.

Deleuze, Gilles. 1995. Negotiations 1972–1990. Translated by Martin Joughin. New York: Columbia University Press.

Deleuze, Gilles. 1997. Essays Clinical and Critical. Translated by Daniel W. Smith and Michael A. Greco. Minneapolis: University of Minnesota Press.

Deleuze, Gilles, and Félix Guattari. 1983. Anti-Oedipus: Capitalism and Schizophrenia. Translated by Robert Hurley, Mark Seem, and Helen R. Lane. Minneapolis: University of Minnesota Press.

Deleuze, Gilles, and Félix Guattari. 1986. Kafka: Toward a Minor Literature. Translated by Dana Polan. Minneapolis: University of Minnesota Press.

Deleuze, Gilles, and Félix Guattari. 1987. A Thousand Plateaus: Capitalism and Schizophrenia. Translated by Brian Massumi. Minneapolis: University of Minnesota Press.

Deleuze, Gilles, and Félix Guattari. 1994. What Is Philosophy? Translated by Hugh Tomlinson and Graham Burrell. New York: Columbia University Press.

Derrida, Jacques. 1979. "Living On / Border Lines." In Deconstruction and Criticism, edited by Harold Bloom, Paul de Man, Jacques Derrida, Geoffrey H. Hartman, and J. Hillis Miller, 75–176. New York: Routledge.

Derrida, Jacques. 1983. "The Principle of Reason: The University in the Eyes of Its Pupils." Diacritics 13, no. 3: 2–20.

Dubiel, Joseph. 1992. "Senses of Sense-Making." Perspectives of New Music 30, no. 1: 210–221.

Dubiel, Joseph. 1997. "On Getting Deconstructed." Journal of Musicology 15, no. 3: 308–315.

Duggan, Lisa. 1992. "Making it Perfectly Queer." Socialist Review 22, no. 1: 11–31.

Edwards, Brent Hayes. 2017. "The Race for Space: Sun Ra's Poetry." In Epistrophies: Jazz and the Literary Imagination. Cambridge: Harvard University Press.

Foucault, Michel. 1977. "Nietzsche, Genealogy, History." In Language, Counter-Memory, Practice, edited by Donald F. Bouchard, 139–164. Ithaca: Cornell University Press.

Foucault, Michel. 1990 [1978]. The History of Sexuality, Vol. 1. An Introduction. Translated by Robert Hurley. New York: Vintage Books.

Freeman, Elizabeth. 2010. Time Binds: Queer Temporalities, Queer Histories. Durham: Duke University Press.

Gill, John. 1995. Queer Noises: Male and Female Homosexuality in Twentieth Century Music. Minneapolis: University of Minnesota Press.

Gleason, Scott. 2013. "Princeton Theory's Problematics." PhD Dissertation, Columbia University.

Guck, Marion. 1994. "Analytic Fictions." Music Theory Spectrum 16, no. 2: 217–30.

Guck, Marion. 1997. "Music Loving, or the Relationship with the Piece." Journal of Musicology 15, no. 3: 343–52.

Halberstam, Judith. 2005. *In a Queer Time and Place: Transgender Bodies, Subcultural Lives*. New York: New York University Press.

Halperin, David. 1995. *Saint Foucault: Towards a Gay Hagiography*. Oxford: Oxford University Press.

Halperin, David. 2003. *How to Be Gay*. Cambridge: The Belknap Press of Harvard University.

Hankins, Sarah. 2014. "Queer Relationships with Music and an Experiential Hermeneutics for Musical Meaning." *Women and Music: A Journal of Gender and Culture* 18: 83–104.

Haraway, Donna. 1988. "Situated Knowledges: The Science Question in Feminism and the Privilege of Partial Perspective." *Feminist Studies* 14, no. 3: 575–99.

Heble, Ajay. 2010. "Why Can't We Go Somewhere There?: Sun Ra, Improvisation, and the Imagination of Future Possibilities." *Canadian Theatre Review* 143: 98–100.

Henderson, Fletcher. 2011 [1961]. *A Study in Frustration (The Fletcher Henderson Story)*. Essential Jazz Classics EJC55511.

Johnson, E. Patrick. 2005. " 'Quare' Studies, Or (Almost) Everything I Know About Queer Studies I Learned From My Grandmother." In *Black Queer Studies: A Critical Anthology*, edited by E. Patrick Johnson and Mae G. Henderson, 124–60. Durham: Duke University Press.

Keeling, Kara. 2019. *Queer Times, Black Futures*. New York: New York University Press.

Kielian-Gilbert, Marianne. 2005–6. "*Meta-Variations* and the Art of Engaging Music." *Perspectives of New Music* 43, no. 2–44, no. 1: 6–34.

Korsyn, Kevin. 2003. *Decentering Music: A Critique of Contemporary Musical Research*. Oxford: Oxford University Press.

Le Guin, Elisabeth. 2005. *Boccherini's Body: An Essay in Carnal Musicology*. Berkeley: University of California Press.

Lee, Gavin. 2020. "Queer Music Theory." *Music Theory Spectrum* 42, no. 1: 143–153.

Lochhead, Judy. 2015. *Reconceiving Structure in Contemporary Music: New Tools in Music Theory and Analysis*. New York: Routledge.

Marx, Karl. 1999. *The Eighteenth Brumaire of Louis Bonaparte*. Translated by Friedrich Engels and Saul K. Padover. [Progress Publishers] Marx/Engels Internet Archive.

Maus, Fred Everett. 1988. "Music as Drama." *Music Theory Spectrum* 10: 56–73.

Maus, Fred Everett. 1993. "Masculinist Discourse in Music Theory." *Perspectives of New Music* 31, no. 2: 264–293.

Maus, Fred Everett. 2004. "Sexual and Musical Categories." In *The Pleasure of Modernist Music: Listening, Meaning, Intention, Ideology*, edited by Arved Ashby, 153–175. Rochester: University of Rochester Press.

McClary, Susan. 2006 [1994]. "Constructions of Subjectivity in Schubert's Music." In *Queering the Pitch: The New Gay and Lesbian Musicology*, 2nd edition, edited by Philip Brett, Elizabeth Wood, and Gary C. Thomas, 205–33. New York: Routledge.

Moten, Fred. 2003. *In the Break: The Aesthetics of the Black Radical Tradition*. Minneapolis: University of Minnesota Press.

Moten, Fred, and Stefano Harvey. 2013. *The Undercommons: Fugitive Planning and Black Study*. London: Minor Compositions.

Mugge, Robert. 1999 [1980]. *Sun Ra: A Joyful Noise*. Winstar CD.

Muñoz, José Esteban. 1999. *Disidentifications: Queers of Color and the Performance of Politics*. Minneapolis: University of Minnesota Press.

Muñoz, José Esteban. 2019 [2009]. *Cruising Utopia: The Then and There of Queer Futurity.* 10th Anniversary Edition, with a new Foreword by Joshua Chambers-Letson, Tavia Nyong'o, and Ann Pellegrini. New York: New York University Press.

Murph, John. 2016. "Exploring Queer Notions Inside Sun Ra's Outer Space Ways." In *Gender and Identity in Jazz*, edited by Wolfram Knauer, 263–275. Darmstädter Beiträge zur Jazzforschung 14.

Newton, Esther. 1979 [1972]. *Mother Camp: Female Impersonators in America.* Chicago: University of Chicago Press.

Nyong'o, Tavia. 2013. "Queer Hip Hop and its Dark Precursors." *Palimpsest: A Journal on Women, Gender, and the Black International* 2, no. 2: 144–146.

Nyong'o, Tavia. 2019. *Afro-Fabulations: The Queer Drama of Black Life.* New York: New York University Press.

Oliveros, Pauline. 1984. *Software for people: Collected writings 1963–80.* Sharon: Smith Publications.

Östersjö, Stefan. 2008. *Shut Up 'n' Play!: Negotiating the Musical Work.* Lund: Malmö Academies of Performing Arts, Lund University.

Randall, James K. 1995 [1972]. *Compose Yourself: A Manual for the Young.* Red Hook: Open Space.

Scherzinger, Martin. 2002. "Feminine/Feminist? In Quest of Names with No Experiences (Yet)." In *Postmodern Music/Postmodern Thought*, edited by Judith Lochhead and Joseph Auner, 141–73. New York: Routledge.

Sedgwick, Eve Kosofsky. 1990. *Epistemology of the Closet.* Berkeley: University of California Press.

Stanley, Thomas. 2014. *The Execution of Sun Ra: The Mysterious Tale of a Dark Body Sent to Earth to Usher in an Unprecedented Era of Cosmic Regeneration and Happiness*, Vol. 2. Waddy: Wasteland Press.

Stover, Chris. 2016. "Musical Bodies: Corporeality, Emergent Subjectivity, and Improvisational Spaces." *M/C Journal* 19, no. 1. https://journal.media-culture.org.au/index.php/mcjournal/article/view/1066.

Stüttgen, Tim. 2014. *In a Qu*A*are Time and Place: Post-Slavery Temporalities, Blaxploitation, and Sun Ra's Afrofuturism Between Intersectionality and Heterogeneity.* Berlin: b-books.

Sullivan, Nikki. 2003. *A Critical Introduction to Queer Theory.* New York: New York University Press.

Sun Ra. 1993 [1973]. *Concert for the Comet Kohoutek* ESP CD 3033.

Sun Ra. 2003 [1974]. *Space Is the Place.* Plexifilm DVD.

Sun Ra. 2005. *Immeasurable Equation: Collected Works*, Vol. 1. Chandler: Phaelos.

Sun Ra. 2009 [1971]. *Sun Ra—Helsinki 1971—The Complete Concert and Interview.* Transparency 0314.

Sun Ra. 2011. *This Planet is Doomed: The Science Fiction Poetry of Sun Ra.* New York: Kicks Books.

Swiboda, Marcel. 2007. "Re Interpretations: Sun Ra's Egyptian Inscriptions." *Parallax* 13, no. 2: 93–106.

Szwed, John. 1998. *Space Is the Place: The Lives and Times of Sun Ra.* New York: Da Capo Press.

Tucker, Sherrie. 2008. "When Did Jazz Go Straight? A Queer Question for Jazz Studies." *Critical Studies in Improvisation / Études critiques en improvisation* 4 no. 2.

Wood, Elizabeth. 2006 [1994]. "Sapphonics." In *Queering the Pitch: The New Gay and Lesbian Musicology*, second edition, edited by Philip Brett, Elizabeth Wood, and Gary C. Thomas, 27–66. New York: Routledge.

Youngquist, Paul. 2016. *A Pure Solar World: Sun Ra and the Birth of Afrofuturism.* Austin: University of Texas Press.

7

The Chronographic Fallacy of Unilinear Music Theory, Or, Un(Re)productive Temporality in *Dichterliebe*

Gavin S. K. Lee

There has always been something profoundly queer about the way I relate to *Dichterliebe*. From the haze of memories of my time spent as a graduate student at Jesus College, Oxford, I recall an episode late at night when a friend and I took a stroll around the tranquil university campus and ended up in the graduate common room listening to Schumann. With the first song *Im wunderschönen Monat Mai* wafting indeterminately through the relative keys A major and F# minor, the opening of *Dichterliebe* embodies none of the urgency—familiar from Burnham's interpretation of Beethoven (1995)—that would ensure the accomplishment of heroic feats. Instead, the poet languishes with love alongside premonitions of suffering, with euphoria and eroticism alongside the denial of anguish, and with archaic images of joy juxtaposed with plaintive utterances—a smorgasbord of affective pathways that would ultimately lead not to the final goals of marriage, family, and reproduction, but to alienation from grief in the form of the coffin within which is buried love and pain, in the final song *Die alten, bösen Lieder*.

Deviating from the linear life trajectories embodied in poetry and music of works such as *Frauenliebe und -Leben*, the male protagonists of iconic German song cycles have often trodden along meandering affective paths of "failure" to marry and produce offspring, life goals that were of great consequence in nineteenth-century Germany as these were the means by which property was consolidated in genealogical lines. Against the instrumental functions embedded in life events, the alternative affective routes of the German Lied embodied the Romantic ideal of an interiority created to

Gavin S. K. Lee, *The Chronographic Fallacy of Unilinear Music Theory, Or, Un(Re)productive Temporality in Dichterliebe* In: *Queer Ear*. Edited by: Gavin S. K. Lee, Oxford University Press. © Oxford University Press 2023. DOI: 10.1093/oso/9780197536766.003.0008

counter the rational, financial purposes of heteronormative kinship.[1] The transhistorical common ground between the different bachelors—that in *Dichterliebe*, on the one hand, and the young graduate students roaming a university campus late night, on the other—is the patriarchal assurance that women are better suited for conventional family life, with women's bodies subject to a battery of legal, cultural, and physical controls and threats, including the threat of sexual assault: to discern this connection between the two contexts, simply consider the freedom of the bachelor students who give not a second thought to their personal safety, on the one hand, and the freedom outside of marriage "enjoyed" (albeit reluctantly) by the protagonist of *Dichterliebe*. Yet nineteenth-century women found ways to resist oppressive forces, sometimes assuming traditionally masculine roles, as Clara Schumann did in her professional and family life (as bread winner, with her composer husband given to bouts of depression and mental instability). From the perspective of normative gender roles, both Robert and Clara are in a sense as queer as the unproductive bachelor of *Dichterliebe*.

There is a transcultural dimension to the relentless movement of queering as well. As an adolescent of color growing up in homophobic surroundings in Singapore, I encountered *Dichterliebe* in the late 1990s at around the same time as I discovered the writings of gay Americans (Edmund White, Paul Monette) in the "Gender Studies" section of my favorite bookshop. I watched MTV playing videos of Backstreet Boys, Boyzone, and other boy bands, and I met up with local gay Singaporeans who I had chatted with through IRC ("Internet Relay Chat," essentially the pre–smart phone Grindr). This was how I assembled a queer life out of scraps in a country where the gay sexual act is criminalized. In that context, *Dichterliebe* became an escape hatch leading to a world beyond the boundaries of my own suffocating context. But I also knew intimately the anguish and grief in the song cycle, as well as the dream-like opening that resonated so much with the hermetic life into which I had sealed myself—the closet that protected my secret. Whatever elements of cultural imperialism that are intertwined with Western art music in the context of European colonization (Singapore was a British colony), and with *Dichterliebe* as a canonic work from that repertoire, are also part of my protective walls of that time.

---

[1] See Kramer (1998, 29) for elaboration of how the German Lied embodied a Romantic interiority against the rational conception of marriage.

In this chapter, I explore the opacity (from a heteronormative perspective) of *Dichterliebe*, articulating its queer temporality that deviates from the reproductive life. Two spheres of temporality had emerged in the longue durée of modernity stretching back to the beginnings of industrialization (Freeman 2010, 5). On the one hand, there was the linear, teleological temporality of the inter-related spheres of work, industrial capitalism and the property-protecting nation-state. On the other hand, the inter-related spheres of domesticity, tradition, and the sacred were temporally cyclic and in that sense timeless or eternal—even as the hands of the life clock continually moved and indicated progression along the appropriate timeline from love to marriage and reproduction (as in *Frauenliebe und -Leben*).[2] From one perspective, the entire edifice of this double time is constituted by and co-constitutive of modernity and capitalism and thus utterly compromised. In response, queer theory has focused on the avant-garde that is "ahead" of the heteronormative status quo, and on an "antiformalism" that disrupts present social forms in anticipation of the future (Freeman 2010, xiii).[3] In contrast, Elizabeth Freeman switches from a modality of negation ("anti-") to one of assembling "cultural debris" (xiii), anchoring her work in the unrealized promise of the political projects of the 1960s and 1970s (historical social "forms"). In Freeman's work, queer temporality emerges when conceptual tinder is applied to archaic movements, shedding light on tangential, contradictory, deviated, and otherwise non-normative paths that emerge within the double time of modernity. Containing (cyclic/linear) temporal debris that may seem familiar but is repositioned aslant and askance, queer temporality is a deviation from the macro temporal cyclicity and linearity identified by Karol Berger (2007) as relational polarities at the emergence of modernity, and also from the entwinement of cyclicity and linearity demonstrated by Bettina Varwig (2012).

In keeping with the multiple valences of debris, I regard *Dichterliebe* as fundamentally queer because of my own adolescent transcultural history, and yet its (to me) queer features are also part of heteronormative structures, resulting in an ambiguity that is very much in keeping with the opening song and with the complexity of any cultural

---

[2] Freeman's argument is made in relation to the United States but the presence of double time in Europe is easily evidenced from, e.g., the stazaic cyclicity of domestic-leaning Biedermeier poetry frequently set by Schubert and Schumann, versus, e.g., the masculine musical linearity in Beethoven's public-facing symphonies (Burnham 1995). This suggests that temporal cyclicity and linearity are available for nineteenth-century composers to draw on in their negotiation of private/public.

[3] Freeman cites Edelman 2004 as an example of "antiformalist" queer theory.

milieu.[4] There is a strong resonance between the regular cyclicity of Heine's stanzaic form, on the one hand, and the conservatism and "smug" domesticity of the Biedermeier generation of early to mid-nineteenth-century Germany, on the other (Brown 2004, 24). In contrast, the earlier poetry of Jena and Heidelberg Romanticism at the turn of the nineteenth century had disrupted the strophic musicality of simple stanzas with structural complexity (with Baroque forms, complex word play, elaborate rhyme, etc.); for instance, Johann Ludwig Tieck's *Abend* (for which there is an incomplete musical setting by Schubert, D. 645, 1819) comprises stanzas and lines of varying lengths. Yet the cyclicity of *Im wunderschönen Monat Mai*—as seen in its stanzaic form, and in the cliched references to spring (flowers, birds) that evoke the cycle of seasons—is arguably belied by an underlying irony that trivializes the extreme conventionality of the poem (Brown 2004, 25).

Irony lends itself as a plausible reading of *Im wunderschönen Monat Mai* because of Heine's famous *Stimmungsbrechung* (breaking of the tone) found near the end of a poem, in which the entire meaning of the foregoing text changes with a reversal. Within the two four-line stanzas of *Wenn ich in deine Augen seh'* (*Dichterliebe* no. 4), the initial promise of the curative powers of love turns into bitter weeping (Table 7.1). This transformation is effected through the simple device of negation, with the word "but" (*doch*) placed at the start of the third line in each stanza. In the first stanza, the negation takes the form of a kiss that completely heals the poet (from his suffering and grief). In the parallel position in the second stanza, however, the negation marks a pivot away from "heavenly bliss" (line 6) such that the very utterance of "doch" (beginning of line 7) changes the entire meaning of the poem. An intense foreboding is introduced in the third line ("But when you say: I love you!"), leading to the last line in which the poet weeps.

According to Adorno (1968, 150), Heine's irony is rooted in the Jewish poet's alienation from an intolerant Germany. During the period that Heine was working on the collection of sixty-five poems *Lyrisches Intermezzo* (from which Schumann selected initially twenty for *Dichterliebe*, before four songs were eliminated), the poet was expelled from the University of Göttingen for antisemitic reasons, leading him to declare that "Everything German disgusts me . . . The German language splits my ears" (Heine 1972, 50). Read against the obstruction of Heine's life path and his exclusion from

---

[4] See Lee 2018 for an exploration of ambiguity as an analytic in studies of gender, sexuality, and popular music.

Table 7.1 Bifurcation of temporalities of fantasy and reality in *Wenn ich in deine Augen seh'*

Wenn ich in deine Augen seh', So schwindet all' mein Leid und Weh'; Doch wenn ich küsse deinen Mund, So werd' ich ganz und gar gesund.	Fantasy (Graph 1 in G major)
Wenn ich mich lehn' an deine Brust, Kommt's über mich wie Himmelslust; Doch wenn du sprichst: ich liebe dich! So muss ich weinen bitterlich.	Reality (Graph 2 in E minor)
	Collision of G major musical fantasy with textual reality of bitter tears (Convergence of Graphs 1 & 2)

German identity, the break in *Stimmungsbrechung* becomes an expression of what Sara Ahmed theorizes as queer phenomenology (Ahmed 2006, 113). Whereas an orient*ation* (toward, e.g., the *Orient*) broadly captures the privilege of the majority (e.g., Western orientalists) to access and organize one's world, "*dis*orientation" (4) is experienced by those like Heine who are excluded, disempowered, and alienated.

The disorientating irony unleashed in lines 7–8 of *Wenn ich in deine Augen seh'* causes the foregoing text to assume a different hue—we now realize that suffering and grief (line 2) did not really vanish with a simple look from the beloved, and the healing kiss (line 4) is the product of a one-sided fantasy. What happens temporally speaking is a bifurcation into two histories: a fantasy and a reality. Musically, Schumann captures the bifurcation by pivoting from G major (with tonicization of the subdominant) in stanza 1 to E minor (lines 5–6) and A minor (line 7) in stanza 2, before returning to G major in the final line, which is not, however, a simple return to fantasy. Although the melody of lines 4 and 8 are similar (with a stepwise descent to scale degree 1 of C major and G major respectively), line 8 expresses the denial of the poet who emotes "bitter tears" with a bravado (continued in the next song *Ich grolle nicht*) that belies reality. Thus lines 4 and 8's melodic cyclicity, which would bespeak of romantic and eventual domestic contentment, is undercut by disorientation sitting at the heart of a song that appears to be unified from a purely musical perspective. As exemplified in Lauri Suurpää's graph (1996, 111), *Wenn ich in deine Augen seh'* can be read as fulfilling the Schenkerian dictum that a tonal work unfolds a single chord that anchors the surface features. In contrast with the perspective that Lied can be understood in a purely musical manner (Ferris 2000, 50), however, I argue that a proper reading of music and text will lead us to an interpretation of irreducible ambivalence that makes unified graphs for many songs untenable. Those who are rejected, whether by race, gender, sexuality—or by a beloved—find ourselves caught between two worlds, gathering debris to chart non-normative detours that contain an eclectic mix of the desire for acceptance, along with the denial of rejection, as in *Wenn ich in deine Augen seh'* (in social terms, this translates as a complex mixture of strategic, inevitable, and perhaps delusional assimilation). Particularly for those around the world in constrictive social spaces that suppress emancipatory projects, it is from this detritus that queer world-making arises, sometimes from ironic shards.

In my view, Schuman's setting of the final line (bitter weeping in G major) gives rise to two interrelated but incompatible expressive meanings: (1) the fantasy of love in the G major of stanza 1, (2) the reality of heartbreak, with the E minor of lines 5–6 assuming a structural importance of such *expressive* magnitude that G major is displaced from a position of tonal primacy— an unorthodox reading that emphasizes the textual *Stimmungsbrechung* as much as or even over the music. Perhaps the best way to represent this temporal fissure is with two separate graphs—one for lines 1–4, a second one for lines 5–7 with E minor shown as the tonal center (with tonicization of the subdominant)—and line 8 shown as the collision of both graphs, with the G major tonality of fantasy sounding out bitter weeping. This representation that is weighted toward the poetry by the alienated poet Heine is of course unSchenkerian. Because of queer temporality (fissures, frays, reversals), *Wenn ich in deine Augen seh'* and *Dichterliebe* as a cycle remain opaque to linear-temporal trajectories, both of the heteronormative life (marriage and reproduction), and of the Schenkerian graph. Nowhere is this more obvious than in opposed Schenkerian renditions of the opening song, with C# ambiguously and continuously traversing the alternating tonal contexts of V/ F# minor and A major. On the one hand, there could be a complete erasure of ambiguity, with Schenker's own graph positioning the bass C# (V/ F# minor) as smoothly leading to the tonic A in the bass arpeggiation (via D and E; see Schenker [1935] 1979). On the other hand, Arthur Komar's Schenkerian graph has been described as "hover[ing] at the margins of musical coherence" (Ferris 2000, 52; Komar 1971). Komar's unorthodox graph shows a thrice repeated C# in the *Urlinie*, supported in the bass by a single stemmed white notehead A—without arpeggiation (other white noteheads)—that is sandwiched by two black-notehead C#s supporting

Example 7.1 Komar's graph for *Im wunderschönen Monat Mai*. © by kind permission of W. W. Norton & Company, Inc

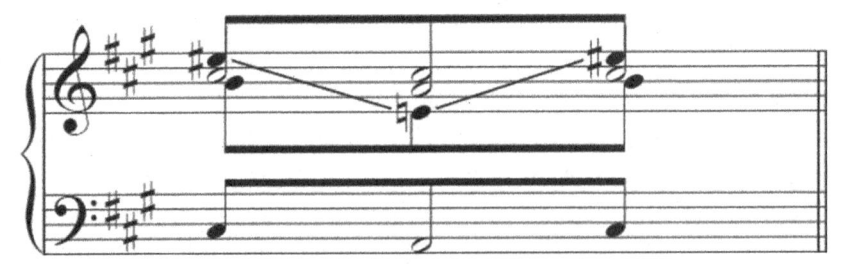

C# dominant 7th; octave traversing voice leading in the treble staff is shown between E#$_5$ – E$_4$ – E#$_5$ (Example 7.1).[5]

Temporal fraying may be hidden in Schenkerian tonal perfection in *Wenn ich in deine Augen seh'* (if one ignores the text), but results in queer-looking graphs for *Im wunderschönen Monat Mai*. In *Wenn ich in deine Augen seh'*, the E minor and A minor of lines 5–7 can reasonably be read as prolongations that are part of a circle of 5ths leading to the final perfect cadence in G major (vi – ii – V – I), and preceding the four ending chords, a conventionally linear-teleological Schenkerian trajectory can be discerned by reading the first stanza as prolongations of I and IV, leading smoothly to the circle of fifths. In contrast, the music of *Im wunderschönen Monat Mai* fully embodies the expressive aesthetic of Heine's *Stimmungsbrechung* even though the specific poem for this song does not contain explicit irony beyond the extreme conventionality of flowers and birds. A simple stanzaic cyclicity (as with *Wenn ich in deine Augen seh'*) is disrupted through the sandwiching and enveloping of the opening song's A major stanzas with the indeterminate V/F# minor of the piano pre-, inter-, and postlude that never lands on the tonic. Unlike *Wenn ich in deine Augen seh'*, however, the temporal fray of *Im wunderschönen Monat Mai* is fully sounded out in tonal meandering, with the poet's articulate moments (containing A major cadences) swimming in a cloud of pianistic indeterminacy (V/F# minor never reaches the tonic). In the prolepsis of the opening song, the eventual rejection and resultant disorientation of the poet (signaled clearly by *Wenn ich in deine Augen seh'*) is prefigured.

Im wunderschönen Monat Mai is perhaps the epitome of the temporal fray (fantasy of love in A major, rooted in a denial of the reality of heartbreak, embodied in the deferring of V/F# minor's tonic goal) that sounds out

---

[5] The analyses by Schenker and Komar are reproduced in Ferris 2000, 52–53.

disorienting social and romantic rejection. The key to Komar's Schenkerian "failure" outlined above is the two valences of rejection that can be discerned here: (1) the ejection of tonal ambiguity by the Schenkerian apparatus, and (2) the rejection by the beloved that leads away from the path of marriage and reproduction. In other words, the tonal meandering that arises from disorientation is delimited by the tendencies of Schenkerian theory toward tonal clarity. I concur with David Ferris, who points out that although the verbal exposition accompanying Schenkerian graphs goes some way in giving voice to the complexities of the temporal experience of music, the graphs themselves often have the effect of ironing out ambiguity[6]—rather than capturing the continuously changing configuration of Husserlian protention and retention (Husserl 1964, 44, 58) at every moment along the flow of musical time, resulting theoretically in an indefinite number of pasts, presents, and futures. In *Dichterliebe*, temporal frays are commonly found at both the surface and structural levels, and thus they produce a multitude of experiences of past, present, and future that are incongruent with a teleological reading aligned with the unilinear presentation in a musical score, with the seemingly incessant succession of beat upon beat and measure upon measure. If one reads a score teleologically, wherein the temporality of music adheres strictly to the horizontal dimension of a score, one succumbs to *chronographic fallacy*, defined as the false assumption of unilinear goal-directedness. The Schenkerian apparatus, which shares the unilinear temporal presentation of the musical score, is subject to chronographic fallacy, as I argue below.

Although the musical score represents relative (to the chosen tempo) rather than absolute, quantitative increments of time, the notes are aligned along an imaginary temporal line extending from the first to the last measure, and thus resonates with the modern, spatial, Newtonian conception of time marked by points (e.g., date, time) on a line that is subject to quantitative measurement (Scherzinger 2019, 242). In linear (non-logarithmic) graphs in general (including math graphs), a straight line is used to represent time, and this model of temporality applies to both musical scores and music-theoretical graphs in which time flows from left to right on the page. While this form of temporal-graphic representation is on one level a convention, there is a sense in which the pragmatic function of linear temporality in a score, that is, denoting notes to be played in sequence, becomes endowed

---

[6] Ferris makes the argument that Schenker's graph for *Aus meinen Thränen spriessen* in *Der freie Satz* (1935) "could not capture the ambiguity of Schumann's effect" as plainly as a verbal passage from the earlier *Harmonielehre* (1906) (Ferris 2000, 41).

with additional symbolic meaning in Schenkerian graphs. Referencing minority-rights discourse, Schenker argued that non-tonic tones do not have "equal rights" as the tonic (Ewell 2020, 4.5.2). This establishes a link between the hierarchy of humans and the hierarchy of tones—tones that are framed by the teleological linear-temporal progression of the bass arpeggiation and *Urlinie*—that is, the necessity that *Ursatz* notes lead inexorably back to the tonic. According to Schenker, blacks are supposedly incapable of producing genius music that elaborates the *Ursatz* (4.5.3). All this implies that the teleological linearity and chronographic dimension of Schenkerian theory have racist hues. (Note that *linear-temporal* progression refers to goal-directed movement from left to right on the page in time, rather than the conjunct motion of voice leading.)

With its tonal ambiguity and lack of harmonic teleology, *Im wunderschönen Monat Mai* cannot be incorporated in the "white racial frame" (Ewell 2020) of orthodox Schenkerian theory. Even the charting of the alternation of V/F# minor and A major is unacceptable from a Schenkerian perspective because of the teleological harmonic foundation of the theory—the alternation is non-developmental, unlike a cadential progression. *Im wunderschönen Monat Mai* is really a multiplicity composed of five sections (of V/F# minor and A major), since a reduction that treats the sections as prolongations of two key regions, V/F# minor and A major, would still be incompatible with an understanding of the disorientation that results precisely in the *veering* between two tonalities. This tonal indeterminacy points to two temporalities—A major sections inhabit the temporality of fantasy, which is continuously interrupted by the barely grasped reality of the non-cadencing V/F# minor. A hypothetical graphic representation that could perhaps capture this disorientation is one in which each of the five sections are placed on five different staves at differing heights on the page.

Schenker's and Komar's graphic analyses of *Im wunderschönen Monat Mai* reveal the chronographic fallacy of Schenkerian theory, wherein each consecutive note is regarded as placed along a *single* unbroken temporal line, and the flow from note to note is endowed with *causal* properties, with prior notes and passages necessarily giving rise to later ones. The unity of the temporal line is demonstrated with the inability of analysts to represent the temporal fray, which is the expressive crux of the song, for example, Komar's V/F# minor – A major – V/F# minor sandwich forces temporal fragments into the unilinear chronograph, squeezing multiplicity into a forced unity.

Hypothetically, if we were to attempt to represent both V/F# minor (i.e., C#) and A major as tonal anchors at a specific point in the graph (say, the beginning of the bass arpeggiation), pragmatic difficulties would arise. There would have to be the notation of either C#-A or A-C# in the bass consecutively (left to right), which would imply a false priority to the first note that would appear to be more prolonged; or, A-C# would have to be notated simultaneously, which would be misinterpreted as a unified A major. These hypothetical notations point to the inability of Schenkerian theory to accommodate more than one key (in the score) or more than one *Stufe* at any given temporal juncture—whereas multiplicity is the essence of tonal ambiguity, standing in contrast to the chronographic unilinearity of one *Stufe* necessarily leading to the next. Although tonal ambiguity is not necessarily indicative of temporal multiplicity, the latter *is* a feature of *Im wunderschönen Monat Mai* with its alternating tonalities, such that (failed) attempts to produce Schenkerian graphs reveals the presumed unities of Schenkerian theory—both (vertical) harmonic-tonal unity, and (horizontal) temporal unity (embodied in the single goal-directed motion of left to right in the graph).

In Freeman's terminology, Schenkerian theory is "chrononormative" (Freeman 2010), embodying a unilinear trajectory, which, if we take Schenker at his word, is tinged with not just racial but heteronormative hues, since it is reproduction that ensures the birth of German geniuses. The double time of nineteenth-century musical Europe comprises domestic cyclicity alongside a public linearity, both of which converged on reproduction, with the bliss of family life and children constituting the affective face of increasingly sophisticated, teleological strategies of population control administered by the state, which exercises "bio-power" (Foucault [1976] 1990, 140) over life and death, from the registering of a baby who grows up to pay taxes and earn tax deductions for marriage and reproduction, to public education of future workers and soldiers. One might say that there is no time for queer temporality (or for queers, for that matter) in the lean, efficient, linear, state-administered progression of life and work cycles that produce babies and workers. Chrononormativity as "the use of time to organize individual human bodies towards maximum productivity" (Freeman 2010, 3) exerts its force through the temporal fissure that structures cyclic domesticity *in relation to* unilinear, productivity-driven work, in a social sphere within which love and marriage lead to the reproduction of the workforce.

A contradiction is found between the efficiency of the unilinear conception of reproduction (from love to future workers), on the one hand, and the affective meanderings of the rejected suitor, on the other, just as the unilinearity of the Schenkerian chronograph contradicts "wasteful" harmonic or temporal ambiguities and multiplicities—rather, Schenkerian theory uses reduction to pare the music down to the *Ursatz*. In relation to this social and musical background, the unproductive temporality of *Dichterliebe* is profoundly queer.

The connection between temporal unilinearity in workforce-building pregnancies and in Schenkerian graphs that embody (German) genius is not as far-fetched as it may initially seem, with the common factor of delimitation guiding both a narrow interpretation of what counts as sex and what counts as genius. Sex came to be defined in the modern era (as early as the eighteenth century) as heterosexual vaginal intercourse, excluding so-called foreplay and non-productive sodomy (Abelove 2003, Morrison 1993). Same-sex relations that could not result in pregnancy came to be understood as the antithesis of the future (Edelman 2004), with the genealogical line truncated. With a parallel logic of reduction to the bare skeleton (just as sex is narrowed down), Schenkerian theory efficiently produces the *Ursatz*, which is cast in a biomusical frame that reveals the connection between Schenker's racist and reproductive discourses—both already discussed elsewhere without being fully integrated, both of which are anchored in the teleological reproductivity of human and musical wombs. Schenker understood background to foreground elaboration in the generative terms of a biological organism that "grows outwards from within" (Schenker [1935] 1979, 6), with diminution emerging from the "*Urlinie*'s motherly womb" (Schenker [1926] 2014, 22)—all of this is phrased in the characteristic language of procreation that is the central metaphor in Schenker's writings (Cook 2007, 277). Also organized around the principle of delimitation, Schenker's conception of race is reflected in his conception of genius as a specifically German trait, with blacks excluded (see above). The conjunction of both race and reproductivity in Schenker's conception of the *Ursatz* is significant, resonating with the putative biological basis of "social Darwinism,"[7] in which race and reproduction are intertwined. In the nineteenth-century adaptation of Darwin's theory of evolution, races—which evolve because of the fact of biological, generational

---

[7] On music and social Darwinism, see Taylor 2007 (79).

reproduction—were assigned different positions in the ladder of progress leading to the pinnacle of Western civilization.[8] With its racial exclusionism, Schenkerian theory's efficient reduction and even "elimination[ism]" (Cook 2007, 217) can be read as a form of "epistemicide" (Grosfoguel 2013) that erodes the culture of others through neglect, instead of making room for multiple voices.

If there is any doubt about the historical connection between race, re-production, and reduction, a material, horrific context may prove to be suggestive—slave labor. Efficiency is key to the rationalized, standardized mass production, workflows, assembly lines, and waste elimination of Fordism and Taylorism, but can in fact be traced to earlier "violent acts of resynchronization" that reorganized the quotidian time of Africans (sleeping, waking, eating, mating, reproducing, dying) into slave labor (Johnson 2002, 152). As Adorno and Horkheimer argued, the instrumental form of rationality that prizes means over ends is the logic of capitalism—in their reading, Odysseus is tied to the lean mast of capitalism so that he is not lost to the seductive but fatally wasteful Siren song (Adorno [1947] 1979, 35). The leanness that is observed both in the resynchronized temporality of slave labor and reproduction, on the one hand, and in "eliminationist" music-theoretical methods, on the other hand, is not necessarily closely correlated, but a consequence of the *universalization* of the capitalist logics that Adorno spent his career critiquing. The unfrayed unilinearity of Newtonian time may be accepted as objective fact, but it also buttressed a progressivist, evolu-tionist, unilinear modern temporality that served as the foundation of racist apparatuses that assigned the highest state of development (progress through time) to Western civilization (Scherzinger 2019, 242), providing rational jus-tification for colonial-imperial conquest and the related theft of capital (land, labor). This is the background against which analytical chronographs should be understood as one expression of the logic of "waste reduction" in the service of production, progress, and asymmetrical prosperity, embodying chrononormativity and symbolizing the maximal productivity of the human body. (It is worth noting that analytical graphs which present the temporal dimension in linear format, as in Schenkerian theory, are distinct from

---

[8] Darwin's cousin Francis Galton thought that welfare and insane asylums promoted the over-breeding of inferior humans, and that society should promote the breeding of superior humans of the respectable class, stopping short of advocating for related state policies. Paul 2006, 230.

musical scores in that the latter serve a pragmatic function for performance whereas graphs endeavor to unveil musical insights that often succumb to the chronographic fallacy of unilinearity.)

Having elaborated on the racial and sexual meanings of Schenkerian chrononormativity, elucidated via songs 1 and 4 of *Dichterliebe*, I turn now in the last portion of this chapter to remarks pertaining to temporality at the cycle level of the work. As pointed out in Ferris 2000 (30), Komar's analysis of the cycle as a whole (Example 7.2) is premised on key unity; in terms of reductive efficiency, this can be understood as both (i) the vertical unity of harmony (with a definite tonality A major identified for the first song, and understood to be prolonged throughout the cycle) and (ii) horizontal unilinearity, with a teleological third progression A – B – C# in the bass, indicating the ending of the cycle in the C# minor/Db major transfiguration of the final song. Aside from the myriad problems identified by Ferris (e.g., the bass C# *Stufe* of the final song leaves the *Ursatz* open-ended and thus has no Schenkerian standing), we can diagnose Komar's forced reading of an idiosyncratic unilinearity in the lower staff as a consequence of chronographic fallacy: building on the fundamental Schenkerian insight of long-range voice leading, Komar proceeded to construct his graph, constrained by the assumption that consecutive *Stufe* necessarily lead to one another from beginning to end. This assumption serves as the premise of the C#-directed progression that requires the insertion of an intermediate B, but this B then has to be conceptualized as an "interruption" because of the continuation of the circle of 5ths modulation between the two songs 5 and 14 in B minor and B major respectively (Komar 1971, 77).[9] Komar's graph lacks an *Urlinie*, applies Schenkerian concepts idiosyncratically, and mismatches with listening experience; in particular, the interruption which lasts more than half of the song cycle prevents any meaningful tonal association to be made between the ending C# and the opening A (Ferris 2000, 32). Chronographic fallacy is a construct underlying Komar's analysis.

Against the postulate of unity, there have been substantial interventions in the study of Romantic aesthetics, particularly with reference to August

---

[9] The keys of the cycle are largely organized in a descending circle of fifths (number of accidentals in the key signature are indicated in brackets): songs 1–2(3#), 3(2#), 4(1#), 5(2#), 6(1#), 7–8(nil), 9(1b), 10(2b), 11(3b), 12(2b), 13(6b), 14(5#), 15–16(4#) (C# minor modulates to the parallel tonic Db major in song 16). The Bb major to Eb minor modulation in songs 12–13 constitutes the only break from the circle of 5ths because of the modal switch to minor in the latter song, but the 5th motion is preserved.

Example 7.2 Komar's graph for *Dichterliebe*. © by kind permission of
W. W. Norton & Company, Inc

Wilhelm Schlegel's concept of the literary fragment as intentionally incomplete, stirring the imagination of the reader who coauthors the work of art by creating relationships between pieces in a collection (cycle of poems or paintings, passages from Schlegel's own aphoristic *Fragmente* 1798) (Ferris 2000, 59; Perrey 2002, 26). Ferris's approach, based on musical parallels such as weak openings or similar formal structure in songs, teases out relationships without assuming unity or unilinear progression, both of which persist in music theory. This is seen in the narrative and tonal graphs of Suurpää's 2014 study (168, 175) of *Winterreise*, which I shall discuss briefly to illuminate the lasting power of chronographic fallacy. Although the chrono-narrative approach is supported by the composition of the text as a cycle by Wilhelm Müller, and Suurpää's analysis possesses a logical structure, it is also evident that there is an underlying assumption of unilinear relationality between consecutive songs, contradicting the fragment-concept. Suurpää posits narrative "kernels" (songs 14–15, 16, 20, 21, 24) that anchor "satellite" songs (song 16 anchors 17–19; song 21 anchors 22–23), with the two kernels (songs 16 and 21) respectively articulating the ideation of death as the final goal (replacing love), and the inability to achieve dignified death. Without formal-poetic means to establish narrative hierarchy (at least none that Suurpää analyzed), and the tenuous link of the satellites to the kernels,[10] however, it may be more productive to entertain relations between non-consecutive songs (e.g., as Ferris demonstrates in his analysis of Schumann's *Liederkreis*, Op. 39). Suurpää's narrative scheme makes even less sense in the light of tonal relations between the songs. The common-tone, neo-Riemannian modulations pointed out by Suurpää create a sense of local groupings but stand in conflict with the chrono-narrative: for example, the satellite group 17–19 modulates from D major to D minor and A major via common tone(s), but this satellite group is detached from (has no common tones with) the putative kernel, song

---

[10] For example, song 19 *Täuschung* about the false promise of warm light from a house is supposed to be a satellite of song 16 *Letzte Hoffnung* in which the protagonist despairs and his hope is buried in a grave—but this is surely just one of many possible interpretations.

16 in E♭ major.[11] Suurpää's summation is that the key scheme in songs 13–24 contributes to the "unified whole" (190) of part two of *Winterreise*, with the shift from common tone modulations (songs 13–16, and 17–19) to stepwise key relations (songs 20–24) indicating the dissipation of the protagonist's goal-directedness, marking the transformation from love to death as the eventual goal (178). The unilinearity of this interpretation is anchored in a restricted understanding of chrono-narrativity that precludes listeners from constructing long-range tonal pairings taking the form of associations rather than prolongations (e.g., the connection between the bright A major of both song 19 about the false promise of warm light from a house, and song 23 about the darkening of the "false suns").

The non-systematic heterogeneity of collections of poems and songs means that unity and unilinearity tend to be inappropriate tenets for analysis of the Romantic song cycle, particularly since it is precisely the *cyclic* temporality of the domestic sphere—to which the Lied belongs—that is meant to ameliorate the harsh teleological, unilinear temporality of capital accumulation through labor, calculated marriage, and reproduction. Forcing unilinearity onto the song cycle means that tangential associations between songs, positioned askance and aslant, may be occluded. Thus Ferris argues instead for an analytical method that pays heed to alternative pairing, using the titular term from Goethe's novel *Elective Affinities* for conceptual explanation (78). By discarding the vertical harmonic unity and horizontal unilinearity of analytical graphs with unified tonality and timeline, new ambiguous and non-prolongational relations that are not representable in a chronograph can come into view. There should be no doubt over the importance of the C# harmonies and tonalities that book-end the cycle, with the connection extending over a heterogeneous mix of structural levels and tonalities: V/F# minor in song 1 is not a tonic harmony and never lands on the implied tonic, whereas C# minor is the initial tonic of song 16. Additionally, there are multiple retentions that are evoked by the postlude of song 16 in D♭ major, which, in addition to recalling the earlier occurrences of C# harmonies and tonalities, is itself a transposition of song 12's postlude. We might also say that the tonal ambiguity of song 1 is a protention of the heterogeneity of structural levels and temporal frays that become relationally entangled in the cycle. Compared with chronographs that obscure elective affinities in favor

---

[11] Suurpää argues that E♭ major of song 16 is linked to G minor of the next kernel, song 20, with the intervening satellites inexplicably unrelated to song 16.

of unilinearity, the ambiguous sonority of C#/D♭ harmonies and tonalities in *Dichterliebe* presents deviations akin to the tonal and affective meandering of the poet who avoids heading straight into production (as a worker) and reproduction (as procreator). The protensive-retensive vagaries of C#/D♭ in *Dichterliebe* is but one instance of the temporal/tonal frays and deviations that are commonplace in musical experience, in which, as the music proceeds, we instinctively sense the copresence of both previous moments and a projected, ever-changing musical future based on the accumulating musical past.

Within the broad modern contexts of industrial capitalism and the related colonial apparatuses of capital accumulation, temporality came to be organized through the prism of a duality, with cyclic domesticity serving as the foil to the linearity of work and workforce reproduction. Against this backdrop, the temporal frays analyzed in this chapter that are created by irony, harmonic ambiguity, and tonal juxtaposition in *Dichterliebe* allow for new possibilities that stand outside of the norm, with non-reproductive protagonists following the path of rejection, alternation, and archaism (fairy tales in song 15). Within the normative structure of the double time of unilinearity and cyclicity, temporal frays are "elective" in the sense that they are not considered to be "necessary" to production and reproduction. In my reading, "elective affinities" imply alternative relationalities that are of great consequence in queer world-making, whether in the form of bachelor uncles at family events who show no interest in starting a family, black youths who escape to the "houses" of New York (a play on the term for aristocratic families) headed by drag queen "mothers," affluent white gay networks of life-long friends in San Francisco, or migrant communities of Asians who escaped from repressive societies. Elective, re-defined kinships (Butler 2002) that non-traditionally reproductive LGBTQ+ people weave in the course of our lives (even if we choose to have babies through reproductive science and adoption) embody an anti-chrononormative temporality that sits at the very heart of Goethe's novel *Elective Affinities*. As pointed out in Gustafson 2002 (79), although Goethe's title is conventionally understood to refer to the repairing of the two opposite-sex couples Eduard and Charlotte, and the Captain and Ottilie, there is a queer and chemical resonance to elective affinities that may shed new light on *Dichterliebe*. Elective affinity was a scientific term used to refer to the substitution of elements of two compounds (AB and CD, each comprised of two elements) in a chemical reaction, which can be represented in the form: $AB + CD \rightarrow AD + BC$

(84). In the novel, the formula is brought up in the characters' conversation, and explicated as follows: Eduard (B) notes that the Captain (C) has been drawing him away from Charlotte (A), resulting in "BC," which connotes a homoerotic deviation, constituting a temporary detour from the eventual opposite-sex repairings of the novel.

The poet of *Dichterliebe* does not mention any close same-sex friend, but his bachelorhood is potentially a little queer. Temporal disruptions permeate the life of many queers who may be out among friends but may also be partially in the closet for various personal and professional reasons, such that irony (appearing straight) and the switching of language and behavioral codes comprise a way of life, resonating with the ambiguity of *Dichterliebe* (and, incidentally, of movies in which human-looking vampires or witches are compelled to hide their true nature). Queer world-making is necessarily eclectic since we queers exist within the confines of chrononormativity, frequently gathering cultural debris to create lifelines we have to construct for ourselves. From that perspective, what is most alluring about the "elective," unnecessary temporal deviations of *Dichterliebe* might be its hint of a queer *secret* hidden by the outwardly opposite-sex-attracted poet, a secret buried in the coffin sunk to the bottom of the sea in the final song.

References

Abelove, Henry. 2003. "Some Speculations on the History of Sexual Intercourse during the Long Eighteenth Century in England." In *Deep Gossip*, 21–28. Minneapolis, MN: University of Minnesota Press.

Adorno, Theodor. 1968/1991. "Die Wunde Heine, sowie Reden über Lyrik und Gesellschaft." *Noten zur Literatur I* (Frankfurt am Main: Suhrkamp). Available as "Heine the Wound." In *Notes to Literature I*, edited by Rolf Tiedemann, translated by Shierry Weber Nicholson, 80–85. New York: Columbia University Press.

Adorno, Theodor, and Max Horkheimer. [1947] 1979. *Dialektik der Aufclärung*. Amsterdam, Netherlands: Querido Verlag. Available as *Dialectic of Enlightenment*. Translated by J. Cumming. London: Verso.

Ahmed, Sarah. 2006. *Queer Phenomenology: Orientations, Objects, Others*. Durham, NC: Duke University Press.

Berger, Karol. 2007. *Bach's Cycle, Mozart's Arrow: An Essay on the Origins of Musical Modernity*. Berkeley: University of California Press.

Brown, Jane K. 2004. "In the Beginning Was Poetry." In *The Cambridge Companion to the Lied*, edited by James Parson, 12–34. Cambridge: University of Cambridge.

Burnham, Scott. 1995. *Beethoven Hero*. Princeton, NJ: Princeton University Press.

Butler, Judith. 2002. "Is Kinship Always Already Heterosexual?" *Differences: A Journal of Feminist Cultural Studies* 13, no. 1: 14–44

Cook, Nicholas. 2007. *The Schenker Project: Culture, Race, and Music Theory in Fin-de-siècle Vienna*. Oxford: Oxford University Press.

Edelman, Lee. 2004. *No Future: Queer Theory and the Death Drive*. Durham, NC: Duke University Press.

Ewell, Philip. 2020. "Music Theory and the White Racial Frame." *Music Theory Online* 26, no. 2, accessed October 5, 2020. https://mtosmt.org/issues/mto.20.26.2/mto.20.26.2.ewell.html.

Ferris, David. 2000. *Schumann's Eichendorff Liederkreis and the Genre of the Romantic Cycle*. Oxford: Oxford University Press.

Foucault, Michel. [1976] 1990. *La Volentè de savoir*. Paris, France: Editions Gallimard. Available as *The History of Sexuality I: An Introduction*, translated by Robert Hurley. New York: Vintage Books (first published by Pantheon Books, New York, in 1978).

Freeman, Elizabeth. 2010. *Time Binds: Queer Temporalities, Queer Histories*. Durham, NC: Duke University Press.

Grosfoguel, Ramon. 2013. "The Structure of Knowledge in Westernized Universities: Epistemic Racism/Sexism and the Four Genocides/Epistemicides of the Long 16th Century." *Human Architecture: Journal of the Sociology of Self-Knowledge* 11, no. 1: 73–90.

Gustafson, Susan E. 2002. *Men Desiring Men: The Poetry of Same-Sex Identity and Desire in German Classicism*. Detroit, MI: Wayne State University Press.

Heine, Heinrich. 1972–. *Heine Säkularausgabe: Werk—Briefe—Lebenszeugnisse XX*, edited by Nationale Forschungs- und Gedenkstätten der klassischen deutschen Literatur in Weimar and Centre National de la Recherche Scientifique. Berlin (East); Paris: Akademie-Verlag and Editions du CNRS.

Husserl, Edmund. 1964. *The Phenomenology of Internal Time Consciousness*. Translated by J. S. Churchill. Bloomington: Indiana University Press

Johnson, Walter. 2002. "Time and Revolution in African America: Temporality and the History of Slavery." In *Rethinking American History in a Global Age*, edited by Tom Bender, 148–167. Berkeley: University of California Press.

Komar, Arthur, editor. 1971. *Dichterliebe. A Norton Critical Score, by Robert Schumann*. New York: W. W. Norton and Company, Inc.

Kramer, Lawrence. 1998. *Franz Schubert: Sexuality, Subjectivity, Song*. Cambridge: Cambridge University Press.

Lee, Gavin, ed. 2018. *Rethinking Difference in Gender, Sexuality and Popular Music: Theory and Politics of Ambiguity*. New York: Routledge.

Morrison, Paul. 1993. "End Pleasure." *GLQ* 1, no. 1: 53–78.

Paul, Diane. 2006. "Darwin, Social Darwinism and Eugenics." *The Cambridge Companion to Darwin*, edited by Jonathan Hodge and Gregory Radick, 219–45. Cambridge: Cambridge University Press.

Perrey, Beate Julia. 2002 *Schumann's* Dichterliebe *and Early Romantic Poetics: Fragmentation of Desire*. Cambridge: Cambridge University Press.

Schenker, Heinrich. [1926] 2014. "Forsetzung der Urlinie-Betrachtungen." In *Das Meisterwerk in der Musik II*. Munich: Drei Masken. Available as "Further Consideration of the Urlinie II." In *The Masterwork in Music II*, translated by Ian Bent, Alfred Clayton, and Derrick Puffett, edited by William Drabkin, 1–22. Mineola, NY: Dover Publications.

Schenker, Heinrich. [1935] 1979. *Der Freie Satz*. Vienna, Austria: Universal Edition A. G. Available as *Free Composition*. Translated and edited by Ernst Oster. New York: Longman Publishers.

Scherzinger, Martin. 2019. "Temporalities." *The Oxford Handbook of Critical Concepts in Music Theory*, edited by Alexander Rehdings and Steven Rings, 234–71. Oxford: Oxford University Press.

Suurpää, Lauri. 1996. "Schumann, Heine, and Romantic Irony: Music and Poems in the First Five Songs of *Dichterliebe*." *Intégral* 10: 93–123.

Suurpää, Lauri. 2014. *Death in Winterreise: Musico-Poetic Associations in Schubert's Song Cycle*. Bloomington: Indiana University Press.

Taylor, Timothy. 2007. *Beyond Exoticism: Western Music and the World*. Durham, NC, Duke University Press.

Varwig, Bettina. 2012. "Metaphors of Time and Modernity in Bach." *Journal of Musicology* 29.2: 154–190.

8

Queering Musical Chrononormativity

Percussion Works of the West Coast Group

Bill Solomon

West Coast Percussion Ensemble as Queer Subcultural Practice

The proliferation of percussion ensemble works from the 1930s and 1940s on the West Coast of the United States was the second wave of Western notated works written for collections of percussion instruments, following a first wave of European works including Edgard Varese's *Ionisation*, George Antheil's *Ballet Mechanique*, and Stravinsky's *Les Noces* in the 1920s. The influence of the European avant-garde was felt throughout the United States by a group of composers loosely and collectively referred to as the West Coast group. Centered around Henry Cowell, a well-connected musician whose activities included composing, publishing, performing, and teaching, were several young composers who were taking an interest in writing music for the newly conceived percussion ensemble: most importantly John Cage and Lou Harrison, along with Johanna Beyer, Ray Green, John J. Becker, and Gerald Strang. The composition and performance of West Coast percussion ensemble works during this period was influenced by modernist European compositional practices but with an intention to create a distinctly US-American musical sensibility while simultaneously developing alongside the burgeoning modern-dance community.[1] This resulted in a repertoire that was largely conceived of and created alongside dancing bodies. It was an experimental practice that developed on the fringes of the musical landscape, diverging from more formalized concertizing practices found in Europe and the United States. Cage, Cowell, and Harrison were three queer men who led

---

[1] For more on the early history of the West Coast percussion ensemble, see Miller 2000 and Siwe 2020.

Bill Solomon, *Queering Musical Chrononormativity* In: *Queer Ear*. Edited by: Gavin S. K. Lee, Oxford University Press.
© Oxford University Press 2023. DOI: 10.1093/oso/9780197536766.003.0009

the charge of organizing percussion concerts and publishing scores of these new works while collaborating with dancers and choreographers, many of whom were also queer.[2]

Considering the concentration of queer individuals in this community of musicians and dancers, the West Coast group can be considered a queer musical subculture that had its own value system and range of influences that operated separately from but existed within a larger ecosystem of modern concert music in the United States. "Subcultures," according to J. Halberstam, "suggest transient, extrafamilial, and oppositional modes of affiliation" (Halberstam 2005, 154). A subculture has its own norms that exist in opposition to larger society, and the West Coast group and their collaborators created work that was informed in part by fascination with non-Western cultures while using artistic practices that derived from Euro-Western lineages. The West Coast's relative proximity to Eastern Asia, along with the large number of Asian immigrants who lived and worked in the United States, exerted a profound influence on the artistic output of the West Coast group. Being located on the Pacific Rim reduced the need for access to Asian culture to be mediated through European colonialist and capitalist mechanisms, particularly as the United States continued to develop its own imperialist prerogatives as it grew to global dominance. Thus, artists working in cities including San Francisco, Seattle, and Los Angeles developed a uniquely US-American sensibility in their interpretation of Asian cultures, which was further deepened within queer subcultures' non-normative familial and kinship structures that existed outside of straight societal norms.

A critical aspect of the queerness of the West Coast musical subculture was a desire to use—or, more pointedly, to appropriate—Asian materials in order to construct an imagined world outside of the sexually repressive United States that would validate their non-normative sexual lives and cultural production. The focus of this chapter will be on how the compositional temporality of the West Coast percussion ensemble repertoire was uniquely influenced by the appropriation of Asian temporalities, particularly as composers reacted against the acceleration of modern temporality that increasingly privileged heteronormative lives. The percussion ensemble repertoire of this period was a product of the forward push of musical modernism while simultaneously a reaction against

---

[2] For more on sexuality in early US-American modern dance, see Foulkes 2002 and Ramsay 1995.

modernity as an attempt to stop or reverse time. The West Coast group fetishized Asian cultures as a way of rearticulating their own Western, white, queer, and male lives in an erotic that reveals a variety of privileges and oppressions within the larger matrix of colonial, racial, sexual, and artistic expressions.

In this chapter, the term "queer" when used in relation to individuals refers specifically to a range of non-normative sexualities among the composers in question situated in the United States during the early twentieth century. Without needing to detail the sexual histories of these composers, broadly speaking, Cage, Cowell, and Harrison had sexual and romantic relationships with men and women, and Cowell also had interactions with underage males. In current terms, we could refer to these shifting sexual practices as gay, bisexual, polyamorous, or pederastic, and thus the term "queer" is employed somewhat anachronistically, but also more as a convenient (if potentially problematic) catch-all term to aid discourse. What is under consideration within the West Coast group is a variety of sexualities that pertained to white cisgendered men. It is telling that the primary subjects here do not include trans, non-male, or non-white individuals. The ways in which these queer white male composers interacted with Asian persons, who were portrayed as racialized and abstracted, in the production of the new percussion ensemble speaks volumes about which lives are privileged in the historical records of US-American music. It would be naïve and incorrect to suggest that there was an absence of non-normative bodies circulating in the same spaces as these composers, and of course there were: lesbian female choreographers, male and female impersonators within the Chinese opera world, and more broadly, a range of gender and sexual identities in various Asian communities that did not necessarily cohere to colonized understandings of sexuality and gender. The centrality of a narrow range of white cisgender male sexualities within the broader range of non-normative sexualities and gender identities is yet another example of white masculine privilege that cannot be overlooked in this discussion. Nonetheless, the word "queer" will continue to be used throughout this chapter "as a placeholder for conceptual tools that are yet to emerge" (Luther 2019, 10), partially out of frustration for a lack of more incisive terminology. This comes with an acknowledgment that even the relatively privileged sexual position gay white men inhabited in relation to less privileged sexual outlaws was still dangerous within the larger context of white, straight society. For example, Cowell's imprisonment at San Quentin from 1936 to 1940 shows that homophobia had real life consequences for queer US-Americans who had to navigate oppression on a daily basis.[3]

The focus on temporality within the realm of aesthetics in this queer subcultural practice requires an analysis that is both specific in its materiality as experienced in the daily lives of the composers and their musical compositions, and broad enough to encompass the diffuse understanding of the affect that the composers were seeking to achieve. Queer theorists have increasingly been attending to temporality in addition to space, particularly in the palpable ways that time is felt by queer individuals. Elizabeth Freeman's concept of queered chrononormativity posits that heteronormativity has leveraged temporality as an oppressive and pervasive tool that impacts the lives of queer people in tangible ways, and the ways in which queers have developed coping tactics as acts of survival and protest in order to exist beyond the rigidity of chrononormativity (Freeman 2010). Freeman defines chrononormativity as "the use of time to organize individual human bodies toward maximum productivity," which brings to the fore how chrononormativity is primarily in service of capitalism and efficient reproduction of heterosexual bodies (Freeman 2010, 3). If queer bodies cannot be seen as productive members of a capitalist society, their desires are seen as a danger to the larger population, and their agency and experience of time are undermined and sabotaged.

As music is an art form inherently concerned with the flow of time, the application of queer temporality theories to musical analysis reveals ways in which power dynamics have influenced compositional practices, particularly through colonialist readings. Freeman further states that chrononormativity is "event-centered, goal-oriented, intentional, and culminating in epiphanies or major transformations" (Freeman 2010, 5), and as such, it follows that chrononormativity filters out non-productive, non-intentional, and non-transformational phenomena. Lives that were viewed as anti-productive, whether queer US-American citizens or Asian immigrants, do not fit within the constraints of chrononormativity; similarly, music that is understood as ateleological, digressive, or non-functional would not conform to the chrononormative dictates that music historically organized into teleologically constructed productive forms and would be summarily dismissed as unimportant or unsuccessful. The concept of queered chrononormativity

---

[3] For more on Cowell's incarceration see Sachs 2012, 275–349.

necessarily includes the (chrono)normative within its scope, as such queered constructions are in reaction to dominant and oppressive forms of temporality imposed by larger heterodominant society. Thus, the use of the term "queered chrononormativity" in relation to the West Coast group acknowledges a particular form of queer temporality that relates (even if in negation) not only to dominant compositional practices, but also to forms of colonial temporality that will be outlined below.

Queer musicians employing methods of composition that run counter to traditional practices were prioritizing the rhythms and temporalities of their bodies and desires, eschewing the demands of heteronormative society and leaning instead into their collective erotics. Deborah Wong defines an erotics as "the place where the affective and the structural come together and where corporeal control is felt and made visible" (Wong 2015, 179). Temporality existed in the zone of erotics for the West Coast group as they manipulated musical time in the act of utopia building in order to more fully realize queer desire and community. Infused with an affectual sense of time-lessness, West Coast erotics did not include Asian bodies except as empty models for imagined non-normative lifestyles; this added a power dynamic that placed the West Coast group in a dominant position in relation to the sources that they heavily borrowed from while also existing as an oppressed group with US-American society. Gamelan in particular provided a formal framework that inspired percussion ensemble compositional practices of stacked temporal layers of ostinatos; the ostinato will be understood as the primary musical unit West Coast composers employed to construct queered chrononormativities. Gamelan and other Asian cultural traditions merged with modernist compositional practices to generate a uniquely US-American expression of experimental music making situated within the larger global forces of colonization that facilitated composers' access to cultures outside of their own through appropriation. Understanding how "the exotic becomes the direct site of exploitation and appropriation" (Ibrahim 2019, 32) within the percussion repertoire will further expand an understanding of how queered temporality and erotics perpetuated racist tropes.

The chapter that follows is divided into three sections. The first section, "Temporality, Queer Bodies, and Percussion," connects an embodied percussion practice to queer temporalities, showing how the West Coast group pursued queered chrononormativity in their compositional practice. "Appropriation and the Transpacific Queer Gaze" delves further into an analysis of how the West Coast group's sexual identity formation was influenced by their exoticized appropriative practices within a colonial context. Finally, "Composing/Constructing Queer Temporality in Cowell's *Ostinato Pianissimo*" examines Cowell's exemplary percussion ensemble work as a case study for analyzing queer chrononormativity. In general, the specific instances found within the early US-American percussion ensemble project are connected with larger power structures to develop a broader context in which to facilitate musical analysis of queered chrononormativity. Temporality is both a diffuse feeling that is influenced by the cultural environment in which one hears and creates music as well as a strictly musical phenomenon that can be described with concrete language. Therefore, toggling between various analytic modes provides a richer understanding of how queer musicians were able to manipulate musical time as a reflection of their identities in relation to other forces that materially impacted their lives.

Temporality, Queer Bodies, and Percussion

The West Coast percussion repertoire experimented with temporality as the materials of musical composition shifted from controllably pitched instruments (e.g., strings, winds, and keyboards) to largely unpitched/ aleatorically pitched instruments, which form the core of the percussion instrumentarium. Without the need to structure compositions around harmonic schema that privileged teleological orientation as found in common practice tonality, the West Coast percussion ensemble compositions dispensed with certain musical forms, particularly sonata-allegro and related forms. Early US-American percussion ensemble works tended to be on the short side (the longest works lasting under ten minutes), and along with the ultramodernist imperative to explore new modes of musical expression, West Coast composers used percussion composition as a site to push beyond the boundaries of received art-music compositional techniques, seeking out new ways to organize their music. In addition to the visual spectacle of percussion ensemble performances, the novelty of the instruments and timbres that were employed—including found objects, gongs, and other ringing metallic sounds—as well as the unique combinations of sounds from instruments collected around the world, were themselves an important aspect of the spectacle that drew audiences and critics to this new performance practice. An overly complex or opaque form would add unnecessary incoherence to the range of previously unheard sounds that were presented in any given composition to a Western audience. Thus, composers needed to find a way to frame the "new" sounds in a musically intelligible way. The need for innovative forms that could make the percussion ensemble both comprehensible and tantalizing to adventurous audiences was a built-in prerogative for the West Coast composers as they imagined the possibilities of percussion-only composition.

Ostinato forms proved to be a successful compositional model in this period due not only to its accessibility for audiences, but for performers, too. The performers of the early percussion ensemble largely comprised modern dancers and composers instead of professional orchestral percussionists or popular music drummers who were not engaged in this music during this time. While the use of ostinatos in percussion ensemble works was largely influenced by cultural impressions from the East mediated via Western colonialist frameworks, it is important to acknowledge the influence of the burgeoning US-American modern dance scene as an emerging practice intertwined with the percussion ensemble. A range of choreographers filtered through the West Coast modern dance scene including Denishawn (Ruth St. Denis and Ted Shawn), Doris Humphrey, Charles Weidman, Lester Horton, Martha Graham, José Limón, Tina Flade, Hanya Holm, Lore Deja, and Bonnie Bird. Modern dance as practiced on the West Coast serves as a useful analogue for understanding the percussion ensemble in several respects, including: the need for danceable forms based on audibly repeating metric structures, a tendency to exoticize Eastern arts practices in contraposition to inherited Western practices, and the creation of social and artistic spaces that welcomed queer sexualities. Cage, Cowell, and Harrison all spent significant time in collaboration with modern dancers, and a large portion of the early percussion repertoire was made explicitly for dance or was directly inspired by modern-dance sensibilities. From this perspective, the ostinato in percussion ensemble repertoire then has multiple sources: as a way of allowing "new" sounds to be introduced to listeners in a comprehensible manner; from modern dance, where an ostinato makes the music danceable; and as a reflection of the fascination with Eastern musics. A further layer of queerness pervades each of these sources, as these ideas were generated and developed within the queer subculture of the West Coast group. As the ostinato became the primary building block of musical structures in the percussion ensemble repertoire, the ostinato can itself be understood as a vehicle for the construction of queer temporality.

Queer approaches to theorizing temporality provide deeper understandings of how queer individuals might construct and perceive time. Influential queer theorists, including José Esteban Muñoz, J. Jack Halberstam, and Elizabeth Freeman, have applied queer conceptions of temporality to analyses of film, art, aesthetics, and embodied experiences. If queer individuals are able to experience and understand time in ways that privilege their queer bodies and desires—as opposed to normative structures of time and temporality that arise from capitalism and heteronormativity— queerness can flourish outside of oppression and build supportive structures that mirror their lives and question hegemonic heteropatriarchy. Chrononormativity, as understood by Freeman, organizes all bodies into productive structures that promote those habits and supportive systems that reproduce heterosexual bodies. To queer chrononormativity means to subvert, reorganize, and/or exist outside of these hegemonic pathways through nonproductive, radical, and unusual temporal means. Chrononormativity, as it existed in the first half of the twentieth century in capitalistic United States for the West Coast composers, would have been experienced in tangible ways over the course of one's life, as there was increasing pressure to be formally educated, get married, have children, and work a steady job as a productive member of society in the correct, predetermined order; any deviation from this plan was considered irresponsible or even dangerous. Further, temporal structures such as days, weeks, and months dictated preferable ways of experiencing time, such as daily activities organized around childrearing and expectations for conducting regular business hours, to the construction of biological calendars designed to coach heterosexual couples how to most efficiently conceive children (Carter 2007, 99). Activities such as these formed the ways in which larger society divided, used, and felt chronometric time. For heterosexual, able-bodied individuals, chrononormativity validated "happiness scripts" (Ahmed 2010) that dictated what a good, white, and capitalist life looked like. For those who existed outside of heterosexuality, these pressures to live in predetermined ways produced friction and were, by many, felt as oppressive.

The act of queering chrononormativity was both a survival mechanism, and a tactic of disidentifying with straight society for those people who chose to live outside of the dictates of normative society, including the queerleaning artistic circles that the West Coast composers moved through. Muñoz defines disidentification as a "mode of dealing with dominant ideology, one that neither opts to assimilate within such a structure nor strictly opposes it; rather, disidentification is a strategy that works on and against dominant ideology" (Muñoz 1999, 11). Muñoz's formulation of disidentification is a tactic employed by racially minoritized artists (mostly identified as queer Black and/or Latin subjects) who used the materials of dominant white culture in subversive ways through performance to critique the structures of power that exploited and discriminated against them. Muñoz points out that *identification* and *counteridentification* are both processes that reaffirm the "conception of power as being a fixed discourse" (Muñoz 1999, 19), whereas *disidentification* questions the fixity of a singular discourse in the first place. Evoking disidentification in the context of the West Coast percussion ensemble allows one to consider the subculture status of the West Coast group in relation to other modernist and institutionalized classical music practices within the United States (including the east coast modernist circle of queer composers including Bernstein, Copland, and Thompson), and how they sought to amplify and subvert the dictates of modernism by composing experimental music. What does not carry over in applying the concept of disidentification to the West Coast composers is the critical aspect of race Muñoz invokes in the subjects he discusses, and rather, it is important to not only acknowledge their white privilege—even as they experience discrimination as queer figures—but further, to understand the ways in which race and exoticism of East Asian cultures impacts an understanding of racial privilege within the works of the West Coast group (discussed further in the following section).

More critical to an understanding of queer temporality, Muñoz reads Heidegger's concept of future possibilities through a queer lens: "I think of queerness as a temporal arrangement in which the past is a field of possibility in which subjects can act in the present in the service of a new futurity" (Muñoz 2009, 19). Essentially, queerness is "a backward glance that enacts a future vision" (Muñoz 2009, 4): queers can construct their own archive in order to orient toward utopian futures that are always just out of reach, "only in the horizon" (Muñoz 2009, 11). Queers construct their own sense of temporality, always moving toward an ever-out-of-reach utopia while gazing backward, as opposed to heteronormative subjects who keep their focus on the manageable and achievable goal-oriented future, prioritizing clear and predictable outcomes. Sarah Ahmed connects the spatiality of the queer (and racialized) gaze to a Muñozian temporality: "The temporality of orientation reminds us that orientations are effects of what we tend toward, where the 'toward' makes a space and time that is almost, but not quite, available in the present" (Ahmed 2006, 20). Because queers understand that their future will never quite materialize—utopia is always just out of reach—they are able to make creative use of the past in unexpected ways. While queer subjects still must experience the linearity of time, the ability to play within and experience some fluidity with various structures of temporality is one tactic of disorientation, particularly within the realm of music composition.

A musical application of Muñozian temporality suggests a fluid experience of temporal simultaneity and provides a specifically queer way of approaching temporality beyond teleological models. As percussion music was freed from harmonic organizing principles due to its lack of clear pitch structures, time and rhythm became the primary way composers approached their work, particularly as seen in the work of Cage. His use of macro- and micro-rhythmic structures, as well as his use of multiple temporal layers (also seen in early percussion works such as Cowell's *Ostinato Pianissimo* (1934) and Johanna M. Beyer's *IV* (1939) can be understood as a movement away from productive directionality, and toward an attempt to achieve what sounds like stasis (to Western ears), or what Kramer refers to as "vertical time" (Kramer 1988, 55). John Latartara defines a temporal layer as "musical material that has a distinct temporal identity created through rhythm, meter, repetition, or accent," and further, that "regularity of time is often de-emphasized and irregularly emphasized through both the superimposition of multiple temporal layers and anomalies within each layer" (Latartara 2007, 101). Musical interest is maintained with localized variances in individual layers, and the unexpected simultaneities that occur among various temporal layers. Much of the West Coast repertoire consists of the layering of multiple ostinatos (or quasi-ostinatos, which are repeating figures that are not exact replications, but have minor variations with similar rhythmic and melodic contours (Solomon 2016, 185–93) as a way to achieve Kramer's vertical time, a temporality that feels non-teleological but is never stagnant. As will be shown in the music of the West Coast group, this type of repetition points toward a sort of utopian horizon of their own design, but never arrives there, hence invoking a queerness that is seeking an alternative to heteronormative ideals of temporal progression.

The West Coast evocation of timelessness through ostinatic repetition is further compounded by the influence of ultramodernism, a US-American movement that influenced forward-leaning aesthetics and rhetoric. Ultramodernism was an accelerationist movement that sought to separate itself from Eurocentric tradition through rigorous experimental compositional practices infused with global music influences (David Nicholls 1990). Cowell was a vocal proponent of ultramodernism, and many of his writings advocated for such forward-leaning practices, including his highly influential *New Musical Resources* from 1930 (Cowell 1996). Cowell's references to "Oriental" music are frequent in his writings as he located non-European sources for the new music he was advocating for in service of a new US-American compositional practice. As he stated in 1927, "Western music has taken one road and Oriental another, going in exactly the opposite direction" (Cowell 1927, 672). The spatiality in this quote situating the West and the Orient as heading in opposite directions can be read alongside Ahmed's understandings of orientations, and how such motion relates specifically to temporality. What does it mean for the West Coast group to have turned away from the road that Western music was (ostensibly) heading in, and instead re-orient geographically and aesthetically toward the Orient as a form of disidentification? Whereas Muñoz says that queers look backward in order to move forwards, perhaps the West Coast group vis-à-vis ultramodernism were looking forward in order to move backward. The racialized and colonial implications of this formation need to be examined in further depth, as the connection between "backward" and "Asian" present a problematic schematic, to say the least; Cowell's comment implies that the Orient is not oriented in the direction of modernity and forward motion, but in some other opposing direction. The West Coast group members were seeking utopia through their art in a Muñozian fashion, but unlike the queers of color who adopted a stance of forward-learning political solidarity, the West Coast group was seeking a way out of an oppressive contemporary society using their white male privilege via ultramodernist aesthetic directives.

Thus, exoticized forms of temporality in the early US-American percussion ensemble were simultaneously reacting against heteronormative modern society while engaging in and influencing *au courant* modernist compositional practices. White male privilege allowed the West Coast group to both engage in and disassociate with prevailing experimentalist practices that existed within and beyond their immediate queer coterie of composers, artists, and dancers to an extended network of other US-American classical composers. The simple musical device of the ostinato sought to freeze time, or at the very least, expand beyond a chrononormative temporality that projected clear directionality into a temporal zone where time need not function in productive ways. The queered chrononormativity of the West Coast group followed from the "backward" gaze toward the East that existed outside more normative conceptions of temporality derived from Eurocentrically oriented traditions. The novelty of compositions largely for percussion instruments alone necessitated the use of ostinatos to allow audiences the capacity to make sense of new sounds using repetition in order to induce familiarity. Critically, the ostinato reveals an erotics by paying homage to the dancing queer bodies that fostered this repertoire, imbuing the music with an embodied sense of sexuality. In the section that follows, a more in-depth look at how East Asian exoticism fed the eroticized imagination of the West Coast composers will be discussed to further understand how sexuality, colonialism, and race were intertwined in the queer temporality of the percussion ensemble.

Appropriation and the Transpacific Queer Gaze

In her book *The Queer Composition of America's Sound*, Nadine Hubbs shows how the circle of New York queer modernist composers including Copland, Bernstein, Thompson, and others looked transatlantically toward Paris for stylistic and aesthetic grounding in their compositional practices (Hubbs 2004). In an analogous manner, the West Coast composers "turned their gaze transpacifically" (Yang 2008, 37) toward Asia for inspiration and alternative models of music creation from their position as queer, male, and white US-Americans. The West Coast of the United States was strongly influenced by Asian immigration in the late nineteenth/early twentieth centuries, and the geographical and affectual proximity between urban queer sexuality and Asian culture connected these two populations who found themselves outside of the dominant heteropatriarchy, particularly in the interwar era as whiteness and heterosexuality consolidated new forms of social and cultural power (Carter 2007). Aspects of West Coast queer identity were subsumed within larger political global movements of colonialism and capitalism, and were embedded in the early percussion ensemble repertoire, particularly when considering non-normative temporalities. Connecting sexuality with appropriation in the West Coast group situates a larger history of Western classical music cultural borrowings that has specific resonances in the repertoire at hand.

San Francisco serves as an example of a city where gay-friendly urban neighborhoods bordered Asian immigrant neighborhoods, in this case Chinatown and the nearby gay neighborhood the Tenderloin (Boyd 2003,

5). Thus, it was common for queer socializing to rub against Asian cultural attractions including musical performances, cuisine, vice entertainments, and casual sexual encounters. Such proximate geography existed within a larger framework of urban centers that white middle-class families viewed as dangerous areas, sites that simultaneously attracted tourism and spectatorship from the same white outsiders who condemned outsider cultures. "The anthropology of tourism," according to Nan Alamilla Boyd, "suggests that sexual and racial or ethnic entertainments function as hegemonic texts for white or western tourists who seek meaning and bring authenticity to their own lives through experiencing cultural practices beyond their own life sphere" (Boyd 2003, 81). White heteronormative society demarcated racialized and sexualized zones as necessary in their own identity formation, separating themselves from communities who did not adhere to their increasingly restrictive norms. In reaction, many white queer men in west coast urban centers, including the Bay Area and Seattle, felt comradeship with Asian immigrants onto whom they projected their own experiences of homophobia and exclusion, although there is little evidence that this sense of community was necessarily reciprocated, as Asian immigrants faced their own set of highly restrictive legal and social regulations that US-resident white gay men did not have to consider.[4] Both within their own localized communities, as well as in imagined utopias across the ocean, the queer West Coast group constructed an idealized Asian Other, a cipher who served as a receptacle for their queer sexualities that were unwelcome within the United States. Discussing Java specifically, Henry Spiller describes this as "Americans' capacity to use the peoples and cultures of Java as a blank screen on which they could project their own values and desires" (Spiller 2015, 13). The evocation of Asian music in the percussion ensemble is partially a result of this longing for a society that accepted queer sexualities and nonnormative lifestyles without engaging with actual Asian lives in any substantial way, as further evidenced by a general absence of Asian musicians in collaborative artistic capacities at the time. The West Coast percussion ensemble was music by and for primarily white audiences and performed by musicians that borrowed heavily from Asian musicians without engaging them beyond the surface level of inspiration. Further impacting this power imbalance was the presence of white male queer sexualities, which added a

---

[4] See Yunhwa Rao 2017, particularly part 1, which details legal and social restrictions that Chinese immigrants faced in the United States.

combination of their feeling of entitlement to Asian culture along with their lived experiences of discrimination due to sexual orientation. The way oppression potentially generates further oppressive actions, in this case homophobia generating racist appropriative and exoticized musical practices, needs to be identified in order to hold such subjects morally accountable for their actions. The West Coast group's failure to understand the impact of their appropriation needs to be registered along with their legitimate experiences of discrimination, not as a way of excusing the latter but by complicating a legacy of white queer artists whose understanding of structural oppression ends at their own experiences.

With this in mind, it is important to acknowledge that the West Coast composers were explicit in their appropriation of Asian musical tropes as white queer men having been exposed to various musical traditions during this period of the mid-1930s to the mid-1940s. This included the use of Asian instruments, aesthetics, and forms that appeared in the percussion repertoire in a variety of ways. They encountered Asian musics in multiple settings, which included recorded and live performances, institutionalized education, interactions with native music practitioners, and, importantly, frequent exposure to other Orientalized Western-produced cultural artifacts that were themselves inspired by Asian arts and culture, particularly from within the modern-dance community.[5] In this phase of the development of the percussion ensemble, Cage, Cowell, and Harrison encountered Asian music, specifically Balinese and Javanese gamelan, Chinese opera, and various Indian and Japanese traditions, which was mediated through a Western colonial positionality, even when native musicians were present. For example, the Golden Gate International Exposition (GGIE) in San Francisco, held from 1939 to 1940, featured daily performances of Javanese gamelan and dance in the Dutch East Indies pavilion in a picturesque setting. World Expos from the late-nineteenth through the mid-twentieth century were cultural colonial formations as sites for displays of national economic and cultural power for the larger public. The GGIE was the first place that Harrison heard live gamelan, and it left a long-lasting impression on him and his compositional output, particularly as the fair attracted gay audiences (Miller 2012, 253). As Mina Yang points out, "thus, when Harrison heard his first live Balinese gamelan orchestra at the 1939 expo, fifty years after Debussy's

---

[5] For more on West Coast group and modern dance encounters with Eastern music in the first half of the twentieth century, see Cohen 2010; Miller 2006, 47–112; Miller and Lieberman 1999, 146–78; Nicholls 1999, 125–28; Yang 2001.

famous introduction to the gamelan at the Paris world fair, the Asian music was encoded with associations that resonated in particularly loaded ways for a young gay Californian composer" (Yang 2008, 37). The strong connection between Asian music and queer culture cannot be understood outside of the colonial frameworks that brought gamelan to San Francisco. This encounter left an indelible mark on Harrison and, as just one such example within the West Coast group, speaks to the complex ways in which appropriation occurred in this social and artistic circle.

The cross-cultural interactions as exemplified by the GGIE existed within a larger framework of colonialism and homosexuality that had been playing out since at least the nineteenth century throughout Europe and the United States, underlining a multifaceted process of how the West Coast composers came to hear live gamelan. At the time of the GGIE, Java was a colony of the Netherlands, and the Dutch East Indies Company had sponsored these performances as an outpost of their global business interests seeking out a larger North American market for their Javanese imports (Spiller 2015, 20). Such colonial enterprises connected international capitalism with exoticized music entertainment in an erotically charged atmosphere that brought international performance to local audiences (Yang 2009, 36–37). There was a strong connection between Java and homosexuality in the imagination of western queers as part of a larger legacy of colonialism throughout the world whereby, as Robert Aldrich notes, "a widespread belief circulated in Europe that homosexuality (and other sexual deviance) was endemic in the non-European world," leading to "the perception, and (to a limited extent) the reality, of the empire as a homosexual playground" (Aldrich 2003, 5). Many men who had sex with men—and some who went so far as to identify themselves as homosexual—actively sought out travel to Java, Bali, and other parts of modern-day Indonesia in the early twentieth century, which had come to be a destination for gay sexual tourism as men hoped to meet up with the locals as well as other Western travelers who had convened there (Boellstroff 2005, 52–54). Homosexual desire was mediated through networks of colonial power, which intersected with the West Coast group in moments such as Harrison hearing gamelan at the GGIE, an occurrence that would not have happened without such mediation. Thus, when Philip Brett observed that "gamelan is a gay marker in American music" (Brett 1994, 238), there are (at least) two levels of exchange at play. On the surface, he suggests that US-American gamelan references in Western concert music were present due to a social network of queer composers who shared similar influences (a process that Hubbs 2004 details). Pushing deeper, one can also understand such references to gamelan by white gay US-American males as reflections of a larger systemic imperial Western tendency to project non-normative sexualities onto racialized others who served as an imaginary salve to anxieties that were experienced at home as sexual outsiders while facilitating exotic and erotic ends. "[US-Americans] shared their awareness of gamelan music . . . filtered through their own desires and self-understandings, with the public at large. The vagueness of American conceptions of 'Java' empowered these individuals to remake Javanese performing arts in their own images" (Spillers 2015, 17).

The West Coast group was implicated within a larger legacy of US-American imperial identity formation as they casually absorbed musical aspects of gamelan into their compositions. Gamelan in particular served as a significant source of musical inspiration in the realm of the percussion ensemble, although other Asian cultures also had material and affective influence upon percussion composition. In many ways, the appropriation that occurred in the percussion ensemble repertoire was pan-Asian with broader syncretic pan-global tendencies, as instruments and ideas from Central/South Americas and Africa were also formative. Chinese and Japanese musical cultures were highly influential in popular and art music throughout the United States, in particular across the west coast, and therefore cannot be ignored.[6] Members of the West Coast group had varying degrees of engagement in scholarly and culturally responsive understandings of specific Asian musical traditions during the early days of the percussion ensemble. Several musical traditions mixed together as the composers collected new ideas, but in many ways, it was the influence of gamelan on temporality that is the easiest to trace, particularly through the use of stratified rhythmic cycles in many early percussion works. Gamelan serves as an entry point to understanding appropriative practices that should also not delimit exploration of broader Asian sources in the repertoire that may not be easily disentangled. Tracing the larger web of influences and how they were manifested within the percussion ensemble repertoire—especially those related to temporality—is a larger project that will spill beyond the boundaries of this chapter, particularly as queerness fades into other relevant issues.

As stated above, Aldrich ties two critical ideas together: first, the problematic colonialist assumption that non-Western societies inherently produce

---

[6] For histories about the influence of Chinese and Japanese music in the US (respectively) see Rao, 2017 and Sheppard 2019.

sexually non-normative bodies, and second, that these bodies were freely available for Western queers to access without consent. Read within a musical context through the percussion works of the West Coast composers, the appropriation of Asian music was an attempt to construct an imagined queer musical utopia using cultural materials that the composers freely felt entitled to use. Conversations around cultural appropriation frequently focus on how the appropriated group loses agency and material gains, or how such appropriation can generate harmful stereotypes that can translate into further discrimination and perpetuate bodily and psychic trauma. In the particularities of the West Coast group, what is of specific interest is how cultural appropriation facilitated queer desire and how that desire was transmogrified through the composition of percussion ensemble works in concrete musical terms. This aligns with Ben Miller's concept of "primitive homopoetics," which he defines as "a metropolitan gay identification with tropes of non-western and non-state peoples and cultures coded as 'primitive' which arose from the colonial regimes of sexuality" (Miller 2020, 110). The "primitive homopoetics" of the West Coast group were concerned with evocations of timelessness and exoticized eroticism via sonic landscapes of Asia. The early percussion repertoire is often understood as a space for exploration of new sounds in novel combinations, but it is possible to also understand it as a refashioning of primitive musical ideals within an urbanized and eroticized context. Miller's connection between colonialism and identity articulates Wong's formulation of an erotics within the realm of Western white male queerness.

Rather than focusing on individual instruments or timbres that composers used in these works, an understanding of how queer temporality functions as an appropriated category helps to tease out a larger colonialist and racist framework that undergirds how West Coast queer communities understood musical time as something itself that could facilitate white male queer erotics. A look at temporal structures in Cowell's *Ostinato Pianissimo* will elucidate what appropriation looks like in more concrete musical terms, merging appropriation and the queer body in percussion composition.

Composing/Constructing Queer Temporality in Cowell's *Ostinato Pianissimo*

The queer temporality that the West Coast composers constructed was a product of colonial attempts to control racialized bodies realized in the specificities of the queer artistic circles in which they created their music. The desire to seek out a utopia where time flowed differently than the teleological time of the capitalist heteropatriarchy meant that the composers needed to control time, much in the way that colonialism controlled racialized bodies. The queered chrononormativity of the West Coast group is constructed time, a deliberate attempt to stop or reverse time in reaction against heteronormativity and its resultant chrononormativity. Of course, control of musical time is an essential aspect of western art music and the prerogative of the composer; this control is at the service of white heteronormativity. Yet for queer musicians, manipulation of temporality is also a tactic of survival and resistance to oppression. To achieve vertical time is not an accident, or an abdication of authorial control; rather, sculpting music to sound as if time has stopped, or to imbue a score with a sense of timelessness is a highly intentional and controlled process. The construction of percussion ensemble scores was generally highly procedural with an emphasis placed on systems and techniques that were outlined by the dictates of ultramodernist composition. If the materials of percussion composition originated (at least partially) from Asian sources, then the control and manipulation of these materials is an act of colonialism insofar as it was white Westerners who created these scores.

An Eastern affect (as felt by West Coast composers) pervades the use of vertical time found in West Coast temporalities primarily due to the use of ostinatos; however, ostinatos by themselves would not be enough to construct the sense of timelessness that the composers were hoping to achieve. Temporal layers moving at different speeds marked by distinct timbral groups are a feature of several percussion ensemble works, including Cowell's *Ostinato Pianissimo* (1934), Harrison's *Fugue* (1942), Beyer's *IV* (1939), and Cage and Harrison's collaboratively composed *Double Music* (1941). If ostinato cycles with varying beat subdivisions are of different lengths, they will repeat independently from other parts, making larger phrase structures difficult to ascertain, if they are even present. *Ostinato Pianissimo* is a prime example of this, where each of the eight parts has a unique ostinato length (in increasing order of 4, 5, 6, 9, 10, 11, 13, and 15 measures of ♩ and rhythmic value (a range from whole notes to sixteenth notes), and at no point in the short work—lasting under four minutes—do all the cycles repeat at the same point (Figure 8.1).

Cowell is very strict in his exact use of ostinatos, although there are slight variations in superimposed accent patterns in some of the parts, such as the

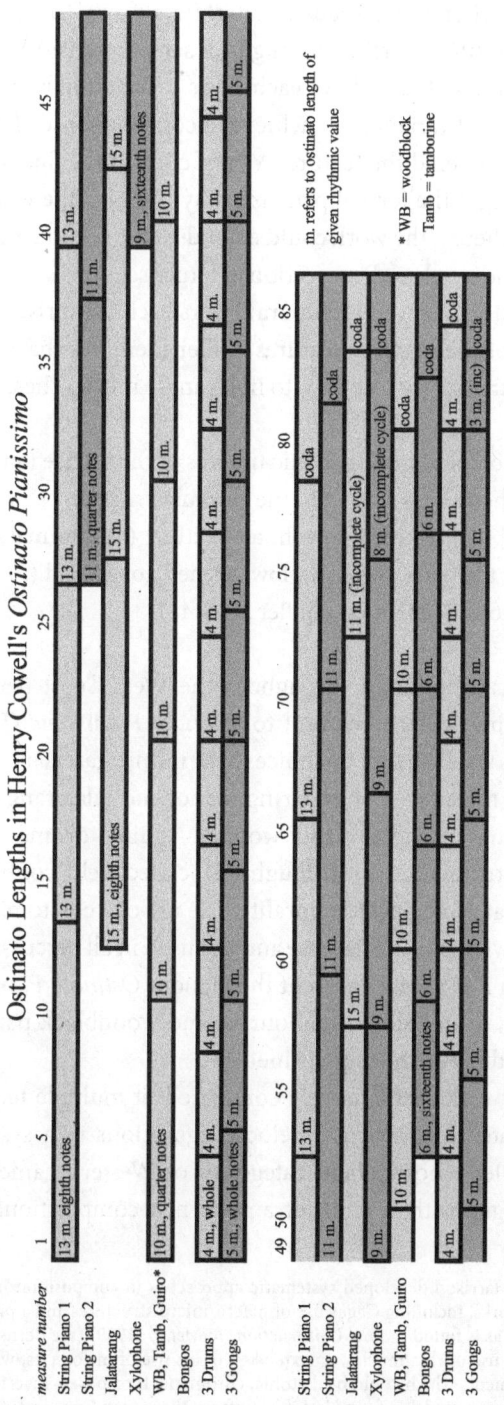

Figure 8.1 Henry Cowell, *Ostinato Pianissimo* (1934), overview of ostinato lengths by instrument

xylophone (which is, referring back to Latartara, a way of "de-emphasiz[ing]" the "regularity of time," further adding to a sense of stasis; Latartara 2007, 101). The combined effect allows each layer to be audibly distinct due to timbral and registral variance but achieves a cohesive sense of stasis once all of the parts have entered the texture. A brief coda in the final few measures of the piece changes the formal plan as a way to finish the work somewhat abruptly, but in theory, the work could extend ad infinitum with unexpected simultaneities and no clear demarcation of larger sections.

The combination of several temporal layers each comprised of their own ostinato is one of the primary features Spiller identifies that US-American listeners were particularly receptive to in Javanese music. These include:

(1) The rich, complex, nonharmonic timbres of the bronze (and bamboo) instruments themselves . . . ; (2) the formulaic nature of melodies and elaborations; (3) a stratified polyphonic texture; (4) a formal framework marked off by the parts played on low-pitched gongs; and (5) a tendency toward ostinato and repetition (Spiller 2015, 41).

These features can be found throughout the West Coast percussion repertoire and are particularly relevant to *Ostinato Pianissimo* (Example 8.1). (1) is present in the instrument choices that mimic gamelan, including the combination of metallic—gongs, string piano, and jalatarang (pitched rice bowls originating in India)—and wooden—guiro, drums, bongos, and xylophone—instruments. (2) through (5) collectively contribute to the overall affect of ateleological temporality. The use of a colotomic gong structure (4) is somewhat of a special case and not used in all percussion ensemble works, although it is notably present throughout *Ostinato Pianissimo* in the combined gong, drum, guiro, tambourine and woodblock parts, and is responsible for audibly anchoring the meter.

In general, a work that is largely comprised of multiple temporal layers that uses ostinatos to construct melodic figurations in a systematic way[7] aligns with Spiller's most salient categories of Western gamelan mimicry. This further aligns with several ultramodernist compositional techniques

---

[7] Both Cage and Harrison developed systematic approaches to composition in their early percussion ensemble works, including Cage's use of macro/micro structures and a process to generate motivic deployment as is found in *First Construction (in Metal)* (1939) (see Bernstein 2002, 71–74, as well as Harrison's use of rhythmicles, an extension of his use of melodicles, which are "motivic neume-like arrangements which could be diatonic, chromatic, transposed, inverted, used in retrograde, or joined to form a mode" as found in *Fifth Simfony* (1941) (von Gunden 1995, 30–31).

Example 8.1 Henry Cowell, *Ostinato Pianissimo* (1934), colotomic instruments, mm. 1–8 (woodblocks, tambourine, guiro, drums, gongs)

that David Nicholls has outlined, including "the use of new or unconventional instruments," "rhythmic complexity, both simultaneous and successive," "independent organization of the various parameters of a musical line or idea," and "large-scale and/or small-scale structuring of form" (Nicholls 1990, 218). The ability for Cowell to refract the concept of gamelan through ultramodernist compositional techniques demonstrates how West Coast composers were able to merge exoticism and Western modernism in the percussion ensemble. Cowell's "primitive homopoetics" are on full display as he constructs this tiny slice of frozen time in such a brief yet potent work, distilling and abstracting the concept of gamelan in service of his urbanized exotic imagination.

Ostinato Pianissimo is one instance of what a Westerner imagines gamelan *might* sound like, which does not necessarily reflect a more culturally responsive experience of hearing gamelan. The sense of stasis in gamelan from a Western perspective results from what Colin McPhee called the "lack of a climax" (referenced in Tenzer 2000, 417). Such an understanding is an orientalist construction and is not necessarily how a native listener would experience the same music. Tenzer articulates this sentiment in response to Kramer's ideas of linearity and nonlinearity and how culturally-centric listening is critical to how one experiences temporality:

> I do not understand *kebyar* as a linear experience in the same way that I or Kramer would understand Beethoven's Opus 132, but I will hold that it is *not* a *nonlinear* one. Regardless of how one in fact hears it, it is fair to state that like Balinese cyclicity, tonal linearity reinforces the values of those conditioned to the culture that engendered it . . . Always caught among these

changeable modes of perception, after decades of listening to both Balinese *gamelan* and tonal music I cannot concede any fundamental opposition between their temporalities . . . Most of my Balinese friends were inexperienced with eighteenth- and nineteenth-century Western art music, and when I played it for them . . . most admitted hearing it as muddled and directionless." (Tenzer 2000, 417–18)

The flatness of *Ostinato Pianissimo* is the result of a failure to hear past the more immediate aspects of gamelan, at least as understood within a Western framework of listening. Tenzer highlights how a sense of temporality is dependent on a personal and cultural familiarity with the given repertoire, and how casual cross-cultural listening can erase otherwise distinctive features that point to larger structures.

Cowell's construction of vertical time is ultimately more of a reaction against Western linearity, including its climaxes and teleology, than it is an attempt to accurately depict gamelan, and it reiterates the vision of Asian bodies as receptacles for Western queer desire. Cowell queers chrononormativity in an act of identity formation against dominant US-American heteropatriarchal forces from within inherited compositional practice by composing in opposition to how he perceived normative and functional musical temporality, which included build-ups, climaxes, formal markers, and harmonic phenomena. *Ostinato Pianissimo* contains none of these components, and Cowell is representative of the West Coast group in orienting himself toward the East while using the tools of modernism to forge novel musical expressions yet denying agency to the cultures from which he appropriates; "constructions of Otherness rely on a temporal and spatial banishment of other cultures from Modernity" (Jordan 1995, 282). In the percussion ensemble's queer utopian vision for an alternative to the forward motion of modernity, the West Coast group ultimately reinscribes colonial and racist structures that maintain Western dominance through essentializing, caricaturing, and excluding the Asian cultures that they sought to honor and emulate.

Conclusion: Imagining Queered Chrononormativities

The temporality that infuses the West Coast percussion repertoire is a historically contingent iteration of queered chrononormativity centered around cyclic forms that veer away from teleological trajectories as a way of creating a sense of timelessness that was informed by a historically contingent queer erotics. The West Coast composers fell into colonialist patterns that had already been laid out for them, absorbing exotic influences into their practice without an awareness that they were acting in an exploitative manner. Their shallow understanding was indicative of racial and colonial privileges that were rewarded in artistic circles that frequently dabbled in exoticism as a sign of avant-gardism and outsider cachet. West Coast percussion composers were constructing an aesthetic experience that borrowed widely and indiscriminately, yet behind the erotics of Asian-facilitated desire was a necessity borne of the materials of percussion, requiring new formal organization that eschewed the tendencies of tonal music due to a lack of standardized pitch content and a charge to follow the path of Western musical modernism. Exoticism, eroticism, modernism, and race come crashing together in the social climate of the interwar period to construct the queered chrononormativity that distinctly belongs to the West Coast percussion repertoire.

The field of percussion has a tendency to indiscriminately absorb instruments and styles from global musics in a continuation of Western accumulative colonialism. Acknowledging the historical forces of power that have generated these practices, as well as the resultant aesthetics that have been born out of their use, is the first step toward a potentially more power-sensitive musicmaking that can reveal the myriad ways that white Western capitalist privilege has consistently relied-upon racialized and indigenous global music practices. Western percussion history and criticism in particular have only begun to reckon with a colonial and racist past that is just around a century old since the earliest pieces were composed, and it is urgent to more broadly consider why the field has held up certain works as exemplary and what they tell us about the field's priorities. Queer theory and other critical approaches including critical race theory, feminism, post/decolonial studies, and disability studies are necessary in order to generate new understandings, particularly as normative music theory has traditionally been applied to percussion works. Today, the works of the West Coast group are viewed as foundational to the percussion ensemble repertoire that followed in its wake, and as the field has moved from experimental to broadly accepted and normalized practice, it is imperative to acknowledge the queer roots of the ensemble and the forms of power that are inscribed in the repertoire.

Expanding beyond percussion, queered approaches to chrononormativity in any musical practice will be dictated by the normative pressures under which they arise. As long as oppressive forces necessitate creative survival responses from queer artists, new forms of temporality will continually come into being, particularly as older forms become co-opted by normativity. Various iterations of queered chrononormativity will not necessarily resemble each other as the processes that produce them are more important than the forms that they take. Starting with queer bodies and their erotics will lead to locating the necessary analytical tools in order to understand how queer individuals and groups are coping with temporal oppression through aesthetic means and reclaiming their agency as they imagine new ways of being in the world.

References

Ahmed, Sara. 2006. *Queer Phenomenology: Orientations, Objects, Others*. Durham, NC: Duke University Press.

Ahmed, Sara. 2010. *The Promise of Happiness*. Durham, NC: Duke University Press.

Aldrich, Robert. 2003. *Colonialism and Homosexuality*. London: Routledge.

Bernstein, David W. 2002. "Music I: to the late 1940s." In *The Cambridge Companion to John Cage*, edited by David Nicholls, 63–84. Cambridge: Cambridge University Press.

Boellstorff, Tom. 2005. *The Gay Archipelago: Sexuality and Nation in Indonesia*. Princeton, NJ: Princeton University Press.

Boyd, Nan Alamilla. 2003. *Wide Open Town: A History of Queer San Francisco to 1965*. Berkeley: University of California Press.

Brett, Phillip. 1994. "Eros and Orientalism in Benjamin Britten's Operas." In *Queering the Pitch: The New Gay and Lesbian Musicology*, edited by Philip Brett, Elizabeth Wood, and Gary C., 235–56. Thomas. New York: Routledge.

Burt, Ramsay. 1995. *The Male Dancer: Bodies, Spectacle, Sexualities*. New York: Routledge.

Carter, Julian B. 2007. *The Heart of Whiteness: Normal Sexuality and Race in America, 1880–1940*. Durham, NC: Duke University Press.

Cohen, Matthew Isaac. 2010. *Performing otherness: Java and Bali on International Stages, 1905–1952*. New York: Palgrave Macmillan.

Cowell, Henry. 1927. "The Impasse of Modern Music: Searching for New Avenues of Beauty." *Century Magazine* 114, no. 6 (October): 671–77.

Cowell, Henry. 1996. *New Musical Resources. With Notes and an Accompanying Essay by David Nicholls*. Cambridge: Cambridge University Press.

Foulkes, Julia L. 2002. *Modern Bodies: Dance and American Modernism from Martha Graham to Alvin Ailey*. Chapel Hill: University of North Carolina Press.

Freeman, Elizabeth. 2010. *Time Binds: Queer Temporalities, Queer Histories*. Durham, NC: Duke University Press.

Halberstam, Judith. 2005. *In a Queer Time and Place: Transgender Bodies, Subcultural Lives*. New York: New York University Press.

Hubbs, Nadine. 2004. *The Queer Composition of America's Sound: Gay Modernists, American Music, and National Identity*. Berkeley: University of California Press.

Ibrahim, Ahmad. 2019. "Under Empire and the Modern State." In *"Queer" Asia: Decolonising and Reimagining Sexuality and Gender*, edited by J. Daniel Luther and Jennifer Ung Loh, 29–43. London: Zed Books.

Jordan, Glenn. 1995. "Flight from Modernity: Time, the Other and the Discourse of Primitivism." *Time & Society* 4, no. 3: 281–303.

Kramer, Jonathan D. 1998. *The Time of Music: New Meanings, New Temporalities, New Listening Strategies*. New York: Schirmer Books.

Latartara, John. 2007. "Cage and Time: Temporality in Early and Late Works." *College Music Symposium* 47: 100–16.

Luther, J. Daniel, and Jennifer Ung Loh. 2019. "Introduction." In *"Queer" Asia: Decolonising and Reimagining Sexuality and Gender*, edited by Luther J. Daniel and Jennifer Ung Loh, 1–26. London: Zed Books.

Miller, Ben. 2020. "On Faggots and Class Struggle." *Pinko* 2: 109–12.

Miller, Leta E. 2000. "The Art of Noise: John Cage, Lou Harrison, and the West Coast Percussion Ensemble." In *Perspectives in American Music, 1900–1950*, edited by Michael Saffle, 215–64. New York: Garland Publishing.

Miller, Leta E. 2006. "Henry Cowell and John Cage: Intersections and Influences, 1933–1941." *Journal of the American Musicological Society* 59, no. 1 (Spring): 47–112.

Miller, Leta E. 2012. *Music and Politics in San Francisco: From the 1960 Quake to the Second World War*. Berkeley: University of California Press.

Miller, Leta E., and Fredric Lieberman. 1999. "Lou Harrison and the American Gamelan." *American Music* 17, no. 2 (Summer): 146–78.

Muñoz, José Esteban. 1999. *Disidentifications: Queers of Color and the Performance of Politics*. Minneapolis: University of Minnesota Press.

Muñoz, José Esteban. 2009. *Cruising Utopia: The Then and There of Queer Futurity*. New York: New York University Press.

Nicholls, David. 1990. *American Experimental Music, 1890–1940*. Cambridge: Cambridge University Press.

Nicholls, David. 1999. "Reaching beyond the West: Asian Resonances in American Radicalism." *American Music* 17, no. 2 (Summer): 125–28.

Rao, Nancy Yunhwa. 2017. *Chinatown Opera Theater in North American*. Urbana: University of Illinois Press.

Sachs, Joel. 2012. *Henry Cowell: A Man Made of Music*. Oxford: Oxford University Press.

Sheppard, W. Anthony. 2019. *Extreme Exoticism: Japan in the American Musical Imagination*. Oxford: Oxford University Press.

Siwe, Thomas. 2020. *Artful Noise: Percussion Literature in the Twentieth Century*. Urbana: University of Illinois Press.

Spiller, Henry. 2015. *Javaphilia: American Love Affairs with Javanese Music and Dance*. Honolulu: University of Hawai'i Press.

Solomon, William. 2016. "Cage, Cowell, Harrison, and Queer Influences on the Percussion Ensemble, 1932–1943." DMA thesis, University of Hartford.

Tenzer, Michael. 2000. *Gamelan Gong Kebyar: The Art of Twentieth-Century Balinese Music*. Chicago: University of Chicago Press.

von Gunden, Heidi. 1995. *The Music of Lou Harrison*. Metuchen, NJ: Scarecrow Press.

Wong, Deborah. 2015. "Ethnology without Erotics." *Women and Music: A Journal of Gender and Culture* 19: 178–85.

Yang, Mina. 2001. "New Directions in California Music: Construction of a Pacific Rim Identity, 1925–1945." PhD diss., Yale University.

Yang, Mina. 2008. *California Polyphony: Ethnic Voices, Musical Crossroads*. Urbana: University of Illinois Press.

QUEER NARRATOLOGY

9

Queer Sexuality and Musical Narrative

Fred Everett Maus

Music as Narrative

In the 1980s, music scholars (I among them) developed a lively discussion of relations between non-programmatic instrumental music and narrative.[1] We wondered whether nonprogrammatic instrumental music, despite its lack of specific external reference, might sometimes be a kind of storytelling. Edward T. Cone, though not emphasizing the term narrative, made influential early contributions in *The Composer's Voice* (1974), which introduced notions of persona and agency, and in essays on Brahms (Cone 1977) and Schubert (Cone 1982) that, in effect, identified plot in short piano pieces.[2] As the field developed, one of its most visible and accomplished scholars was Anthony Newcomb, whose essays on Schumann, Chopin, and Mahler offered an array of different approaches to musical narrative.[3] Susan McClary, an innovative contributor on narrative throughout the 1980s, broke new ground with her book *Feminine Endings* (1991), recasting narrative interpretation as a resource for feminist music criticism.[4]

Contexts for narrative approaches were various. Narrative-like descriptions of music from the same historical milieux as specific musical compositions could support narrative interpretation as a project of recovering historical meanings.[5] General structural studies of literary and vernacular narrative, in the tradition of Russian Formalist and Structuralist theorists, could

---

[1] As it developed, the conversation almost all took place around interpretation of Western art music, and that is still where the approach seems to be most at home.

  Drama may be a more precise concept than narrative for this area of study. See Maus 1988, 56–73, and 1997, 293–303. But music scholars generally refer to the area as "music and narrative." The term "narrative" has connotations that could be misleading, but by now many scholars share a broad understanding of ways that narrative or drama can relate to music.

[2] Cone 1974; 1977, 554–74; 1982, 233–41.

[3] Newcomb 1984, 233–50; 1987, 164–74; 1992, 118–36; 1994, 84–101; 1997, 131–53.

[4] McClary 2002. First published 1991.

[5] Newcomb, "Once More 'Between Absolute and Program Music,'" is a clear example of this historicizing approach.

Fred Everett Maus, *Queer Sexuality and Musical Narrative* In: *Queer Ear*. Edited by: Gavin S. K. Lee, Oxford University Press. © Oxford University Press 2023. DOI: 10.1093/oso/9780197536766.003.0010

suggest analogous generalizations for music, for instance about types of musical plot structures. The resemblance between music theory discourse and narratologists' formalist abstraction and rule-seeking was suggestive.[6] Less scientific styles of literary studies could also provide models, for instance in Cone's accounts of musical persona, drawing on Wayne Booth's work, and musical gesture, drawing on R. P. Blackmur.[7] Feminist studies of narrative in literature and beyond contributed to McClary's thought.[8] Less academically, musicians and music lovers were familiar with everyday practices of storytelling as a way of interpreting music. Listeners and writers have often, intentionally or spontaneously, consciously or less consciously, imagined story-like events as they hear music; E. M. Forster provided a famous example in *Howard's End*.[9] A performance instructor might offer narrative to encourage vividness in students' performances; McClary, long before writing about musical narrative, used narrative description in her role as a chamber music coach.[10] Donald F. Tovey's critical writing from the early twentieth century often moved into vivid storytelling and was influential for some contributors to narrative-oriented criticism, not least for a group of music scholars associated with Princeton University—Cone, Joseph Kerman, Charles Rosen, Leo Treitler.[11] Partly through Tovey's influence, Kerman and Rosen wrote in ways that could be associated with later narrative interpretations of music.[12] Finally, during the 1980s and after, "music and narrative" was named and debated in professional music studies as a critical approach and a research field.[13]

---

[6] Newcomb's recurring invocation of plot archetypes is a clear example. Patrick McCreless developed comparisons and contrasts between musical and literary structures (1988, 1–29; 1991, 35–73). I explored formalist and structuralist resources (1991, 1–34).

[7] Cone 1974, 4, 163.

[8] In particular, McClary drew on the feminist narratology of Teresa de Lauretis (2002 14–15, 140).

[9] Forster's character Helen, hearing Beethoven's Fifth Symphony in a concert creates a vivid story about goblins while hearing the third and fourth movements (2000, 26–28).

[10] "I began my own interrogation of music and narrative long before I had read any literary theory, back in the mid-1960s when I worked as a chamber-music coach. When I played the piano by myself, I intuited certain ways of 'making sense' in music, and it was only when I encountered others whose performances sounded inert that I started devising verbal strategies for explaining scores. I was repeatedly flabbergasted when good technical musicians failed to notice struggle or miraculous arrivals or anything other than just . . . notes on the page, and I understood my job as pointing up these events and explicating the contexts." McClary 1997, 23.

[11] Princeton graduates from subsequent generations have also been active in music and narrative studies—Anthony Newcomb, Carolyn Abbate, and I. Long-time faculty member Scott Burnham (now at CUNY) has worked in similar ways. Music scholars are accustomed to thinking of a "Princeton School" of intensely elaborated formalist music theory oriented around Milton Babbitt's work. We should think of another "Princeton School" as well, oriented around music criticism, narrative studies, Cone, and Tovey (see the latter's vivid storytelling in Tovey 1935–39).

[12] Kerman 1967; Rosen 1971. Rosen's favored concept was drama rather than narrative. Kerman responded to subsequent developments (1992, 80–101).

[13] For my general accounts of the development of this field, see Maus 2001 and 2005, 466–83.

Another productive contribution to music criticism was the study of musical topics, following Leonard Ratner's influential treatment in 1980.[14] Topics are recognizable recurring stylistic features of passages of music, associated with meanings and thus making up a vocabulary of meaningful signs. Identification of topics, by connecting specific meanings with moments in a composition, could contribute to a narrative account.[15]

In general (and beyond specifically narrative orientations), studies of musical meaning have often centered on emotional experience or emotional expression as the central link between musical sound and human life. A focus on narrative offers a different emphasis, finding in instrumental music a series of events that go together in a story-like way and exhibit a range of human-like qualities—emotion, of course, but also thought, purpose, action and reaction, character traits, and more. Detailed technical analysis can add specificity to a musical narrative that attributes recognizable human meaning, and early studies of music and narrative by Cone, Newcomb, McClary, Treitler, and others leaned heavily on analysis. Thus, the study of music and narrative could narrow the discursive gap between technical analysis, on one hand, and critical interpretation, on the other. Noted contributors to this area included some people primarily identified as music historians along with others identified as music theorists. The approach sometimes seemed to bring musical interpretation closer to literary criticism, the latter field often a point of reference when music scholars advocated for music criticism.

The study of music and narrative has ranged from relatively systematic generalization (Seth Monahan, Byron Almén, Robert Hatten) to imaginative, improvisatory verbalization that should perhaps not be called "theory" or "analysis" (Tovey, and perhaps J. K. Randall above all).[16] Epistemologies of such work range from an aspiration to historical knowledge (Newcomb) to reports of personal experience (Philip Brett).

Queer Musical Stories

McClary's *Feminine Endings* was not the first scholarly feminist writing on music, but it has often been praised as the first book of feminist music

---

[14] Ratner 1980.

[15] See, e.g., Allanbrook 1992, 125–71.

[16] See, e.g., Monahan 2013, 321–71; Almén 2008; Hatten 2018; Randall 1976, 424–517. In Randall's text as first published, some pages are out of order (see errata: 1977, 1).

criticism. Many of its central arguments relied on narrative interpretations. Before *Feminine Endings*, McClary wrote about musical narrative in contexts other than gender and sexuality. Her first published essay, "Pitches, Expression, Ideology: An Exercise in Mediation," linked three components: musical structure as described in analytical terms, expressive patterns recurring across a group of early nineteenth-century compositions, and broad issues in nineteenth-century European culture.[17] The ideological issues were "problems of discontinuity, loss of confidence in the individual's ability to determine his or her fate, and the turn from rational processes to the irrationality characteristic of Romanticism," and "a dual perception of external versus internal realities and an inability (or reluctance) to reconcile them adequately."[18] Essays on Mozart and Bach followed, each taking as a central example a movement of a concerto; in McClary's accounts, solo keyboard parts embodied protagonists interacting with external social forces.[19]

Feminine Endings continued to use a narrative approach in relation to social concerns, now issues of gender and sexuality. McClary's much-discussed account of sonata form articulated a narrative of masculine subjectivity, potentially subverted by femininity, regaining control through domination of pitch structure. The familiar structural plan of key relations, involving a narrative of destabilization and reassertion of control, interacted with an interpretation of gendered associations of different types of musical material, akin to a topical analysis (McClary used the terms "semiotics" and "codes"). As always in her work, she inflected this general plan subtly to match the details of individual compositions. McClary also drew attention to parallels between musical and sexual experience, associating a purposeful drive toward climax and resolution with a normative masculinity and masculine sexuality, hearing in alternative temporalities an evocation of different sensual and sexual subjectivities.

The same critical approaches shaped McClary's two major contributions at the beginning of queer music criticism. She described the first movement of Tchaikovsky's Fourth Symphony in terms of a protagonist, associated with Tchaikovsky himself, caught between two destructive forces.[20] The protagonist does not exhibit heroic masculinity, as in many sonata form pieces, but

---

[17] McClary 1983, 76–86.

[18] McClary 1983, 82.

[19] McClary 1986, 129–69; McClary 1987, 13–62.

[20] Throughout this essay, I am not concerned to judge the truth of the analyses that I discuss. I ask how the authors shape their arguments and how queerness is relevant to their positions.

is set apart from it. An "appoggiatura-laden, limping theme . . . hypersensitive, vulnerable, indecisive"[21] embodies the protagonist, who is "victimized both by patriarchal expectations and by sensual feminine entrapment."[22] The reference to a "limping" theme draws in physical disability, perhaps in association with the idea of homosexuality as deficiency, perhaps also linking to sexual impotence. The frightening military fanfares of the introduction establish extreme masculinity as an antagonist in this story, and the second theme evokes a threatening, exoticized femininity. Obviously, semiotic features were crucial in this interpretation. McClary's detailed narrative traced the interplay of these contrasting gendered characteristics through the movement.

McClary's essay on the second movement of Schubert's "Unfinished" Symphony argued differently, though again the interpretation emphasized a contrast with the more usual gendered narratives of sonata form. Qualities of movement and pleasure were central, resulting in part from choices of pitch structure. In general,

> Schubert tends to disdain goal-oriented desire per se for the sake of a sustained image of pleasure and an open, flexible sense of self—both of which are quite alien to the constructions of masculinity then being adopted as natural, and also to the premises of musical form as they were commonly construed at the time.[23]

McClary found these qualities in the Andante of the "Unfinished" Symphony, which

> appears to drift freely through enharmonic and oblique modulations, rather than establishing a clear tonic and pursuing a dynamic sequence of modulations; identities are easily shed, exchanged, fused, and reestablished.[24]

Such music is very different from the heroic style of the first movement of Beethoven's Symphony No. 3, often taken as a supreme model of musical design. In its persistent drive through vicissitudes toward final triumph, the

---

[21] McClary 2002, 71 ("Sexual Politics in Classical Music" chapter).
[22] McClary 2002, 76 ("Sexual Politics in Classical Music" chapter).
[23] McClary 2006, 223.
[24] McClary 2006, 223.

Beethoven movement is a model of striving and achievement. In contrast, McClary followed Schubert's Andante through various changes—an opening that evokes a "porous ego," briefly disturbed by an "abrupt intrusion of authority" (again, masculinity figures as an antagonist); a section in which formation of a definite identity and a corresponding harmonic stability feel like constraints, "a kind of prison"; an escape from this, identity dissolving into interacting characters who once again "float" through a series of key changes.

The Schubert analysis, unlike the Tchaikovsky analysis, was strongly affirmative. None of the three interacting entities in McClary's Tchaikovsky narrative—the wounded protagonist, patriarchal force, and dangerously seductive femininity—could be simply celebrated, though the narrative could arouse empathy. Where Tchaikovsky was read as depicting a painful situation, McClary saw Schubert musically constructing an enchanting image of an alternative masculine subjectivity: Schubert's music affirms difference. (The slogan might be: "We're here, we're sensuous and non-teleological, get used to it.") Alongside this positive image McClary also noted Schubert's darker compositions, his "victim narratives." These offer enticing images of pleasure, but then the pleasure is punished.[25]

McClary was drawn to think about Schubert in relation to sexuality in part because of Maynard Solomon's then-recent argument that Schubert was homosexual,[26] but also because of an observed phenomenon of contemporary listeners who wondered, just from their experience of the music, whether Schubert was gay.[27] And she responded to a long tradition that depicted Schubert's music as somehow troubled in relation to masculinity.[28] As research on Schubert's sexuality developed, McClary acknowledged that Solomon's arguments for Schubert's homosexuality were not conclusive, and she preferred to emphasize Schubert's musical construction of a distinct, alternative masculine subjectivity.[29] At the same time, she noted resonances between Schubert's subjectivity, as we can experience it through his music, and twentieth-century queerness. In looking for an analogue of Schubert's characteristic effects, she turned to critic Earl Jackson's account of "gay male sexuality" and its expression in contemporary literature,[30] and she compared

---

[25] McClary 2006, 225.
[26] Solomon 1989, 193–206.
[27] McClary 2006, 205–6.
[28] McClary 2006, 209, 213, 227.
[29] This was the argument that appeared in McClary's final version of the essay in *Queering the Pitch*.
[30] McClary 2006, 223–24.

Schubert's victim narratives to the work of famous modern queer literary writers.[31]

McClary's essays on Tchaikovsky and Schubert are foundational classics of queer music studies, merging technical analysis with rich narrative resources. Philip Brett's account of the slow movement of Schubert's Sonata in C for piano, four hands is a third exemplary study in queer musical narrative. Brett's essay, published in 1997, identified itself as the first intervention by a lesbian or gay scholar (by which he meant an out lesbian or gay scholar) in what had become a heated discussion of Schubert and sexuality.[32] Brett wrote about Schubert to ask, among other questions, what Schubert's music might mean to modern gay men. This question is somewhat independent of historical speculation about Schubert's life. Brett reflected on his performances of piano music for four hands with a younger gay male friend. He began by noting the potential eroticism and deviancy in the four-hand medium itself, with its domestic setting, its frequent reliance on transcriptions with their aura of inauthenticity, and the physical closeness of the partners who must merge their embodied musicalities into a single performance.[33]

Brett's description of Schubert's music gave close attention to the opening section, where he frequently named details with reference to gender and sexuality and the imagery of twentieth-century gay life ("nervous tenor," "drama queen," "diva," "impetuous transvestite soprano").[34] Moments of harmonic equivocation led Brett to identify "a fluctuation, a vacillation, a carefully constructed undecidability," which Brett associated with

> the intense confusion of thought and feeling that is connected with the image of the emasculated male in the age of sensibility and that, for different reasons, homosexual children and adolescents grow up with today.[35]

Odd repetitions of the closing cadence in this first section suggested distraction, which Brett again linked to the age of sensibility and to modern gay men, who sometimes need to perform distraction in order to slip out of an immediate unsustaining environment.

---

[31] McClary 2006, 226.
[32] Brett 1997, 150.
[33] Brett 1997, 153–55.
[34] Brett 1997, 157.
[35] Brett 1997, 159.

Brett's description of the opening section depicted an ambivalent subjectivity while issuing reminders that the interpretation arose from the interaction of two twentieth-century gay men with Schubert's music. Brett's larger narrative centered on three points in the rest of the movement when disquieting music appears, returning each time with increasing intensity until, finally, "all hell breaks loose . . . in a texture as reductive, nihilistic, and terrifying as anything in nineteenth-century music."[36] Or, to put it in more emotional terms,

> The brutal dissonance and hollow timbre represent the sheer rage of the powerless subject who is hopeless, the out-of-control moments that are never revealed, or the terrifying fantasy of their revelation ("Is this what would happen if I really let it all out?").[37]

Brett and his piano-duet partner were both familiar with these feelings, though in somewhat different ways, as twentieth-century gay men of different ages, from different national and economic backgrounds. Presumably, as Brett observes, Schubert drew on some related range of emotional experience to be able to write this music; this may have been due to his illness with syphilis, perhaps also the non-normative sexuality suggested by Solomon.

Brett emphasized, not just these moments of dysregulation, but especially the way the music responds to them afterward. The first two times, the troubled passage is closed off abruptly by polite, conventional cadences, described as a "cover-up gesture." Brett found this to be

> even more poignant than the irresolute wanderings that have preceded it. Virtuosos in the art of "passing," and of pleasing all and sundry, my partner and I manage to produce a particularly smug cadential gesture while both, I suspect, feeling its latent pain and incongruity.[38]

After the third, most intensely painful turn to dark emotion, the piece ends by seeming to grope unsuccessfully for another pleasant, superficial cadential resolution.

McClary's and Brett's interpretations varied in their claims to truth. McClary's vivid, firmly stated descriptions seemed to aim for historical truth,

[36] Brett 1997, 163–164.
[37] Brett 1997, 164.
[38] Brett 1997, 160–161.

even as she acknowledged that other experiences of the music were possible. Brett was especially clear about the subjective components of his reading of Schubert: as mentioned, the analytical portion of the essay was about a Schubert piece as perceived by two twentieth-century gay men. Memorably, Brett stated that "Criticism is radical in musicology because it is personal and has no authority whatsoever."[39]

The three interpretations varied, as well, in the way they brought queerness into musical narratives. McClary understood the Tchaikovsky movement in terms of strongly gendered codes. Her Schubert analysis depended less on semiotics, more on a construction of time and pleasure that contrasts with struggle and goal-orientation. As often in *Feminine Endings*, she interpreted music in relation to temporal patterns of sensuality and sexuality. Brett's description turned to a complex pattern of emotional experience—painful feelings that emerge from a suppressed state, which are then suppressed again through the imposition of a compliant false self. This interpretation did not match the music directly with sexual feelings, but rather with the emotional consequences of social stigma and conformity.

None of these narrative patterns has an inevitable association with men desiring men. The Tchaikovsky, as McClary read it, most clearly depicts gender failure, inadequacy in relation to strongly marked images of masculinity and femininity. (Such gender failure is, to be sure, central to some conceptions of homosexuality.) Present-oriented pleasure and the dissolution of ego, as found in the Schubert symphony, are accessible to people other than gay men. Management of stigma and of socially unacceptable rage, as heard in Schubert's four-hand piano piece, could be part of many lives. The point is not that one can reliably discover homosexuality from evidence in any of this music; McClary and Brett were very clear on this. Such an inquiry would be a performance of the epistemology of the closet, preoccupied with secrets, clues, and detection.[40] What McClary and Brett did was different: regarding sexuality, they asked how certain music could make sense in relation to gay lives. Given that we know that Tchaikovsky was homosexual, that Schubert may have been, or may have been set apart from dominant norms of masculinity in other ways, and that some present-day listeners and performers are gay men, what might this music mean in such lives?

[39] Brett 1997, 171.
[40] This pattern of thought was influentially articulated in Sedgwick 2008.

The Beginnings of "Music and Narrative": Edward T. Cone

I return now to the work of Cone and Newcomb. As mentioned, both made crucial early contributions to the development of music and narrative studies. Both were gay men, out in their social lives but not referring openly to their sexual identities in their published work as music scholars. They maintained this personal/professional dichotomy during the growth of queer music studies from the late 1980s on, a movement in which they did not participate. Nonetheless, I want to ask whether their pioneering work on music and narrative owed a debt to their gay male subjectivities.

I will comment shortly on Cone's essay "Schubert's Promissory Note: An Exercise in Musical Hermeneutics," which relates Schubert's *Moment musical No. 6* to sexual temptation and deadly consequences. It is Cone's only explicit treatment of music in relation to sexuality.[41] First, though, I want to mention several texts about Cone by other writers. These publications are not about music as narrative, but they provide a backdrop of material that positions the discreet Cone, one way and another, in various relations to gender and sexuality.

In 1995, Cone's partner of many years, philosopher George Pitcher, published a memoir, *The Dogs Who Came to Stay*, about the couple's adoption of a stray dog and her puppy, and their life with the two dogs over many years.[42] This book is the most extensive public document of Cone's personal life. It never identified Cone and Pitcher as lovers, instead introducing them as "two middle-aged bachelors," "sharing this handsome Victorian house."[43] By the end, Pitcher named the quartet of humans and dogs as a family; a queer family, as I would say but Pitcher did not, with two non-human children and two human fathers; one dog also brings a maternal quality to the group.[44] Throughout, it is a moving book about love. The men's love for their dogs was described in touching detail. The love between Cone and Pitcher was never mentioned as such. Instead, the book quietly exemplified the men's relationship through the continuous thoughtful attention they gave to each other. The two were rarely separated, and they made all decisions together, about the dogs and about other matters such as the long trips that they took

[41] Cone 1982.

[42] Pitcher 1995).

[43] Pitcher 1995, 4. I note that the word "handsome" has been displaced from male attractiveness onto a big old house.

[44] Pitcher 1995, 158.

together. The book did not mention friendships or other relationships that competed with their mutual involvement. The narrative did not grant to either man any sexual experiences or attractions. *The Dogs Who Came to Stay* is an affecting book about a family, but with a gap at its center, a book in which the love between the two parents dared not speak its name.[45] In the somewhat unlikely context of a book-length memoir about loving relationships, it followed the same rule of nondisclosure about personal sexuality as Cone's writings about music. No doubt this reticence made the book enjoyable for dog-lovers who would not have welcomed open identification of Pitcher and Cone as gay.

Near the beginning of *Feminine Endings*, McClary commented on a passage in *Musical Form and Musical Performance* in which Cone worried over a detail in a Chopin polonaise. Cone suggested a performance strategy for an "incorrigibly feminine" cadence; a certain way of playing could make the cadence sound a bit stronger, "if not precisely masculine." As McClary aptly put it, "Cone is concerned here with 'butching up' a polonaise."[46] In what Cone no doubt understood as a technical discussion, McClary caught more than a whiff of misogyny, an aversion to musical qualities associated with femininity.[47]

In his essay on Schubert, Brett subjected Cone to a bit of sexuality-based teasing. Cone wrote in *The Composer's Voice* about the intimacy of four-hand piano performance, which he called "the blending of two players into a single four-handed monster" and "a marriage rather than a mere friendship." Brett drew out some sexual implications, concluding that Cone's comments are "surely as close as musicology of a perfectly respectable kind can come to exploring the (deviant) sexuality surrounding music without advertising what it is doing."[48] Brett expressed sincere admiration for Cone's willingness to describe the potential sex-adjacent closeness and awkwardness of four-hand performance, but there was something else in Brett's words. Brett

---

[45] The book includes twelve photographs of the dogs. Pitcher appears in a few of them, Cone in a few others. No photo includes both men. This makes sense, of course, if one member of the couple was in a photo that the other man took. But it is striking that they felt no need to gather the whole family for at least one image.

[46] McClary 2002, 10.

[47] I spoke with Cone in 1991, shortly after the publication of *Feminine Endings*, at a retirement party for J. K. Randall. He asked whether I had read *Feminine Endings* and what I thought of it. The part he wanted to talk about, it turned out, was McClary's passage about masculine and feminine cadences. He was grumpy. "It's just a metaphor," he said.

[48] Brett 1997, 154.

had persistent distaste for, and sometimes anger at, his contemporaries in musicology who maintained a strict separation between queer lives and unqueer music studies. Coming from Brett, "perfectly respectable" would not be a purely positive phrase; it could be heard in this context as implying "closeted."

Twice before, I have interpreted Cone's ideas in relation to gender and/or sexuality. In "The Disciplined Subject of Musical Analysis," I wrote about the psychology of listening in *The Composer's Voice*. As I summarized it:

> A listener's imaginative experience . . . has a strange multiple conscious-ness, conjoining an awareness of submission (the persona's power over them) with a thrill of identification with power (even though that power takes effect, in part, by domination of themself). To this doubled experi-ence is added, I suppose, a third aspect, a listener's awareness that the whole configuration is, to some extent, fictional and consensual, a chosen style of imaginative submission rather than a literal subjection to force. And the whole complex configuration seems to be itself an object of desire.[49]

I likened this listening to the eroticization of power relations in sadomas-ochism, citing a practical manual on the bottom role in sadomasochism that enthusiastically described a similar combination of submission and identification.[50]

In "Time, Embodiment, and Sexuality in Music Theory," I reflected on Cone's contrast between "synoptic comprehension" of musical structure and "immediate apprehension" of music. His distinction came at the end of *Musical Form and Musical Performance*, a book that mostly addressed the communication of musical structure through reflective performance decisions. I likened Cone's contrast to McClary's characteristic opposition be-tween goal-driven drama and present-oriented pleasure, summarized above in relation to Schubert. In writing about Schubert, McClary interpreted the second type of temporality as an alternative masculinity; elsewhere she often associated similar qualities with women and the feminine. As I paraphrased it, Cone

---

[49] Maus 2004, 35. At the time of writing, the pronouns she/her/hers were considered a good solu-tion to the default masculine pronoun of older usage. This is no longer true; I have substituted they/them/theirs in the quoted passage.

[50] Maus 2004, 35–36.

distinguishes between, on one hand, a "lust for inventing structures" (a phrase he borrows from [his heterosexual Princeton colleague] J. K. Randall), on the other hand, an "unholy delight" in "the successive notes and smallest fragments, as they turn up moment after moment." This is, for Cone, an unusually frisky moment, in which he acknowledges the eroticism of musical experience, apparently on condition that the acknowledgment be almost unnoticeably brief. Structure, according to Cone, is an object of desire, or "lust," while the moment-by-moment experience of music offers "delight," inviting what Cone also calls a "healthily hedonist attention to the musical surface." Like McClary, he links his musical opposition to experiential qualities associated with stereotypes of gendered sexual subjectivities [though perhaps without consciously perceiving the connection to gender and sexuality as such].[51]

McClary used her opposition to categorize different kinds of music. Cone's account was about contrasting attentional styles, not primarily musical styles. Some music does not invite or reward synoptic perception, but otherwise both kinds of perception are available for most music, and Cone recommended developing both, even while his book focused on the synoptic and structural.

In these five examples we see, first, Pitcher writing at length about his life with Cone while carefully refraining from mention of their sexual relationship, and then four examples of commentators nudging Cone's writing toward more explicit connections with gender and/or sexuality. McClary found Cone unselfconsciously reproducing a negative gender stereotype; she brought it to the surface. Brett and I found Cone linking music and sexuality in insightful ways but holding back from stating connections to sexuality openly, as we went on to do. In writing such passages, was Cone conscious of relations between sexuality and music?

"Schubert's Promissory Note" was different. By the end, the essay associated Schubert's *Moment musical* No. 6 with sexual temptation and syphilis, incurable in Schubert's time. Before turning to the Schubert piece, the essay began with a bold general theory of musical meaning, developing ideas previously stated in the last section of *The Composer's Voice*. A composition, Cone stated, does not have a single definite meaning; it has expressive potential, a range of possible meanings.[52] People experience specific meanings in their

---

[51] Maus 2009, 69–70. I have added a few new words, shown in square brackets, to the quoted text.
[52] Cone 1982, 239.

encounters with music because of the interaction between their personal concerns and the expressive potential of the music. A listener or performer will spontaneously choose from the range of possible meanings some specific meaning that resonates with their own life. Musical meaning is, to a large extent, personal and variable. But, Cone emphasized, it is constrained by the determinate expressive potential of the composition, held firm by musical structure: "If verbalization of true content—the specific expression uniquely embodied in a work—is possible at all, it must depend on close structural analysis."[53]

These generalizations yield the plan for Cone's analysis of the *Moment musical*. First, Cone described the piece, mostly in technical language. The salient issue, for Cone, was a chromatic note, E natural, that disturbs the calm diatonic context of A-flat major. The music keeps coming back to E natural or F flat in ways that are increasingly expansive and finally destructive. Next, Cone gave a relatively abstract description intended to summarize the expressive potential:

> As I apprehend the work, it dramatizes the injection of a strange, unsettling element into an otherwise peaceful situation. At first ignored or suppressed, that element persistently returns. It not only makes itself at home but even takes over the direction of events in order to reveal unsuspected possibilities. When the normal state of affairs eventually returns, the originally foreign element seems to have been completely assimilated. But that appearance is deceptive. The element has not been tamed; it bursts out with even greater force, revealing itself as basically inimical to its surroundings, which it proceeds to demolish.[54]

Call this Narrative 1. In its generality— "an element," "a situation," "possibilities," "state of affairs"—this description resembles the language of narratology, abstracting from the details of more determinate stories. Next, Cone filled this outline with a more specific description, which on his general account should show his "personal contact" with the music based on the

---

[53] Cone 1982, 235. The same emphasis on a determinate structure that limits appropriate personal content appears in Cone 1974, 171.

[54] Cone 1982, 239–40. Cone's opening words, "as I apprehend the work," are confusing. The level of expressive potential is supposed to be the objective part of the interpretation, the shared foundation for personal interpretations. But Cone seems to introduce subjectivity even here. Perhaps he was not fully committed to the idea of a non-relative expressive potential. Or perhaps he meant only that he was doing his best to grasp that solid foundation; but the language sounds relativistic.

"personal context" that he brought. Cone associated the foreign element with "the occurrence of a disquieting thought to one of a tranquil, easy-going nature. Disquieting, but at the same time exciting, for it suggests unusual and interesting courses of action."[55] Call this Narrative 2. Cone took a further step: the sequence of events

> can be taken as a model of the effect of vice on a sensitive personality. A vice, as I see it, begins as a novel and fascinating suggestion, not necessarily dangerous though often disturbing. It becomes dangerous, however, as its increasing attractiveness encourages investigation and experimentation, leading to possible obsession and eventual addiction.[56]

Call this Narrative 3. It moved the argument toward an interpretation that Cone speculatively attributed to Schubert; it is not clear whether it was also continuing the account of Cone's own personal interpretation or moving away from Cone. It brought a startling specificity—vice! Already in the initial purportedly technical analysis, Cone oriented the narrative toward sensuality:

> The melodic and rhythmic flexibility that has gradually insinuated itself into the preceding phrases is now at its most ingratiating . . . The restrained, carefully measured satisfactions of the opening have been gradually transformed by the development into the more sensuous delights of a berceuse.[57]

And in Narrative 2, Cone already suggested that the protagonist's exploration reveals "hitherto unknown and possibly forbidden sources of pleasure."[58] Narrative 3 added the idea of vice, and Cone finally proposed a specific meaning drawn from Schubert's own life, in what we can call Narrative 4, a story about Schubert's sexual encounters and their horrifying consequence in syphilis.[59]

It was daring of Cone to connect the desolate ending of this piece, and some other irruptions of "dread" in Schubert's later music, with Schubert's

---

[55] Cone 1982, 240.
[56] Cone 1982, 240.
[57] Cone 1982, 237.
[58] Cone 1982, 240.
[59] Cone 1982, 240–41. This series of interpretations, moving closer and closer to sexual experience and arriving there at the end of the essay, feels a bit like a seduction.

syphilis; it is a moving and plausible biographical interpretation.[60] Cone's emphasis on vice was more problematic. Cone explained: "I stress this interpretation, not for any moralistic reason, but because of its bearing on the final step in my investigation," that is, the connection with Schubert's illness. But the term "vice" is intrinsically moralistic, and Cone had no good reason to pass moral judgment on Schubert's sexual activities.[61]

Beyond his reference to vice, Cone seemed to moralize in his narratives of temptation and punishment (Narrative 2 and especially Narratives 3 and 4). The basic Narrative 1 of expressive potential was more neutral, describing a strange element that returns and becomes destructive. Temptation and its consequences entered as Cone turns to more personal interpretations and introduced a protagonist, whose explorations of "unusual and interesting courses of action" led to catastrophe. Narrative 2 and perhaps Narrative 3 were where expressive potential interacted with Cone's personal concerns, according to Cone's own account of the personal origins of musical meaning; in other words, sensuous pleasure and its dangers were, it seems, his personal contributions to the meaning—if one assumes that his interpretation of the piece follows his account of expressive potential rather than diverging from it.[62]

Cone's essay was brilliant in some respects, in other ways questionable. His acceptance of individual variation in the experience of musical meaning was realistic and liberating. In that part of his argument Cone turned away from an assertion of critical authority in favor of personal contextualization. He theorized the kind of interpretation that Brett's essay practiced. At the same time, Cone insisted that acceptable personal meaning must be based on musical structure as revealed by analysis; an accurate perception of structure

---

[60] McClary 2006, 225–26, and Brett 1997, 164, praised Cone for making this connection.

[61] I am grateful to Lawrence Kramer for identifying this reference to vice as a disconcerting aspect of the essay (personal communication, August 30, 2018). It is true that Schubert's friends were critical of his sensual pleasures. See Solomon 1989, "Franz Schumann and the Peacocks of Benvenuto Cellini," 193–94. But scholars do not need to accept those judgments.

While Cone seems to have identified with the moralizing judgment against vice, some of his language points in another direction. The temptations in the story sound enchanting and suggest personal growth—the sensuous delights of a berceuse, unsuspected possibilities, unusual and interesting courses of action, hitherto unknown sources of pleasure, a novel and fascinating suggestion. I am grateful to Arved Ashby for drawing my attention to this (personal communication, January 3, 2022). Cone's concept of vice was in tension with his implicit acknowledgment of the attractiveness and potential value of the protagonist's explorations. And Cone's description twice associated the return to the opening music with "duty" ("dutifully," 237; "duty," 240), a drab description that again attributes value, by contrast, to the exploratory.

[62] The divergence would come in offering interpretations of meaning that did not reflect Cone's own personal associations but something else.

was necessarily the foundation of any appropriate personal meaning. And it seemed that the structure of a given piece of music was determinate rather than, itself, open to multiple interpretations. I dissent from the part of Cone's position that tethered all acceptable personal meanings to a uniform foundational musical structure. I would prefer to move in the opposite direction, beginning with respectful attention to personal interpretations, whatever they may be, and then, if analysis is desired, asking what aspects of the music, accessible through analysis, are taken up by an interpretation.

In exemplifying personal interpretation of the *Moment musical*, Cone's essay stopped short of the explicitly personal. That is, we are not told what, in Cone's life, provided the context for his narratives of temptation, vice, and dreadful outcome. Musicologists in the early 1980s would not have expected Cone to offer a full disclosure of his relation to these matters. But I note that some years later, Brett, writing in a context where intimate personal disclosure was more possible (though certainly not normative), gave a much more specific account of the personal context into which he received Schubert's music.

Now if one asks, as I did at the beginning of this section, how "Schubert's Promissory Note" might relate to Cone's gay male subjectivity, the answer is in part obvious, in part obscure. Here and in the subsequent discussion of Newcomb, I do not draw on detailed knowledge of these writers' lives. My suggestions are based on generalizations about the lives of twentieth-century gay men and other LGBTQ+ subjects—specifically, about people growing up in respectable, mostly homophobic twentieth-century Euro-American settings. They are based on the experiences that could occur within certain cultural resources of identities, events, psychologies, and narratives. Recall, too, that Cone was born in 1917 and grew up in the South in a particularly homophobic time, amid widespread pathologizing of homosexuality. Someone growing up gay, lesbian, or bisexual in such a society was likely to experience same-gender sexual attraction, when it arose, as, on one hand, alluring, on the other hand, discontinuous or incompatible with much of their environment, and therefore possibly quite frightening. This fits well Cone's description of "a strange, unsettling element" that "persistently returns" and blossoms into "ingratiating" music offering "sensuous delights." In Cone's continuation to topics of disease and disaster, the account becomes obscure and problematic. It seems we are to understand Cone as having some unspecified personal relation to the distressing conclusion of this composition. It is possible to fill in details of a story that might match Cone's personal situation, but what I can offer is purely conjecture. Here is one version. In this story about a young gay man, call it Narrative 2A, there is incompatibility between the serenity of the protagonist's familiar world and a dawning awareness of forbidden sexual appetites, leading to delightful but dangerous sexual exploration. The protagonist finds himself in an impossible situation, unable to reconcile two aspects of his life that both seem indispensable. The outcome, which could be understood as fearfully imagined or as real, is a catastrophe in which neither his initial placid identity and environment nor his unfettered enjoyment of a new sexual life can survive. The music provides a vivid image of this catastrophe.

Thinking of Cone's essay in relation to gay identity raises questions of context and chronology. Might Cone have thought of Schubert as homosexual? Musicological discussion of Schubert's sexuality and its relation, or not, to interpretation of his music had a spectacular boom after Solomon's essay "Franz Schubert and the Peacocks of Benvenuto Cellini" appeared in print in 1989, several years after Cone's essay.[63] An earlier essay by Solomon, also speculating about Schubert's homosexuality, was published in 1981 but generated less conversation among musicologists.[64] Cone could not have read either of these in print before finishing his essay, though information about Solomon's ideas may have circulated earlier. Apart from Solomon's research, there is a long tradition of thinking of Schubert as "different," sometimes formulated as an issue about masculinity. And gay men have sometimes felt a strong affinity with Schubert simply based on the music, feeling it as close to their own sensibilities.[65] Working with public materials, we have no way of knowing whether Cone felt such a connection. Possibly people who were close to Cone personally knew more about this.[66]

Cone's essay was published in spring 1982. Its first readers would have been aware of the beginnings of what became the AIDS epidemic, initially reported in summer 1981. But awareness of the newly identified syndrome could not have influenced Cone's essay, which was received by *19th-Century Music* on April 7, 1981.[67] In a less specific way, though, Cone's essay has a deep connection to HIV/AIDS. One response to the epidemic was a moralistic condemnation of the sexual activities through which illness was spread, perpetuating

---

[63] Solomon 1989.

[64] Solomon 1981, 137–54.

[65] McClary 2006, 209, 224; Fisk 2022, 339–45.

[66] Surely, during the 1990s musicological dust-up about Schubert's sexuality, Cone must have talked with his close musical friends about Schubert and sexuality.

[67] Christina Acosta, personal communication, August 30, 2018.

and intensifying long phobic traditions associating non-normative sexuality with illness and death. Another response was a fierce reaffirmation of the value of sexual freedom, and of gay and promiscuous sex, and a defiant rejection of the conflation of sexual activity, disease, and death.[68] Cone's essay, with its unmistakable association of forbidden pleasure, vice, demolition, and death, seems to be on the wrong side of this debate. To end the essay, Cone quoted critic Edmund Wilson on Oscar Wilde's stories that seem to encode syphilis: "In the end . . . the horror breaks out: the afflicted one must recognize himself and be recognized by other people as the odious creature he is, and his disease or disability will kill him." To be ill through a sexually transmitted disease is to be an odious creature. And Cone quoted from *King Lear*: "The gods are just, and of our pleasant vices / Make instruments to plague us." Justice leads from pleasant vices to plague. This was not the sex-positive discourse that was needed in 1982 and that we continue to need. Possibly Cone understood himself to be reporting traditional moralizing attitudes, rather than endorsing them, but the essay offers no clarity on this.

Thus, there are aspects of "Schubert's Promissory Note" that one might not want to reproduce today. Nonetheless, in the essay a gay music scholar introduced a pluralist account of musical meaning, in itself a celebration of diversity; he openly associated music, through detailed description, with sensuality and sexuality; and he made a frank connection between Schubert's syphilis and a recurring quality of dread in his music. These brave, innovative ideas came together in a pioneering contribution to the not-yet-named music and narrative research field. Cone's position as a gay man in the largely heterosexual Princeton University Department of Music, and in the masculine-toned fields of composition and music theory, may have fostered a sense of difference that emboldened such suavely dissident work.[69] The same can be said of examples discussed earlier. In "Feminism, Music Theory, Time, and Embodiment," I suggested that Cone, writing about the "unholy delight" of immediate sound, turned away from a masculine emphasis on structure. In "The Disciplined Subject of Musical Analysis," I made a contrast between Cone in *The Composer's Voice* and Allen Forte in "Schenker's Conception of

---

[68] Crimp 2002, 43–82; Crimp 2002, 43–82; Bersani 2010, 3–30; Patton 1996. Bersani's essay provocatively retained a connection between sexuality and death, but in the sense of self-loss rather than physical, bodily death.

[69] During the discussion after my conference presentation of "Feminism, Music Theory, Time, and Embodiment" (Köln, 2008), McClary made this point with regard to Cone's work in general. I am indebted to her formulation. See Maus 2009, 70.

Musical Structure." Forte's essay described musical structure in terms of relations of control and subordination among musical elements and had little to say about listening. Cone, I argued, shared a concern with power relations but added a description of a musical listener who experiences a complicated, pleasurable play of submission and identification. In these two examples, Cone intervened in a discourse that was thoroughly masculine by adding something different.

To reformulate what I said about McClary's and Brett's analyses of Tchaikovsky and Schubert: my question is not whether one can tell from Cone's writing that he was a gay man. Rather, knowing that Cone was gay, we can ask what aspects of his writing might make sense, indeed might be deeply meaningful, in relation to that. I suggest that valuable insights in Cone's work were shaped by his lived experience outside masculine heteronormativity.

The Beginnings of "Music and Narrative": Anthony Newcomb

Newcomb's essays on music and narrative proposed meanings for large-scale compositions, relating successions of musical events to human stories. The stories he told were broadly accessible; still, they are particularly evocative in relation to LGBTQ+ lives, and my suggestion is that Newcomb's life as a gay man prepared him to find those meanings.[70]

Newcomb's sustained narrative interpretations invariably concerned music that does not follow familiar formal patterns. In Chopin's Polonaise-Fantasy, "the aspect of *formal segmentation* and *formal function of the segments* . . . offers puzzles that have baffled analysts since Leichtentritt attempted a formal segmentation of the piece in 1921."[71] The last movement of Schumann's String Quartet, Op. 41, No. 3 "lay[s] bare . . . the conventions of the rondo scheme in order to turn them upside down . . . The attentive listener is forced to move beyond static recognition of formal schemata to dynamic questioning of formal procedures."[72] Newcomb used narrative interpretation to "solve" such compositions that do not conform to familiar

---

[70] I began my discussion of Cone by turning to several existing musicological publications that related his work to gender and sexuality. I am not aware of any similar publications regarding Newcomb.

[71] Newcomb 1994, 87.

[72] Newcomb 1987, 174.

formal patterns. No doubt, such pieces could show with special clarity the value of interpretive tools beyond conventional formal theory.[73]

In twentieth-century European and American cultures, and by and large to the present, people of non-normative sexuality or gender have found ourselves surrounded by stories of normal lives, understood as heterosexual, and must recognize, often in isolation, that our own lives will be different. At best, we LGBTQ+ people find our own life-patterns and come to regard them as equal in value to straight lives, and perhaps as having their own idiosyncratic intelligibility. (This does not mean we have stepped outside of cultural narratives; the story of ad hoc intelligibility is itself a culturally embedded narrative about LGBTQ+ people.) Newcomb's work on narrative depended on analogies between life patterns and musical forms. His championing of formally non-normative music can be seen as a beautiful, if inexplicit, queer-affirming practice.[74]

In "Once More 'Between Absolute and Program Music': Schumann's Second Symphony," Newcomb wrote about the whole symphony, but the analysis focused most intensely on a final movement that does not conform to any familiar formal pattern. It makes sense, instead, through the special narrative that it embodies, understood in relation to the entire symphony. The first movement has "an atmosphere of internal uneasiness and struggle."[75] The second movement, a bustling *perpetuum mobile* in its main sections, has "an unstable, contradictory character ... This antic scherzo is in fact not what it appears to be."[76] The slow movement resolves these tensions and ambiguities; its opening theme, "which utterly dominates the third movement, remains fundamentally unchanged in character and identity."[77] This stability arrives in a state of deep grief. The third movement has solved the problem of achieving a consistent, noncontradictory identity. There remains the question of whether one can move past the sadness; the movement ends in "resignation and near stasis."

---

[73] From Newcomb's selection of examples, one might get the impression that some pieces are adequately understood through technical analysis, while others need a narrative description. In my view, this would be an error. For one thing, familiar formal patterns have their own narrative implications. And beyond its formal pattern, familiar or not, any piece will have innumerable individual features not accounted for in the formal classification and inviting *ad hoc*, perhaps narrative description. See Maus 1991, 17–19.

[74] The Moment musical that Cone discusses is also, of course, formally distinctive, with the dramatically altered return to its initial A section.

[75] Newcomb 1984, 242.

[76] Newcomb 1984, 242.

[77] Newcomb 1984, 243.

Newcomb's interpretation of the fourth movement is persuasive and moving. He described it as initially signaling a light rondo form and a happy ending, and then, through its increasingly weighty development section and expansive retransition, transforming into an emotionally complex, unconventional sonata form. The music that occupies the formal position of a recapitulation, rather than returning to the opening of the movement, works with a theme that emerged during the development and eventually reconnects with the introduction that opened the symphony.

This unusual structure conveys a psychological progression. The beginning of the fourth movement, boisterous and cheerful, is shockingly incongruous after the grief of the third movement. It seems to turn away willfully from the emotions of the immediately preceding music. It could be felt as manic denial.[78] The sense of denial becomes more specific as the movement introduces an incongruously brisk, cheerful version of the third movement's main theme, directly evoking past suffering and trivializing it. After a brief return to the opening theme (supporting for the moment the sense of a rondo), the ensuing development section takes on a newly serious tone. It returns to the theme of the third movement, now serious again, in an intense developmental style with modulations and imitation. This leads to a somber cadence. As Newcomb noted, the cadence re-creates the "resigned melancholy" of the end of the third movement.[79] Thus, it offers a second chance for the music to respond to that state, and this time a quietly affirmative theme appears, feeling like a response to the sadness rather than a dismissal. In a further-developed form, this theme will take the place of the boisterous first theme when the time comes for the recapitulation. The basic psychological narrative of the movement, then, concerns an initial denial of grief, followed eventually by acknowledgment of that sadness and a more appropriate affirmative response. In its final form, the new theme of the development and recapitulation has "a character of serene power and confidence."[80]

It is easy to see how this narrative might relate to the life experiences of a gay man. The first two movements depict a condition of "internal uneasiness and struggle" and "an unstable, contradictory character." The third movement achieves integration and stability, but in a state of dejection. This is a common pattern in the lives of sexual minority subjects, as we experience

---

[78] "Manic denial" is my language for what Newcomb describes. I also hear manic denial in the second movement's "antic scherzo," though Newcomb does not make this point.

[79] Newcomb 1984, 244.

[80] Newcomb 1984, 245.

confusion and then, with clarification about our sexuality, perhaps a state of mourning for our failure to meet the norms that surround us. There is a risk of denial of the insights into oneself and of the accompanying sadness. The fourth movement, after initial denial, fully acknowledges the sadness and then find a way to move past it to a new, positive identity. It does so by setting aside conventional forms and coming up with something new. Similar psychological states and progressions can arise for non-queer subjects, but I want to emphasize the ordinariness of such a narrative for LGBTQ+ people (in the specific twentieth-century settings that I have mentioned).

Newcomb's description of the first movement of Mahler's Symphony No. 9 had some similarities to "Schubert's Promissory Note." The opening of the movement explores the contrast of "diatonic purity with a subverting, corrupting chromaticism."[81] At first the addition of chromatic notes to the D major theme is brief and quiet. But the

> foreign tones then bring about a rapid slippage into an agitated, unstable contrasting idea full of chromatic tones and local leading-tone tensions . . . The effect of these first forty measures of the score is one of a placid stability undermined.[82]

In the lengthy movement, the working out of this opposition is complex. Newcomb identified a repeating pattern of subversion, crisis, and collapse, followed by an attempt to start again, to find a way back to the opening material. Eventually the music can "confidently integrate" chromatic notes into "a stable and sustained D major." This is a resolution, but there is sadness in this outcome. The first movement is "a farewell to childhood and to primal innocence," a story of

> growth through to young adulthood—and of the inevitable hardening and toughening that comes with this process, the inevitable loss of gentle innocence and openness to love and the learning of self-protective strategies that come with its storms and crises.[83]

---

[81] Newcomb 1992, 121.

[82] Newcomb 1992, 121. Compare Cone's reference to "the occurrence of a disquieting thought to one of a tranquil, easy-going nature."

[83] Newcomb 1992, 124.

Newcomb was noncommittal about the nature of the events that push the protagonist beyond childhood. There was no suggestion, as in Cone's narrative, that sexuality is the force that initially undermines "placid stability."[84] Newcomb's description emphasized the inevitability of these changes, and by implication their universality. But he did not comment on Mahler's emotional extremity, appropriate no doubt to some people's experience of adolescence, disproportionate to others'. One group for whom the passage out of childhood can be especially fraught is, of course, LGBTQ+ people, who sometimes find that a prior sense of ease and trust within our family and social world becomes impossible, and for whom childhood "openness to love" may yield painfully to confusion, secrecy, and "self-protective strategies."

In the second movement, the protagonist "throws himself into the physical sensuality and distractions of the modern urban world." Its events include "a collapse of out-of-control sensuality" and "the near rape done by the second dance (and tempo), which . . . proceeds to run more out of control than ever, tumbling down its chains of deceptive cadences under increasingly intoxicated waltz figurations."[85] Now, sexuality has entered Newcomb's narrative as a destructive form of self-loss, indeed as something that seems to assault the protagonist. Newcomb associates the cheerless bustle of the third movement with "the bright, competent adult." Near the end of the movement, a radical change, "a vision," interrupts the momentum, showing the possibility of something different and evoking the beginning of the first movement.[86] The fourth movement takes on an intricate task of recovering the concerns of the first movement, but from an adult perspective; the childhood world cannot be simply reinstated.[87]

Newcomb's descriptions of the Mahler and Schumann symphonies both centered on the temporary disavowal of significant experience, followed by acknowledgment and response. In the Mahler, the disavowal happens in the second and third movements, which both turn away from inwardness, the memory of childhood, and the experience of grief, to become absorbed instead in worldly experiences. The immersive, dangerous intoxication and sensuality depicted in the second movement are especially close to major issues of Western urban gay life in the twentieth century.

---

[84] As I hear it—this is not Newcomb's reading—the first intrusion of Mahler's intensely chromatic music suggests stress and suffering, but not sexuality. In contrast, when that music appears a second time, it enters a state of erotic exuberance, mingling pleasure and pain and not ending happily.

[85] Newcomb 1992, 125. Newcomb 1997 is a fascinating detailed exploration of this movement.

[86] Newcomb 1992, 127.

[87] Newcomb 1992, 131–32.

Newcomb's essays on narrative were consistently impersonal in style and marshalled many kinds of evidence to argue for interpretations that aspired to historical truth. Nonetheless, I suggest that they also had connections to Tony Newcomb the person. Thus, I am interpreting Newcomb's work in terms of personal sources of meaning, as emphasized explicitly by Brett and Cone but not Newcomb. The stories Newcomb found in Schumann and Mahler are unexpected and subtle. Without challenging his goal of recovering historical meanings, we can wonder what drew him to the specific musical works he wrote about, and how he found his way to the interpretations he offered. My suggestion is that for a gay man, the plot lines that Newcomb attributed to this music would be near at hand, thoroughly familiar from gay life experiences, Newcomb's own or those of people he knew. Newcomb would not need to be conscious of these connections in order to draw on these real-life plot archetypes.

The essays I have discussed by Brett, Cone, and Newcomb all organized their readings of musical works around a contrast between a significant personal truth—rage, sexual desire, self-knowledge accompanied by sadness, childhood and its transience—and something else that hides or distracts from that truth. Gay men and other queer people in European and American settings, from the twentieth century and beyond, typically forming our identities in unwelcoming surroundings, are likely to have a bone-deep familiarity with such contrasts.

Listening for the Self

Critics like McClary and Brett have intentionally combined narrative interpretation of music with queer themes. But also, I have proposed that some of the foundational musicological texts about music and narrative have unstated connections with the queerness of their authors. Does narrative interpretation of music have a special relation to queerness, and if so, how?

As mentioned, forming stories in relation to music is not just a musicological project; it is a vernacular practice, something people do in everyday life. It can have a special importance for young people who are or will become LGBTQ+ subjects. Proto-queer young people often try to understand who we are in environments that do not provide adequate concepts or where nonheteronormative identities are stigmatized. We try to understand ourselves by finding aspects of the external world that seem to illuminate our own experience. Intense explorations of library materials may be part of this—a longstanding resource presently under cruel attack by US right-wing activists. Various mass media may help with investigations, conscious or unconscious, of queer identity, such as comic books and animation (Sailor Moon or the X-Men, for example, in very different ways).[88] We may be drawn to music that seems to offer solutions—perhaps not answers that can be verbalized, but at least a sense of belonging that may be missing from much of our environment. Popular music may serve in this way, offering, for example, many pop divas and gender-benders. Now-classic studies by Wayne Koestenbaum and D. A. Miller explored such relations to opera and musical theater.[89] The internet, of course, has offered unprecedented opportunities for self-formation and community among gender and sexuality nonconformists. Classical instrumental music can also invite such intimacies, through performance, listening, or composing; this may have been more common in the past, given the shifting cultural role of classical music, but as a music teacher of young adults I know well that such relations still exist. Charles Fisk has written eloquently about this use of music:

> As an adolescent in the early 1960s too ashamed of my strong sexual attraction to other men to imagine ever acting upon it, I felt recognized by Schubert's music. Like the tenderness in that music, mine, too, was endangered. If I felt and expressed that tenderness with a man, I would risk disgrace. And if I tried to develop and express it with a woman, I would risk exposure as an impostor. But it was as if Schubert's music, of its own compassionate accord, embraced me in its loving presence. Reassuring me of my capacity for love, his music lifted me from my shame and restored to me a sense of personal value.[90]

Out of this affinity with Schubert's music, Fisk fashioned narratives, identifying strongly with their protagonists. In the opening of Schubert's B-flat Piano Sonata,

> If one hears the opening, hymnlike theme as being sung by an angelic chorus, one might then imagine that a member of that chorus, drawn to the mysteriously alluring trill, enters the realm, the remote key of Gb Major, to

---

[88] On countercultural trends in superhero comics, see Fawaz 2016.
[89] Koestenbaum 1993; Miller 2000.
[90] Fisk 2022, 340.

which it beckons. At first, this seems a realm of enchantment in which that singer can linger without harm for a spell before rejoining the group. But when he returns, he is cast out before reaching a cadence with the chorus, hurled back into the once-alluring G-flat realm, now transformed into an F#-minor scene of banishment.[91]

Kip Pegley, writing at a time when they identified as a butch lesbian, recalled their fascination as a seventeen-year-old with the first movement of Stravinsky's Symphony in C: they

> felt that this work in particular reflected the way in which her life was going to develop as a lesbian: it could be graphed within a rigid box (analogous with her strict environment) and sections "developed," but not in the traditional sense (family or children). Finally, and most importantly, she did not sense closure at the end of sections. Instead, she heard juxtaposed areas that functioned as interruptions—a pattern that she thought was inevitable in her life.[92]

Of course, people who are not queer can also relate to music in this way, listening for resonances with themselves. (There is a major branch of music therapy, the Bonny Method of Guided Imagery and Music, based on this widespread capacity for personal construction of meaning in relation to music.[93]) But the pain and confusion of young LGBTQ+ people can make the quest for identity through music especially urgent. It should not surprise us that a gay man, Cone, theorized such personal listening, nor that Newcomb, another gay man, was prominent in translating musical stories into scholarly inquiry.

I mentioned that some studies of music and narrative have worked toward systematic generalization while others, less theoretical in tone, seem like expressive verbal improvisations. More specifically, some narrative studies of music seek general theories of music and narrative; others commit to a

---

[91] Fisk 2022, 344. This is another story of diatonic security broached by alluring, dangerous chromaticism.

[92] Pegley and Caputo 2006, 309.

[93] For Helen Bonny's foundational work, see Bonny 2002. For many further explorations, see Grocke 2019. Since 2013 I have studied the Bonny Method of Guided Imagery and Music in professional training courses. This has been, for me, a continuously rewarding immersion in and reflection on subjective responses to music, and it has shaped the sensibility from which I wrote this essay. I am grateful to my teachers Cara Marinucci and Erin Johnson, and to my wonderful classmates, all so insightful about psychology, psychotherapy, and music.

rich, individualized understanding of a specific composition, often using *ad hoc* linguistic means. I believe these approaches can result from very different motivations. Detailed responses to individual pieces sometimes come from a convergence of personal and musical meaning, articulating something significant in the listener's and writer's life through a personally resonant description of music. In contrast, theoretical studies reflect, perhaps, a conception of knowledge as embodied in a lucid, abstract, systematic set of general statements. A writer could be strongly oriented to one kind of motivation or the other, or of course both.[94]

It is not rare for critics to interpret works of art in relation to the queerness of the artist. It is less common to interpret art criticism in relation to the nonnormative sexuality of the critic, as I have done with Cone and Newcomb, though there has been splendid work of this kind.[95] In closing, I want to mention an excellent recent composer-oriented study, because it touches on many of the topics of the present essay. In " 'Au Fond d'un Placard': Allusion, Narrative, and Queer Experience in Poulenc's *Ier Nocturne*," Campbell Shiflett considers a piano piece by Francis Poulenc in relation to the composer's homosexuality. The piece is formally unconventional; Shiflett wants to be "sensitive to its difference" rather than "straightening out the nocturne's kinks, correcting its disorientations, and fixing its meaning"; any attempt to do the latter would refuse the queerness of the music.[96] Shiflett associates the piece with what he calls a "coming-out narrative,"[97] not about public disclosures but about coming out to oneself, the recognition and acceptance of one's own sexuality.[98] The opening section of the *Nocturne* is diatonic and pastoral in character. Tensions arise, associated with increased chromaticism; Shiflett associates the succession with childhood innocence disrupted by sexuality. Near the end, a coherent and thoroughly chromatic passage seems to offer the possibility of a positive adult sexuality, though the *Nocturne* ends in instability. Shiflett deepens this reading by drawing on biographical information

---

[94] Many texts, like the essays by Newcomb discussed above, combine theoretical formulations with detailed interpretations of individual compositions. My own early-career studies of narrative (in particular "Music as Drama," "Music as Narrative," and "Narrative, Drama and Emotion in Instrumental Music") were oriented to theory, and the musical examples were not particularly personal. For some comments on the style of "Music as Drama," and an alternative style in the later essay "Love Stories," see Maus 2020, https://www.gmth.de/zeitschrift/artikel/1035.aspx.

[95] I am thinking especially of D. A. Miller on Roland Barthes, Eve Kosofsky Sedgwick on Henry James's *The Art of the Novel*, and Philip Brett on Miller 1992; Sedgwick 2003, 35–65; Brett 2002, 177–88.

[96] Shiflett 2020, 202.

[97] Shiflett 2020, 202.

[98] Shiflett 2020, 215.

along with Poulenc's musical self-allusions that link the *Nocturne* with his earlier and later compositions. Shiflett's epistemology is complex, as he goes through the steps to create a responsible biographical/historical reading, while stating that the meanings are irreducibly elusive and, in part, mirror back his own complex subjectivity.

Shiflett's essay picks up aspects of the older texts I have discussed here, developing them in sophisticated ways. Most generally, it offers an overtly queer musical narrative, as did McClary and Brett. It mulls over the relation between the critic's life experiences, the composer's life, and the musical interpretation. It works with an unclassifiable musical structure, offering to respect its queer individuality. And most specifically, like Cone's essay about Schubert and Newcomb's essays about Mahler, it finds a narrative of childhood and the intrusion of adulthood, now identified explicitly as a representation of queer experience, evoked once more through the opposition of diatonic and chromatic music. I see the essay as a welcome unclosetng of aspects of Cone's and Newcomb's interpretations, as well as a respectful successor to their critical practices.

Shiflett identifies the narrative of youthful innocence endangered by maturation as a pastoral topos. Similarly, I want to emphasize the cultural embeddedness of all the queer narratives I have discussed. For example, the conception of childhood and youth as a time of serenity subject to invasion by sexuality and worldly experience, brought into musical interpretation by Cone and Newcomb, is a particular cultural construction; there are other ways to think of young people, and they might also provide resources for thinking about music.[99]

In the early 1990s, impressed by recent advances at the Oakland meeting of the American Musicological Society (1990) and the first Feminist Theory and Music conference (1991), I said to Suzanne Cusick, then my colleague at the University of Virginia, that it was exciting to be present at the beginning of queer musicology. She paused for a moment, and then murmured: "Unless that's what we have had all along, and we didn't know it." In part, this remark was about LGBTQ+ composers and other musicians studied by musicologists without mention of their non-normative sexualities or genders. But also, there was a significant presence of LGBTQ+ music scholars, among them many gay men, whose identities were never openly part of their professional

---

[99] See Stockton 2009. Psychoanalysis has often contested common concepts of childhood innocence; Melanie Klein's work is a particularly rich resource.

work. Philip Brett noted that gay music scholars who maintained a wall between the personal and the professional inhibited the development and acceptance of feminist and queer research.[100] I do not mean to exempt Cone or Newcomb from this charge. Recall Cone's response to *Feminine Endings* (as mentioned in an earlier note).[101] And, more dangerously, in 1990 Newcomb was Chair of the AMS Program Committee that considered turning down the session proposal "Composers and Sexuality." Brett learned of the possible rejection and threatened to picket at the meeting unless the session was accepted.[102] In that crucial field-defining session, Gary C. Thomas, McClary, Malcolm Hamrick Brown, and Brett presented on Handel, Schubert, Tchaikovsky, and Britten.[103]

But I have been making a different point. If my speculations about the work of Cone and Newcomb are on the right track, gay subjectivity made foundational contributions to the study of music and narrative—not explicitly, probably not intentionally, but crucially. We can take pride in these achievements of queer musicology.[104]

References

Allanbrook, Wye Jamison. 1992. "Two Threads through the Labyrinth: Topic and Process in the First Movement of K. 332 and K. 333." In *Convention in Eighteenth- and Nineteenth-Century Music: Essays in Honor of Leonard G. Ratner*, edited by Allanbrook, Janet M. Levy, and William Mahrt, 125–71. Stuyvesant, NY: Pendragon.

Almén, Byron. 2008. *A Theory of Musical Narrative.* Indianapolis: Indiana University Press.

Bersani, Leo. 2010. "Is the Rectum a Grave?" In *Is the Rectum a Grave? And Other Essays*, 3–30. Chicago: University of Chicago Press; first published 1987.

Bonny, Helen. 2002. *Music Consciousness: The Evolution of Guided Imagery and Music*, edited by Lisa Summer. Gilsum, NH: Barcelona Publishers.

Brett, Philip. 1997. "Piano Four-Hands: Schubert and the Performance of Gay Male Desire." *19th-Century Music* 21, no. 2 (Autumn): 149–76.

---

[100] Brett 2006, 16. See also Brett 1997, 151–52.

[101] See note 47.

[102] McClary 2006, 3. Brett's criticism of homosexual musicologists who reject sexuality as a topic for musicology, part of his paper for the 1990 session (later published in *Queering the Pitch*), was no doubt directed partly at Newcomb; see note 100.

[103] I described the session and its role in the development of queer music studies in Maus 2022, 6–7. McClary's conference paper developed into the essay on Schubert that I discussed here.

[104] For support and valuable responses as this essay developed, I am grateful to Arved Ashby, Charles Fisk, Gavin S. K. Lee, Susan McClary, Kip Pegley, and Campbell Shiflett. The first version of this paper was presented at the Queer Resource Group session at the 2015 meeting of the Society for Music Theory.

Brett, Philip. 2006. "Musicality, Essentialism, and the Closet." In *Queering the Pitch: The New Gay and Lesbian Musicology*, ed. Philip Brett, Elizabeth Wood, and Gary C. Thomas, 2nd ed., 9–26. New York: Routledge.

Brett, Philip. 2002. "Musicology and Sexuality: The Example of Edward J. Dent." In *Queer Episodes in Music and Modern Identity*, edited by Sophie Fuller and Lloyd Whitesell, 177–88. Urbana: University of Illinois Press.

Cone, Edward T. 1974. *The Composer's Voice*. Berkeley: University of California Press.

Cone, Edward T. 1977. "Three Ways of Reading a Detective Story—or a Brahms Intermezzo." *The Georgia Review* 31, no. 3 (Fall): 554–74.

Cone, Edward T. 1982. "Schubert's Promissory Note: An Exercise in Musical Hermeneutics." *19th-Century Music* 5, no. 3 (Spring): 233–41.

Crimp, Douglas. 2002a. "How to Have Promiscuity in an Epidemic." In *Melancholia and Moralism: Essays on AIDS and Queer Politics*, 43–82. Cambridge, MA: MIT Press. First published 1987.

Crimp, Douglas. 2002b. "Mourning and Militancy." In *Melancholia and Moralism: Essays on AIDS and Queer Politics*, 43–82. Cambridge, MA: MIT Press. First published 1989.

Fawaz, Ramzi. 2016. *The New Mutants: Superheroes and the Radical Imagination of American Comics*. New York: NYU Press.

Fisk, Charles. 2022. "Endangered Tenderness: Schubert, Chopin, and Schumann." In *The Oxford Handbook of Music and Queerness*, edited by Fred Everett Maus and Sheila Whiteley, 339–52. New York: Oxford University Press.

Forster, E. M. 2000. *Howard's End*. New York: Penguin Books. First published 1910.

Grocke, Denise E., ed. 2019. *Guided Imagery and Music: The Bonny Method and Beyond*. Dallas, TX: Barcelona Publisher.

Hatten, Robert. 2018. *A Theory of Virtual Agency for Western Art Music*. Bloomington: Indiana University Press.

Kerman, Joseph. 1967. *The Beethoven Quartets*. New York: Knopf.

Maus, Fred Everett. 1988. "Music as Drama." *Music Theory Spectrum* 10: 56–73.

Maus, Fred Everett. 1991. "Music as Narrative." *Indiana Theory Review* 12 (Spring and Fall): 1–34.

Kerman, Joseph. 1992. "Representing a Relationship: Notes on a Beethoven Concerto." *Representations* 39: 80–101.

Koestenbaum, Wayne. 1993. *The Queen's Throat: Opera, Homosexuality, and the Mystery of Desire*. New York: Poseidon Press.

Maus, Fred Everett. 1996. "Love Stories." *Repercussions* 4, no. 2: 86–96.

Maus, Fred Everett. 1997. "Narrative, Drama and Emotion in Instrumental Music." *Journal of Aesthetics and Art Criticism* 55, no. 3 (Summer): 293–303.

Maus, Fred Everett. 2001. "Narratology, Narrativity." *Grove Music Online*. https://doi.org/10.1093/gmo/9781561592630.article.40607.

Maus, Fred Everett. 2004. "The Disciplined Subject of Musical Analysis." In *Beyond Structural Listening: Postmodern Modes of Hearing*, edited by Andrew Dell'Antonio, 13–43. Berkeley: University of California Press.

Maus, Fred Everett. 2005. "Classical Instrumental Music and Narrative." In *A Companion to Narrative Theory*, edited by James Phelan and Peter Rabinowitz, 466–83. Oxford: Blackwell.

Maus, Fred Everett. 2009. "Feminism, Music Theory, Time, and Embodiment." In *Dichotonies: Music and Gender*, edited by Beate Neumeier, 61–73. Heidelberg: Winter Verlag.

Maus, Fred Everett. 2020. "Defensive Writing in Discourse about Music." *Zeitschrift der Gesellschaft für Musiktheorie* 17, no. 1. https://www.gmth.de/zeitschrift/artikel/1035.aspx

Maus, Fred Everett. 2022. "Introduction." In *The Oxford Handbook of Music and Queerness*, edited by Fred Everett Maus and Sheila Whiteley, 1–31. New York: Oxford University Press.

McClary, Susan. 1983. "Pitches, Expression, Ideology: An Exercise in Mediation." *Enclitic* 7, no. 1 (Spring): 76–86.

McClary, Susan. 1986. "A Musical Dialectic from the Enlightenment: Mozart's Piano Concerto in G Major, K.453, Movement 2." *Cultural critique* 4 (Fall): 129–69.

McClary, Susan. 1987. "The Blasphemy of Talking Politics during Bach Year." In *Music and Society: The Politics of Composition, Performance, and Reception*, edited by Richard Leppert and McClary, 13–62. Cambridge: Cambridge University Press.

McClary, Susan. 1997. "The Impromptu That Trod on a Loaf: Or How Music Tells Stories." *Narrative* 5, no. 1 (January): 20–35.

McClary, Susan. 2002. *Feminine Endings: Music, Gender, and Sexuality*. 2nd ed. Minneapolis: University of Minnesota Press. First published 1991.

McClary, Susan. 2006a. "Constructions of Subjectivity in Schubert's Music." In *Queering the Pitch: The New Gay and Lesbian Musicology*, edited by Philip Brett, Elizabeth Wood, and Gary C. Thomas, 2nd ed., 205–33. New York: Routledge. First published 1994.

McClary, Susan. 2006b. "Introduction." In Philip Brett, *Music and Sexuality in Britten*, edited by George E. Haggerty, 1–9. Berkeley: University of California Press.

McCreless, Patrick. 1988. "Roland Barthes's *S/Z* from a Musical Point of View." *in theory only* 10, no. 7: 1–29

McCreless, Patrick. 1991. "The Hermeneutic Sentence and Other Literary Models for Tonal Closure." *Indiana Theory Review* 12 (Spring and Fall): 35–73.

Miller, D. A. 1992. *Bringing Out Roland Barthes*. Berkeley: University of California Press.

Miller, D. A. 2000. *Place for Us: Essay on the Broadway Musical*. Cambridge, MA: Harvard University Press.

Monahan, Seth. 2013. "Action and Agency Revisited." *Journal of Music Theory* 57, no. 2 (Fall): 321–71.

Newcomb, Anthony. 1984. "Once More 'Between Absolute and Program Music': Schumann's Second Symphony." *19th-Century Music* 7, no. 3 (April 3): 233–50.

Newcomb, Anthony. 1987. "Schumann and Late Eighteenth-Century Narrative Strategies." *19th-Century Music* 11, no. 2 (Autumn): 164–74.

Newcomb, Anthony. 1992. "Narrative Archetypes and Mahler's Ninth Symphony." In *Music and Text: Critical Inquiries*, edited by Steven Paul Scher, 118–36. Cambridge: Cambridge University Press.

Newcomb, Anthony. 1994. "The Polonaise-Fantasy and Issues of Musical Narrative." In *Chopin Studies 2*, edited by John Rink and James Samson, 84–101. Cambridge: Cambridge University Press.

Newcomb, Anthony. 1997. "Action and Agency in Mahler's Ninth Symphony, Second Movement." In *Music and Meaning*, edited by Jenefer Robinson, 131–53. Ithaca, NY: Cornell University Press.

Patton, Cindy. 1996. *Fatal Advice: How Safe-Sex Education Went Wrong*. Durham, NC: Duke University Press.

Pegley, K., and Virginia Caputo. 2006. "Growing Up Female(s): Retrospective Thoughts on Musical Preferences and Meanings." In *Queering the Pitch: The New Gay and Lesbian*

Musicology, edited by Philip Brett, Elizabeth Wood, and Gary C. Thomas, 2nd ed., 297–313. New York: Routledge. First published 1994.

Pitcher, George. 1995. *The Dogs Who Came to Stay*. New York: Dutton.

Randall, J. K. 1976. "How Music Goes." *Perspectives of New Music* 14, no. 2, and 15, no. 1: 424–517. See also errata in *Perspectives of New Music* 15, no. 2 (Spring–Summer 1977): 1.

Ratner, Leonard G. 1980. *Classic Music: Expression, Form, and Style*. New York: Schirmer Books.

Rosen, Charles. 1971. *The Classical Style: Haydn, Mozart, Beethoven*. New York: Viking.

Sedgwick, Eve Kosofsky. 2003. "Shame, Theatricality, and Queer Performativity: Henry James's *Art of the Novel*." In *Touching Feeling: Affect, Pedagogy, Performativity*, 35–65. Durham, NC: Duke University Press.

Sedgwick, Eve Kosofsky. 2008. *Epistemology of the Closet*. 2nd ed. Berkeley: University of California Press. First published 1990.

Shiflett, Campbell. 2020. "'Au Fond d'un Placard': Allusion, Narrative, and Queer Experience in Poulenc's *Ier Nocturne*." *The Journal of Musicology* 37, no. 2 (Spring): 197–230.

Solomon, Maynard. 1981. "Franz Schubert's 'My Dream.'" *American Imago* 38, no. 2 (Summer): 137–54.

Solomon, Maynard. 1989. "Franz Schubert and the Peacocks of Benvenuto Cellini."*19th-Century Music* 12, no. 3 (Spring): 193–206.

Stockton, Kathryn Bond. 2009. *The Queer Child, or Growing Sideways in the Twentieth Century*. Durham: Duke University Press.

Tovey, Donald F. 1935–39. *Essays in Musical Analysis*, Volumes. 1–6. Oxford: Oxford University Press.

10

"Legendary In-Reading"

Musical Meaning, Analysis, and Biography in Edward Prime-Stevenson's Music Criticism and Sexology

Kristin Franseen

In the privately printed novel *Imre: A Memorandum* (ca. 1905–1906), Xavier Mayne's narrator Oswald comes out to his friend and soon-to-be lover Imre von N. by recounting his early life, previous relationships, and encounters with sexology. Throughout this account (which takes up most of the short novel's second chapter), Oswald references many touchstones of nineteenth-century gay history and literature ranging from Plato to Walt Whitman. One of the few figures Oswald mentions twice—first in a memory of the role music played in his personal coming out and shortly later in a list of great figures of the queer past—might strike some readers as surprising. In a comment on his artistic self-education, Oswald remarks, "I had half-divined it in the music of a Beethoven and a Tschaikovsky before knowing facts in the life-stories of either of them—or of a hundred other tone-autobiographists" (Prime-Stevenson 2003, 84).

Taken in isolation, the inclusion of Ludwig van Beethoven alongside Tchaikovsky as a figure in queer history might seem bizarre or uninformed, the speculation of a medical man who knew little of Beethoven's biography. In the introduction to *Imre*, Mayne positions himself as the sympathetic recipient of Oswald's and Imre's shared memoirs. The subtitle "a memorandum" even suggests the sexological case studies collected by the likes of Richard von Krafft-Ebing, Havelock Ellis, and Magnus Hirschfeld. Mayne's other book on homosexuality, *The Intersexes: A History of Similisexualism as a Problem in Social Life* (ca. 1908–1909), suggests vague medical credentials, with its use of case studies and dedication to Krafft-Ebing. Xavier Mayne, however, was in reality far from uninformed on the subject of music. "Mayne" was in fact the pseudonym of American music critic, novelist, and amateur sexologist Edward Ireneus Prime-Stevenson (1858–1942). Despite legal

Kristin Franseen, *"Legendary In-Reading"* In: *Queer Ear*. Edited by: Gavin S. K. Lee, Oxford University Press.
© Oxford University Press 2023. DOI: 10.1093/oso/9780197536766.003.0011

training, he pursued a professional life as a music critic for *The Independent* and *Harper's Weekly* and published fiction, research, and essays on a variety of subjects during the 1880s and 1890s. A large inheritance from a maternal uncle around the turn of the century allowed him to live a life of relative leisure in Europe, where he lived in various Italian and Swiss hotels, lectured on a variety of subjects, and arranged for the private printing and distribution of his books (see Figure 10.1).

James Gifford, editor of the Broadview Literary Texts edition of *Imre* observes that "the bachelorhood of Ludwig van Beethoven . . . continually intrigued EPS the music critic" (Prime-Stevenson 2003, 89n1). Throughout his fiction, music criticism, and sexological work, Prime-Stevenson returned multiple times to the possibility of queer readings of Beethoven, both through reinterpreting certain biographical anecdotes and letters and through the potential secret meanings he attached to the composer's piano sonatas and symphonies. These writings simultaneously raise questions about how music scholars should deal with more dubious claims about musical meaning and provide rare evidence of queer modes of musical analysis in the first half of the twentieth century. While they reveal some awareness of (and desire for) a kind of queer symphonic canon decades before such concerns were openly addressed in academic musicology and theory, they also are frequently poorly cited, essentialist, and reflective of Prime-Stevenson's personal musical preferences and biases. This chapter will provide a brief overview of Prime-Stevenson's (and his known readers') general writings on Beethoven and queer musical meaning before focusing more specifically on the questions of the framing of Beethoven's Ninth presented in the short story/analytical program note "Prince Bedr's Quest." I will conclude by considering his later efforts to express a deeply personal philosophy of listening to instrumental music in light of more recent work on queer listening practices. Ultimately, I argue that Prime-Stevenson's fascination with

Boys' Adventure Stories: White Cockades (1887), Left to Themselves (1891)

Sentimental fiction: Her Enemy; Some Friends—and other Personages: Stories and Studies Mostly of Human Hearts (1913), Dramatic Stories to Read Aloud (1925)

Amateur Sexology: Imre: A Memorandum (ca. 1905–6), The Intersexes: A History of Simisexualism as a Problem in Social Life (ca. 1908 or 1909)

Music Criticism: Long-Haired Iopas: Old Chapters from Twenty-Five Years of Music Criticism (1927), A Repertory of One Hundred Symphonic Programmes (1932)

Figure 10.1 Prime-Stevenson's Major Works

the possibility of queer readings of Beethoven reflected both a desire to shape a kind of queer musical canon formation through a printed repetition and preservation of queer gossip and a complicated approach to listening that other approaches to musical meaning and emotion at the time could not wholly satisfy. These kinds of readings (while likely never as widespread as Prime-Stevenson would eventually claim) were not wholly invented by him, but reflective of the use of Beethoven's music to suit a variety of personal and political interpretations during this period and beyond.

To have some idea of the context of "Prince Bedr's Quest" as a work of queer musical analysis, it is helpful to trace references to Beethoven across Prime-Stevenson's writings and the works of some of his colleagues and contemporaries. The passage from *Imre* mentioning Beethoven, Tchaikovsky, and "other tone autobiographists" was excerpted in the socialist philosopher Edward Carpenter's *The Intermediate Sex: A Study of Some Transitional Types of Men and Women* (1908, 168) alongside other writings theorizing sexual identity. Beyond suggesting one arm of Prime-Stevenson's intended readership and distribution channels for "Mayne's" quasi-sexological writing, the inclusion of this reference suggests that Carpenter found such a statement relevant to his own interest in historical, literary, and anthropological writings on the value of what he called "intermediate types" in society. In my recent articles in *19th-Century Music* and *Music & Letters* on Prime-Stevenson as a nostalgic queer biographer (Franseen 2020a and b), I connect Carpenter's and Prime-Stevenson's writings on Beethoven in terms of a broader search for queer biography and Prime-Stevenson's deep personal nostalgia for the New York concert scene of the 1890s. It was in New York where Prime-Stevenson had a number of personal and professional relationships that profoundly shaped his later work and where he likely first encountered the queer gossip surrounding Tchaikovsky.[1] Prime-Stevenson's reinterpretation of historical anecdotes about Beethoven alongside the then-current gossip surrounding Tchaikovsky's sexuality and death reflects the importance of reading as a queer practice. I argue that Prime-Stevenson's intention in repeating the same references to specific composers and works across his

---

[1] Prime-Stevenson's obituary for Tchaikovsky, published in *Harper's Weekly*, suggests that the two met multiple times during the composer's time in New York, although Tchaikovsky appears surprisingly infrequently in Prime-Stevenson's later collected music criticism. He writes that "[only] a few days before he left New York in 1891 he remarked cordially, to one who had met him frequently during his brief visit, 'I shall surely come over here again and see what you are all doing in music here, and how well you may be liking what I am doing.' His unexpected death reminds the writer of the kindly remark, and of the cancellation of a courteous hope and a splendid career." E. I. S. 1893, 1112.

sexological writings, overtly gay fiction, and music criticism was to construct a kind of queer music historical canon not otherwise available in print. His personal wealth, strategic use of self-publishing, and connections to elite musical, literary, and sexological circles gave him a unique level of authorial control in printing and distribution through venues not widely available to other queer authors and scholars. Yet thinking of Prime-Stevenson only in terms of the written word risks missing the threads of musical meaning that run throughout his musical descriptions and assumptions that his readers are also themselves listeners. I think it is useful to think of Prime-Stevenson's queering of Beethoven in particular through two lenses: (1) the appeal of applying secret meanings to canonical works and (2) the promotion of listening and amateur performance. Taken together, these form a kind of queer analysis that had the potential to go beyond the "acceptable" approaches to musical biography and interpretation available during Prime-Stevenson's lifetime.

Secret Meanings

Despite the unconventionality of his writings on Beethoven, Prime-Stevenson seemed to see his reading of Beethoven as grounded in the documentary evidence. In a preface to a selection of Beethoven's letters included in a mainstream literary anthology, he emphasized the importance of reading composers' letters as a way of understanding their humanity and creative process:

> His correspondence holds up the mirror to his own nature, with its extremes of impulse and reserve, of affection and austerity, of confidence and suspicion. It abounds, too, in that brusque yet seldom coarse humor which leaps up in the Finale of the Seventh Symphony, in the Eighth Symphony's waggery, the last movement of the Concerto in E flat. They offer likewise verbal admissions of such depressions of heart as we recognize in the sternest episodes of the later Sonatas and of the Galitzin Quartets, and in the awful Allegretto of the Symphony in A. They hint at the amorous passion of the slow movements of the Fourth and Ninth Symphonies, at the moral heroism of the Fifth, at the more human courage of the "Heroic," at the mysticism of the Ninth's tremendous opening. In interesting relation to this group, and merely of superficial interest, are his hasty notes, his occasional

efforts to write in English or in French, his touches of musical allusiveness. (Prime-Stevenson 1917, 1750)

This is not in and of itself a queer reading of Beethoven, but it suggests something vital about Prime-Stevenson the musicologist and analyst that became even more overt in his fiction and sexology: the role of a personal connection with musical and primary sources in grounding his various claims about musical and historical meaning. Only a few years after *Imre*, "Xavier Mayne" would expand upon his queer Beethoven interpretation in a non-fictional context within a brief passage in his monumental history of homosexuality *The Intersexes*.[2] The book's section on music (in a chapter on "the aesthetic professions") is only a few pages long but provides a curious blending of turn-of-the-century sexological writings on music, queer biographical gossip, and musical meaning (not to mention Prime-Stevenson's own musical preferences). Some of this gossip is unsurprising and resonates with discussions of queer musicality in mentions of Tchaikovsky by Carpenter, E. M. Forster, and others:

> The death of the brilliant and unhappy Russian composer Tschaikowsky has been affirmed (if denied with equal conviction) as a suicide, not a sudden illness, in consequence of terror of a scandal that hung over him— a relative being spoken of as the persecutor. Some homosexual hearers of Tschaikowsky's last (and most elegiac) symphony, known as the "Pathetic" claim to find in it such revelations of a sentimental-sexual kind that they have nicknamed the work the "Pathic" Symphony. Brahms and the colossal Bruckner have been characterized as "the ultimate voices in a homosexual message by symphonic music"; even if one sub-consciously uttered. (Prime-Stevenson, ca. 1908/9, 396–97).

Prime-Stevenson clearly does not limit himself to the most recent or heavily documented queer gossip, even when it comes to claims about "homosexual hearers." Based on the possibilities of "revelations of a sexual-sentimental kind," he conflates biography, gossip, and the potential for queer musical meanings that could be found through historical research, musical analysis, and listening:

---

[2] The implications, potential sources, and both documented and imagined readership for "Mayne's" queer musical claims in *The Intersexes* are explored in greater detail in Franseen 2020, 300–20.

Composers present homosexual types: during either all their lives, or a portion of them. The supreme secret of the noble-natured and moral Beethoven seems to have been an idealized homosexualism. In Beethoven's sad latest days, can be traced a real passion for that unworthy nephew Carl: who, it is said, once sought to extort money from Beethoven, on threats to disclose an [*sic*] homosexual relationship! Beethoven's beautiful sonata, Opus 111, in often called among German and Austrian Uranians, "The Uranian Sonata," from some legendary "in-reading" of the work. (Prime-Stevenson, 1908/9, 396)

Despite Prime-Stevenson's occasional references to Tchaikovsky and clear awareness of the gossip surrounding the composer's death in Anglo-American gay circles, Tchaikovsky does not occupy a major role in his music criticism. Instead, he seems preoccupied with using the then-popular gossip about Tchaikovsky as a way for making similar claims about secret meanings in works by other composers as a form of queer interpretation. As with Tchaikovsky and the *Pathétique*, "Mayne" suggests an unusually direct parallel between biography and music in moving toward a queer reading of Beethoven's Piano Sonata, op. 111. While he shies away from specific musical details, he claims that it is not just him, but others (the unspecified "Austrian and German Uranians" that are his only citation for this claim) who truly understand a kind of hidden message in Beethoven's music.

"Prince Bedr's Quest" and "Xavier Mayne's" Beethoven

For a critic who promoted hidden readings and secret meanings, Prime-Stevenson appears to have had some reticence surrounding the issue of authorial voice and (auto)biography. In both his fiction and non-fiction writings on instrumental music, he appears at some points to favor discussing the music "itself." In the introduction to *Long-Haired Iopas: Old Chapters from Twenty-Five Years of Music-Criticism*, he dismisses discounting both familiar historical anecdotes and his own numerous personal encounters with famous musicians as "merely souvenirs" that have little to do with the act of listening or the memories of past performances (1927, ix). Yet, when it comes to some aspects of symphonic music—namely, the question of cultivating musical understanding—Prime-Stevenson is often eager to either point to biographical sources or make claims around authorial intent. This perhaps explains some of the odd structure and intertextual aspects of "Prince Bedr's Quest," as well as the problems with considering "Bedr" as a work of analysis. To fully unpack "Bedr's" reading of Beethoven's Ninth and associations with other works by Prime-Stevenson on queer listening, one must first understand the metafictional and intertextual references at play in the story's publication and framing.

"Prince Bedr's Quest: As Hinted in Beethoven's Ninth Symphony?" is the concluding chapter of the first section of the book, which focuses largely on nineteenth-century Viennese music. Although presented alongside the revised versions of Prime-Stevenson's earlier lectures and newspaper columns that make up the bulk of *Iopas*, the essay is actually a somewhat strange work of fiction organized according to the following structure (see Figure 10.2):

While the remainder of the anthology consists of poetry and nonfiction attributed to Prime-Stevenson and clearly expressing his public authorial persona and stated opinions as a music critic, "Bedr" begins with an account

Introduction (unmarked)	Oswald and narrator (Imre?) in Vienna.
"This prefatory to a tale in the score"	The young Prince Bedr is introduced and departs on his quest on the urging of a mysterious, mocking dervish in a green robe.
"I. Allegro non troppo – un poco maestoso"	Bedr visits with friends in other lands and undertakes philosophical studies, only to find "a taste of bitterness, the edge of unsatisfied desire" and continue his journey (51).
"II. Molto Vivace"	Bedr finds temporary happiness in nature, only to be put off by "a leering centaur" and the revelation that nature is "just existence" (53)
"III. Adagio Molto e Cantabile"	Bedr nearly becomes engaged to the daughter of the king of the Country of the Sunset. He sees a vision of the dervish (accompanied by a trumpet call) commanding him to renounce earthly love.
"IV. Presto, selon le caractére d'un récitatif"	The dervish now appears "cheerful" and (following each change of tempo) confirms that he has passed all the tests needed to receive enlightenment. He takes Bedr's hand and grants him a vision of the universe. The story concludes by claiming Bedr never married, returned tohis kingdom as a wise ruler, and lived to be a hundred.

Figure 10.2 Plot Outline of "Prince Bedr's Quest"

from an unnamed narrator describing his and his friend Oswald's Beethoven tourism and musical interests:

> It was after another of our Viennese days, passed in prowling about what is left of Beethoven's homes and haunts in "Alt-Wien"—Heiligenstadt, the Kahlenberg, those low-ceilinged rooms in the ancient Schwarzspanierhaus. My friend Oswald and I fell upon an old Beethoven question fantasy—that is to say, how far ought imagination to interpret the Ninth Symphony; to make it a thing of definite emotional meaning, construing it as "programmatic music." Neither Oswald nor I are of kindly feeling towards confessedly "programme" scores . . . But we two musical idlers, particularly as real lookers-on in Vienna, are by no means the first who have become introspective of the Ninth. (Prime-Stevenson 1927, 45)

The Oswald mentioned by this narrator is likely the same Oswald who narrated *Imre* (and who, according to the preface to that novel, sent his and Imre's life stories as a case study for "Mayne"). In the novel, Imre von N. has personal connections to Vienna and briefly saw a Viennese psychiatrist. The reappearance of these characters in this seemingly nonfictional context is unusual, although not entirely unexpected. Prime-Stevenson reused specific characters and allusions across his self-published fiction—Imre himself reappears as a minor character in the 1913 short story "Madonnesca," and multiple short stories and essays published by Prime-Stevenson cite "Xavier Mayne" as an expert on sexology and ostensibly separate person from the author. One of the lengthiest (and oddest) self-citations in Prime-Stevenson's work appears in *The Intersexes*, where "Mayne" cites his own novel ("the psychological romance already referred to in this study several times, on account of its aim at serious suggestiveness") as evidence of what "Mayne" views as the complexities and contradictions inherent to really knowing gay history:

> What a contrast are these to the heroes and heroic intellects of Greece and Rome! To a Themistocles, an Agesilaus, an Aristides and a Kleomenes; to Socrates and Plato, and Saint Augustine; to Servetus and Beza; to Alexander, Julius Cæsar, Augustus, and Hadrian; to Sweden's Charles the Twelfth, to Frederick the Great, to indomitable Tilly, to the fiery Skobeleff, the austere Gordon, the ill-starred Macdonald; to great Oriental princes; to the brightest lyrists and dramatists of old Hellas and Italia; to Shakespeare, (to Marlowe also, as we can well believe) Platen, Grillparzer, Hölderlin, Byron,

Whitman; to an Isaac Newton, a Justus Liebig—to the masterly Jérôme Duquesnoy, the classic-souled Winckelmann; to Mirabeau, Beethoven, to Bavaria's unhappy King Ludwig;—to an endless procesion [*sic*] of "exceptional men," from epoch to epoch! As to these and innumerable others, whose hidden, and inner lives have proved without shadow of doubt (however rigidly suppressed as "popular information") or by inferences vivid enough to silence scornful denial, that they belonged to Us. (Prime-Stevenson 1908/9, 558–59)

In any event, the additional inclusion of Imre and Oswald in *Long-Haired Iopas* further ties the work to Prime-Stevenson's pseudonymous sexological writings, works that he otherwise acknowledged under his own name only as "important studies in a branch of the psychiatrics of sex" (Prime-Stevenson 1913, 2003). It also appears to maintain the fiction (constructed in *Imre*) that Imre and Oswald are independent people merely corresponding with "Mayne"/Prime-Stevenson—perhaps even his sources for the queer Beethoven reading presented in *The Intersexes*. Whether this particular self-citation is a half-hearted attempt to distance himself from his pseudonym, a game for those who knew the works of both Prime-Stevenson and "Mayne," or an eclectic combination of the two, "Bedr" is unique for being the only ostensibly *nonfiction* works by Prime-Stevenson to go so far as to de-fictionalize one of his own characters to express and confirm his heterodox musical opinions!

The rest of the story—an Orientalist fantasia corresponding to the movements of Beethoven's Ninth Symphony—has strong homoerotic overtones, featuring a Turkish prince named Bedr ultimately choosing the wisdom offered by a travelling mystic (later revealed to be a djinn disguised as a dervish) over his planned marriage, making "a sudden vow not to wed, for a long season to come—as indeed became his case. And in great gladness for the rest of his long life—though the gladness was one that he never explained to anyone whomsoever" (Prime-Stevenson 1927, 57–58). Overtly, the story is one of ascetic devotion, with Bedr experiencing various types of worldly experiences before finding himself unsatisfied and moving onward. Each "movement" of the story applies tempo indications corresponding to those of the symphony to Bedr's journey and personal development. There is nothing particularly new or shocking in the emotional trajectory of the story, as Bedr embarks a journey from physical luxury to an exploration of nature to romantic love to eventual universal brotherhood and spiritual fulfillment. Similar (and far more musically detailed) readings can be found in the far more mainstream analyses of the symphony by the likes of Rosa Newmarch and Donald Francis Tovey. Where Prime-Stevenson differs notably from his contemporaries is in his creation of a program "by" one half of a fictional gay couple who earlier expressed interest in secret meanings within Beethoven's works.

If one understands where Oswald and Imre originated—and, perhaps, is also familiar with the discussions of Beethoven present in "Mayne's" other work—it is not so much that Prime-Stevenson is presenting "Bedr" as a uniquely queer story (although Bedr's rejection of marriage and grasping the mystic's hand at his moment of enlightenment are certainly suggestive). Rather, Prime-Stevenson appears to be trying to find a way around the problems of evidence that continued to vex his queer musical project, problems that would reappear with the emergence of a more formalized queer musicology at the end of the century.

Even the subtitle of the short story "As Hinted in Beethoven's Ninth Symphony?" suggests multiple ambiguities with its end punctuation and pointed use of "hinted." The obvious reading is that the personal journey undertaken by Bedr is the story "hinted" at in the symphony, with its use of tempo indications and the claim in the opening that "so curiously did each detail that we finished our romancing almost ready to query seriously whether Beethoven's own thought had not been busy through the same fantastic literary inspiration when meditating the complex and dramatic episodes of the Ninth" (Prime-Stevenson 1927, 45–46). Yet, if one reads the opening with Oswald and Imre *as* a part of Prime-Stevenson's "fantastic literary inspiration," the "hint" may instead be back toward Oswald's inclusion of Beethoven as one of the "tone autobiographists" who guided him toward self-realization and acceptance of his sexuality. In this vein, Oswald and Imre appear to be taking part in the kind of gossip that would lead to "Mayne's" claims about a "Uranian" Sonata and seemingly deliberate (mis)reading of Beethoven's life and letters. Yet this experimentation also goes beyond biography. Imre and Oswald express in their "programme" the same questions that "Mayne" hints at in his vague references to queer gossip about Beethoven's music. Imre's stated disdain for programmatic music thus comes across as a challenge not to finding programs in instrumental music but in being told what to think and how to feel about the meanings we find as listeners. What, he asks, do we hear in instrumental music, even when society tells us certain meanings are impossible? How can one listen to, research, and write about music queerly when such a reading is impossible or limited to a few acknowledged narratives of repression and tragedy? Whose musical conversations and experiences do and do not get preserved in program notes or printed in musicological journals? What works and modes of expression lend themselves more easily (or safely) to queer reinterpretation. These questions are reminiscent of some of Philip Brett's concerns about the presence of a limited set of "acceptable" queer frameworks for musical analysis and biography in the reception histories of Tchaikovsky and Britten and the debates surrounding the act of extending a queer lens to Schubert. "A lesbian and gay musicology," Brett observed in "Musicality, Essentialism, and the Closet," "will want to interrogate both terms [homosexuality and musicality] unceasingly as it re-searches our history, proposes new theories of music, and devises a new pedagogy. It is not the evidence, but the right to interpret it, to which we have to lay claim" (Brett 2006, 22). While Prime-Stevenson was certainly no critic of the German musical canon, his move from reading Beethoven's life through the dominant (tragic and troubled) lens that contemporary queer gossip applied to Tchaikovsky to reading Beethoven's music as the vehicle for Oswald's and Imre's continued life together suggests a new paradigm is at play, one that allowed for multiple possible valid (and potentially queer) musical encounters.

Listening and Performance

What did these possible meanings actually do when considered during the act of listening? In other words, what did Prime-Stevenson (or his characters or his anonymous—and possibly apocryphal—informants) actually hear that was queer in Beethoven's music? With all of this talk of autobiographical hints, it is tempting to ask whether Prime-Stevenson's linking of sexuality, romance, and instrumental music had any personal basis. For all his readings (and creation) of historical and musical anecdotes, Prime-Stevenson's personal feelings on the musical experience are often hidden behind his professional personas: "Mayne" the sexologist, Oswald and Imre the fictional correspondents, and Prime-Stevenson the former music critic. Yet Prime-Stevenson's later nostalgic fiction—privately printed under his own name, but with occasional references to Oswald, Imre, and "Mayne"—presents a more overtly queer and romantic view of amateur listening and performance, particularly in the short story "Once: But Not Twice." Although written during the 1910s and published in the privately printed anthology *Her Enemy* in 1913, it is set in the 1890s and imagines thinly veiled versions of Prime-Stevenson (depicted here as Douglas Macray) and his estranged friend, former student, and one-time lover Harry Harkness Flagler (Bertram Jaques) reconnecting years after the latter's marriage, finally agreeing upon a meeting at the opera that tragically never materializes.[3] While pondering their state of affairs, the nostalgic Macray looks back on their bonding over attending concerts and playing the piano together. The depiction of Macray's and Jaques's imagined domestic and symphonic music-making aligns well with other early twentieth-century literary depictions of homosocial or homoerotic pianistic experiences, such as Lisl von Herzogenberg's Brahms arrangements as described by Ethel Smyth in *Impressions that Remained* and the pianola performance of Tchaikovsky presented in E. M. Forster's *Maurice*.[4] While many literary historians, including Gifford and Graham Robb, have noted the similar uses of music in scenes of queer awakening and seduction in both *Imre* and *Maurice*, it is worth expanding on the significance of this shared symphonic space as a site of musical-sexual encounter. Across the nineteenth century (until the birth of commercial recording), piano four-hands pieces and arrangements of symphonic works served as a medium for romantic musical connections as well as a site of considerable anxiety around gender and sexuality. In his consideration of accounts of piano duets in *Four-Handed Monsters*, Adrian Daub admits that, since the actual experiences of piano four-hands were by nature private and ephemeral, any attempt to reconstruct their meanings through literary sources is a "questionable bridge to the past" (Daub 2014, 8–9). This ephemerality is both a limit to understanding the role of queer performance and listening in Prime-Stevenson's work—where such readings often blend with those more acceptable to his non-queer public—and a feature of his repeated attempts to record his own musical understanding.

---

[3] The fictional scenario presented in "Once: But Not Twice" differs in a few significant ways from the historical account. Although the two indeed became estranged for a lengthy period following Flagler's marriage to Anne Lamont, the dedication in *Repertory* suggests that the two eventually reconciled socially, remarking upon their long acquaintance and musical appreciation "from earliest youth." That dedication also notes Flagler's continued musical philanthropy and presidency of the New York Philharmonic Society, a position he held in various forms from 1914 to 1934. In Prime-Stevenson's short story, Macray dies before the lovers can reconcile.

[4] For more on the queer domestic performances described by Smyth and Forster, see the third chapter of my dissertation, "Ghosts in the Archives: The Queer Knowledge and Public Musicology of Vernon Lee, Rosa Newmarch, and Edward Prime-Stevenson" (McGill University, 2019).

While listening to Tchaikovsky or Brahms in the concert hall might suggest a communal experience with all other people—performers and listeners—in the hall as part of publicly acceptable interpretation, the intimate, often domestic setting for private duet performance is open to much more personal musical responses. In "Once: But Not Twice," Prime-Stevenson links his characters Macray and Jaques's shared symphonic appreciation and sexual ecstasy in the experience of playing through piano four-hands arrangements, noting that "such musical evenings and the sweet sound of those orchestras and singers that fifteen years . . . are less tenderly green in my thought than our quiet hours of duets and extemporizing and—oh, audacious word!— composing together, in that quiet roomy second floor back we shared" (Prime-Stevenson 2003, 165). Prime-Stevenson's image of composition as an almost orgasmic experience leads to a collaboration between the lovers, with their shared arrangement and composition serving as Macray's only tangible reminder of their past. At least in Prime-Stevenson's fictionalized account, music appears as a queer practice in multiple forms: listening, interpretation, and composition.

There is little surviving evidence of the real Prime-Stevenson and Flagler engaging in amateur performance or composition together, but they both were heavily involved in the orchestral and operatic life of New York City: Prime-Stevenson as a music critic and Flagler as the eventual president of the New York Philharmonic. Prime-Stevenson dedicated at least three works on musical subjects to Flagler: "Once: But Not Twice," the essay "Long-Haired Iopas," and the book *A Repertory of One Hundred Symphonic Programmes.* All three works emphasize the importance of listening in order to understand aspects of music or music history that might otherwise seem ineffable. In particular, the list of composers and works in "Once: But Not Twice" suggests a shared secret program that unlocks not only Macray's and Jaques's musical interests but also the true depths (unknown to the *New York Times* reporter who writes Macray's obituary at the end of the story) of their relationship:

> What a pair we were to work out our course together through Mozart's E Flat Symphony, *à quatre mains!*—or become most stupendously excited in storming through the finale of Beethoven's Fifth! Trembling with an ecstasy, that two high-strung young natures made no attempt to conceal, whole nights went to Schumann, to Schubert, to Brahms, to Tschaikovsky, to Franck! To this day, I can never hear Brahms's noble Third Symphony but

I am curried back to one evening when we first played it through together.
(Prime-Stevenson 2003, 165)

This image of bringing together romance, performance, and musical associations finds some echoes in late twentieth-century experiments in queer musical meaning. In "Piano Four-Hands: Schubert and the Performance of Gay Male Desire," Brett observes that his own performance-based analysis of Schubert's Grand Duo and promotion of a queer reading of Schubert's biography are "if . . . a projection, it is at least a recognizable and understandable one that has served its purpose for generations of closeted homosexuals on the lookout for support from the past, or in my case, administering a nasty jolt in a timely manner" (Brett 1997, 169). Prime-Stevenson's forays into musical meaning in both his fiction and nonfiction appear to contain similar aims: seeking a queer past lurking not very far beneath the surface of accepted musical canons, reflecting a (real or imagined) romance conducted along musical terms, and delivering a "jolt" to strictly heterosexual readings of musical experiences, meanings, and histories. In the case of "Once: But Not Twice," one might see this "jolt" as particularly aimed at Flagler, whose marriage and social position placed him in very different musical circles from both the imagined private performances and compositions of Macray and Jaques and imaginative literary-analytical collaboration of Oswald and Imre. Through fiction, Prime-Stevenson could reimagine and relive queer musical moments that were all too fleeting in life and rarely safe to record.

The practice of experiencing a shared set of works and composers as a shared romantic experience is also reflected in some aspects of Prime-Stevenson's last known work, *A Repertory of One Hundred Symphonic Programmes*. Ostensibly a conventional guide to how to listen to recorded music and consisting primarily of curated "playlists" of specific recordings of different movements from an eclectic (and expansive) collection of symphonic and operatic works, the prefatory and appendices also suggest something of Prime-Stevenson's personal listening habits. In *Repertory*, one sees the phonograph as a kind of time machine, sonically transporting him back to the New York Philharmonic or the Metropolitan Opera, or forward to a musical reunion with others during times when war and his own failing health made transatlantic travel impossible.

When Prime-Stevenson shifts from writing about particular concerts to recordings, the possibility for he and his readers (including, one presumes, Flagler) uniting across temporal and geographical distance expands greatly.

Unlike the scattered references in his fiction, *Repertory* contains few outward signs of being connected to his research on the history of sexuality. Described on the title page as "for public auditions of the orthophonic phonograph-gramophone: with a prefatory on programme-making and conducting," the work presents several paradoxes in its scope and intent (Prime-Stevenson 1932). *Repertory* is a guide to music appreciation and listening that grew out of a series of combination lecture-phonograph listening sessions (dubbed "auditions") that the author apparently held in his hotel suite in Florence. Despite this supposedly public goal, the book was privately printed and distributed in a manner similar to that used for "Mayne's" queer writings. Although many of Prime-Stevenson's favorite composers are included, there is precious little about the grouping of his programs that immediately suggests these concerts as faithfully reproducing his "queer canon." Nonetheless, the book is significant for the lengthy dedication to Flagler and for Prime-Stevenson's thoughts on the value of the phonograph for private and semi-private musical gatherings. Beyond that, taken alongside works like *The Intersexes* and *Iopas*, it can be understood as the culmination of Prime-Stevenson's attempts to understand musical meanings and experiences of listening in a deeply personal way.

Although the phonograph recording neatly erases the bodies of the performers, Prime-Stevenson's guide brings into clearer focus the presence of the auditors and the "conductor" of the gramophone recital, promoting "shadow-conducting" (so long as it does not distract from the music), encouraging discussion of the works and their connections, and emphasizing the auditory and spiritual intimacy between the auditors and the composer. One review of *One Hundred Symphonic Programmes* in *Music and Letters* questioned Prime-Stevenson's instructions because "the blessing of the machine, for many, is precisely this absence of the distracting human form" (Goddard 1933, 391). Even as Prime-Stevenson instructs the "conductor" on how to guide the listeners through his record collection, however, he cautions against centering the conductor over the experience of listening. To this aim he also promotes a quasi-mystical intimacy between listener and composer, one that is unencumbered by the distracting atmosphere of the concert hall:

> For, one of the supreme qualities of a gramophonic concert, as contrasted with hearing the same music from an orchestra in a concert hall, is the superior intimacy, closeness of attention, fixedness of interest, absortion [*sic*] of all that the music means and conveys to ear and psychos; as there is not any

of the sub-conscious distraction of attention that is inevitable in a public concert-hall, for the auditors. . . . It is worthwhile to remember that when music is heard in presence of a public audience, the message of a master-musician is to others, as well as to you; but when you are hearing, just by yourself alone, then Bach, Mozart, Beethoven, Brahms—they are speaking to you, in an individualized, personal interview, what they mean by their score. For such great honour to you, your phonograph is the mystic, faithful medium. (Prime-Stevenson 1932, 26–27)

With the exception of these instructions on how to set up phonograph "auditions" and appendices, *One Hundred Symphonic Programmes* is largely a compilation of playlists with no further commentary. Some are grouped thematically by composer (Mozart, Bach, Wagner, Verdi, Johann Strauss), genre ("light modern classics," "popular" classics), or nationality (Italian, French, German, Spanish), but most are a juxtaposition of different genres, composers, eras, and national styles. Some familiar names from *The Intersexes* and *Long-Haired Iopas* appear frequently, including Beethoven, Brahms, Bruckner, and Wagner.

In addition to some lengthier passages included in the appendices, Prime-Stevenson intersperses quotations from various sources throughout the book in a manner similar to the interpolated poetry and prose quotations used to delineate sectional divisions within *Long-Haired Iopas*, explaining that:

The citations recurring, from the volume mentioned—miscellaneous studies and essays dealing with music and musicians—have been included in response to many requests from guests of the author, at his phonographic concerts, to which the Prefatory refers. It is hoped that such explanation may be sufficient excuse and—apology. (Prime-Stevenson 1932, 50)

While the majority of these quotes are taken from the essays in *Long-Haired Iopas* (although notably not "Prince Bedr's Quest"!), Prime-Stevenson also includes quotations on music from Shakespeare and a couple of lengthy excerpts from Verdi's letters. Given Prime-Stevenson's description of sharing these materials with his audiences, it is likely that the "auditions" included readings from Prime-Stevenson's music criticism, poetic dialogues and narrative poems, and (perhaps) fiction as means of illustrating his musical observations alongside silent listening to the selected recordings. The reprints and expansion of his public lectures presented in *Long-Haired Iopas* and short stories in the fictional anthology *Dramatic Stories to Read Aloud* (1924) demonstrate his love of speech as a form of performance closely tied to the musical experience. This would also explain the inclusion of poetic, fictional, and dramatic texts in *Long-Haired Iopas*, as well as some of his more unusual approaches to musical narrative and tangents on music history. Much like the historical and musical gossip he cites, these spoken performances of musical analysis and observation were unrecorded and remain lost to history.

In the preface, Prime-Stevenson repeatedly attempts to justify the book's publication by citing "urgent requests . . . that a discreet publicity of the large repertory on which I have drawn for my programmes, may advisably be made; for the use of a wider contingent of auditors" (Prime-Stevenson 1932, 3–4). At times, however, Prime-Stevenson remarks that his advice may be applied by a solitary listener, "the gramophonist himself," potentially revealing his private listening practices. *Repertory* can be seen as a revisiting of music (and people) from the past using the new phonograph technology and building on Prime-Stevenson's theories of queer musical experience, the symphony, and music appreciation. The playlists and approach to listening Prime-Stevenson espouses in *Repertory* also closely align with his earlier writings on musicality, homosexuality, and the New York symphonic scene in the 1890s. This imagined time and space existing within the experience of symphonic listening also connects with other homosocial and homoerotic accounts of domestic music-making and appreciation from the early decades of the twentieth century.

The specific musical references in Prime-Stevenson's work are not unique to him, of course, and their inclusion in his works dedicated to specific people suggests a sort of imagined—if geographically dispersed—musical community. Literary historian Graham Robb notes the popularity of novels on the *Tristan and Isolde* subject among queer readers, but also observes that:

> The instinctive perception of sympathy—even unintended—was especially strong in music. Gay tastes were remarkably consistent. The names of certain composers appear again and again in letters and novels: Beethoven (sonatas), Chopin (nocturnes), Wagner (*Lohengrin*, *Parsifal*, and *Tristan*), Tchaikovsky (the *Symphonie pathétique*), and fin-de-siècle French composers: Debussy, Delibes, Gounod, Massenet.
>
> The key ingredients seem to have been a melodious melancholy and something oxymoronic in the emotions: grandiose and sentimental,

ostentatious and discreet. The sexuality of the composer was not of primary importance, though both Forster and Prime-Stevenson suggest that Tchaikovsky's sexuality was audibly encoded in the bars of the *Symphonie pathétique*. Music could convey quite precisely what could never be said in print. (Robb 2005, 228)

Although several scholars in musicology and word-music studies have examined the ways in which music functioned as a useful and important code within fin-de-siècle queer communities (especially those with the means and leisure time to frequent the symphony or the opera), for Prime-Stevenson, it is clear that the shared experiences of the concert hall went beyond the merely symbolic act of recognizing a particular set of shared references.[5] The shared act of listening is also potentially a way for future readers to grasp the queer symphonic meanings he expresses elsewhere in his music criticism and fiction, perhaps even reading these works prior to listening to a particularly relevant movement or passage. Prime-Stevenson's writing and rewriting of queer music histories could thus be merged with a kind of queer listening that could go beyond his individual memories and experiences.

Reading a Queer Beethoven across Carpenter and Prime-Stevenson

While Prime-Stevenson's queer reading of Beethoven is certainly the one of the most overt and eclectic of this kind, he was neither the only such person to propose an alternate reading of Beethoven's music that aligned well with potential queer subjectivities nor the only to claim a queer biographical interpretation of Beethoven himself. Carpenter's work seems to have had an impact on both Prime-Stevenson's musical and sexological interests, despite the obvious differences in their personal politics, public engagement with sexology and sex reform activism, and personal circumstances. These readings share a few things in common: a focus on readings (and counter-readings) of masculinity and sexuality in instrumental music, an awareness of conflicting and seemingly unresolvable narratives surrounding Beethoven's personal

[5] See, for example, the chapter on queer audiences in Deutsch 2015, the comparisons between music and sexuality in Brett 2002, and the treatment of literary depictions of musicality and homosexuality in Law 2004.

life, and a desire to understand and/or claim awareness of the composer's emotional state while writing.

Carpenter's writings on Beethoven are not overtly queer in their analysis, but reflect a view of Beethoven's music as expressing something both "indescribable" and potentially sensual in ways that align with the goals of his work toward sex reform and utopian vision. His own analysis of the Ninth Symphony (published in 1898) presents a similar kind of journey to enlightenment to that put forth in "Prince Bedr's Quest," with a similar claim to understanding Beethoven the man after listening:

> The mood of feeling thus reached and expressed by Beethoven in his last period became something like the solution of the enigma of life. And I cannot but think that he has (almost deliberately) expressed this in his Ninth Symphony. (Carpenter 1898, 199)

Unlike Prime-Stevenson's depiction of Bedr as an enlightened ruler, Carpenter presents a more democratic vision of the conclusions found in the final movement, "a sense of Equality and Freedom which gives the soul habitation everywhere" (200). Like Prime-Stevenson, however, Carpenter quickly associates the long-standing fascination with the Ninth and desire to find some deeper meaning within it with Beethoven's psychology in a way that is reminiscent of the alleged acts of creativity and romantic fantasizing that produced "Bedr":

> If this "programme" (to use that expression had been the result of a mere mental argument, or brain process, I should think little of it. It would not have raised the Ninth Symphony above the level of Berlioz, or of much of Wagner's work. But if it was, as I venture to think, the embodiment of Beethoven's own experience of life (idealised and dramatized), the pictured evolution of his own heart, that perhaps explains to use the overpowering impression and fascination that this great creation carries with it. (Carpenter 1898, 201)

As previously mentioned, Carpenter's later writings on homosexuality mention Beethoven only in a quotation from "Mayne's" fiction. Yet the fact that Carpenter saw "Mayne's" claim about Beethoven as a "tone autobiographist" as worth inclusion alongside more decidedly non-fictional accounts from medical case studies suggests that he was intrigued (if, based on his lack of further comments, perhaps not wholly convinced) by the directions in which Prime-Stevenson took his musical "idealized and dramatised" notions of Beethoven's music as queer self-expression. For his part, Prime-Stevenson returned the favor in citing *The Intermediate Sex* in a footnote to *The Intersexes*, one of his few direct citations in a work that largely lacks a clear sense of documented sources:

> In making the foregoing references to belles-lettres that in colouring are more or less immediate to the topic of this book, its authour[6] [*sic*] is well aware of how incomplete and arbitrary they may seem. Many names and titles inevitably must be absent that are of much interest and importance. The reader in fact is asked to accept what is offered as only a small contribution to a suitably general survey. Especially from the field of essays, philosophic studies and so on, there has been no room here, at the date when these pages go to press, to include several recent allusions of value. For a single English instance a special word is due to Mr. Edward Carpenter's new little volume "The Intermediate Sex: A Study of Some Transitional Types of Men and Women." . . . (Prime-Stevenson 1908/9, 387n9)

Beyond the sheer oddness of a citation within a footnote apologizing for a *lack* of citations, this short note gives some sense of a network of readers that Prime-Stevenson could imagine reading his works and sharing his literary, historical, and (perhaps) musical tastes and interpretations. If the "Austrian and German Uranians" and characters like Oswald, Imre, Macray, and Jaques existed solely within Prime-Stevenson's imagination, the limited few who had access to his body of self-published works might at least share in their adventures, loves, and interests through a network built on reading and listening.

Attempts to trace those who read Prime-Stevenson's self-published works have been limited, and they largely depend on those surviving copies annotated by previous owners. In "What Became of *The Intersexes*?," James Gifford traces the book's current archival holdings and known early owners, noting Prime-Stevenson's determined attempts to get the volume into the

---

[6] Prime-Stevenson consistently added a "u" to "author" in nearly all of his self-published works. In his review of *Iopas*, J. A. Fuller Maitland noted that "Though the typography seems to have undergone a process of Europeanisation (at times almost to excess, as in the case of 'author'), the writer's American nationality is not disguised. For this and other reasons the book is not very easy reading, but it is well worth the trouble." Fuller Maitland 1928, 84.

collections of major libraries, the hands of sympathetic sexologists and activists, and members of his social circle in Italy and beyond. While Gifford uncovers a great deal about the kinds of individuals who owned copies—a loose network that included eccentric scholars, scandalous poets, and free-loving anarchists—these names reveal little of what Prime-Stevenson's readers thought of his claims. A few of these owners, including William Smith and Theodore Schroeder, annotated their copies with "further examples of scandals to complement Stevenson's collection" (Gifford 2011, 27).[7] In the rare surviving personal copies of his works, Prime-Stevenson engaged in a similar practice, perhaps tied to his plans for additional publications and distribution. The copy of *Iopas* gifted to Dartmouth College in 1938 (alongside inscribed copies of *Her Enemy* and *Repertory*) contains numerous typed and handwritten annotations and corrections, as well as a bound copy of a lengthy "literary agent's press-circular" with excerpts from French, British, and American reviews of the book. These reviews—some of them in mainstreams scholarly outlets like *Music & Letters*—frequently be-moan the book's limited edition, although almost none touch directly on the queer allusions in Prime-Stevenson's discussions of Beethoven and Wagner. Prime-Stevenson's extensive annotations and interest in documenting the musicologists, conductors, and critics who read his work suggest to me that he at one point was considering a second, perhaps more broadly accessible printing. Just as his writings on listening increasingly imagine a future where a variety of queer musical meanings are possible, the never-realized new volume hinted at would have imagined a world where one attempt at queer music theory emerges from the shadows.

Conclusions

In thinking about the context, content, and imagined future readership for Prime-Stevenson's queer Beethoven project, I want to resist the assump-tion that his alternative readings of Beethoven feed into some kind of uto-pian vision of the man or his music as universal. Such a claim would ignore the historical, artistic, and political specificities of both Beethoven and

---

[7] Some of these annotations further reveal that "Mayne's" identity was not as unknown as the use of a pseudonym for sensitive materials might normally suggest. Underneath the name Xavier Mayne on the title page, Schroeder wrote in his copy (now part of the Special Collections of the University of Wisconsin-Madison) "(probably) E. I. Prime-Stevenson."

Prime-Stevenson, including the latter's own numerous prejudices, limitations, and biases as a theorist: his stated and unstated views of "music" as meaning primarily the Western art music produced in Germany, France, and Italy during the eighteenth and nineteenth centuries (and specifically excluding all forms of popular music), his elitism, his use of exoticist and orientalist cliches, to name but a few. For all that his queer approach to Beethoven might initially seem radical to those used to an outright denial of queerness in music history, Prime-Stevenson's queering of the German canon never questions the existence of musical canons in the first place.

But I do want to consider Prime-Stevenson's Beethoven writings in terms of a kind of imagined utopianism within his own work, of bringing together seemingly disparate threads in order to consider what kinds of musical meanings might be possible. As a work of analysis, "Prince Bedr's Quest" is confusing, meandering, and fairly unoriginal in terms of its basic musical details, which are scant and depend on the reader associating tempo designations in the symphony with particular moments in the extramusical story. Yet its intertextual connections to Prime-Stevenson's pseudonymous works, fiction, and later guide to listening all present a kind of queer musical framework that adds additional layers to an otherwise simplistic story. Across his career and in different literary genres, he seems to have experimented with different approaches to queer musical meaning: biographical claims, appeals to gossip, claims of hearing something hidden or subconscious, and (ultimately) a more speculative call for the act of shared listening.

Thinking about Beethoven in connection with later musicological anxieties surrounding queer musical meaning provides a moment of reflection for when, why, and how music scholars tend to address the intersections of identity and compositional practice. While generally associated with the so-called Schubert debates that took place in the pages of *19th-Century Music*, *Schubert durch die Brille*, and the *New York Review of Books* (not to mention at events hosted by the American Musicological Society and the 92nd Street YMHA), gendered and sexualized readings of Beethoven and Schubert date back to at least the posthumous reminiscences published by Schubert's friends and associates.[8] Despite persistent tropes of tragic heterosexual love

---

[8] For a thorough overview and analysis of many of these primary sources and their later reinterpretation across the late nineteenth and early twentieth centuries, see Messing 2006–7). Messing traces the origins of the supposedly "girlish" character originally attributed to Schubert by Robert Schumann alongside other loaded gendered terminology used to describe Schubert's life and music (often in contrast with Beethoven) through the writings of various later critics, novelists, and scholars. Of particular interest to the project of historicizing a queer reading of Schubert prior to

in popular fictional treatments the lives of both composers—Schubert in *Das Dreimaderlhaus* and Beethoven in *Immortal Beloved*—analyses of their works are not free of these associations. Some of Prime-Stevenson's interest in Beethoven may have been to claim a canonical composer as a part of his queer musical circle, reinforcing some of the biases Brett observed in his evaluation of how musicology had addressed Tchaikovsky's homosexuality:

> The one composer we have been allowed to "know" about in the period is Tchaikovsky. But the disclosing of the Russian composer's sexuality and the careful covering over (or ignoring) of the tracks around Schubert surely has to do with the processing of music by scholarship as a male and predominantly German art. A Russian composer could be homosexual, indeed one so close to Teutonic mastery probably had to be homosexual, because that would allow the exotic, decadent, and effeminate quality of the music to be held up (as I remember it being held up to me in my youth) as a warning. The central German canon must at all costs be preserved in its purity. (Brett 2006, 15)

Prime-Stevenson's relationship to this canon is complex. He at once challenges the presumed heteronormativity associated with the "male and German art" of nineteenth-century symphonic literature, while reinforcing a great deal of musical gatekeeping. He repeatedly makes grand claims for widespread queer readings of Beethoven that are only hinted at elsewhere and remain unsupported by the historical literature. I also find myself wondering whether or not there is an element of safety and self-protection in his identification with Beethoven's music and various (mis)interpretations of the composer's personal life. In his more guarded (or, as in the case of "Bedr," more securely coded behind multiple layers of fiction) appreciations of Beethoven's "masculine" music (as it was frequently described), Prime-Stevenson was admiring another man across history in a way that was socially sanctioned, even celebrated, within public musical life. Perhaps this is why his initial conflation of Beethoven and Tchaikovsky is so strange and troubling—to know Tchaikovsky's biography and to still identify so strongly with his music would have required an explanation that Prime-Stevenson was unable to give under his own name and beyond the very select, very limited

---

the late twentieth century are the chapters in volume 1 on Schubert's contested place in sanitized Victorian music histories and in volume 2 on the rise of German sexological approaches to music.

queer musical circles he inhabited. In *The Apparitional Lesbian*, Terry Castle identifies within "an alternative universe—the opera house—in which many of the more restrictive norms governing ordinary female-female experience were temporarily suspended" (Castle 1993, 202). A gay love for Beethoven could similarly be simultaneously privately queer and publicly acceptable.

Current approaches to queer musicology have not entirely resolved the question of biography and identification in analysis. In his keynote workshop on queer music theory at the 2017 meeting of the LGBTQ Music Study Groups at Edge Hill University, David Bretherton observed that some of the far more recent queer analyses of Schubert are also not particularly uncomplicated when it comes to making the case for queer musical meanings—they are bound up in various assumptions about gender and sexuality in both the 1990s and 1810s; intersect with historical documentation of masculinity, student life, and sex work in early nineteenth-century Vienna; and may or may not reflect one's own experiences of performing, researching, or listening to Schubert. In a similar manner, Prime-Stevenson's attempts to find "the ultimate homosexual message" in the piano sonatas and symphonic music of Beethoven (as well as Brahms and Bruckner) reveal something about what he sought in his listening and analytical practices. First and foremost, he sought a history, one that reinforced his own experiences—and, not infrequently, his prejudices—and connected his sense of self with the music and stories he found most appealing.

As I revisit these conclusions in the year 2021, we have just completed a so-called Beethoven Year, the 250th anniversary of Beethoven's birth. This occasion was not without its controversies and contentious moments. On social media, several music researchers expressed longstanding skepticism toward the risk of positioning of Beethoven's music as universal, especially given the rise in right-wing populism and the appropriation of "symphonies" as a white nationalist dogwhistle.[9] Still others saw in the valorization of

---

[9] Linda Shaver-Gleason provides an overview of the racist appropriation and celebration (often for political purposes) of the perceived whiteness of the European past, the erasure of composers of color, and the limits of tokenistic efforts at a more inclusive classical music under a definition that still centers the exceptionality of white male geniuses as the creators of "Great Music." See "Who Wrote the Symphonies, and Why Should It Matter?," https://notanothermusichistorycliche.blogspot.com/2018/09/who-wrote-symphonies-and-why-should-it.html. For a more historical illustration of what the music research fields lose when they (actively or passively) practice exclusion, see Philip Ewell's February 2021 Twitter project "Erasing Colorasure in Music Theory," which draws attention to Black music theorists and composers "who may have been of interest to American music theory, had American music theory ever been truly interested in blackness" (Twitter post, February 1): https://twitter.com/philewell/status/1356367978078597120.

Beethoven the tacit approval of a kind of musicological nostalgia, when one could "safely" ignore concerns of identity, oppression, and inclusivity in favor of "only" focusing on the music. How, then, to understand the idiosyncrasies and eccentricities present in the trace of an analysis that is simultaneously so laughably misguided and daringly brave, radical in its specific claims and conservative in its general scope, anticipatory of the paradigm-shifting methodologies of the New Musicology and reflective of the author's devotion to finding himself in a canon many of us would care to dismantle (or, at the very least, greatly expand beyond the limits of what Prime-Stevenson would recognize as music)? I am reminded here of another infamous question surrounding Beethoven's identity in the popular imagination, one that routinely makes the rounds on social media (to the consternation of many involved in what is known as "musicology twitter") and that is also grounded in the biases and gatekeeping of conventional music research. Dominique-René de Lerma traces the spread of stories promoting (as he titles his brief debunking of the rumor for the *Black Music Research Journal*) "Beethoven as a Black Composer," observing that the rumors surrounding Beethoven's racial identity frequently conflate documented history, misreadings and counter-readings of biography, iconography, and speculation. In a manner similar to Prime-Stevenson's assertion of a queer musical canon through repetition in the absence of evidence or scholarly recognition, Jamaican historian Joel Augustus Rogers (1880–1966) argued in numerous books published from 1941–52 that Beethoven had African ancestry. De Lerma ultimately notes that, while Rogers "circumstantial or speculative" claims "deserve notice," established genealogical research disproves his thesis (de Lerma 1990, 120).

Yet this rumor was allowed to spread—in fact, continues to spread—in part because of the neglect of composers of color by the music research fields (and the realm of "classical music" more broadly). In his analysis of far more recent social media repetitions of the myth of the Black Beethoven, Nicholas Rinehart argues that such ahistorical claims are:

> claims to legitimacy, claims to accomplishment, claims to genius, claims to participation and inclusion. The figure of Black Beethoven is perhaps most significant because it is a radically desperate attempt to accomplish what historical whitewashing has totally failed in doing. This desperation, this need to paint Beethoven black against all historical likelihood is, I think, I profound signal that the time has finally come to make a single, concerted, organized, rigorous, dynamic, and robust effort at fundamentally reshaping

the classical canon and reconsidering and reimagining the history of Western art music, period. (Rinehart 2011, 130)

Could one make a similar point about Prime-Stevenson's queer readings of Beethoven? Like Rogers, Prime-Stevenson grappled with a desire for history and a deep personal love of music within a social framework that told him that his analytical lens and the experiences that informed them were unspeakable and unworthy of serious consideration. The main lesson those of us looking to the histories of musicology, theory, and biography for alternative or counter-narratives of musical meaning can take from a figure like Prime-Stevenson is to expand our frameworks for understanding musical knowledge—even when said knowledge is dubious, incomplete, or outright incorrect. "Subconscious utterances" aside, Beethoven, Brahms, and Bruckner are not figures in our queer musical history—but was does it say about Prime-Stevenson that he so passionately wanted to be able to read and hear otherwise? What does it say about the possibilities for queer musical understanding in his lifetime and the limits of biographical and musical knowledge (even for a more "known" figure like Tchaikovsky)? What do we risk as musicologists and theorists when we ignore this kind of reading? More disturbingly, what continued untruths do we unknowingly perpetuate by considering certain kinds of claims beneath our notice? Part of the problem with Prime-Stevenson's analyses is that they are frequently unverifiable, but another part is that it is all too easy to assume that no one was doing queer musical analysis before it became reasonably possible to publish it within accepted academic outlets. As someone with an interest in the kinds of eccentric analyses practiced by Prime-Stevenson and others outside of the academy, I am wary of inadvertently reinforcing false narratives or assuming that any relevant and challenging questions within our field have never been asked before now. "Prince Bedr's Quest" tells us far more about Prime-Stevenson and the world in which he lived (or wished possible) than it does about the historical Beethoven or the Ninth Symphony. But the questions this kind of work raises are certainly worth asking, by both queer theorists and music theorists—and those who are both—alike.

References

Anonymous [probably Edward Prime-Stevenson]. [1913]. "Stevenson, Edward Prime-." In *Who's Who in America*, 7th ed., 2002. Albert Nelson Marquis. Chicago: A.N. Marquis.

Anonymous [probably Edward Prime-Stevenson]. 1927(?). "Literary Agent's Press-Circular: Long-Haired Iopas: Old Chapters from Twenty-Five Years of Music Criticism, by Edward Prime-Stevenson." Bound in the endpapers of Prime-Stevenson, *Long-Haired Iopas: Old Chapters from Twenty-Five Years of Music Criticism.* Copy #77. Dartmouth College Library. Florence: Privately Printed.

Bretherton, David. 2017. "An Introduction to 'Queer Music, Queer Theory, Queer Music Theory.'" Presented at Music, Queer, Intersections: Annual Symposium of the LGBTQ+ Music Study Group. May 26–27, 2017. Edge Hill University.

Brett, Philip. 1997. "Piano Four-Hands: Schubert and the Performance of Gay Male Desire." *19th-Century Music* 21, no. 2: 149–76.

Brett, Philip. 2002. "Musicology and Sexuality: The Example of Edward J. Dent." In *Queer Episodes in Music and Modern Identity,* edited by Sophie Fuller and Lloyd Whitesell, 177–88. Urbana and Chicago: University of Illinois Press.

Brett, Philip. 2006. "Musicality, Essentialism, and the Closet." In *Queering the Pitch: The New Gay and Lesbian Musicology,* 2nd ed., edited by Philip Brett, Elizabeth Wood, and Gary C. Thomas, 9–26. New York: Routledge.

Carpenter, Edward. 1898. "Beethoven and his Earlier Sonatas." In *Angel's Wings: Essays on Art and Its Connection to Life,* 140–75. London: Sonnenschein and Co.

Carpenter, Edward. 1908. *The Intermediate Sex: A Study of Some Transitional Types of Men and Women.* London: Allen & Unwin.

Castle, Terry. 1993. *The Apparitional Lesbian: Female Homosexuality and Modern Culture.* New York: Columbia University Press.

Daub, Adrian. 2014. *Four-Handed Monsters: Four-Handed Piano Playing and Nineteenth Century Culture.* Oxford: Oxford University Press.

Deutsch, David. 2015. *British Literature and Classical Music: Cultural Contexts, 1870–1945.* London: Bloomsbury Academic.

E. I. S. [Edward Prime-Stevenson]. 1893. "Peter Iltitsch (sic) Tschaikowsky." *Harper's Weekly,* Vol. 37 (November 18): 1112.

Ewell, Philip (@philewell). 2021. "Erasing Colorasure in Music Theory." Tweet. February 1. https://twitter.com/philewell/status/1356367978078597120.

Franseen, Kristin. 2020a. "'Onward to the End of the Nineteenth Century': Edward Prime-Stevenson's Queer Musicological Nostalgia." *Music and Letters* 101, no. 2: 300–20.

Franseen, Kristin. 2020b. "Queering Musical Biography in the Writings of Edward Prime-Stevenson and Rosa Newmarch." *19th-Century Music* 44, no. 2: 100–18.

Franseen, Kristin. 2019. "Ghosts in the Archives: The Queer Knowledge and Public Musicology of Vernon Lee, Rosa Newmarch, and Edward Prime-Stevenson." PhD diss., McGill University.

Gifford, James. 2011. "What Became of The Intersexes?" *Gay and Lesbian Review* 18, no. 5: 25–27.

Goddard, Scott. 1933. *A Repertory of 100 Symphonic Programmes.* By Edward Prime-Stevenson. Florence: The Giutina Press (privately printed). *Music and Letters* 14, no. 4: 391.

Law, Joe. 2004. "The 'perniciously homosexual art': Music and Homoerotic Desire in *The Picture of Dorian Gray* and Other Fin-de-Siècle Fiction." In *The Idea of Music in Victorian Fiction,* edited by Sophie Fuller and Nicky Losseff, 173–98. Burlington, VT: Ashgate, 2004.

de Lerma, Dominique-René. 1990. "Beethoven as a Black Composer." *Black Music Research Journal* 10, no. 1: 118–22.

Maitland, J. A. Fuller. 1928. Review of *Long-Haired Iopas* by E. Prime-Stevenson. *Music and Letters* 9, no. 1: 84.

Messing, Scott. 2006–7. *Schubert and the European Imagination*. Rochester: University of Rochester Press.

Prime-Stevenson, Edward. (as Xavier Mayne). 1905–6. *Imre: A Memorandum*. Naples: Privately Printed.

Prime-Stevenson, Edward. (as Xavier Mayne). 1908–9. *The Intersexes: A History of Similisexualism as a Problem in Social Life*. Rome, Florence, or Naples: Privately Printed.

Prime-Stevenson, Edward. 1913. *Her Enemy, Some Friends—and other Personages: Stories and Studies Mostly of Human Hearts*. Florence: Privately Printed.

Prime-Stevenson, Edward. 1917. "Ludwig van Beethoven (1770–1827)." In *The World's Best Literature*, Vol. 3, edited by John Cunliffe and Ashley Thorndike, 1750–62. New York: Knickerbocker; Toronto: Glasgow, Brook, and Co.

Prime-Stevenson, Edward. 1927. *Long Haired Iopas: Old Chapters from Twenty-Five Years of Music-Criticism*. Florence: Privately Printed.

Prime-Stevenson, Edward. 1932. *A Repertory of One Hundred Symphonic Programmes*. Florence: Privately Printed.

Prime-Stevenson, Edward. 2003. *Imre: A Memorandum*. Edited by James Gifford. Peterborough, ON: Broadview Literary Texts.

Rinehart, Nicholas. 2013. "Black Beethoven and the Racial Politics of Music History." *Transition: An International Review* 112: 117–30.

Robb, Graham. 2005. *Strangers: Homosexual Love in the Nineteenth Century*. New York: Norton.

Shaver-Gleason, Linda. 2018. "Who Wrote the Symphonies, and Why Should It Matter?" *Not Another Music History Cliché!* September 27. https://notanothermusichistorycli che.blogspot.com/2018/09/who-wrote-symphonies-and-why-should-it.html.

11

Animating Indeterminate Agency

Vivian Luong

> We choose words, and thereby shape texts in particular ways in order to persuade our readers or listeners—including our students—to adopt our way of looking at things. It behooves us to be aware of what we ask others to accept . . . *each of us needs to consider what story to tell.* (Guck 1994, 230; emphasis mine)

> We write to be in reverb with word and world. (Berlant and Stewart 2019, 131)

If the Analytical Stories We Tell Are Worldings, Can We Write Better Worlds?

The site of encounter between listener and music—what we call "musical experience"—has been and remains contested ground in music theory. How can our words responsibly and faithfully reflect our encounters with music? What are the effects of these stories we tell? And what purpose do our analytical accounts serve?[1]

As my opening quotation from Marion A. Guck's "Analytical Fictions" (1994) suggests, our descriptions of these encounters matter because they reveal our situated orientations to the world. Or in Guck's words, analyses illuminate "our way of looking at things" (1994, 230).[2] In generating and sharing

---

[1] Earlier versions of this research were presented at the 2017 and 2018 annual meetings of the Society for Music Theory and were funded by a diversity, equity, and inclusion writing grant through the School of Music, Theatre, and Dance at the University of Michigan. I would also like to thank the individuals who have generously read and shared their thoughts about this piece: Marion A. Guck, Gavin S. K. Lee, Stephen Lett, Desirée Mayr, and Angela Ripley.

[2] Guck's insistence on the subjective and situated aspects of music theory in this article connect with her more explicitly feminist writings on the connections between personal experience

---

Vivian Luong, *Animating Indeterminate Agency* In: *Queer Ear.* Edited by: Gavin S. K. Lee, Oxford University Press.
© Oxford University Press 2023. DOI: 10.1093/oso/9780197536766.003.0012

our prose with fellow music scholars, we share not only our observations about a composition, but also traces of ourselves, our histories, and our worlds.

This quote from "Analytical Fictions" also alludes to the effects of our written analyses on others. Building on philosopher Kendall Walton's concept of "fictions" (1990), Guck notes how our analyses invite readers to envision our stories about a piece and thus take on our preferred relationships with it (Guck 1994a, 18). When we share an analysis at a conference, in a publication, or during a class, we are asking our audience to imagine worlds alongside us. This can be a lot to ask of one another, as Guck suggests.

In thinking about the effects of our analytical stories, I also sense a connection between our analytical fictions and anthropologist Kathleen Stewart's concept of "worldings" (2007, 2010, 2014). For Stewart and her collaborator Lauren Berlant, worldings are also sites of encounter like that of musical experience. More specifically, the term describes the emergence of temporary worlds constructed from the convergence of bodies, forces, and things as we go about our daily routines. Worldings can result from an unexpected encounter on the street, a conversation during an office hour, or rumination on a philosophical concept, which are all scenes that Berlant and Stewart write about in *The Hundreds* (2019), a collection of coauthored prose-experiments.

As performed in this text, writing about worldings involves attuning to these moments in terms of their textures, form, and affects. Following this ethos of writing, we:

> add something, delete something, substitute tenses; [we] rearrange clauses and phrases, remember another thing that happened that made this thing more of an event, *and with each change the world offered to [our] readers shifts*. (Berlant and Stewart 2019, 60; emphasis mine)

Similar to Guck's depiction of analytical fictions, Berlant and Stewart's approach to writing involves carefully listening for the resonance of words and worlds as summarized in my second opening quotation. The words that we choose, the subjects and actions that we reanimate from our encounters with music—these are decisions that craft worlds. With this weight of responsibility, I join these authors in urging fellow music theorists to reflect on the broader consequences of our writerly choices.

and professional writing. See "A Woman's (Theoretical) Work" (1994b) and "Music Loving, Or the Relationship With the Piece" (1996), which are both contemporaneous with "Analytical Fictions."

Attuning to the worldings of our prose, this chapter suggests that our analytical tones and forms affect not only our relationships with musical works, but also our ability to envision what is possible and what can be otherwise. If analyses are imaginings of our worlds, what are the worlds that we have chosen to write into existence? What other possibilities have these decisions foreclosed? And what would it take to write better worlds?

To examine these consequences and offer alternative futures, I will take seriously Guck's as well as Berlant and Stewart's emphasis on the world-making potential in storytelling. As a contribution to an edited collection on queer music theory, this chapter focuses primarily on how our modes of analytical storytelling affect the survival of queer music theory as well as queer music theorists. Recent publications by Gavin Lee (2020), Maus (2020b), and Danielle Sofer (2020) identify various structural barriers that contribute to the attrition of queer scholars and scholarship. These obstacles include micro- and macroaggressions in everyday professional settings, lack of institutional and professional mentoring, and a policing of what counts as music theory and as queer music theory.

For the purposes of solidarity and coalition building, I will also consider how our writing impacts the thriving of minoritized subjects in the field at large. This chapter seeks to be in dialogue with ongoing conversations on issues of diversity and inclusion in music theory. Interlocutors with my work include scholarship that has illuminated music theory's relationship to settler-colonialism (Attas 2020), white supremacy and anti-blackness (Ewell 2020 and 2021), sexism (Hisama 2021), and ablelism (Straus 2011 and 2021), among other systems of oppression. This chapter has also benefited from cross-disciplinary dialogue facilitated by Project Spectrum, a graduate-student-led collective—especially their 2020 symposium, "Diversifying Music Academia: Building the Coalition."

Since the study of music-theoretical storytelling typically falls under the purview of music and narrative scholarship, this chapter examines a central concept in this area of study—musical agency. In an attempt to trace a different story from this term, I begin with Fred Everett Maus's assertion that *indeterminate musical agency*—the elusive identity of who acts in musical experience—is a fundamental quality of analytical language (1988). Here, I note that Maus's insistence of music's power to elude us aligns with contemporaneous feminist and queer interventions in the field.

However, subsequent responses to Maus have often obscured this connection to issues of gender and sexuality. Instead, they approach agential ambiguity as a challenge to be solved with anthropocentric solutions. In particular, the hierarchical taxonomies offered by authors such as Seth Monahan (2013) and Robert Hatten (2018) establish worldings in which the higher status of human agents is continually assumed over that of nonhuman musical agents. As I will illustrate alongside post-humanist interventions, this notion of human-centric agency is entangled with the historical and continued negation of marginalized subject positions—such as queer identities—deemed "sub-human, in-human, [or] non-human" (Anzaldúa 1987, 40; quoted in Luciano and Chen 2015, 186). This post-humanist scholarship then calls for a radical rethinking of agency away from its anthropocentric prerequisites to generate more just and equitable relations in the world (Braidotti 2006 and 2019).

Returning to indeterminate agency as an opening to imagine worlds otherwise, this chapter then re-animates the term to illuminate its queer post-humanist resonances. To do so, I situate Maus's observations on agency in the context of feminist and queer interventions in music theory by Maus himself as well as Guck (1994b, 1996) and Suzanne Cusick (1994a, 1994b). I then link these authors' descriptions of music's erotic *animism* with the concept of *animacy* developed by queer theorist and linguist Mel Y. Chen (2012). Resisting the human-oriented hierarchy of animacy in linguistics, Chen points to instances when language subverts the agential status quo as opportunities to rethink who and what matters for biopolitical and ethical ends. Thinking with Chen, I suggest that the purpose of analytical writing goes beyond knowledge production and affirmations of the human self. Rather, our writing always invites readers to imagine and enact particular worlds. To conclude, I situate this orientation to writing in dialogue with Black, Indigenous, and other minoritized interventions to build better, more liberatory worlds.

Agency (Human and Otherwise)

Let us start this story about indeterminate agency as other scholars have before me—by tracing the key contributions in Maus's "Music as Drama" to the field of music theory. Maus begins this article by outlining two related binary oppositions rooted in music analysis—musical structure versus musical affect and technical versus emotive descriptions of music. According to these conceptualizations of analysis, musical structure and technical descriptions align more with the domain of professional music theorists, while only amateurs or music lovers would favor affect and emotion.

Through an analysis of the opening measures of Beethoven's Op. 95 String Quartet, however, Maus collapses these divisions (1988, 60–72). In this section of the article, he demonstrates and reflects on how music analysts habitually use non-technical language to attribute feelings, thoughts, and motivations to musical events. Thematic sections might have loud, clumsy outbursts (1988, 60). Rhythmic patterns lurk and interrupt. Pitches antagonize or desire one another. Thus, an analysis cannot be a mere technical explanation of an autonomous musical structure. Rather, it is a narration of a series of dramatic actions experienced during moments of listening (1988, 70).

But if musical works and descriptions of them contain actions, who exactly is behind these acts? Instead of producing an overarching theory that maps specific musical scenarios onto specific types of musical agents, Maus asserts that the identity of musical agents is *indeterminate*. Analyses, according to Maus, often contain agential evasions in which the identity of who acts vacillates from the listener-analyst to particular pitches, motives, and even the entire piece itself (1988, 60). Who acts in a musical analysis is always dependent on the particular context of the listening experience that informs it.

> As the listener discerns actions and explains them by psychological states, various discriminations of agents will seem appropriate, but never with a determinacy that rules out other interpretations. The claim is not that *different listeners* may interpret the music differently (though they undoubtedly will), but rather that a *single* listener's experience will include a play of various schemes of individuation, none of them felt as obligatory. (1988, 68; emphasis in original)

Our analyses can even leave the identity of musical agents unnamed at times. These agential omissions, Maus asserts, add merit to our analyses in their faithfulness to actual musical experience:

> [Agential] evasions might seem to be *omissions*, gaps that a fuller analysis would fill. I suggest, however, that the gaps belong in the analysis, that they record an aspect of musical experience. The evasions reflect a pervasive *indeterminacy* in the identification of musical agents. (1988, 68; emphasis in original)

In other words, the agential indeterminacy in our writing honors our encounters with music during which we do not always have a firm grasp of who is acting on whom. These agential omissions belong in music analysis because they reflect the ephemeral aspects of our personal encounters with music. As well, they acknowledge and account for the power that music wields over us during acts of listening.

In summary, Maus asserts in "Music as Drama" that the actions that emerge during a particular musical encounter are beyond our predetermined efforts to entirely control and know all that happens in experience. As such, music analyses reflect these experiences of indeterminacy through agential inconsistencies in our writing. In one moment, a particular form of a sonic agent motivates an action. During another, some other musical agent takes over the reins. And then immediately after that, the identity of who acted might simply be unclear. Analyses are affective traces of a listener's engagement with a multiplicity of musical agencies.

This acknowledgment of the limited power of an analyst to determine *who* exactly they are dealing with can be frustrating and unsettling, as evidenced by subsequent attempts to clarify the concept of indeterminate agency. This work often pins down the elusive qualities of musical agency with detailed taxonomies. And by examining these classification schemes, I suggest that we can illuminate the discipline's current imaginings of the world.

Monahan's article "Action and Agency Revisited" seeks to tame the "chaos" of agential indeterminacy by merging the concept with Edward T. Cone's earlier theory of musical personae from *The Composer's Voice* (Monahan 2013, 323).[3] In so doing, Monahan embeds Maus's observations of indeterminate agency within a unified, hierarchical model of agent classes (see Figure 11.1a). At the top, we have the analyst as the ultimate human agent, followed by the fictional composer persona (our interpretation of the historical composer), then the work persona (the personification of the piece itself). Finally, Monahan allocates Maus's indeterminate agents—the individuated elements of a piece such as pitches, motives, and themes—to the bottom of this scheme.

In this depiction of a music-analytical world, Monahan fixes indeterminate agency with downward, unidirectional arrows that represent which agents can act on others (Figure 11.1b). Here, human analysts can act on

---

[3] "[W]ith [Maus's] emphasis on ephemerality and 'indeterminacy,' it does paint a somewhat chaotic picture of our analytical practice, with fictional agents flitting in and out the discursive frame in a kind of interpretive free-for-all, regulated only by the analyst's whim" (Monahan 2013, 323).

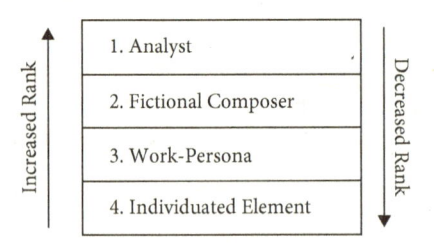

Figure 11.1a Seth Monahan's hierarchy of musical agent classes (2013, 334)

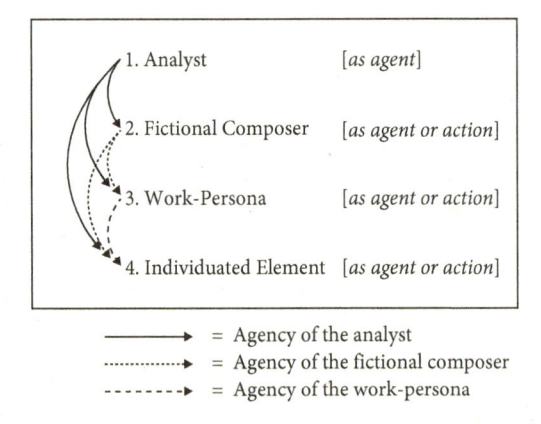

Figure 11.1b Monahan's summary of normative action/agent relations (2013, 338)

the fictional composer, work persona, and musical elements, but the flow of agency is not, Monahan tells us, usually reversed so that lower-level agents can act on higher-level ones.

Robert Hatten's approach to the problem of indeterminacy follows a similar logic. Building on his earlier work on musical meaning and interpretation in which agency appears as a secondary concept (1994, 2004), Hatten more fully expands on his understanding of the term in his 2018 book *A Theory of Virtual Agency for Western Art Music*. As the title of this book suggests, Hatten's depiction of agency similarly divides agents into a hierarchy that places the "actual" agency of listeners, performers, composers, and teachers over the myriad of "virtual" musical agents (Figure 11.2).

For Hatten, the term "virtual" denotes the ways in which musical agency "simulate[s] the actions, emotions, and reactions of a human agent" in our

---

Actual agents

Listener
Performer (with performative agency [Hatten 2004])
Composer
Teacher/coach

Virtual agents
Persona (e.g., the "composer's voice" [Cone 1974])
Subjectivity (as integrative, self-reflexive consciousness)
Narrative (staged by "shifts in level of discourse" [Hatten 1994])
Actors (with roles in a dramatic trajectory)
    Internal, principal (e.g., "protagonist" [Hatten 2004]); stable identity (active or reactive)
    External (e.g., "Fate")
Agents (with human characteristics)
    Primary
    Secondary (Clater 2009)
Actants (prior to agential identity)

Figure 11.2 Robert Hatten's delineation of actual versus virtual musical agents (2018, 34)

experiences of music (2018, 1). The study of musical agency is then about *our* attribution of "movement, agency, emotional expression, and even subjectivity" to music (2018, 1). Through Hatten's words, he builds a world in which musical agency is modeled after the human—or at least, as I will demonstrate below, a particular image of the human. The purpose of anthropomorphizing and personifying music, as Hatten asserts, is to help us work through our emotional and psychological well-being and our sense of self (2018, 288).

This human-centered study of musical agency rests also at the foundation of Monahan's orientation to musical experience. He understands the work persona as a stand-in for the analyst to work through their listening encounter with a piece of music:

> It seems to me that the very conceit of the work-persona may have arisen, at least in part, as a response to the sensation that what is happening in the music is happening *to us* and even *within us*. The fictional work-persona provides a means of encapsulating that experience while also depersonalizing it, placing it at a safe objective distance through ostensible universalization. (2013, 351)

Through hierarchical taxonomies and the centering of human experience, Monahan's and Hatten's perspectives align with other contemporary theories of musical agency (BaileyShea 2012; Cox 2016; Howe 2016; Klorman 2016; Newcomb 1997; Zbikowski 2018) that place the "real" power of human agents over the "fictional" or "virtual" agency of nonhuman musical elements. However, I suggest that viewing music's capacity to affect listeners as a product of human perception is only one way to orient to the problem of agential indeterminacy. In particular, these authors' solutions adhere to an anthropocentric model of agency rooted in white, Western traditions of philosophy, literary theory, and cognition research, in which the qualities of intentionality, rationality, and sentience serve as prerequisites (Anscombe 1957; Davidson 1963).[4] But by treating the ambiguity of musical agency through these perspectives, I suggest that we as a discipline are passing over an opportunity to rethink agency and the human entirely, and with that, a chance to write different worlds.

I wish to articulate this alternate possibility by bringing music and agency scholarship into closer contact with critical post-humanisms (Braidotti 2006; Ferrando 2013; Wolfe 2010). This term gives name to the shared aim across many areas of thought—such as Black studies, Indigenous studies, and feminist new materialisms, in addition to queer theory—to illuminate exclusionary notions of the human that pervade many aspects of our lives. Critical post-humanisms as a broad area of study offers a variety of reasons as to why this image of the human limits and harms. This chapter will focus on two points from this scholarship. First, this area of thought notes how this definition of the human inaccurately represents an anthropocentric hierarchy of agency. This perspective erases our coevolution and contingency with other life forms, the environment, and technology (Alaimo 2008; Barad 2007; Bennett 2009; Kirby 2008). As a result, these authors argue that any form of politics or knowledge produced with this assumption of the human will be ineffective in that it does not accurately address the way things actually are.

Second, this scholarship points out the structural inequities that result from delineating between who counts as human—a category that was often not given to historically dehumanized and minoritized subjects, such as Indigenous, queer, and racialized peoples (Anzaldúa 1987; Belcourt 2020; McNay 2016; Puar 2017). For example, Dana Luciano and Chen's essay on "queer inhumanisms" depicts this notion of the human thusly:

---

[4] These examples are not representative of *all* responses to Maus's work. Some scholars have tried to build on rather than resolve the problem of indeterminate musical agency. See, e.g., Gadir 2018.

> [The human] is usually associated with the Enlightenment subject . . . he is rational, bounded, integral, sovereign, and self-aware. This is the figure to whom rights and citizenship are granted; this is the default figure that grounds and personifies norms of behavior, ability, and health; this is the figure around which we ordinarily construct notions of political and social agency. (2015, 190)

The work of cultural theorist and philosopher Sylvia Wynter (2003) also intervenes in the consequences of this very specific understanding of the human. In particular, she notes the problematic equation of the human as a broad category of possibility with a specific iteration of the human as "Man," a figure passed down since the Renaissance that brought forth colonial projects that continue to subjugate Black, Indigenous, and other minoritized life (2002, 264). As Walter D. Mignolo observes in his essay on Wynter's notion of Man as Human:

> Wynter's writings demonstrate that Western epistemology built itself on a concept of Human and Humanity that, in turn, served to legitimate the epistemic foundation that created it. That is, Human and Humanity were created as the enunciated *that projects and propels to universality the local image* of the enunciator. The enunciator assumes, and thus, postulates, that his concept of Human and Humanity is valid for every human being on the planet. However, once the universality of the Human has been postulated— and we encounter this formulation in many official documents telling us that humans are "all born equal"—hierarchies are needed and put into place to establish differences between all who were "born equal." Indeed, after we are born, we inhabit a world made of inequality. (2015, 109; emphasis in original)

Returning to the theme of storytelling as practices of worldings in this chapter, I contend that tales of this exclusionary human are also retold through established theories of musical agency. And by continuing to take a certain image of the human as a given, we as a field participate in creating "a world made of inequality." To support this argument, let me return once again to Monahan's and Hatten's responses to indeterminate musical agency. While their respective approaches carefully situate their theories within the domain of Western music and music theory (Monahan 2013, 321–22; and Hatten 2018, 6–10), there remain momentary slippages and erasures in both texts that reinforce the universalization of the human critiqued by Wynter, Luciano and Chen, and other critical post-humanists. To be clear, my reading below does not intend to frame Monahan, Hatten, and members of our discipline at large as intentionally exclusionary. Rather, I hope that my reading of these texts below will serve as an invitation for all of us to contemplate the broader effects and values of our work, and who we seek to serve with our scholarship (Reed 2020).

In the beginning of Monahan's article, we as readers are immediately launched into a thought experiment in order to situate the problem of musical agency: how would a non-Western or a culturally naïve Western listener react to the indeterminate musical agency that permeates written analyses? Focusing specifically on Joseph Kerman's 1966 analysis of the first movement of Beethoven's String Quartet in A minor, op. 132, Monahan imagines that Kerman's "dizzyingly inconsistent" and "haphazard" attributions of musical agents would confound us non-Western, non-acculturated readers (2013, 321–22). Yet, according to Monahan, in returning to our "real" positionalities—people who would likely read the *Journal of Music Theory*, the publication in which this article appears—we would think of Kerman's musical descriptions as ordinary due to our shared history and training as music analysts. As Monahan writes, "we can navigate Kerman's prose with ease and even admiration," which "testifies to our long-standing comfort" with such ambiguous agential depictions (2013, 322). From this established commonality, Monahan then offers his hierarchical theory of musical agency as a way to explain our experiential tendencies.

But who counts under the category of "we as music analysts" who are situated at the top of Monahan's agential hierarchy? And what kind of world does this image of the analyst construct? Before answering these questions, it is important to note that Monahan performs great care and concern with avoiding the pitfalls of universalism and prescriptivism. He writes, "[i]t is not my aim to lay out a normative model of how 'we' experience (or ought to experience) music agentially, nor is it to codify how analysis ought to be written in the future" (326). However, my reading observes a tension between this aim and the article's bracketing out of gendered and queer aspects in musical agency, which are presented as outliers in musical experience.

Some of these exceptions, according to Monahan, include experiencing the composer-persona (the second-highest agent in the hierarchy) as an embodied agent in our analyses:

fictional composers tend not to be [corporealized], at least in music-analytical discourse; their actions are more often construed as entirely cerebral, in keeping with what Suzanne Cusick (1994a, 15) has called the "mind-mind game" so intrinsic in many masculine-gendered conceptualizations of art music. There are exceptions of course, like Marx's (1863) analysis of the op. 132 quartet or Cone's (1982) reading of Schubert's A♭-major *Moment Musicale*—both of them instances in which a composer's physical illness is thought to impact his mental activity. *But for the most part; analysts have been interested in fictionalized composers mainly as minds rather than bodies.* (2013, 332; emphasis mine)[5]

As well, Monahan also asserts a similar negation of the analyst's body in our writing:

Though as a culture, we analysts seem content to depict ourselves mainly as disembodied minds. With a few notable exceptions—mainly critics who reflect substantially on the bodily basis of musical performance, such as Marion Guck, Suzanne Cusick, and especially Alexandra Pierce (e.g., 2007)—*music analysts rarely invite us to imagine them engaged in physical activity.* Thus, both ostensibly extramusical agent classes (analyst and fictional composer) tend to be realized mainly in cerebral, noncorporeal terms. (2013, 333n14)

In these moments of exception, Monahan cites foundational feminist and queer music-theoretical texts without identifying them as such: Cone's "Schubert's Promissory Note," Guck's "Analytical Fictions," and Cusick's "Feminist Theory, Music Theory and the Mind/Body Problem."[6] In each case, the body as a site of political and disciplinary intervention is neutralized and excised as an anomaly. For example, Guck's and Cusick's contributions are framed not only as "rare," but also as concerned with "musical performance" instead of feminist critiques of the field. While brief, I suggest these instances point toward the construction of a particular world, in which minoritized experiences of agency are deemed uncommon or made invisible, while the

---

[5] Monahan 2013 erroneously cited the first volume of A. B. Marx's *Ludwig van Beethoven: Leben und Schaffen.* The correct citation for the second volume, published in 1863, is given here.

[6] While Cone's piece is not explicitly queer, other scholars have pointed to as an opening for subsequent queer readings of Schubert (Brett 1997; McClary 1994 and 1997)

desire to hierarchize and fix in place musical experience are presented as the commonsensical norm.

Hatten's book on agency also contains similar normalizing approaches regarding the human and musical agency. I will focus on two instances that occur in the opening section of the book, in which Hatten contextualizes his theory of virtual musical agency by tracing particular narratives surrounding the history of the human. First, in this introduction, Hatten lays out a set of presuppositions that form the foundation of his theory. Here, he writes that at the basis of his theory is the axiom that:

> humankind's cognitive capacities to hear music as expressive, and thus as expressed by a virtual source with which humans can identify in some fashion, have been in place since the earliest records of human responses to music: from the Hebrew Bible (Jubal's lyre, Miriam's harp) to Greek theories of ethos. (2018, 6)

With this gesture, the capacity for humans to perceive music as animated is immediately subsumed by and equated with Hatten's concept of virtualizing music. This conflation is further naturalized through pointing to evidence of virtual musical agency in these early moments of human history. This conceptual move can be likened to what Wynter calls the "overrepresentation of Man" that I have discussed above, wherein the Western subject with its capacities, histories, and inclinations becomes a stand-in for all humans and human experience.[7]

At the same time, Hatten's list of presuppositions also contains exceptions to what kinds of human experience are addressed in his theory. Nearing the end of the book's introduction, Hatten expresses a regretful omission in the remainder of his text: In addition to popular music and other non-Western art music genres, experiences of (virtual) agency that intersect with "gender, . . . gender orientation, race, religion, nationality, and marginalized communities or cultural groups" will not be addressed (2018, 10). He concludes this admission with an assurance that, despite this gap, he nonetheless "trust[s] the basic concepts of virtual agency may be of use" to scholarship on these areas of experience (2018, 10).

---

[7] This use of the Man as Human returns at the end of Hatten's book in a section titled "The Earliest Evidence of Virtualizing in Humans" (290).

However, alongside critical post-humanisms, I argue that the orientations to music and musical agency as hierarchical, as virtual and Western-subject-centric are not given and do not work to explain many other kinds of experience. As a woman and queer music theorist of non-white and non-Western descent, I find that such descriptions of musical experience and analysis run counter to my own relationship to music and relations in the world. And I suggest that what we take as commonsense and commonplace in main-stream musical agency scholarship might not speak to other experiences as well. In fact, following Wynter's and other's work, these patterns of thought erase differences. These gestures continue to universalize and de-situate bodies, which are all mechanisms that therapist and trauma scholar Resmaa Menakem identifies in the reinforcement of a white-body supremacy—the structural elevation of white bodies as the standard from which other bodies' humanity and agency are measured (2017, 5). I wonder then about the possibilities we are foreclosing by entangling musical agency with such an image of the human and how might we find models to imagine musical agency otherwise?

We might find inspiration in critical post-humanisms' turn toward alter-native cosmologies, for example, from actor network theory (Latour 1987; Latour and Woolgar 1986) to the animist and relational ethics embodied in Indigenous thought (Kimmerer 2013; Robinson 2020; TallBear 2019; Todd 2016; Watts 2013). In these heterogeneous approaches to decentering the human, I suggest that there might be other ways to envision and write our worlds. These ways of writing are exemplified in Berlant and Stewart's ethnographies of worldings discussed above. As well, Saidiya Hartman's speculative histories of black, queer, and femme resistance offer another roadmap to conceptualize agency beyond its implicitly white, Euro-centric, cis-heteronormative restrictions (2008, 2019).

This chapter joins this diverse collective of critical post-humanist thought by reanimating the associations of the word "indeterminacy" with being unfixed and unbound. Latent in indeterminate musical agency is an invi-tation to reconsider the kinds of power, agency, and worldings perpetuated by established music-theoretical orientations. This transformative poten-tial in indeterminate musical agency will become more evident when we resituate "Music as Drama" in the context of the early work of feminist and queer music theory from the 1990s. In these writings, the acknowledgement of music's power to affect us—its agency—becomes a central way into the critique of music theory's heteronormative and patriarchal tendencies. So in order to bring these implicit concerns of "Music as Drama" into the foreground, my story now turns to its sequel, "Hanslick's Animism" (1992), which I will read alongside its feminist and queer contemporaries by Guck (1994b) and Suzanne Cusick (1994b).[8]

Animism

The link between "Music as Drama" and "Hanslick's Animism" appears at the end of the former article. As he concludes, Maus offers a brief reading of a passage from Peter Kivy's *The Corded Shell* (1980) to shift from the term "agency"—an entity's capacity to act—to "animism": an entity's liveliness, sentience, and possession of a soul (Maus 1988, 73n27).[9] In order to understand the agency expressed in music-analytical language, Maus suggests that future work could study the animistic tendencies in established music-theoretical texts. And it appears that "Hanslick's Animism" takes up this cause.

In this later article, Maus is again concerned with the traces of music analysts' intimate relationships with music in their discourse. He complicates Hanslick for queer ends by emphasizing descriptions of erotic musical animism that appear in his 1854 text, *On the Musically Beautiful*. In these moments, Maus points to descriptions that betray Hanslick's efforts to control his prose—sections that vivify inanimate objects with thoughts, feelings, and even anthropomorphic bodies equipped with circulatory systems, limbs, and sexual desire.

Since Maus's reading of a particular excerpt by Hanslick encapsulates his argument concisely, I will share this extensive quotation here. For context, the quote is Hanslick's attempt to describe musical beauty through a comparison of music with the interweaving lines of arabesque patterns. He writes:

We follow sweeping lines, here dipping gently, there boldly soaring, approaching, and separating, corresponding curves large and small, seemingly incommensurable yet always well connected together, to every part a counterpart, a collection of small details but yet a whole.

---

[8] Maus 2020 also draws more robust connections between "Music as Drama" with his later work in feminist and queer music theory.

[9] The passage that Maus cites appears in Kivy 1980, 58–59.

How let us think of an arabesque not dead and static, but coming into being in continuous self-formation before our eyes! How the lines, some robust and some delicate, pursue one another! How they ascend from a small curve to great heights and then sink back again, how they expand and contract and forever astonish the eye with the ingenious alternation of tension and repose! There before our eyes the image becomes grander and more sublime.

Finally, let us think of the lively arabesque as the dynamic emanation of an artistic spirit who unceasingly pours the whole abundance of his inventiveness into the arteries of this dynamism. Does this mental impression not come close to that of music? (Hanslick 1986, 29; reproduced in Maus 1992, 280–81)

While there is much that can be discussed regarding race and orientalism in Hanslick's relationship with the animated body of the arabesque, I will focus here on the ambiguously gendered eroticism brought out in Maus's particular reading. Similar to the indeterminacy of musical agency, in which the identity of agents can sometimes move from smaller parts, such as pitches and motives, to larger sections, such as themes, Hanslick's description of arabesque moves between different levels of parts and wholes. He starts by following the gentle dipping, curved lines themselves. Then these lines interact with each other moving from a small curve to "great heights," painting—according to Maus—heteronormative erotic imagery of contrasting "robust and delicate" lines moving together (1992, 280–81). Finally, as a whole, the arabesque is imbued with a life force, which Maus interprets as a spiritually animated phallus with which Hanslick so lovingly interacts (1992, 281–82).

This sexually charged description betrays the more well-known argument in Hanslick's writings, in which he attempts to do away with extra-musical language in musical writing. Maus then maps this failure and Hanslick's own moralistic discomfort with musical-sexual description onto contemporary music theory, which continues to struggle to rein in the animism of music in analytical language. Instead of attempts to censor and maintain control, Maus advocates that music theorists should embrace the fact that our analytical language will always reflect our personal and sometimes erotic relationships with music. By acknowledging this, perhaps we can also then understand how gender and sexuality are factors that are deeply involved in the practices of music theory (Maus 1992, 282–83 and 292n20).[10]

This image of music as an agent doing things to us also aligns with the musical animism depicted in other feminist and queer music scholarship at the time. For example, Cusick theorizes the queer eroticism of performance by emphasizing the work that her body does to release the power of music and its messages of musical pleasure and joy (1994b). Focusing particularly on her experience of playing the fourth variation in J. S. Bach's *Canonic Variations on "Vom Himmel hoch"*, she depicts the circulation of power during the performance in which "who's on top" (1994b, 78)—the piece or herself—is indeterminate: "Power circulates freely across porous boundaries; the categories player and played, lover and beloved, dissolve" (1994b, 78). Here, the animism of music affirms her liveliness as well: "I have felt most fully alive, most fully myself... when I have *become* the music" (1994b, 78).

This orientation to music's power and the cocreation of our sense of self is also akin the pleasurable work of listening and writing about musical experience described in Guck's article "A Woman's (Theoretical) Work":

> And doing this work [writing about one's personal experience with a piece] gives great pleasure. I make myself all ears, give myself up to the piece, let it carry me away. When the sounds of the piece end, I carry myself back by asking "just what was that like? What could I tell someone else so that they too could hear that effect?" I play it at the piano, I make up momentary dances—I give myself up to it now as it has become a part of me. (1994b, 38)

In these intimate performing, listening, and analytical relations, the continual flow of agency and power are integral. These accounts contrast mainstream approaches to musical agency described above by centering music's central role to the formation of our subjectivities in addition to music-theoretical knowledge.

For these authors, these moments when music and human merge not only produce sensations of pleasure and subjectivity, but also provide an opening for political and disciplinary transformation. As Cusick writes:

---

[10] See also Maus 2020a, 69–71.

> I suspect for all of us the originating joy of it [interacting with music] comes from assuming more varied positions than we think we're allowed in regular life, positions that enable us to say yes or no, to immerse, to initiate, to have simultaneous but independent climaxes, *to escape a system (maybe it was always the phallic economy) of bewildering fixed categories*, to wallow in the circulation of pleasures that are beyond danger and culturally defined desires. (1994b, 80; emphasis mine)

Through writing and reading others' accounts of this joy, early feminist and queer music scholarship hoped for and sought to build a world beyond musically "thinking straight."

So far, I have illustrated a concern shared across early feminist and queer music theory regarding the relationship between music-theoretical language and experiences of music's agency. In "Music as Drama," Maus details the power of language to animate and reflect the agency of the music itself in experience. As well, by insisting on the indeterminate qualities of agency in musical language, Maus destabilizes the image of the all-knowing, all-powerful music analyst, since they cannot always control the agential slippages in their discourse. Then through reading "Hanslick's Animism" alongside other feminist and queer writings by Cusick and Guck, I demonstrated how the animating tendencies of music-theoretical language have repercussions for issues of gender and sexuality in our field.

While the personal style of writing performed by Maus, Guck, and Cusick attempts to balance the agencies of the listener and music, the post-humanly queer potential in musical agency remains only partly actualized. In particular, the value of music and our relationships with it remain rooted in their capacity to shape *our* sense of self and identity. Musical experience as worldings then remain centered on human subjectivity and meaning-making. Bringing this work into dialogue with other perspectives from critical post-humanisms, I would like to explore other ways to approach the animistic qualities of music. What would it be like to radically care for music while honoring its status a nonhuman entity? Following this line of thought might then lead us closer to envisioning differently queer worlds.

Animacy

Having traced a connection between agency to animism, I have arrived at a third concept in my queer genealogy of musical indeterminacy—animacy.

Traditionally a linguistic concept, animacy denotes the quality of life-ness, sentience, or humanness of a noun or noun phrase through grammatical and syntactical conventions of a language (Chen 2012, 24). According to certain linguists such as John Cherry, grammars across many languages adhere to an animacy hierarchy. As illustrated in Figure 11.3 below, these hierarchies are often structured with humans at the top, followed by animals, then inanimate objects, and at the bottom, incorporeal concepts. The hierarchies developed in music and agency scholarship appear to follow this logic with human agents, particularly, the analyst, placed at the top. These agential orderings were illustrated earlier in Monahan's classification of agent classes in Figures 11.1a and 11.1b and in Hatten's division of actual versus virtual agents in Figure 11.2.

Chen challenges this view by focusing on moments in which animacy subverts this anthropocentric hierarchy—moments during which language is used to dehumanize people of particular marginalized identities or phrases that intentionally or unintentionally animate animals, objects, and concepts. For Chen, these moments hold vital biopolitical and ethical potential to upend our current world. To clarify this possibility, I will draw on an example from Chen's writings to illustrate the effects of these slippages in animacy, which I will then connect to music theory's version of agency.

In their work, Chen theorizes from a position of having multiple chemical sensitivity and heavy-metal poisoning—a condition in which their body builds up and recirculates toxins acquired from their surroundings rather

Humans	Adult > Nonadult Male/MASC gender > Female/FEM gender Free > Enslaved Able-bodied > Disabled Linguistically Intact > Prelinguistic/Linguistically Impaired Familiar (Kin/Named) > Unfamiliar (Nonkin/Unnamed) Proximate (1p & 2p pronouns) > Remote (3p pronouns)
Animals	Higher/Larger Animals > Lower/Smaller Animals > Insects Whole animal > Body part
Plants	Plants
Inanimates	Motile/Active > Nonmotile/Nonactive Natural > Manmade Count > Mass
Incorporeals	Abstract Concepts, Natural Forces, States of Affairs, States of Being, Emotions, Qualities, Activities, Events, Time Periods, Institutions, Regions, Diverse Intellectual Objects

Figure 11.3 Based on John Cherry's animacy hierarchy (2002, 2014)

than filtering them out. As their body accrues toxins, their modes of relating and delineating between humans, objects, and self break down. In one example, Chen narrates an account of their everyday experience with this condition, describing the ceaseless negotiation of bodily boundaries that Chen enacts with fellow pedestrians, as well as tobacco smoke, whiffs of perfume, and car fumes.

As we follow them along their day, the accumulated toxins from Chen's activities have become too much. And as a result, they enter a state in which

> anyone or anything that I manage to feel any kind of connection with, whether it is my cat or a chair or a friend or a plant or a stranger or my partner, I think they are, and remember they are, all the same ontological thing. (2012, 202)

In a case of mistaken animacy, Chen recounts the subsequent shock when they learn that they had amorously snuggled with the arms and back of a couch during this toxic episode, while thinking that it was the arms and back of their human partner. Chen writes:

> Have I performed the inexcusable: have I treated my girlfriend like my couch? Or have I treated my couch like her, which fares only slightly better in the moral equations? After I recover, the conflation seems unbelievable. But it is only in the recovering of my human-directed sociality that the couch really becomes an unacceptable partner. (2012, 202–3)

The reoccurrence of such moments, as Chen notes, forces them to rethink notions of intimacy and animacy. This toxic, post-human intimacy is one that does not differentiate, that does not rely on a heartbeat or the traditional requirements of human subjectivity and intentionality.

I contend that these fleeting moments of anyone-anything intimacy share similarities with musical experience during which we encounter indeterminate musical agency. Various sonic events do things to us, and us to them. And when we come out of the interaction, just as Chen leaves their toxic state, we immediately reenter a human-centric logic that limits our ability to grasp what has just occurred. But what if we were to pause for a moment before jumping back into this seemingly commonsense ordering of the world? What might the problem of indeterminate musical agency offer us then? With these questions and Chen's toxically amorous relations with the couch, we appear to have left the orbit of usual music-theoretical inquiry. To conclude this section, let me walk us back to my original call to rethink music's indeterminate agency to suggest future experiments with worldings.

An exploration of music's nonhuman animacy might lead us to examine the concept of toxicity, which is integral to Chen's notion of post-human animacy. Toxicity as a term conjures images of encounters that are harmfully and too closely intimate: an invasion, a contamination, the breaking down of bodily, social, or state borders by some previously external agent. Furthermore, these scenarios animate typically less-animate subjects and objects—from molecules and particulates to queer and racialized others. These re-orderings of agency upset the traditional animacy hierarchy and the impenetrable Western human subject, both of which help to uphold intersecting structures of inequity:

> There is, indeed, something "unworlding" that might be said to take place in the cultural production of toxic notions. A "normal" world's order is lost when, for instance, things that can harm you permanently are not even visible to the naked eye. Temporal orders become Moebius strips of identity: How could it do this to me? And yet in that instant, the "me" that speaks is not the "me" before I was affected by it. (2012, 203)

For Chen, this potential "unworlding"—the unraveling and restructuring of worlds—presents a way into theorizing queerness alongside other dehumanized positions shaped by ablelist, racist, and settler-colonialist logics (2012, 207–8). In other words, toxicity holds the possibility for coalition- and world-building otherwise, which Chen describes with term "toxic worlding" (2012, 196).

Following the alternative lineage of agency that I have traced so far, if listening is about opening ourselves up to indeterminate musical animacy—if it is boundless, porous, and limitless—might it also be toxic in this sense? And if so, what then? I suggest that thinking listening with toxic animacy offers us a way to reconsider a similar kind of potency in our professional activities of listening. Listening as the process of encountering and engaging with indeterminate musical agencies is something that we pride ourselves in doing and in teaching as music theorists. It is a commitment shared across all of the music-theoretical literature discussed in this chapter—from Monahan's and Hatten's mainstream theories of musical agency to those offered by Maus,

Guck, and Cusick. Listening deeply and carefully is an activity that I also celebrate in my own work (Luong 2017). And this is in part due to how feminist and queer music theory has theorized the queer potential of listening as moments of open receptivity to sound.

But figuring indeterminate musical agency as a toxic agent also reframes the stakes of our listening habits in a different light. In particular, toxicity is not purely utopian. Rather, it exists as an ambivalent and tenuous political concept—one that attracts an "explosion of resentful, despairing, painful, screamingly negative affects" in addition to those of pleasurable and loving connection (2012, 211). For example, what I have omitted so far from my retelling of Chen's narrative are the negative affects that accompany their toxic condition. They write:

> A few pedestrians cross my path, and before they near, I quickly assess whether they are likely (or might be the "kind of people") to wear perfumes or colognes or to be wearing sunscreen. I scan their heads for smoke puffs or pursed lips pre-release . . . In an instant, quicker than I thought anything could reach my organs, my liver refuses to process these inhalations and screams hate, a hate whose intensity each time shocks me. (2012, 199)

The intimacies that cross animacy lines, which are afforded by Chen's multiple chemical sensitivity, our living conditions in this particular world, and our professionalized capacities to listen, can also lead to violent refusal and resistance.

In the context of our disciplinary reactions to musical agency, resistance manifests itself in a reflexive return to Western cosmologies of the human, self, and world. Instead of orienting toward indeterminate musical agency's potential for unworlding and "not thinking straight" (Cusick 1994b), scholarship on music and agency has mostly de-animated the concept and removed its toxic unworlding potency. From this deadened version of agency, we can then proceed with the status quo—to extract disciplinary value from our encounters with music and retrench in the current state of affairs.

This way of orienting to disciplinary knowledge production performs a mode of relating critiqued in a long history of Indigenous scholarship and activism (Tuck and Yang 2012, 2014). I sense, specifically, a connection between our habitual deactivation of musical agency's potent potential with Dylan Robinson's theorization of settler listening practices depicted in the term "hungry listening" (2020). Thinking with the Halq'eméylem adjective for settler/white person methods and things (shxwelítemelh), Robinson notes the origins of this term with "xwelítem" or "starving person," which encapsulates the insatiable white-settler hunger to consume Indigenous peoples and lands (2020, 2–3, 47–54). This hunger maps onto practices of listening (xwélalà:m) that appropriate Indigenous musics to reify the Western colonialist vision of the way things are.

Robinson then establishes methods for critically listening otherwise through centering situated relation-building (2020, 68). Furthermore, his decolonial project involves slowing down and resisting the pull toward satisfying a hunger for "felt confirmations of square pegs in square holes, for the satisfactory fit as sound knowledge slides into its appropriate place," such as the neatly separated ranks of the animacy hierarchy detailed above (2020, 51). Robinson's critique of fast-paced knowledge consumption (2020, 53) shares affinities with Chen's insistence to sit with the "wiliness" of toxic animacy to imagine queerness otherwise (Chen 2012, 237). I situate this chapter alongside these authors' interventions to ask music theorists to also pause and consider what we take to be commonsense orderings of our disciplinary worlds.

Finally, this reading of Robinson with Chen highlights once again the importance of writing and wordings in the creation of new worlds. Robinson calls for experimentation with performative writing that approaches the interconnected relations of listener, music, and space (2020, 81). Here, he draws a roadmap for Indigenous and non-Indigenous coalition through building on the subjective writing of feminist and queer music scholars, whose contributions also rest at the foundation of this chapter. Inspired by Robinson's construction of decolonial tools through feminist and queer music scholarship, I suggest that queer music theory could also respond in kind by placing ourselves in further relation to Indigenous and other positionalities to write better worlds into being.

Wordings and Worldings Otherwise

> When we want to imagine *otherwise* possibilities—*otherwise* worlds—we must abolish the very conceptual frame that produces categorical distinction and makes them desirable; we have to abolish the modality of thought that *thinks* categorical distinction as maintainable. (Crawley 2020, 28–29; emphasis in original)

This chapter began with an invitation to contemplate the resonances between word and world in our analytical stories. Then, by narrowing in on the issue of indeterminate musical agency as an example, I shared a different tale of the concept's otherwise potential through reanimating its feminist and queer history, and its potential for coalition with other minoritized perspectives. To conclude, I will reflect on the term "otherwise" that has been scattered throughout this chapter in order to answer what might it mean for us to write worlds otherwise in music theory.

Like my reconceptualization of "indeterminacy" as unfixed and unbound, my use of the word "otherwise" is intended to evoke a similar "boundlessness" theorized in the introduction to Tiffany Lethabo King, Jenell Navarro, and Andrea Smith's edited collection *Otherwise Worlds: Against Settler Colonialism and Anti-Blackness* (2020, 14–21). Throughout this introductory essay, King, Navarro, and Smith meditate on the various facets of the otherwise as: "something else, or anything else; something to the contrary" (2020, 8), "in all ways, but the one mentioned" (2020, 10), "in other ways" (2020, 12), and "if not, or else" (2020, 13). Alongside these visions of the otherwise and Ashon Crawley's contribution to this collection quoted above, I suggest that thinking musical agency otherwise would involve unsettling the commonsense world offered by music theory ("something else, or anything else" and "in all ways, but the one mentioned") so that we can devise new and other ways of ordering the world ("in other ways").

Furthermore, engaging with the otherwise would require us to acknowledge and be accountable to the pressing imperative of doing so ("if not, or else"). In this chapter, I have reanimated indeterminate musical agency so that we can acknowledge and reckon with the colonizing, racist, and sexist structures that our work can engender. What are the consequences of maintaining our disciplinary divisions, such as text versus context, and of asking whether something or someone counts in music theory? What if we were to think of music theory's worlds as continually otherwise, open-ended, and unmaintainable? Might we then abolish our conceptual frames?

Pursuing these questions to an otherwise will require different modes of analytical storytelling, alternate tones, forms, and temporalities to conjure worlds into being. Through my attempt here to untether musical agency from its Western human confines, I hope that we can continue to enliven the concept and follow it to some otherwise worlds.

References

Ahmed, Sara. 1996. "Beyond Humanism and Postmodernism: Theorizing a Feminist Practice." *Hypatia* 11, no. 2 (Spring): 71–93.

Alaimo, Stacy. 2008. "Trans-Corporeal Feminisms and the Ethical Space of Natural." In *Material Feminisms*, edited by Stacey Alaimo and Susan Hekman, 237–64. Bloomington: Indiana University Press.

Anscombe, G. E. M. 1957. *Intention*. Cambridge, MA: Harvard University Press.

Anzaldúa, Gloria. 1987. *Borderlands/La Frontera: The New Mestiza*. San Francisco: Aunt Lute Books.

Arvin, Maile, Eve Tuck, and Angie Morrill. 2013. "Decolonizing Feminism: Challenging Connections between Settler Colonialism and Heteropatriarchy." *Feminist Formations* 25, no. 1: 8–34.

Attas, Robin. 2020. "Review of Dylan Robinson, *Hungry Listening: Resonant Theory for Indigenous Sound Studies* (University of Minnesota Press, 2020)." *Music Theory Online* 26, no. 4 (November). https://mtosmt.org/issues/mto.20.26.4/mto.20.26.4.attas.html.

BaileyShea, Matthew L. 2012. "Musical Forces and Interpretation: Some Thoughts on a Measure of Mahler." *Music Theory Online* 18, no. 3 (September). https://mtosmt.org/issues/mto.12.18.3/mto.12.18.3.baileyshea.html.

Barad, Karen. 2007. *Meeting the Universe Halfway: Quantum Physics and the Entanglement of Matter and Meaning*. Durham: Duke University Press.

Belcourt, Billy-Ray. 2015. "Animal Bodies, Colonial Subjects: (Re)Locating Animality in Decolonial Thought." *Societies* 5, no. 1: 1–11.

Belcourt, Billy-Ray. 2020. *A History of My Brief Body*. Toronto: Hamish Hamilton.

Bennett, Jane. 2009. *Vibrant Matter: A Political Ecology of Things*. Durham, NC: Duke University Press.

Berlant, Lauren, and Kathleen Stewart. 2019. "44. Fish in Drag." In *The Hundreds*, 60. Durham: Duke University Press.

Braidotti, Rosi. 2006. *The Posthuman*. Cambridge, UK: Polity.

Braidotti, Rosi. 2019. "A Theoretical Framework for the Critical Posthumanities." *Theory, Culture, & Society* 36, no. 6: 31–61.

Brett, Philip. 1997. "Piano Four-Hands: Schubert and the Performance of Gay Male Desire." *19th-Century Music* 21, no. 2: 149–76.

Chen, Mel Y. 2011. "Toxic Animacies: Inanimate Affections." *GLQ: A Journal of Lesbian and Gay Studies* 12, nos. 2–3: 265–86.

Chen, Mel Y. 2012. *Animacies: Biopolitics, Racial Mattering, and Queer Affect*. Durham, NC: Duke University Press.

Chen, Mel Y. 2014. "Brain Fog: The Race for Cripistemology." *Journal of Literary & Cultural Disability Studies* 8, no. 2: 171–84.

Cherry, John. 2002. "Animism in Thought and Language." PhD diss., University of California, Berkeley.

Cone, Edward T. 1974. *The Composer's Voice*. Berkeley: University of California Press.

Cone, Edward T. 1982. "Schubert's Promissory Note: An Exercise in Musical Hermeneutics." *19th-Century Music* 5, no. 3: 233–41.

Coole, Diana, and Samantha Frost, eds. 2010. *New Materialisms: Ontology, Agency, and Politics*. Durham, NC: Duke University Press.

Cox, Arnie. 2016. *Music and Embodied Cognition: Listening, Moving, Feeling, and Thinking*. Bloomington: Indiana University Press.

Crawley, Ashon. 2020. "Stayed|Freedom|Hallelujah." In *Otherwise Worlds: Against Settler Colonialism and Anti-Blackness*, edited by Tiffany Lethabo King, Jenell Navarro, and Andrea Smith, 27–37. Durham, NC: Duke University Press.

Cusick, Suzanne G. 1994a. "Feminist Theory, Music Theory, and the Mind/Body Problem." *Perspectives of New Music* 32, no. 1 (Winter): 8–27.

Cusick, Suzanne G. 1994b. "On a Lesbian Relationship with Music: A Serious Effort Not to Think Straight." In *Queering the Pitch: The New Gay and Lesbian Musicology*, edited by Philip Brett, Elizabeth Wood, and Gary C. Thomas, 67–83. New York: Routledge.

Davidson, Donald. 1963. "Actions, Reasons, and Causes." *Journal of Philosophy* 60: 685–700.

Ewell, Philip. 2020. "Music Theory and the White Racial Frame." *Music Theory Online* 26, no. 2 (September). https://mtosmt.org/issues/mto.20.26.2/mto.20.26.2.ewell.html.

Ewell, Philip. 2021. "Music Theory's White Racial Frame." *Music Theory Spectrum* 43, no. 2: 324–29.

Ferrando, Francesca. 2013. "Posthumanism, Transhumanism, Antihumanism, Metahumanism, and New Materialisms: Differences and Relations." *Existenz* 8, no. 2 (Fall): 26–32.

Gadir, Tami. 2018. "Understanding Agency from the Decks to the Dance Floor." *Music Theory Online* 24, no. 3 (September). https://mtosmt.org/issues/mto.18.24.3/mto.18.24.3.gadir.html.

Giffney, Noreen, and Myra J. Hird, eds. 2008. *Queering the Non/Human*. Burlington, VT: Ashgate.

Graybill, Roger C. 2018. "Facilitative Agency in Performance." *Music Theory Online* 24, no. 3 (September). https://mtosmt.org/issues/mto.18.24.3/mto.18.24.3.graybill.html.

Guck, Marion A. 1989. "Beethoven as Dramatist." *College Music Symposium* 29: 8–18.

Guck, Marion A. 1994a. "Analytical Fictions." *Music Theory Spectrum* 16, no. 2 (Autumn): 217–30.

Guck, Marion A. 1994b. "A Woman's (Theoretical) Work." *Perspectives of New Music* 32, no. 1 (Winter): 28–43.

Guck, Marion A. 1996. "Music Loving, Or the Relationship with the Piece." *Music Theory Online* 2, no. 2 (March). http://www.mtosmt.org/issues/mto.96.2.2/mto.96.2.2.guck.html.

Guck, Marion A. 2006. "Analysis as Interpretation: Interaction, Intentionality, Invention." *Music Theory Spectrum* 28, no. 2 (2006): 191–209.

Hartman, Saidiya. 2008. "Venus in Two Acts." *Small Axe* 12, no. 2 (June): 1–14.

Hartman, Saidiya. 2019. *Wayward Lives, Beautiful Experiments: Intimate Histories of Riotous Black Girls, Troublesome Women, and Queer Radicals*. New York: W. W. Norton and Company.

Hanslick, Eduard. 1986. *On the Musically Beautiful*. Translated by Geoffrey Payzant. Indianapolis: Hackett Publishing Company.

Hatten, Robert S. 1994. *Musical Meaning in Beethoven: Markedness, Correlation, and Interpretation*. Bloomington: Indiana University Press.

Hatten, Robert S. 2004. *Interpreting Musical Gestures, Topics, and Tropes: Mozart, Beethoven, and Schubert*. Bloomington: Indiana University Press.

Hatten, Robert S. 2018. *A Theory of Virtual Agency for Western Art Music*. Bloomington: Indiana University Press.

Hisama, Ellie. 2021. "Getting to Count." *Music Theory Spectrum* 43, no. 2: 349–63.

Howe, Blake. 2016. "Music and the Agents of Obsession." *Music Theory Spectrum* 38, no. 2: 218–40.

Kerman, Joseph. 1966. *The Beethoven Quartets*. New York: Norton.

Kimmerer, Robin Wall. 2013. *Braiding Sweetgrass: Indigenous Wisdom, Scientific Knowledge, and the Teaching of Plants*. Minneapolis: Milkweed Editions.

King, Tiffany Lethabo, Jenell Navarro, and Andrea Smith. 2020. "Beyond Incommensurability: Toward an Otherwise Stance on Black and Indigenous Relationality." In *Otherwise Worlds: Against Settler Colonialism and Anti-Blackness*, edited by Tiffany Lethabo King, Jenell Navarro, and Andrea Smith, 1–26. Durham, NC: Duke University Press.

Kirby, Vicky. 2008. "Natural Convers(at)ions: Or, What if Culture was Really Nature All Along?" In *Material Feminisms*, edited by Stacey Alaimo and Susan Hekman, 214–36. Bloomington: Indiana University Press.

Kivy, Peter. 1980. *The Corded Shell*. Princeton, NJ: Princeton University Press.

Klorman, Edward. 2016. *Mozart's Music of Friends: Social Interplay in the Chamber Works*. Cambridge: Cambridge University Press.

Latour, Bruno. 1987. *Science in Action: How to Follow Scientists and Engineers Through Society*. Cambridge, MA: Harvard University Press.

Latour, Bruno, and Steve Woolgar. 1986. *Laboratory Life: The Construction of Scientific Facts*. Princeton, NJ: Princeton University Press.

Lee, Gavin. 2020. "Queer Music Theory." *Music Theory Spectrum* 42, no. 1: 143–53.

Liboiron, Max, Manuel Tironi, and Nerea Calvillo. 2018. "Toxic Politics: Acting in A Permanently Polluted World." *Social Studies of Science* 48, no. 3: 331–49.

Lochhead, Judy. 2020. "Music's Vibratory Enchantments and Epistemic Injustices: Reflecting on Thirty Years of Feminist Thought in Music Theory." *Zeitschrift der Gesellschaft für Musiktheorie* 17, no. 1: 15–29.

Luciano, Dana, and Mel Y. Chen. 2015. "Has the Queer Ever Been Human?" *GLQ: A Journal of Lesbian and Gay Studies* 21, nos. 2–3: 182–207.

Luong, Vivian. 2017. "Rethinking Music Loving." *Music Theory Online* 23, no. 2 (June). https://mtosmt.org/issues/mto.17.23.2/mto.17.23.2.luong.html.

Marx, Adolphe Bernhard. 1863. *Ludwig van Beethoven: Leben und Schaffen*, Vol. 2. Berlin: Otto Janke.

Maus, Fred Everett. 1988. "Music as Drama." *Music Theory Spectrum* 10 (Spring): 56–73.

Maus, Fred Everett. 1989a. "Agency in Instrumental Music and Song." *College Music Symposium* 29: 31–43.

Maus, Fred Everett. 1989b. "Introduction: *The Composer's Voice* as Music Theory." *College Music Symposium* 29: 1–7.

Maus, Fred Everett. 1992. "Hanslick's Animism." *Journal of Musicology* 10, no. 3 (Summer): 273–92.

Maus, Fred Everett. 1993. "Masculine Discourse in Music Theory." *Perspectives of New Music* 31, no. 2 (Summer): 264–93.

Maus, Fred Everett. 2020a. "Defensive Discourse in Writing about Music." *Zeitschrift der Gesellschaft für Musiktheorie* 17, no. 1: 65–80.

Maus, Fred Everett. 2020b. "LGBTQ+ Lives in Professional Music Theory." *Music Theory Online* 26, no. 1 (March). https://mtosmt.org/issues/mto.20.26.1/mto.20.26.1.maus.html.

McClary, Susan. 1994. "Constructions of Subjectivity in Schubert's Music." In *Queering the Pitch: The New Gay and Lesbian Musicology*, edited by Philip Brett, Elizabeth Wood, and Gary C. Thomas, 205–34. New York: Routledge.

McClary, Susan. 1997. "The Impromptu That Trod on a Loaf: Or How Music Tells Stories." *Narrative* 5, no. 1: 20–35.

McNay, Lois. 2016. "Agency." In *The Oxford Handbook of Feminist Theory*, edited by Lisa Disch and Mary Hawkesworth, 39–60. New York: Oxford University Press.

Menakem, Resmaa. 2017. *My Grandmother's Hands: Racialized Trauma and the Pathway to Mending Our Hearts and Bodies*. Las Vegas, NV: Central Recovery Press.

Mignolo, Walter D. 2015. "Sylvia Wynter: What Does It Mean to Be Human?" In *Sylvia Wynter: On Being Human as Praxis*, edited by Katherine McKittrick, 106–23. Durham, NC: Duke University Press.

Monahan, Seth. 2013. "Action and Agency Revisited." *Journal of Music Theory* 57, no. 2 (Fall): 321–71.

Newcomb, Anthony. 1997, "Action and Agency in Mahler's Ninth Symphony, Second Movement." In *Music and Meaning*, edited by Jenefer Robinson, 131–53. Ithaca, NY: Cornell University Press.

Puar, Jasbir. 2017. *The Right to Main: Debility, Capacity, Disability*. Durham, NC: Duke University Press.

Reed, Alissandra. 2020. "Who Does Your Scholarship Serve?" Paper presented at the Annual Meeting of the Music Theory Society of New York State, virtual conference.

Robinson, Dylan. 2020. *Hungry Listening: Resonant Theory for Indigenous Sound Studies*. Minneapolis: University of Minneapolis Press.

Sofer, Danielle. 2020. "Specters of Sex: Tracing the Tools and Techniques of Contemporary Music Analysis." *Zeitschrift der Gesellschaft für Musiktheorie* 17, no. 1: 31–63.

Stewart, Kathleen. 2007. *Ordinary Affects*. Durham, NC: Duke University Press.

Stewart, Kathleen. 2010. "Afterword: Worlding Refrains." In *Affect Theory Reader*, edited by Melissa Gregg and Gregory J. Seigworth, 339–53. Durham, NC: Duke University Press.

Stewart, Kathleen. 2014. "Tactile Compositions." In *Objects and Materials: A Routledge Companion*, edited by Penny Harvey, Eleanor Conlin Casella, Gillian Evans, Hannah Knox, Christine McLean, Elizabeth B. Silva, Nicholas Thoburn, and Kath Woodward, 119–27. New York: Routledge.

Straus, Joe. N. 2011. *Extraordinary Measures: Disability in Music*. New York: Oxford University Press.

Straus, Joe. N. 2021. "Music Theory's Therapeutic Imperative and the Tyranny of the Normal." *Music Theory Spectrum* 43, no. 2: 339–48.

TallBear, Kim. 2019. "Caretaking Relations, Not American Dreaming." *Kalfou* 6, no. 1 (Spring): 24–41.

Todd, Zoe. 2016. "An Indigenous Feminist's Take on The Ontological Turn: 'Ontology' Is Just Another Word for Colonialism." *Journal of Historical Sociology* 29, no. 1 (March): 4–22.

Tuck, Eve, and K. Wayne Wang. 2012. "Decolonization is not a Metaphor." *Decolonization: Indigenity, Education & Society* 1, no. 1: 1–40.

Tuck, Eve, and K. Wayne Wang. 2014. "R Words: Refusing Research." In *Humanizing Research: Decolonizing Qualitative Inquiry with Youth and Communities*," edited by Django Paris and Maisha T. Winn, 223–48. Los Angeles: SAGE Publications.

Walton, Kendall L. 1990. *Mimesis as Make-Believe: On the Foundations of the Representational Arts*. Cambridge: Harvard University Press.

Watts, Vanessa. 2013. "Indigenous Place-Thought & Agency amongst Humans and Non-Humans (First Woman and Sky Woman go on a European World Tour!)." *Decolonization: Indigeneity, Education & Society* 2, no. 1: 20–34.

Wolfe, Cary. 2010. *What is Posthumanism?* Minneapolis: University of Minnesota Press.

Wynter, Sylvia. 2003. "Unsettling the Coloniality of Being/Power/Truth/ Freedom: Towards the Human, After Man, Its Overrepresentation—An Argument." *CR: The New Centennial Review* 3, no. 3: 257–337.

Zbikowski, Lawrence M. 2018. "Performing Agency: A Response." *Music Theory Online* 24, no. 3 (September). https://mtosmt.org/issues/mto.18.24.3/mto.18.24.3.zbikow ski.html.

Index